MOLECULAR FORENSIC

ENCYCLOPAEDIA OF FORENSIC SCIENCE - 3

MOLECULAR FORENSIC

By

Ashok Kumar

Dept. of Zoology

Bundelkhand University

Campus Department

Jhansi (India)

DISCOVERY PUBLISHING HOUSE PVT. LTD.

NEW DELHI-110 002

First Published – 2009
Reprinted – 2017

ISBN: 978-81-8356-422-9 (Set)

ISBN: 978-81-8356-566-0

Molecular Forensic

Published by:
DISCOVERY PUBLISHING HOUSE PVT. LTD.
4383/4B, Ansari Road Darya Ganj
New Delhi - 110 002 (India)
Phone: +91-11-23279245, 43596064-65
Fax: +91-11-23253475
E-mail: discoverypublishinghouse@gmail.com
sales@discoverypublishinggroup.com
web: www.discoverypublishinggroup.com

Printed at:
Infinity Imaging Systems
Delhi

Preface

The present title *"Encyclopaedia of Forensic Science"* has been written for undergraduate, post-graduate students and those engaged in pharmaceutical, pathological, and clinical research. Actually the explosion of new technologies with their vast potential has brought with it the need for forensic scientists to equip themselves and their laboratories with a whole array of new expertise. With the high discriminating power of the DNA systems has come high potential in evidentiary terms, high profile status for many investigations, and not least, a high degree of professional scruting of evidence produced by such technology. The present book provides protocols for the major methods of DNA analysis that have been introduced for identity testing in forensic laboratories. It also deals with the developments intersecting with the neighbouring fields of law inforcement and the justice system. This book will prove a useful guide for public awareness, health authorities, professional and industrial organizations. The aim of writing this book has .been to show how it is possible to enjoy the benefits of technology in detecting the criminals. The language used in it is simple and lucid, and illustrations are clear and labelled.

To make the work more comprehensive and informative, the author has consulted many authoritative books, research journals, abstracts, monographs etc., so there can be no claim to originality except in the .manner of treatment.

The author expresses his thanks to his friends and colleagues whose continue inspirations have initiated him to bring out this book.

The author expresses his gratitude to Mr. Wasan and staff of M/s Discovery Publishing House Pvt. Ltd. for their whole hearted co-operation in the publication of this book.

In the mean time, the author will remain sincerely responsible for any shortcomings of the book and be grateful to the readers for their suggestions and constructive criticism for the continuous betterment of the book. He takes this opportunity to appeal to the readers to send their suggestions straightaway to his Publisher.

Author

CONTENTS

1

INTRODUCTION

The end result of decomposition of humans is more intimately familiar and perhaps of greater interest to forensic pathologists than to any other group whose duties include the evaluation and investigation of postmortem remains on a routine basis. From such remains, the forensic pathologist may be asked to make an evaluation of the cause and manner of death and, perhaps, how long the body had been *in situ*. These determinations may be challenging, even for the experienced investigator, depending on the condition and location of the remains. The extent, pattern, and nature of decomposition in a specific circumstance may be of great significance and utility in the forensic investigation of a death. Conclusions and inferences drawn from the investigation can be the subject of scrutiny, consideration, and documentation.

Clearly, an understanding of the processes of decomposition can be of benefit for such purposes as estimation of the postmortem interval, recognition of postmortem artifacts, and in an overall evaluation of the death scene. For the forensic pathologist faced with the even more complex issues associated with partial remains, such as the lower extremity, knowledge of the mechanistic processes of decomposition may facilitate an understanding of the specific circumstances of the death in question.

Because the physical appearance and sequence of decomposition events has been extensively detailed and reviewed in the forensic literature, the focus of this chapter is to explore the biochemical reactions and processes that provide the ultimate basis for the visible (or otherwise detectable) evidence of the decomposition with which we regularly deal with in medicolegal contexts.

There are many macroscopic processes or events that can impact the fate of postmortem remains in an unpredictable and variable nature, such as physical disruption, scavenging, and deliberate or accidental burial. However, the common underlying sequence of biochemical events provides a basis for understanding decomposition as a logical progression of natural processes. It is anticipated that an enhanced understanding of the biochemistry of decomposition of human remains will be useful to some investigators, and facilitate the evaluation, and extraction of useful information from the seemingly unpredictable and chaotic processes lying at the center of a crime or death scene.

Life can be viewed in its essence, as an energy-utilizing sequence of interrelated chemical reactions whereby order and structure, of truly magnificent scope and complexity, is derived from an intricate and multifaceted process of breakdown, combination, synthesis, and modification or rebuilding of biomolecules from an otherwise random or partially organized collection of both simple and more complex available molecules, ions, and atoms. The maintenance of life—or more accurately, the maintenance of the underlying order, as reflected in molecular and macromolecular structures—requires the continued input and utilization of energy. The interlinked reactions of life comprise overall, an endothermic process both in total and on an individual basis. Clearly, the termination of a life results in the cessation of the flow of energy available to maintain, support, and reproduce the molecules, structures, and biochemical processes of the organism.

Organic biomolecules are—as considered from the temporal perspective of days, months, or years—extremely fragile and ethereal constructions, readily broken apart by relatively small amounts of thermal, electrochemical, or electromagnetic energy. Within living organisms, the molecules of life are primarily "*reduced*," in the chemical sense, in that they are hydrogen-rich and able to react with molecular oxygen either directly or via intermediate molecules as electron donors or "*reducing agents.*" Indeed, a major form of energy storage in living cells is long-chain carbohydrate molecules. The energy potential of such molecules, which is released upon oxidation, is readily demonstrable in the burning wax of a candle, the fat stores of animals preparing for winter hibernation, and the utilization of geochemical (although essentially biological in origin) oil and its refinement product, gasoline.

Despite the reduced state of most biomolecules, our earthly environment provides an oxidizing atmosphere and (generally) oxygenated aqueous ecosystems. In such a system, the ultimate fate of organic molecules is the corresponding oxidation products of component atoms. Hydrogen yields water and other oxidized products such as hydrogen sulfide. Carbon ultimately yields carbon dioxide. Nitrogen and other elements yield corresponding oxide forms. The facility with which organic molecules are able to transfer single electrons to molecular oxygen provides the underlying basis for aerobic life, given that the energy of that transfer is captured and made available to the organism in the form of high-energy molecules, such as *adenosine triphosphate* (ATP).

The relative fragility of organic molecules necessitates active biological structures to maintain some degree of flux at the molecular level, in that the molecules from which such structures are comprised are always degrading (albeit at different rates). Damaged or degraded molecules are then constantly being replaced by newly synthesized (or otherwise acquired) versions of the same molecule (with the rate of repair dependent to an extent on the health and age of the individual). Complex and elegant enzymatic systems exist to perform the functions of evaluation, repair, and/or replacement of biomolecules.

As a consequence of death, the molecules created by the organism that serve as the building blocks of its corporeal body, internal structures, and organs—both on the macro and micro scale—must, as noted above, ultimately undergo oxidation and degradation in an environment where the normal repair and replacement mechanisms are no longer operative. The process in total, whereby the structures and biomolecules of an organism become less organized or broken down—either by chemical or biochemical processes—and the constituent molecules and atoms are made available to new life, is referred to as "*decomposition.*" The extent to which this process is dependent on the chemical nature of the surroundings is readily illustrated by the recovery of well-preserved specimens—both human and otherwise—from bogs (or, more accurately, peat excavations of ancient bogs). The subsurface ecosystem of a bog is severely oxygen depleted and acidic, resulting—for any unfortunate individual trapped therein—in a preservative entombment that precludes normal molecular oxidative degradation and will not support the aerobic life forms (nor many anaerobes) necessary for a complete decomposition process.

In contrast to the synthetic functions of the living organism, postmortem decomposition of the body is reflective of a collection of physical and degradative biochemical processes that will be situationally dependent for any given body. To an extent, the temporal sequence, and even occurrence, of particular decomposition events in a specific situation will be the result of the combined effects of environmental conditions and the physical setting of the body, as well as the physical actions associated with death. Similarly, the rate at which changes will occur—correlating with the physical state of the remains at any point—will also be a function of those circumstances. With the exception of physically disruptive processes, decomposition is essentially a biological and biochemical phenomenon, mediated by enzymes that are already present in the body, by digestive enzymes and the activities of exogenous flora and fauna colonizing the remains.

All of the processes are driven by the stored chemical energy that the decomposing body represents. This chapter is devoted to understanding—in a general but mechanistic and biochemical sense—the nature of the decomposition processes to which remains of the lower extremity may be subjected.

Decomposition Sequence

In the absence of physical disruption and in unfrozen, unpreserved tissue, the processes of decomposition follow a reasonably predictable pattern. The breakdown of body tissues consists primarily of two processes: *autolysis* and *putrefaction*. *Autolysis* is an aseptic phenomenon caused by the release and subsequent uncontrolled activity of intracellular enzymes that hydrolytically break down cellular constituents that may serve as catalytic substrates. The autolytic process sets the stage for the subsequent massive transformation of previously (more or less) solid tissue to gas, liquid, and salt products during the septic process of putrefaction.

In contrast to autolysis, *putrefaction* is the consequence of a "*population explosion*" of xenobiota in the body, as various organisms (both micro- and macrobiological endogenous and invasive plants, animals, and fungi) compete for the available energy the decomposing tissues represent. Although the difference between autolysis and putrefaction may be relatively clear and definable on a molecular level, the distinction between the processes in an actively decaying corpse may be considerably less so, with both functions occurring to some extent simultaneously.

Although recognizing that there may be significant variations in the time course of the decompositional process within any specific corpse, generally five stages of decomposition have been identified in unpreserved bodies:

1. Fresh (~0–2 d): Begins at the moment of death and includes the autolytic processes. Usually relatively few changes are readily observable on a macrobiologic scale. This stage ends with the beginning of putrefaction. Generally, insect infestation and utilization of the corpse is not extensive at this stage.
2. Bloated (~2–6 d): Begins as the processes of putrefaction start to produce enough gaseous by-products to start inflating the abdomen and other soft tissue. This activity reflects the geometric rates of growth of invasive and/or opportunistic organisms—primarily anaerobic bacteria—in the corpse. Insect activity may be significant during this stage and particularly enhanced as fluids start to seep from the body.
3. Decay (~5–11 d): Begins as the skin of the abdominal wall ruptures or is otherwise breached, thereby allowing the release of trapped putrefactive gases. This process may be facilitated by insect feeding or other scavenger activities. The body may appear moist and blackened. During this stage, a significant loss of soft-tissue mass will occur, primarily as a consequence of maggot feeding activity. Toward the end of the decay stage, the body will begin to dry and the insect population may shift somewhat toward scavenging and predatory beetles.
4. Postdecay (~10–25 d): The nature of the postdecay process is a function of the degree of moisture available in the immediate surroundings of the body. In dry climates, remains will be primarily bones, dried skin, and cartilaginous materials. In moist regions, byproducts of decomposition may remain in the vicinity of the body (e.g., in adjacent soil) for an extended period of time.
5. Dry state (~>25 d): This is generally defined as the stage at which only bones and hair remain, and no significant odor distinct from normal soil or forest duff is readily discernable.

Autolysis

Autolysis is the "*self-digestion*" of the cell. In the context of postmortem decomposition, it refers to the process by which catabolically active enzymes are able to act on cellular organelles and molecular components that would not normally serve as substrates. The release of these enzymes from their subcellular locations marks the beginning of an irreversible process that will eventually result in the complete reduction of the newly dead organism to the remnants of decomposition, available to serve as food for other life forms that can derive energy and nutrients from the decaying corpse. The potential for the autolytic, enzymatic breakdown of cellular biomolecules exists in every cell as a consequence of the presence of the biochemical machinery necessary to process nutrients, degrade toxic species, and recycle structural and functional molecules and, indeed, entire cellular organelles. That tissues differ in rates of autolytic processes can be understood in terms of differential enzyme complements and reflects the functional distinctions of the tissues. Hence the liver, with a broad spectrum of highly active catabolic enzymes, undergoes rapid autolysis, whereas tissues with more limited biochemical activity, e.g., muscle, tend to degrade more slowly.

Interestingly, the essentially aseptic nature of the autolytic process can be understood on reflection that the "*aging*" process used to enhance the flavor and texture of certain meats and game produce a tenderized yet not microbially contaminated product. The operation of autolytic processes in a manner that is protected from either infection or other means of contamination is primarily responsible for the change in physical properties of the muscle mass.

Clearly some mechanism for isolating or segregating the activities of catabolic enzymes with generalized substrate capability is required in the cell, because the maintenance of intracellular structures is in the interest of the organism. The primary segregating elements for catabolic enzymes and processes within the cell are the lysosomes, peroxisomes, and, to a lesser extent, mitochondria. An understanding of autolysis and hence of the entire decomposition process requires familiarity with the enzymatic complements and mechanism for the release of enzymes from these subcellular organelles after the death of the organism.

Subcompartmentalization of catabolic enzymes within the lysosomes, peroxisomes, and other subcellular vesicles protects the operating molecular machinery of the cell from the degradative potential of these enzymes. In addition to the limitation of activity by intracellular segregation, there is elegant additional protection of intracellular constituents. The activity of the lysosomal hydrolases is optimal at an acidic pH (~5.0), which is significantly distinct from the somewhat more basic pH (~7.2) of the surrounding cytosol.

With the death of the organism and the associated circulatory failure, there is a concomitant failure of oxygen transport and delivery to cells. Molecular oxygen serves as the terminal electron acceptor in the electron transport chain in biochemical reactions known collectively as oxidative phosphorylation. This sequence of connected reactions is the primary source of high-energy ATP molecules in the body, which in turn provide the energy for a multiplicity of cellular functions by hydrolysis of phosphate ester linkages. A consequence of oxygen deprivation is the failure of oxidative phosphorylation to take place, causing a shift in cellular metabolism favoring anaerobic glycolysis, a fermentative process which acts to compensate for the energy deficit. Anaerobic glycolysis results in the conversion of glucose to pyruvate and eventually to lactate. The elevation in lactic and pyruvic acid levels in the cell causes the intracellular pH to decline and the intracellular buffering capacity to become quickly overwhelmed. As the glycolytic process continues, intracellular glucose is rapidly depleted, as is the glucose polysaccharide glycogen; thus, it eventually deprives the cell of even this limited resource of ATP production. Anaerobic glycolysis is less efficient than oxidative phosphorylation, in that it leaves an incompletely oxidized product (lactate) and it is further limited to the available substrate, endogenous glucose, and molecules that can be readily converted to glucose, e.g., glycogen.

The consequences of the limitation in ATP synthesis are multifaceted and ultimately devastating for the cell. Many cellular transport mechanisms depend on ATP to provide the energy required to drive energetically unfavorable processes. Many nutrients and other molecules essential to the life of the cell are actively transported across cellular membranes by mechanisms that require ATP hydrolysis. The cellular membrane potential, ranging from approx -10 mV to as much as -90 mV (depending on the tissue or cell type) is also maintained by the action of the sodium-potassium ATPase pump; termination of the activity of this structure allows intracellular sodium to accumulate while potassium diffuses out of the cell through permanent membrane ion channels. As the membrane potential disappears, calcium ions enter the cell (a key indicator and perhaps contributor to the impending death of the cell). The intracellular accumulation of solute ions occurs concomitantly with cell swelling, a function of an increase in the intracellular water content, which is driven by osmotic pressure. Typical necrotic changes in the cell, such as vacuolization and dissociation of cellular organelles, further characterize the cellular demise. Of major significance for autolysis is the disruption of the lysosomal membrane consequential to intracellular acidification and ionic changes. The leakage of the lysosomal acid hydrolases into an acidic environment at a now near-optimal pH for hydrolytic activity facilitates the enzymatic breakdown of cellular components and membranes.

Lysosomes have a single limiting membrane, and the intravesicular pH is maintained at approx 5.0 (corresponding to the optimal pH for hydrolytic enzymes) by a membrane-bound hydrogen ion pump. Lysosomes typically contain a broad spectrum of enzymes capable of hydrolytically cleaving polysaccharides, proteins, nucleic acids, lipids, phosphoric acyl esters and sulfates. Lysosomal action is primarily mediated as a consequence of the fusing of a primary lysosome with an intracellular vesicle produced via phagocytosis (for extracellular materials) or by the analogous budding of an intracellular membrane (for intracellular materials). The fused product is referred to as a *digestive vacuole*, and it is in this protected environment that complex biomolecules are hydrolytically "*de-constructed*".

As previously noted, the capability of the cell to rapidly degrade molecules of significant size and complexity requires compartmentalization and segmentation of the process. The integrity of the lysosomal membrane also prevents the unwanted destruction of other intracellular components, the loss of which could have a negative impact on the viability of the cell. Clearly a loss of lysosomal membrane integrity can result in the appearance within the cytosol of a significant and indiscriminant hydrolytic function with the potential to damage cellular organelles, membranes, and other important biomolecules.

Peroxisomes function primarily in the breakdown of lipids, with long chain fatty acids (>20 CH_2 groups) processed essentially exclusively within these organelles. Medium-chain fatty acids (~ 10–20 CH_2 groups) may be degraded in either mitochondria or peroxisomes. Although the reactions of the mitochondria and peroxisome are similar in many respects, some significant differences serve to point out the functional distinctions. The mitochondrial oxidative phosphorylation process oxidizes flavin adenine dinucleotide, reduced $(FADH)_2$, to yield FAD, with $FADH_2$ regenerated by the oxidation of a fatty acyl CoA molecule. In contrast peroxisomal $FADH_2$ is generated by the same enzyme-catalyzed reaction but oxidized in the process of the reduction of molecular oxygen to hydrogen peroxide, a potentially cytotoxic molecule.

Peroxisomes contain significant quantities of the protective enzyme catalase, the activity of which breaks hydrogen peroxide down to water and oxygen. In the peroxisome, unsaturated fatty acyl CoA molecules are converted to the hydroxy analogs, which are subsequently oxidized to their corresponding ketones by means of hydroxy fatty acyl dehydrogenase with the concomitant formation of NADH. In the absence of an active electron-transport chain and associated cellular synthetic processes, there is no metabolic "*sink*" for the reducing equivalents and nicotinamide adenine dinucleotide is exported to the cytosol. Therefore, peroxisomal catabolism of fatty acids represents a source of both acetyl CoA and reducing equivalents in the form of nicotinamide adenine dinucleotide. Significant for the autolytic process, the enzymatic systems contained in the peroxisome represent the catabolic potential for fatty acids and also for the production of active oxygen species, e.g., hydrogen peroxide. The peroxisomal membrane suffers the same fate in the necrotic cell as the lysosome, with the leakage of its enzymatic machinery into the cytosol, where it becomes available to further catalyze the destruction of cellular components.

Failure of respiration and hence, cellular oxidative phosphorylation, is therefore the key trigger in the autolytic process. Termination of the availability of high-energy molecules that are routinely required to maintain the integrity of the cell, key cellular components and processes (e.g., membranes), synthetic capability, and ion and molecular pumps causes significant changes in the biochemical operation of the cell. This process ultimately leads to the lysis of intracellular organelles, of particular significance being lysosomes and peroxisomes, and the release of their constituent enzymes into the cytosol, where their catalytic actions can break down and destroy the very molecules that had previously served to define the living cell and functions in it.

Rigor Mortis

The postmortem depletion of cellular energy stores leading to autolysis also produces a well-recognized macro-scale phenomenon characterized by the stiffening of voluntary and involuntary muscles, known as rigor mortis. Mechanistically, this process is the result of association of the muscle proteins actin and myosin as intracellular pH decreases to less than approx 6.5 and calcium—normally sequestered in the *sarcoplasmic reticulum* (SR)— leaks into the cytosol as the SR membrane is compromised during autolysis. Cytosolic calcium then binds to troponin, causing a conformational change that results in the "*unmasking*" of myosin binding sites on the actin molecule. In living cells, the subsequent dissociation of the actin–myosin complex is promoted by ATP as part of the normal sequence of events that results in muscle contraction. However, in the ATP-deficient postmortem environment in dead or dying cells, the actin–myosin complex remains until it is either denatured or enzymatically degraded. The process causes the "*death stiffness*" of muscles, or rigor mortis. In contrast to active muscle contraction, there is no process of actin-myosin translocation in rigor mortis and, hence, no shortening of muscle fibers. Thus, rigor is characterized by muscles that are stiff but not contracted. Although rigor mortis occurs in the muscles, it is readily detectable only when the affected muscles are connected to central joints, such as the knees.

Livor Mortis

Lividity is a discoloration of the skin—generally to a dark purple—that results from the pooling of deoxygenated blood in the veins and capillary beds of the body as circulation fails. This process occurs in direct response to gravitational forces. The blood remains fluid after death as a consequence of the release of plasmin, a fibrinolytic enzyme, from the vasculature and serous surfaces. This process depletes the blood of fibrinogen, thereby eventually rendering the blood permanently incoagulable (~30–60 min after death, depending on the ambient temperature). Blood, by providing an ideal liquid growth medium, facilitates the rapid growth of xenobiotics during the putrefaction stage and serves as a conduit for the spread of microbes throughout the body.

The characteristic color of body surfaces during lividity is reminiscent of cyanosis, i.e., the bluish discoloration of skin, nail beds, and mucous membranes that develops in clinical settings as a consequence of inadequate oxygenation. In the postmortem environment, the continued kinetically driven dissociation of oxygen from the hemoglobin molecule continues, changing the absorption spectra of the blood and producing the characteristic and readily observable change in color.

Putrefaction

The result of autolysis is the development of a slightly acidic, anaerobic, nutrientrich environment, with significant degradation of biomolecules at the cellular level. In this fertile milieu, devoid of normally protective and defensive cells and barriers, the proliferation of both invasive and opportunistic endogenous micro-organisms can be rapid and extensive. Ultimately, bacterial growth can affect and transform all the tissues in the body, being limited only by environmental factors, such as temperature and humidity.

The decomposition processes that begins as bacteria proliferate results in the production of gases and other metabolic products. These consequences of microbial growth result in some of the characteristic color changes, bloating, and odor changes that are universally recognized as the hallmarks of a decaying body and are collectively referred to as *putrefaction*. On the molecular level, the actions of microbial degradation transform the complex biomolecules of the body into gases, liquids, and simple molecules. Putrefaction results in the complete (albeit gradual) loss of structural integrity and recognizability of tissues and, indeed, the ultimate reduction of those tissues into their component molecules, molecular fragments, and atoms.

The primary source for the opportunistic microbiological colonization in the decomposing body is the microbially rich environment of the gastrointestinal tract. These enteric micro-organisms can cross the failing membrane barriers, a process that is facilitated by the autolytic degradation of body tissues, and migrate and proliferate throughout the body. Hence, the pronounced impact of autolytic processes on the structural integrity of the cellular membranes and the end of the viability of regular "*defensive*" or protective cells (e.g. macrophages and neutrophils) as a function of pH changes and the loss of available oxygen, provides the basis for the population explosion the putrefactive period represents. Characteristic microbial species observed during putrefaction include various Bacilli and *Pseudomonas*, *Bacterioides fragilis*, *Eschericia coli*, *Clostridium perfringens*, *Proteus mirabilis*, *Staphylococcus epidermidis*, and *Staphylococcus faecalis*.

Although the primary source of anaerobes in decomposition processes is the intestinal tract, other organisms—such as those found in the respiratory tree—may be present and able to take advantage of the conditions for growth. Naturally, any significant antemortem infection (e.g., septicemia or pneumonia) will give the causative agent a "*head start*" on the putrefactive process and may therefore result in an unusual microbiological population, at least during the initial stages of decomposition. The rate of putrefaction will vary with temperature, which will affect primarily the rate of enzymatic activity, with acceleration occurring until temperatures become inconsistent with the maintenance of protein structures.

In the absence of a septic condition, putrefaction begins in the stomach and intestines. The gastric mucosa and intestines acquire a dark purple-brownish color as a result of the release of heme compounds. The mucosal epithelium of the airways becomes deep red, and a hemolytic plum coloration may be noted in the myocardium and large blood vessels, again a result of the release of heme. Changes in organ structure are readily apparent, as seen in the thinning and softening of the myocardium. The liver develops a honeycomb pattern as a result of extensive gas formation. The brain similarly goes through a structural disintegration process that may proceed to complete liquefaction. The spleen becomes exceptionally soft and may extrude through its delineating capsule. The lungs become filled with and surrounded by fluid.

Putrefactive processes are generally first represented by the generation of a greenish color—a consequence of the formation and accumulation of sulphhemoglobin in the abdominal wall where it coincides with the large intestine. Eventually, the discoloration spreads over the entire abdominal wall and may extend over the entire body. Coincident with this color change is the appearance of the superficial veins of the skin as a pattern of lines often described as "*marbling.*" As the process continues, the skin eventually acquires a dark pigmentation that may range from a red-tinged greenish color through purple to black.

The skin color changes are accompanied by structural disintegration of the tissue that results in the characteristic skin-slippage that accompanies the process of decomposition. Large sections of epidermis may be dislodged as a consequence of even a small amount of shear. The newly exposed basal layers appear moist and pinkish and may take on a yellow–tan parchment appearance when they dry. Blisters as large as 20 cm may develop. These blisters are generally filled with a dark fluid and gases of putrefaction and may be easily disrupted to expose a dermal surface similar to that seen as a result of skin-slip.

Putrefaction is often characterized by pronounced bloated, distended bodies as a consequence of the formation of gas in the stomach, intestine, and abdominal cavity. The gas, a consequence of microbial action, is composed of hydrogen sulfide, methane, carbon dioxide, ammonia, and hydrogen, and is responsible for the characteristic odor of putrefaction, along with low molecular-weight organic compounds, including mercaptans, indoles, and the aptly named cadaverine and putrescine. This gas invades all body tissues and causes a generalized swelling to occur, which is characteristically crepitant to palpation. The pressure generated by the evolution of this gas may contribute to the separation of necrotic tissue layers.

At the molecular level, it is the ability of the bacterial species to secrete enzymes into their immediate environment that provides both the basis for the delivery of nutrients back to the microbe, yet also results in the degradation of biomolecules in the vicinity of the organism. These *exoenzymes* are responsible for the significant denaturation and breakdown of proteins into their constituent amino acids, which may be taken up and utilized, or further catabolized by the microbial population. The gas that characterizes the putrefactive process arises as a direct consequence of protein breakdown. Sulfur-containing amino acids are readily reduced to yield hydrogen sulfide, which plays a significant role in the production of the greenish sulfhemoglobin pigmentation and the reaction with reduced (ferrous) iron (released from the iron transport protein transferrin or the iron storage protein ferritin) that produces a black precipitate of ferrous sulfide. Ornithine—a four-carbon diamine amino acid—and lysine, its five-carbon analog, are readily decarboxylated to produce carbon dioxide, but more significantly for humans and "*cadaver dogs*" results in the production of the four-carbon "*putrescine*" and five-carbon "*cadaverine*," which are associated with a decomposing body.

Formation of Adipocere

Adipocere is a decomposition product of adipose tissue and may be an extensively formed a consequence of the putrefactive process in the presence of appropriate environmental conditions—generally high humidity or an aqueous environment coupled with relatively warm temperatures, conducive to the growth of putrefactive organisms. The formation of adipocere is a specific consequence of bacterial action, in which triacyl glycerols and other fatty esters are enzymatically hydrolyzed to produce both fatty acids and salts. Other bacterial reactions that will subsequently affect the chemical composition and physical nature of the final product are hydrogenation, stereo-isomerization, hydration, and dehydrogenation. The physical nature of the material (increasingly hydrophobic as a consequence of the reactions noted above) limits additional breakdown and utilization of the high-energy molecules. The final nature of adipocere varies with the extent of hydration and the fatty acyl cation. Sodium salts produce a relatively soft material, whereas potassium salts are harder. Replacement of sodium with calcium creates an insoluble, somewhat brittle material. Hence, the adipocere may vary from a grayish white, relatively soft, greasy substance to a crumbly, friable material as the water content is reduced.

Mummification

Mummification (or dehydration of tissues) is neither a direct consequence of autolysis or putrefaction but is, in a sense, a competing process. As a function of environmental conditions, the rate at which water evaporates from the body or from exposed sections of the body can be rapid enough to reach a point where dehydration of individual tissues precludes the bacterial action of putrefaction. However, such tissues are subjected to slow oxidative processes that result in the characteristic darkening of the tissues. Internal organs in circumstances of mummification may be somewhat preserved, but usually have undergone some degree of autolysis and putrefactive changes because of the relatively protected and hydrated conditions. Clearly, conditions favoring the dehydration of bodies will facilitate mummification, but the effects of cold should not be discounted. When microbial activity is sufficiently slowed by temperature, the evaporation (or sublimation from frozen tissues) of water in a low-humidity environment may provide conditions for partial or complete mummification.

Factors Affecting Decomposition Processes

The dependence of the processes of decomposition on physical environmental factors, such as humidity and temperature, was noted previously in this chapter. However, the "*contamination*" or poisoning of the decomposing remains—either deliberately via an embalming process or accidentally by leaching of adjacent metal ions or the deposition of the body in a matrix that is unable to support microbial growth—can severely inhibit or effectively preclude any appreciable amount of decomposition.

2

QUANTIFICATION OF DNA

DNA extraction has two main aims: firstly, to be very efficient, extracting enough DNA from a sample to perform the DNA profiling - this is increasingly important as the sample size diminishes - and secondly, to extract DNA that is pure enough for subsequent analysis - the level of difficulty here depends very much on the nature of the sample. Once the DNA has been extracted quantifying the DNA accurately is important for subsequent analysis.

DNA EXTRACTION

There are many methods available for extracting DNA. The choice of which method to use depends on a number of factors, including the sample type and quantity; the speed and in some cases ability to automate the extraction procedure; the success rate with forensic samples, which is a result of extracting the maximum amount of DNA from a sample and at the same time removing any PCR inhibitors that will prevent successful profiling; the chemicals that are used in the extraction - most laboratories go to great lengths to avoid using hazardous chemicals; and the cost of the procedure. Another important factor is the experience of the laboratory staff.

General Principles of DNA Extraction

The three stages of DNA extraction can be classified as (i) disruption of the cellular membranes, resulting in cell lysis, (ii) protein denaturation, and finally (iii) the separation of DNA from the denatured protein and other cellular components. Some of the extraction methods commonly used in forensic laboratories are described below.

Chelex 100 resin

The Chelex 100 method was one of the first extraction techniques adopted by the forensic community. Chelex 100 is a resin that is composed of styrene–divinylbenzene copolymers containing paired iminodiacetate ions. The resin has a very high affinity for polyvalent metal ions, such as magnesium (Mg^{2+}); it chelates the polyvalent metal ions and effectively removes them from solution.

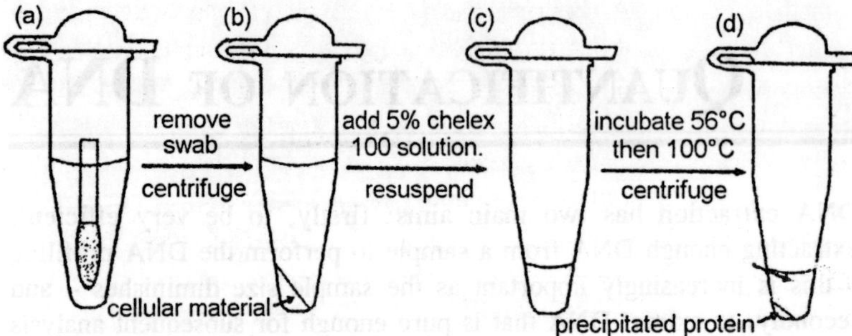

Fig. 2.1. The Chelex 100 extraction is quick and easy to perform. (a) The cellular material is added to 1 ml of TE and incubated at room temperature for 10-15 minutes. (b) The tube is centrifuged at high speed to pellet the cellular material and the supernatant is removed. (c) The pellet of cellular material is resuspended in 5% Chelex, the tube is incubated at 56°C for 15-30 minutes and then placed in a boiling water for 8 minutes. (d) The supernatant contains the DNA and can be used directly in a PCR.

The extraction procedure is very simple, the Chelex 100 resin, which is supplied as beads, is made into a 5% suspension using distilled water. The cellular material is incubated with the Chelex 100 suspension at 56 ª%C for up to 30 minutes. Proteinase K, which digests most cellular protein, is often added at this point. This incubation is followed by 8–10 minutes at 100°C to ensure that all the cells have ruptured and that the protein is denatured. The tube is then simply centrifuged to pellet the Chelex 100 resin and the denatured protein at the bottom of the tube, leaving the aqueous solution containing the DNA to be used in PCR. The Chelex 100 suspension is alkaline, between pH 9.0 and 11.0, and as a result DNA that is isolated using this procedure is single stranded.

The major advantages of this method are: it is quick, taking around 1 hour; it is simple and does not involve the movement of liquid between tubes, thereby reducing the possibility of accidentally mixing samples; the cost is very low; and it avoids the use of harmful chemicals. Importantly, it is amenable to a wide range of forensic samples. The DNA extract produced using this method is relatively crude but sufficiently clean in most cases to generate a DNA profile.

Silica based DNA extraction

Within molecular biology generally, the '*salting out*' procedure has been widely used. The first stage of the extraction involves incubating the cellular material in a lysis buffer that contains a detergent along with proteinase K. The commonly used detergents are *sodium dodecyl sulfate* (SDS), Tween 20, Triton X-100 and Nonidet P-40. The lysis buffer destabilizes the cell membranes, leading to the breakdown of cellular structure. The addition of a chaotropic salt, for example 6-M guanidine thiocyanate or 6-M sodium chloride, during or after cell lysis, disrupts the protein structure by interfering with hydrogen bonding, Van der Waals interactions, and the hydrophobic interactions. Cellular proteins are largely insoluble in the presence of the chaotropic agent and can be removed by centrifugation or filtration. The reduced solubility of the cellular protein is caused by the excess of ions in the high concentration of salt competing with the proteins for the aqueous solvent, effectively dehydrating the protein. Commonly used commercial kits, for example, the Qiagen kits, exploit the salting-out procedure; the methods to isolate the DNA after the cellular disruption vary widely.

Several DNA extraction methods are based on the binding properties of silica or glass particles. DNA will bind to silica or glass particles with a high affinity in the presence of a chaotropic salt. After the other cellular components have been removed the DNA can be released from the silica/glass particles by suspending them in water. Without the chaotropic salt the DNA no longer binds to the silica/glass and is released into solution. The silica method in particular has been shown to be robust when extracting DNA from forensic samples; it is also amenable to automation.

The advantage of the silica based salting-out methods are that they yield high molecular weight DNA that is cleaner than DNA from Chelex 100 extractions. As with Chelex 100 extractions, no highly toxic chemicals are involved. The process takes longer than the Chelex 100 and involves more than one change of tube and so increases the possibility of sample mixing and cross-contamination.

Phenol-chloroform-based DNA extraction

The phenol–chloroform method has been widely used in molecular biology but has been slowly phased out since the mid 1990s, largely because of the toxic nature of phenol. It is still used in some forensic laboratories; in particular it is still widely used for the extraction of DNA from bone samples and soils.

Cell lysis is performed as in the previous method. Phenol-chloroform is added to the cell lysate and mixed and the phenol denatures the protein. The extract is then centrifuged and the precipitated protein forms a pellicle at the interface between the organic phenol–chloroform phase and the aqueous phase; this process is repeated two to three times or until there is no visible pellicle. The DNA is then purified from the aqueous phase by ethanol precipitation or filter centrifugation. The method produces clean DNA but has some drawbacks: in addition to the toxic nature of phenol, multiple tube changes are required and the process is labour intensive.

FTA paper

FTA paper was described as a method for sample collection and storage, particularly from buccal swabs and fresh blood samples. Once a sample is applied to the FTA paper it is stable at room temperature for several years. Cellular material lyses on contact with the FTA paper and the DNA becomes bound to the paper. To analyse the DNA sample, the first step is to take a small region of the card, normally a 2-mm diameter circle, place it into a 1.5-ml tube and the non-DNA components are simply washed off, leaving only DNA on the card. The small circle of FTA paper is then added directly to a PCR. The FTA paper extractions are very simple to perform and do not require multiple tube changes, thus reducing the possibility of sample mixing.

DNA Extraction from Challenging Samples

The extraction of the many samples encountered in the forensic laboratory, including blood and shed epithelial cells, can be carried out routinely using any of the above techniques. There are however some sample types that require variations on the basic techniques.

Semen

Semen is one of the most commonly encountered types of biological evidence. The extraction of DNA from the spermatozoa is complicated by the structure of the spermatozoa. DNA is found within the head of the spermatozoa that is capped by the protective acrosome, which is rich in the amino acid cysteine - a large number of disulphide bridges form between the cysteines in the acrosome. Proteinase K, which is a general proteinase, cannot break the disulphide bonds and this reduces the efficiency of the extraction. The addition of dithiothreitol (DTT), a reducing agent that will break the disulphide bonds, greatly increases the release of spermatozoa DNA.

Another complication with semen is that it is often recovered as a mixture of spermatozoa and epithelial cells. The acrosome can be an advantage in these cases as it is possible to perform differential lysis: the epithelial cells are broken down by mild lysis conditions and the spermatozoa can be effectively separated from the lysed epithelial cells.

Hair shafts

Hair shafts that have been pulled out often possess a root that is rich in cellular material and DNA can be extracted using any of the commonly used techniques - plucked roots have been shown to contain as much as 0.5 μg of DNA. Hair that has been shed when it is in the resting telogen phase often contains no cellular material around the root. The hair shafts are composed of keratin, trace metals, air and pigment - cell fragments, including DNA can get trapped in the matrix of the hair and provide enough DNA to produce a profile. However, hair is notoriously difficult to analyse and in many cases it is only possible successfully to profile mitochondrial DNA, although nuclear DNA can, in some cases, be recovered.

The hair shaft, like the spermatozoa acrosome, is rich in disulphide bridges and requires either mechanical grinding or the addition of a reducing agent such as dithiothreitol that will break the disulphide bonds and allow proteinase K to digest the hair protein and release any trapped nucleic acids. Once released the DNA can be extracted using the salting-out procedure or organic phenol–chloroform based extraction. Alternative methods include digestion in a buffer containing proteinase K followed by direct PCR or dissolving the hair shaft in sodium hydroxide and, after neutralization, the released DNA is concentrated using filter centrifugation.

Because the hair shaft contains very low levels of DNA it is prone to contamination but unlike many other types of biological evidence with low levels of DNA it is possible to clean the hair shaft prior to DNA extraction. Several methods have been used to clean hair including washing in mild detergents, water and ethanol and also using a mild lysis step in the same way as is used in the differential extraction of semen.

Hard tissues

Following murders, terrorist attacks, wars and fatal accidents it is desirable to group together body parts from individuals when fragmentation has occurred and ultimately to identify the deceased. If the time between death and recovery of the body is short then muscle tissues provide a rich source of DNA, which can be extracted using, for example, any of the Chelex, salting-out and organic extraction methods. If, however, the soft tissues are displaying an advanced state of decomposition they will not provide any DNA suitable for analysis. When the cellular structure breaks down during decomposition, enzymes that degrade DNA are released and the DNA within the cell is rapidly digested. This process is accelerated by the action of colonizing bacteria and fungi.

Osteocytes are the most common nucleated cells in the bone matrix. In the teeth odontoblasts within the dentine and fibroblasts in the cell rich zone of the pulp cavity provide a source of nucleated cells. The hard tissues of the body, bone and teeth provide a refuge for DNA. In addition to the physical barriers, the hydroxyapatite/apatite mineral, which is a major component of the hard tissues, stabilizes the DNA which becomes closely bound to the positively charged mineral – this interaction limits the action of degrading enzymes.

Hard tissues provide an advantage over other forms of biological material because they have a surface that can be cleaned to remove any contaminating DNA by using detergents to remove any soft tissue, followed by physical abrasion soaking in sodium hypochlorite (bleach), and exposure to strong ultraviolet light.

After cleaning, the bone/tooth material is normally broken down into a powder by drilling or grinding under liquid nitrogen. The resulting material is decalcified using 0.5-M EDTA either before or at the same time as cell lysis. The organic phenol–chloroform and the silica binding extraction methods are commonly used to extract the DNA. The process of extracting DNA from bone samples takes much longer than with any other type of sample.

Quantification of DNA

After extracting DNA an accurate measurement of the amount of DNA and also the quality of the DNA extract is desirable. Adding the correct amount of DNA to a PCR will produce the best quality results in the shortest time; adding too much or not enough DNA will result in a profile that is difficult or even impossible to interpret. This is especially important when profiling forensic samples, when it is very difficult to know the state of preservation of the biological material and also, in many cases, it is difficult to estimate how much cellular material has been collected. It is less important to quantify

DNA when using some reference samples - where similar amounts of DNA can be expected to be extracted each time as there are not very many variables. Even so, many laboratories will still quantify the DNA from reference samples as part of their standard analysis. In response to the importance of quantification of samples recovered from the scene of crime, the DNA Advisory Board in the USA adopted rules that made quantification of human DNA mandatory.

The quantity of DNA that can be extracted from a sample depends very much on the type of material. Each nucleated cell contains approximately 6 pg of DNA: liquid blood contains 5000–10 000 nucleated blood cells per millilitre; semen contains on average 66 million spermatozoa per millilitre (the average ejaculation produces 2.75 ml of semen). Biological samples recovered from the scene of crime are not usually in pristine condition and can often consist of a very small number of shed epithelial cells; consequently, the amount of DNA that can be recovered can be extremely low and difficult to quantify.

Visualization on agarose gels

A relatively quick and easy method for assessing both the quantity and quality of extracted DNA is to visualize it on an agarose gel. Agarose is a polymer that can be poured into a variety of gel forms - mini gels approximately 10 cm long are sufficient to visualize DNA. The gel is submerged in electrophoresis buffer and the DNA is loaded into wells that are formed in the gel by a comb; an electric current is applied across the gel and the negatively charged DNA migrates towards the anode. The agarose gel forms a porous matrix and smaller DNA molecules move through the gel more quickly than do larger DNA molecules. Dyes that intercalate with the DNA double helix, such as ethidium bromide, can be added to the gel either before or after electrophoresis, the amount of intercalated dye is proportional to the quantity of DNA. An alternative dye, DAPI (4',6-diamidino-2-phenylindole), can be added directly to the DNA before electrophoresis. This migrates through the gel bound to the minor groove of double stranded DNA. DNA is visualized by placing the gel on a transilluminator that emits UV light at 260 nm.

Quantification standards can be run along side the unknown samples to allow the DNA concentrations to be estimated. In addition to showing the presence of DNA, the size of the extracted DNA molecules can also be estimated. High molecular weight DNA can be seen as a single band while degraded DNA or DNA that has been sheared during extraction appears as a smear. This makes comparison to the standards difficult as the DNA is spread out over a range rather than in a single band.

The advantages of agarose gel electrophoresis are that it is quick and easy to carry out and also gives an indication of the size of the DNA molecules that have been extracted. The disadvantages are that quantifications are subjective, based on relative band intensities; it is difficult to gauge the amounts of degraded DNA as there is no suitable reference standard; total DNA is detected that can be a mixture of human and microbial DNA, and this can lead to over estimates of the DNA concentration; it cannot be used to quantify samples extracted using the Chelex method as this produces single stranded DNA and the fluorescent dyes that intercalate with the double stranded DNA do not bind to the single stranded DNA.

Ultraviolet spectrophotometry

DNA absorbs light maximally at 260 nm. This feature can be used to estimate the amount of DNA in an extract and by measuring a range of wavelengths from 220 nm to 300 nm it is also possible to assess the amount of carbohydrate (maximum absorbance 230 nm) and protein (maximum absorbance 280 nm) that may have co-extracted with the sample. The DNA is placed in a quartz cuvette and light is shone through; the absorbance is measured against a standard. A clean DNA extract will produce a curve; if the DNA extract is clean, the ratio of the absorbance at 260 nm and 280 nm should be between 1.8 and 2.0.

Spectrophotometry is commonly used for quantification in molecular biology laboratories but has not been widely adopted by the forensic community. The major disadvantage is that it is difficult to quantify small amounts of DNA accurately using spectrophotometry, it is not human specific and other chemicals, for example, dyes from clothing and humic acids from bone samples, can interfere with the analysis.

Fluorescence spectrophotometry

Ethidium bromide or DAPI (4',6-diamidino-2-phenylindole) can be used to visualize DNA in agarose gels – these are both examples of chemicals that fluoresce at much higher levels when they intercalate with DNA. In addition to staining agarose gels, fluorescent dyes can also be used as an alternative to UV spectrophotometry for DNA quantitation. A range of dyes has been developed that can be used with fluorescent microplate readers and these are very sensitive. The PicoGreen dye is specific for double stranded DNA and can detect as little as 25 pg/ml of DNA. When PicoGreen binds to DNA the fluorescence of the dye increases over 1000-fold – ethidium bromide in comparison increases in fluorescence 50–100-fold when it intercalates with double stranded DNA. PicoGreen is very sensitive and is a powerful technique for quantifying total DNA – it does however have the drawback that it is not human specific.

Hybridization

Hybridization based quantification methods have been widely used in forensic genetics since the early 1990s, in particular a commercially available kit Quantiblot. Extracted DNA is applied to a positively charged nylon membrane using a slot or dot blot process; the DNA is then challenged with a probe that is specific to human DNA. A commonly used target is the D17S1 alpha satellite repeat that is on human chromosome 17 in 500–1000 copies. The probe can be labelled in a number of ways including colorimetric and chemiluminescent.

A series of standards is applied to the membrane, and comparison of the signal from the extracted DNA with the standards allows quantification. The advantage of hybridization-based methods is that the quantification is human specific – agarose gel electrophoresis and spectrophotometry detect total DNA and forensic samples that have been exposed to the environment for any length of time are prone to colonization by bacteria and fungi.

The hybridization systems do suffer from a lack of sensitivity. For samples producing a negative result in many cases it is still possible to generate a profile after PCR. The analysis of the results is also subjective, leading different operators to come to different conclusions. In addition to the limited sensitivity, the process is labour intensive, taking approximately 2 hours to produce the blot. Hybridization-based methods are being widely replaced by real-time PCR systems.

Real-time PCR

When generating a DNA profile, the PCR products are normally analysed at the end point after 28–34 cycles. It is, however, possible to monitor the generation of PCR products as they are generated – real time. This was first developed using ethidium bromide: as PCR products are generated in each cycle, more ethidium bromide intercalates with the double-stranded DNA molecule and fluoresces under UV light. The increase in fluorescence can be detected using a suitable '*camera*'. Increasingly sensitive assays have been developed, such as SYBR Green and the TaqMan system. Using SYBR Green, as PCR products are generated, the dye binds to the double-stranded product and the fluorescence increases. The TaqMan system uses a different approach, with two primers and a probe; the probe is within the region defined by the primers and is labelled on the 5' end with a fluorescent molecule and on the 3' end with a molecule that quenches the fluorescence. As the primers are extended by the *Taq* polymerase, one of them meets the probe, which is degraded by the polymerase, releasing the probe and the quencher into solution - efficient quenching of the fluorescent molecules only occurs when they are in close proximity on the probe molecule.

As more PCR products are generated, more fluorescent molecules are released and the fluorescence from the sample increases. Real-time assays are highly sensitive, human specific and are not labour intensive.

DNA IQ System

A novel approach to quantification is used in the commercially available DNA IQ Isolation System. The isolation method is based on salting-out and binding to silica: a very specific amount of silica coated beads is added to the extraction and these bind a maximum amount of DNA; therefore, when the DNA is eluted from the beads the maximum concentration is known. It has the advantage of combining the extraction and quantification steps but has the disadvantage of not being human specific.

3

Analysing Minisatellite DNA

Over 20 years have passed since the development of DNA fingerprinting, which marked the beginning of forensic DNA typing. Since then, human tandem repeat DNA sequences have become the preferred choice for forensic DNA analysis. These repeat sequences are classified into minisatellites (*variable number tandem repeats*, VNTRs) and microsatellites (*short tandem repeats*, STRs). In this chapter, we will discuss the historical and current forensic applications of such tandem repeats.

Minisatellites

'DNA Fingerprinting' using Multi-locus Probes (MLPs)

Roughly 3 % of the human genome is comprised of tandem repeats that – with the exclusion of *satellite DNA* – can be classified into two groups according to the size of the repeat unit and overall length of the repeat array. Human *minisatellites* or VNTR loci have repeat units ranging in length from 6 bp to more than 100 bp depending on the locus, with arrays usually kilobases in length. Human GC-rich minisatellites are preferentially found clustered in the recombination-proficient subtelomeric regions of chromosomes. Some minisatellite loci show very high levels of allele length variability.

The accidental discovery of hypervariable minisatellite loci detectable with MLPs in 1984 by Sir Alec Jeffreys launched a new age in forensic investigation. These minisatellites were detected by hybridization of probes to Southern blots of restriction-enzyme-digested genomic DNA, to reveal *restriction fragment length polymorphisms* (RFLPs). A common 10–15 bp '*core*' GC-rich sequence shared between different minisatellite loci allowed MLPs to detect a wide array of minisatellites simultaneously, producing multi-band (barcode-like) patterns known as '*DNA fingerprints*'.

Using only a single MLP designated 33.15, the match probability between unrelated individuals was estimated at $<3 \times 10^{-11}$, and in the case of two MLPs (33.15 and 33.6) that detect different sets of minisatellites the match probability is $<5 \times 10^{-19}$. These probabilities are so low that the only individuals possessing identical DNA fingerprints are *monozygotic* twins. The MLPs have proven their use in paternity testing and immigration cases. However, a significant drawback associated with MLPs is the requirement for several micrograms of high-quality genomic DNA in order to obtain reliable DNA fingerprints. Because forensic specimens are often old and yield small quantities of degraded DNA, MLPs are not generally suitable for forensic analysis, although they were successfully implemented in a number of early criminal investigations.

DNA Profiling using Single-locus Probes (SLPs)

To circumvent the limitations of MLPs, specific cloned minisatellites were used as SLPs to produce simpler '*DNA profiles*' and were applied in criminal case-work even before MLPs were commercially established as the standard method for paternity testing. Since each SLP detects only a single minisatellite, it produces two band (two allele) patterns, but is still highly polymorphic due to the use of hypervariable minisatellites. Single-locus probes have considerable advantages over MLPs in analysing forensic specimens. The method is far more sensitive, with the limit of band detection at around 10 ng of genomic DNA. Mixed DNA samples such as semen in vaginal swabs can be analysed with relative ease because the original DNA (from the victim) has only two bands and subsequent autoradiography will reveal whether the profile has more than two bands. Secondly, because allele sizes can be estimated and included in databases, the comparison of samples does not require side-by-side electrophoresis, which overcomes the inter-blot comparison problem associated with DNA fingerprinting. However, owing to continuous allele size distribution and the resolution limits of agarose gel electrophoresis, SLP allele sizing cannot be done with absolute precision. Two procedures for determining allele frequencies and match probabilities in the face of measurement errors are the floating-bin and the fixed-bin methods.

The true discriminating power of SLPs was compromised for no appropriate reason by genetically inappropriate calculations based on the '*ceiling principle*' or '*interim ceiling principle*' invented by the National Research Council of the United States; these calculations were abandoned in 1996.

Amplified Fragment Length Polymorphisms (AFLPs)

Some minisatellite loci with relatively short (~1000 bp) alleles can be amplified via *polymerase chain reaction* (PCR) to yield AFLPs. Before PCR-based typing of microsatellite loci was established, one such minisatellite locus called *D1S80* was used extensively within the realm of forensic DNA analysis. In the *D1S80* system, fragments between the range of 14–42 repeat units (16 bp per repeat) are amplified to yield alleles considerably smaller than the fragments normally analysed in DNA fingerprinting and profiling.

In contrast to RFLP analysis, *D1S80* alleles fall into discrete size classes and thus can be compared directly to a standard composite of most alleles (an *allelic ladder*) on the same gel. This was a significant improvement that was also employed in subsequent STR systems. In *D1S80*, the amplified DNA fragments were commonly detected using a silver stain, with the final profile usually showing two bands from which the numbers of repeat units can be easily estimated. Although the *D1S80* locus in particular contains four common alleles with frequencies of > 10% in Japanese people, the likelihood of discrimination between two unrelated individuals is still high.

This has been the preferred locus for analysing forensic specimens worldwide. In addition to this locus, PCR-based methods utilizing commercial kits that exploit *single nucleotide polymorphisms* (SNPs), including *HLA-DQ*α and the five PolyMarker loci (*LDLR*, *GYPA*, *HBGG*, *D7S8* and *Gc*), were popularly used in the 1990s. Recently, the National Institute of Police Science (Japan) developed a novel genotyping method that involves PCR and fluorescent-labelled primers detected by capillary electrophoresis. This method has allowed for higher accuracy since the results are not prone to human error.

However, after the detailed evaluation of allele frequency data in the world population at *D1S80* and increasing practical usage of multiplex STR systems, *D1S80* has been gradually abandoned in favour of STRs.

Minisatellite Variable Repeat (MVR)-PCR

The majority of minisatellite loci consist of heterogeneous arrays of two or more repeat unit types (MVRs) that differ slightly. The human hypervariable minisatellites characterized to date vary not only in the number of repeat copies (allele length) but also in the interspersion pattern of variant repeat units within the array. This internal variation provides a highly informative approach to the study of allelic variation and the processes of mutation. Interspersion patterns can be determined by MVR mapping and this reveals far more variability than allele length analysis.

The first MVR mapping was developed at locus *D1S8* (minisatellite MS32). This particular minisatellite consists of a 29 bp repeat unit showing two classes of MVR that differ by a single base substitution, resulting in the presence or absence of an *Hae*III restriction site. Extremely high levels of variation in the interspersion patterns of two types of repeat within the alleles have been revealed by *Hae*III digestion of PCR-amplified alleles. Subsequently, a technically simpler version of a PCR-based mapping system (MVR-PCR) was invented. In addition to a primer at a fixed site in the DNA flanking the minisatellite, this assay reveals the internal variation of repeats by using an MVR primer specific to one or more types of variant repeat. The MVR-specific primers at low concentration will bind to just one of their complementary repeat units in the PCR, thus MVR locations will be represented as an array of sequentially sized, amplified DNA fragments. To analyse two different types of repeat, MVR-PCR uses a single flanking primer plus two different MVR primers to generate two complementary ladders of amplified products corresponding to the length between the flanking primer and the location of one or other of the repeat types within the minisatellite repeat array. In order to prevent the progressive shortening of PCR products by internal priming of the MVR-specific primers, '*tagged*' amplification that uncouples MVR detection from subsequent amplification is used.

The MVR-PCR products are separated by electrophoresis on an agarose gel and detected by Southern blotting and hybridization to an isotope-labelled minisatellite probe. The PCR reaction for each of the two MVR-specific primers is carried out in a separate tube, and products are loaded in adjacent lanes in an agarose gel. Some work has been done that involves the labelling of variant primers with different-coloured fluorescent tags and amplifying both sets of MVR products in a single reaction, to facilitate comparison of the complementary MVR profiles. The MVR-PCR technique has revealed enormous levels of allelic variation at several human hypervariable minisatellites: MS32 (*D1S8*), MS31A (*D7S21*), MS205 (*D16S309*), CEBl (*D2S90*), g3 (*D7S22*), YNH24 (*D2S44*), B6.7 and the insulin minisatellite.

At a minority of loci such as MS32, where almost all repeat units are of the same length, a diploid MVR map of the interspersion patterns of repeats from two alleles superimposed can be generated from total genomic DNA and encoded as a digital diploid code. Since different length repeats will cause the MVR maps of each allele to drift out of register, most minisatellites are not amenable to this diploid coding, and instead only single allele coding is possible. Both single allele and diploid codes are highly suitable for computer databasing and analysis.

Allele-specific MVR-PCR methods have been developed to map single alleles from total genomic DNA using allele-specific PCR primers directed to polymorphic SNP sites in the DNA flanking the minisatellite. These SNP primer pairs are identical, with the exception of a 3′ terminal mismatch that corresponds to the variant flanking base. This method is extremely expedient since it does not involve the time-consuming separation of the alleles by agarose gel electrophoresis. Another added advantage of allele-specific MVR-PCR is its ability to recover individual-specific typing data from DNA mixtures.

The MVR-PCR technique is the best approach for exploiting the potential of hypervariable minisatellite loci because of the unambiguous nature of MVR mapping and the generation of digital MVR codes suitable for computer analysis. Code generation does not require standardization of electrophoretic systems, is immune to gel distortions and band shifts, does not involve error-prone DNA fragment length measurement and does not require side-by-side comparisons of DNA samples on the same gel.

For these reasons, MVR-PCR is well-suited for use in forensic analysis. The potential for forensic applications have been demonstrated by obtaining authentic diploid MVR coding ladders from only 1 ng of genomic DNA from blood-stains, saliva stains, seminal stains and plucked hair roots. This is done by determining the source of saliva on a used postage stamp, by making MVR coding ladders quickly without any need for blotting and hybridization and by maternal identification from remains of an infant and placenta. While forensic samples in general contain partially degraded DNA, MVR-PCR does not require intact minisatellite alleles. Such DNA samples yield truncated codes due to the disappearance of longer PCR products, but these codes are still compatible with the original allele information. Although replicate runs on the same sample and reading consensus codes are required, reliable codes can be obtained from as low as 100 pg of genomic DNA by MVR-PCR at MS32.

The MVR-PCR method at MS32 and at minisatellite MS31A has also been applied to paternity testing. The potential for establishing paternity in cases lacking a mother was demonstrated by a major contribution to the paternity index made possible by the extremely rare paternal alleles at these two loci. Similarly, these rare alleles proved vital in confirming the relationship between a boy and his alleged grandparents despite an inconsistency (i.e. mutant allele) between the father and grandparents at one of the STR loci. Significant germline mutation rates to new length alleles have been observed at some hypervariable loci, which will generate false paternal exclusions in about 1.8% of paternity cases. In such cases, allele length measurements do not allow the distinction of non-paternity from mutation. In contrast, detailed knowledge of the mutation processes, coupled with MVR analysis of allele structures, can help distinguish mutations from non-paternity. This theory was tested at MS32 using both real and simulated allele data. Since MVR-PCR allows information to be recovered from at least 40 repeat units, a mutant paternal allele will be identical to the progenitor paternal allele - with the exception of the first few repeats. Most germline mutation events altering repeat array structures are targeted to this region, most likely due to its proximity to a flanking recombination hotspot that appears to drive repeat instability. Thus, a mutant paternal allele in a child will tend to resemble one of the father's alleles more than most other alleles in the population. This approach is unlikely to work at extremely hypervariable minisatellite loci such as CEB1 and B6.7, given their very high rate of germline instability coupled with complex germline mutation events that can radically alter allele structure in a single mutation event.

The MVR-PCR technique reveals enormous levels of variation, unmatched by any other single-locus typing system. At MS32, for example, almost all alleles in several ethnic populations surveyed were different. However, different alleles can show significant similarities in repeat organization. Heuristic dot-matrix algorithms have been developed to identify significant allele alignments and have shown that approximately three-quarters of alleles mapped to date can be grouped into over 100 sets of alignable alleles, indicating relatively ancient groups of related alleles present in diverse populations. Some small groups of alleles can display a strong tendency to be population-specific, consistent with recent divergence from a common ancestral allele. In most groups, the 5′ ends of the aligned MVR maps show most variability due to the existence of the flanking recombination hotspot, therefore MVR allele analysis at MS32 can serve not only as a tool for individual identification but also for giving clues regarding the ethnic background of an individual. Another locus that provided a clear and detailed view of allelic divergence between African and non-African populations is MS205. A restricted set of allele families was found in non-African populations and formed a subset of the much greater diversity seen in Africans, which supports arguments for a recent African origin for modern human diversity at this locus. Very similar findings emerged from MVR analyses of the insulin minisatellite, again pointing to a major bottleneck in the 'Out of Africa' founding of non-African populations.

Finally, MVR-PCR has been developed at the Y-chromosome-specific variable minisatellite *DYF155S1* (MSY1), with potential for extracting male-specific information from mixed male/female samples. This marker is also useful for paternity exclusion and, if adequate population data are available and the allele is rare, can be used in individual identification and paternity inclusion.

Unfortunately, MVR-PCR has rarely been used in forensic analysis despite its simplicity, considerable discriminatory power and its ability to reveal enormous levels of variation.

Microsatellites

As with minisatellites, microsatellites are tandemly repeated DNA sequences and are also known as simple sequence repeats or STRs. They consist of repeat units of 1–5 bp typically repeated 5–30 times. Most microsatellite loci can be efficiently amplified by standard PCR since the repeat regions are shorter than 100 bp. Some microsatellites can display substantial polymorphism - though far less than at the most variable minisatellites - and are found abundantly through-out the human genome, which contains over a million of these loci. Microsatellites are particularly suitable for analysing forensic specimens containing degraded and/or limited amounts of DNA. The first forensic application of microsatellites involved typing the skeletal remains of a murder victim, followed by the identification of Josef Mengele, the Auschwitz '*Angel of Death*'. Although the spurious shadow or stutter bands often observed at dinucleotide repeat loci can make interpretation difficult, small PCR products can be sized with precision by *polyacrylamide gel electrophoresis* (PAGE). Because interpretation can sometimes be difficult, current typing systems employ the use of microsatellites with repeat units 4 bp long to minimize problems of stuttering. The microsatellite approach allows very high throughput via multiplex PCR (single-tube PCR reactions that amplify multiple loci) and fluorescent detection systems have been developed to allow substantial automation of gel or capillary electrophoresis and DNA profile interpretation.

Microsatellite analysis is highly sensitive and can even recover information from a single cell. Discrete allele sizes, combined with automated electrophoresis and interpretation, make unambiguous assignment of alleles possible. For these reasons, the USA, most European nations and numerous other countries have established ever-growing databases. In the United Kingdom, 10 autosomal STR loci plus the amelogenin sex test, typed using the '*second-generation multiplex*' (SGM) Plus system, are used in forensic practice. The SGM Plus loci generate random match probabilities of typically 10^{-11} between two unrelated individuals in the three UK racial groups. The US FBI CODIS (Combined DNA Index System) uses 13 STRs plus amelogenin. These loci produce extremely low random match probabilities. For example, around 60% of Japanese individuals show match probabilities of 10^{-14}–10^{-17}. In 2003, the Japanese National Police Agency (NPA) introduced a nine-microsatellite locus system, which uses some CODIS loci, for analysing forensic specimens. From allele frequencies at these nine loci, around 60% of Japanese individuals have match probabilities of 10^{-9}– 10^{-11}. This particular system also detects X–Y homologous amelogenin genes to reveal the sex of a sample. Recently, new multiplexes that amplify 16 loci in a single reaction, including amelogenin, have been commercially developed. These systems produce even lower match probabilities without sacrificing sensitivity, and it is likely that such systems will remain the standard for analysing specimens in both forensic applications and paternity tests. The Japanese NPA has taken initiative in implementing this system in its forensic applications since 2006.

In situations where a direct comparison between evidence and a suspect is being made, mutation rates are an insignificant issue. However, with comparisons between relatives in parentage testing and kinship analysis – such as victim identification in mass disasters – mutational events may lead to false negatives. In comparison to minisatellites, the mutation rate in most microsatellites is much lower, 0.2% at the most. Consequently, microsatellites are better suited for paternity testing as long as a greater number of loci are used compared with minisatellites, in order to compensate for the relatively low level of polymorphism at each locus.

In recent years the development of commercialized kits has reduced what once was a painstaking task into a simple procedure. Since its inception, these kits have achieved new heights in quality and the microsatellite systems commercially available today have a high standard of sensitivity. Unfortunately, the forensic specimens that we encounter in the field are often degraded or fragmented. As a result, when amplification of DNA is attempted at loci yielding relatively long PCR products, we often fail to retrieve any PCR products, making it impossible to determine the genotypes of these particular loci. To remedy this situation, innovative PCR techniques known as '*mini-STRs*' are currently being developed, which involve bringing primer annealing sites closer to the microsatellites in order to shorten the PCR products, and selecting loci with relatively short allele length distributions. Recently, two different parallel strategies have emerged in Europe. The first employs a 13-STR loci multiplex incorporating three mini-STRs into the currently used multiplex test. The second strategy employs a multiplex of six high-molecular-weight STRs (also in current use), modified to provide smaller amplicons with an additional two loci of high discriminating power. Eventually, the two strategies will merge to provide a single multiplex of 15 STR loci. In this section, we have addressed the applications of autosomal microsatellites; however, microsatellites in the Y chromosome (YSTRs) are of equal importance and should not be ignored. Detailed information on forensic microsatellites can be obtained at STRBase.

In the future, technological advances, along with newer and more improved methods, may give rise to an alternative typing platform utilizing SNPs. This could greatly accelerate typing and offers the potential for DNA analysis to be conducted at the scene of crime. However, even with the introduction of an alternative typing platform, the multiplex microsatellite markers employed today will remain in use for the time being, primarily because millions of DNA profiles - such as those contained in national databases - were generated with STR loci and will require ongoing maintenance.

4

ENDOGENOUS NUCLEOBASE

The past decade has witnessed an emerging appreciation for the complexity of DNA damage caused by agents arising as consequence of the normal physiology of human cells. These so-called *endogenous DNA* lesions span the full range of chemical reactions, including oxidation, reduction, halogenation, alkylation, nitrosation and hydrolysis, with damage affecting both the nucleobase and deoxyribose moieties of DNA. A recent review by De Bont and van Larebeke addresses many of the endogenous base lesions with a thorough compilation of estimates of the quantities of lesions in mammalian cells and tissues.

While lesions derived by oxidation of purines and pyridines have received significant attention over the past 20 years, it is only recently that lesions derived from lipid peroxidation products and nucleobase deamination have emerged as both complex and multifaceted. This chapter will focus on nucleobase deamination in light of recent technical advances in analytical methods to quantify nucleobase deamination products, as well as several recent observations on the stability of these DNA lesions and the diverse mechanisms of their formation.

Nucleobase deamination by any mechanism results in the formation of xanthine, hypoxanthine and uracil, with nitrosative mechanisms leading to the formation of oxanine, abasic sites and DNA cross-linking. This chapter addresses the diversity of mechanisms involved in nucleobase deamination in DNA and RNA, with an update on the currently known mechanisms and discussion of several novel pathways that may influence the cellular burden of these toxic and mutagenic DNA lesions.

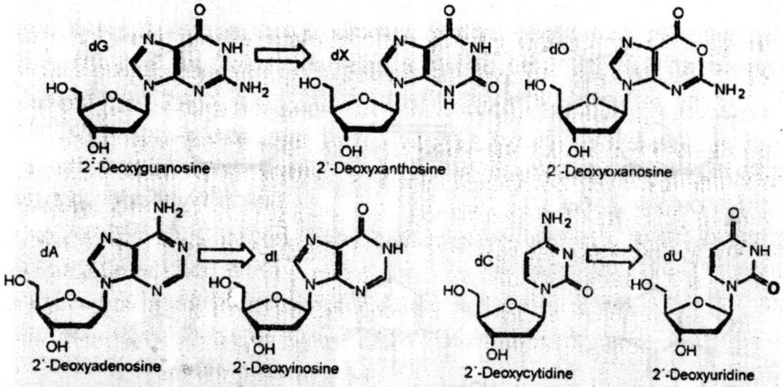

Fig. 4.1. Nucleobase deamination products as 2′-deoxyribonucleosides.

Stability of dX to Depurination

One factor contributing to the relatively slow progress in studies of nucleobase deamination has been the presumed, though unsubstantiated at the time, instability of dX toward depurination. Two recent studies, however, have confirmed that, at neutral pH, dX is a relatively stable lesion capable of contributing to the mutagenic burden of cells. Suzuki and coworkers observed that dX was approximately 40-fold less stable to depurination than dG at pH 4 and 37°C, but without knowledge of the temperature- and pH-dependence of dX depurination, it is not possible to extrapolate the data to biological conditions. In more rigorous studies, Termini and coworkers observed that, at acidic pH, depurination of dX occurred an order of magnitude more rapidly than dG in a single-stranded oligodeoxynucleotide, but found depurination to occur at a rate similar to that of dG at neutral pH. Vongchampa et al. determined the pH-dependence of dX depurination kinetics in the form of a 2′-deoxynucleoside, and as single- and double-stranded oligodeoxynucleotides. At neutral pH, dX in double-stranded DNA has a half-life of ~2 years, with the depurination rate constant inversely proportional to pH. This behavior is similar to the pH-dependence for depurination of dG and dA in DNA observed by Lindahl and Nyberg and it is consistent with the two depurination processes: an acid-catalyzed protonation of dX at pH <7 with a depurination rate constant of 2.6×10^{-5} s^{-1} and a pH-independent hydrolysis at pH >7 with a rate constant of 1.3×10^{-8} s^{-1}. The latter value is ~100-fold greater than the analogous rate constant of ~10^{-10} s^{-1} for depurination of dG and dA in DNA at 37°C and pH 7. Though Vongchampa et al. observed a 5-fold increase in dX stability upon incorporation into a single-stranded

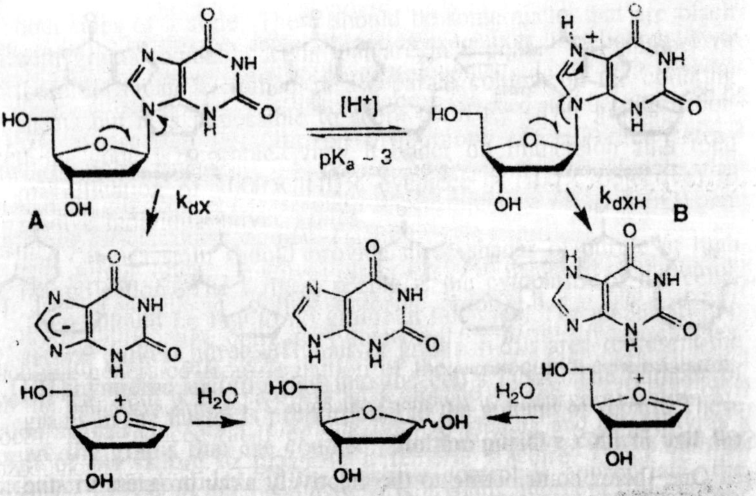

Fig. 4.2. Pathways for depurination of dX.

oligo, they observed a much smaller reduction in the rate of dX depurination in double-stranded oligodeoxynucleotide than the expected 3- to 4-fold reduction based on depurination of dG and dA in DNA. One explanation for the lack of a stabilizing effect may be related to the relatively low pKa of ~5.6 for the N^3 of dX, which, at pH 7, would result in a negative charge for ~95% of the xanthine bases and destabilization of the helix.

These studies point to a role for dX in the mutagenicity of base deamination products. With a half-life of 2 years, endogenously formed dX residues, if not repaired, can be expected to undergo depurination to the extent of only 3% and 11% in one and four months, respectively. Given the relatively slow rate of cell division in tissues such as the human colon, the bulk of dX residues in a cell will be present during cell replication and may thus contribute to mutagenesis.

Analytical Methods and Artifacts

A variety of methods have been developed to quantify nucleobase deamination products, but few have the necessary sensitivity and reproducibility required to measure DNA lesions occurring with frequencies below 1 per 10^6 nucleotides (nt) and all are subject to artifact due to the activity of nucleobase deaminase enzymes that are ubiquitous in prokaryotic and eukaryotic cells. Several efforts to measure uracil have employed *high-performance liquid chromatography* (HPLC) quantification, ^{32}P post-labeling of 2′-deoxyribonucleosides released from DNA, and uptake and labeling of DNA with ^3H-uridine or ^3H-2′-

deoxyuridine. These methods suffer from artifacts of cytosine deamination, RNA-derived uracil contamination and high variability, and all are not sensitive enough to detect background levels of dU in DNA.

As with other DNA and RNA lesions, the most sensitive and accurate methods for the quantification of nucleobase deamination products employ a gas or liquid chromatograph coupled to a mass spectrometer (GC/MS, LC/MS, LC/MS/MS). This approach combines the resolving power of chromatography with the sensitivity and rigor of mass spectrometry for identifying specific chemical species, with sensitivities to 5 lesions per 10^8 nt in 50 μg of DNA. GC/MS approaches have been used to quantify uracil, xanthine and hypoxanthine as free bases. LC/MS methods have been developed for oxanine and dO, inosine in RNA, dX, dI and dU in DNA.

The major hurdle to accurate quantification of nucleobase deamination products in DNA and RNA is the activity of deaminase enzymes present in all cells. The most notable recent example is the dC deaminase activity termed activation-induced cytidine deaminase (AID). As will be discussed earlier, this enzyme performs a critical function in immunoglobulin diversification by apparently causing sequence selective cytidine deamination either in DNA or RNA. Other nucleobase deaminase activities include the adenosine deaminase involved in RNA editing and purine nucleotide metabolism, and guanine deaminase involved in purine base salvage pathways. These enzymes have the potential to cause deamination of nucleobases in DNA during cell manipulations, DNA isolation and during DNA processing. We encountered significant dA deaminase activity as a contaminant of commercial sources of alkaline phosphatase, as well as adventitious dC deaminase activity in human B-lymphoblastoid TK6 cells, which is not surprising given the expression of AID protein in B cells.

The solution to the problem of undesirable deaminase activity is the use of deaminase inhibitors. As shown 3,4,5,6-tetrahydrouridine (THU) is a specific and potent inhibitor of C/dC deaminase that decreases the detected level of dU when present during processing of TK6 cell DNA for LC/MS analysis. Coformycin is a specific inhibitor of adenosine deaminase that effectively inhibits dI formation without interfering with alkaline phosphatase activity when added during DNA processing. While we have not yet encountered adventitious dG deaminase activity in *Escherichia coli*, yeast, mouse or human cells, the availability of guanine deaminase inhibitors, azepinomycin and 4,6-

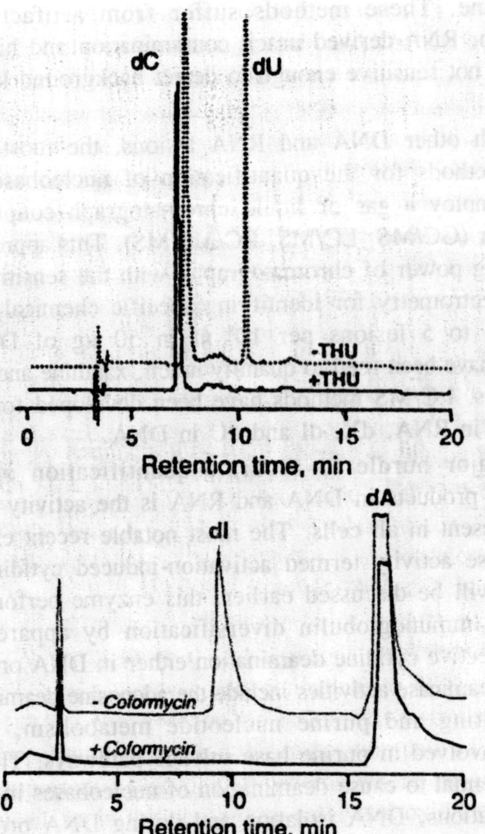

Fig. 4.3. HPLC analysis of THU inhibition of dC deaminase activity (upper) and coformycin inhibition of dA deaminase activity (lower). Dashed line: no inhibitor; solid line: presence of inhibitor.

diamino-8H-1-hydroxyethoxymethyl-8-iminoimidazo[4,5-e][1,3]diazepine, suggests that its emergence would not pose an insoluble problem. It is important to consider that these inhibitors have not seen widespread use in published analytical methods for nucleobase deamination products, so there is some question about the accuracy of the quantities of dX, dI and dU determined *in vitro* and *in vivo*.

Simple Hydrolytic Mechanisms

In addition to exogenous agents such as bisulfite, there are three major endogenous mechanisms for nucleobase deamination. As illustrated, the simplest is hydrolytic deamination that occurs in all aqueous environments and that has been the subject of numerous reviews

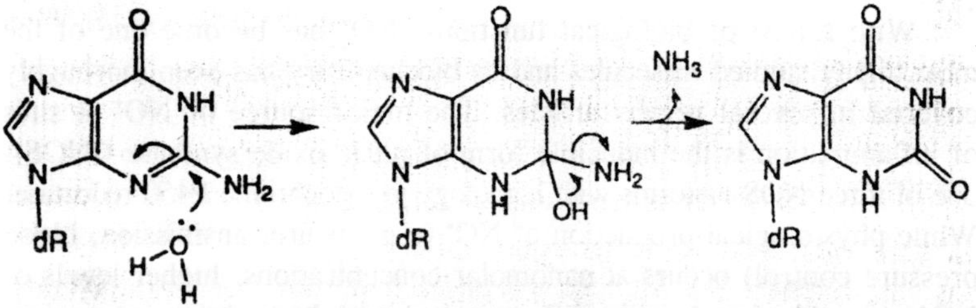

Fig. 4.4. Hydrolytic deamination of dG to form dX.

that obviate repetition here. The propensity for hydrolytic deamination of DNA occurs in the order 5-methyl-dC > dC > dA > dG, with a half-life for dC in the range of 10^2–10^3 years for single-stranded DNA and 10^4–10^5 years in double-stranded DNA. C^5-Methylation of dC increases the rate of deamination by 2- to 20-fold. The high rate in dC and 5′-methyl-dC has been proposed to account for the fact that C→T mutations at CpG sites represent the most common human mutation, though CpG motifs have also been observed to be hotspots for reactions by a variety of genotoxic chemicals.

Nitrosative Deamination and Inflammation

While there are established environmental sources of nitrosating agents, endogenous agents may represent the major source of nitrosative stress in humans. Epidemiological studies demonstrate an association between chronic inflammation and increased cancer risk, such as the links between inflammatory bowel disease and colon cancer, *Helicobacter pylori* infection and gastric cancer and *Schistosoma haematobium* infection and bladder cancer. The strongest evidence for a mechanistic link between inflammation and cancer involves the generation of *reactive oxygen species* (ROS) and *reactive nitrogen species* (RNS) by macrophages and neutrophils in response to cytokines and other signaling processes arising at sites of inflammation. These chemical mediators of inflammation cause damage to surrounding host tissue by oxidation, nitration, halogenation and deamination of biomolecules of all types, with the formation of toxic and mutagenic products leading to somatic mutations associated with malignant transformation, with additional contribution mechanisms that are independent of genotoxicity. Of particular importance here are the RNS arising from *nitric oxide* (NO) production by activated macrophages, the chemistry of which leads, along one pathway, to nitrosating species capable of nucleobase deamination in DNA and RNA.

NO$^{\bullet}$ Biochemistry

With a host of biological functions, NO$^{\bullet}$ has become one of the most highly studied molecules and its biochemistry has been thoroughly covered in several review articles. The major source of NO$^{\bullet}$ at sites of inflammation is the inducible form of nitric oxide synthase (iNOS), one of three NOS isoforms with homology to cytochrome P450 reductase. While physiological production of NO$^{\bullet}$ (e.g., neurotransmission, blood pressure control) occurs at nanomolar concentrations, higher levels of NO$^{\bullet}$ are associated with inflammation and host defenses against microbes. Macrophage cultures activated with lipopolysaccharide and INF-γ *in vitro* have been shown to produce NO$^{\bullet}$ at a rate of ~6 pmol s^{-1} per 10^6 cells or 4×10^6 molecules of NO$^{\bullet}$ per cell. The data regarding biologically relevant levels of NO$^{\bullet}$ are not firm, but it is generally assumed that steady-state concentrations of NO$^{\bullet}$ do not exceed ~1 μM at sites of inflammation. With inflammation lasting months or years, local epithelial cells are thus exposed to significant quantities of ROS and RNS. While NO$^{\bullet}$ is released from macrophages in combination with many other species (e.g., hydrogen peroxide, tumor necrosis factor, cytokines), studies with NO$^{\bullet}$ scavengers point to NO$^{\bullet}$ as the key mediator of macrophage-induced cytostasis.

In chronically inflamed tissue, high local levels of NO$^{\bullet}$ are available for reaction with oxygen or superoxide to generate a multitude of reactive species. The biological effects of NO$^{\bullet}$ ultimately depend on the complexity of the cellular milieu, including concentrations of superoxide and oxygen, enzymes such as catalase and superoxide dismutase, antioxidants such as glutathione, and the diffusion distances between generator cells and target cells. In general terms, however, the reactions of NO$^{\bullet}$ fall along three major pathways in biological systems: (1) diffusion and intracellular consumption; (2) auto-oxidation to form nitrous anhydride, N_2O_3; and (3) reaction with superoxide to form peroxynitrite, $ONOO^-$. $ONOO^-$ can oxidize and nitrate DNA and may potentially cause strand breaks through attack on the sugar-phosphate backbone.

Background on N_2O_3-induced Nucleobase Deamination

The oxidation of NO$^{\bullet}$ by molecular oxygen leads to the formation of N_2O_3 and a number of other nitrosating agents, including the nitrosonium ion (NO^+), nitrous acidium ion ($NO\text{-}OH_2^+$), NOX and N_2O_4, that are favored in gas-phase reactions or under highly acidic conditions. However, while acidified solutions of NO_2^- will generate nitrosating agents, deamination of DNA bases at physiological pH in cells is likely mediated primarily by N_2O_3. In addition to forming N-nitrosamines, this powerful nitrosating agent will react with the primary and heterocyclic amines in DNA bases to cause conversion of cytosine to uracil (2′-deoxyuridine, dU), guanine to xanthine (2′-deoxyxanthosine, dX) and oxanine (2′-deoxyoxanosine, dO; observed with HNO_2 at low pH), 5-methylcytosine to thymine and adenine to hypoxanthine (2′-deoxyinosine, dI), as well as abasic sites and inter or intra-strand G–G cross-links. The reactivity of DNA bases with N_2O_3 is reversed relative to hydrolysis and the abasic sites arise by nitrosation of the N^7-dG and N^7 or N^3 of dA that destabilizes the glycosidic bond and leads to depurination. While nitrosative deamination of dC and dA appear to involve straightforward chemistry, the formation of dO and dX has been the subject of some controversy.

Unusual Chemistry of N_2O_3-induced Deamination of dG

The chemistry of nitrosative deamination of nucleobases in DNA has proven to be both complicated and experimentally challenging to de fine. The simplest mechanism, and the one likely to account for formation of dU from dC and dI from dA, involves nitrosation of exocyclic amines in the nucleobases with subsequent nucleophilic substitution of N_2 by water. The observed formation of abasic sites likely involves similar N-nitrosation of the N7 positions of dG and dA. However, it is now clear that the decades-old assumption of a simple guaninediazonium ion intermediate common to xanthine and G–G cross-links is incorrect and that a more complicated mechanism exists to account for chemistry. The major challenge to this simple model is the observed formation of two deamination products of dG: dX and dO in reactions involving nitrosative chemistry. Suzuki et al. originally described the formation of dO in reactions of nucleosides and DNA with nitrite under acidic (pH$<$4) conditions and subsequently described the physicochemical and biological properties of dO. Shuker and coworkers also observed the formation of oxanine base in reactions of 2′-deoxyribonucleotides and calf thymus DNA with millimolar concentrations of the mutagenic nitrosating agent, 1-nitrosoindole-3-acetonitrile (NIAN).

These observations stand in contrast to our inability to detect dO in DNA exposed to $NO^\bullet$ and O_2 under conditions approaching those thought to exist at sites of chronic inflammation, as discussed shortly. Using a sensitive LC/MS method and the addition of deaminase inhibitors, we quantified dX, dI, dO and dU in DNA that was exposed to steady-state concentrations of 1.3 μM $NO^\bullet$ and 190 μM O_2

(calculated steady-state concentrations of 40 fM N_2O_3 and 3 pM NO_2) in a recently developed reactor that avoids the anomalous gas-phase chemistry of NO•; the presence of a headspace containing air in earlier delivery systems alters the chemistry of NO• by biasing the formation of N_2O_3 and allowing formation of N_2O_4. Under these conditions, dX, dI and dU were formed at nearly identical rates (k = 1.2×10^5 M^{-1} s^{-1}) to the extent of ~80 lesions per 10^6 nt after 12 h exposure to NO• in the reactor. However, dO was not detected in NO•-exposed DNA at a level of >6 lesions per 10^8 nt, except when the DNA was exposed to nitrite at pH 3.8. This result and the observations of Suzuki et al. suggested a pH-dependent partitioning of the reaction intermediate leading to either X or O. Indeed, it is likely that low pH accounts for Shuker's observation of O formation in DNA exposed to NIAN. In those studies, the observation of extensive depurination of dG, dA and dO suggests an acidic condition arising from weak buffering (0.5 mM Tris) in the presence of millimolar concentrations of NIAN and its degradation products, conditions that would favor the formation of dO in DNA. What has not been explained yet is the observation of dO formation in nucleosides and nucleotides at near-neutral pH by Suzuki and co-workers and possibly by Shuker and co-workers, though the latter studies were again performed under weakly buffered conditions.

To explain these observations, as well as to account for the sequence specificity of dG–dG cross-links formed during nitrosative deamination and the predominance of dX over dO under most conditions, Glaser and coworkers recently proposed an attractive model based on currently available computational data and the experimental results discussed above. The model begins with the basic diazotization of the N_2 position of dG to form diazonium ion 2. In environments not involving double-stranded DNA (e.g., free nucleoside, nucleotide, single-stranded DNA), the diazonium ion can undergo nucleophilic displacement by a water molecule to form dX or it can lose N_2 and undergo pyrimidine ring opening to form cation 3. The latter pathway is the only one leading to dO. In double-stranded DNA, however, base pairing with cytosine is proposed to provide base catalysis for a rapid deprotonation of the dG diazonium ion, with subsequent rapid ring opening to form cyanoimine 4.

Perhaps the weakest point in the model is that subsequent addition of water to 4 in double-stranded DNA leads to formation of 6 rather than 5, with consequential formation of dX rather than dO due to limited C–N bond rotation of 6. Nonetheless, the model adequately accounts for most if not all of the observed deamination products under different conditions. Of course, the model is easily tested by defining the complete product spectra in nucleoside, single- and double-strand DNA forms of dG at a range of pH values. The model would predict that, while dX will always predominate, the proportion of dO should be highest in nucleoside reactions of dG and lowest in double-stranded DNA under biological conditions of pH.

N_2O_3-induced Nucleobase Deamination In Vitro and In Vivo

In addition to dX, both dI and dU have been observed in bacterial and mammalian cells exposed to NO• *in vitro* and in activated macrophages. The major problem with most previous studies of nitrosative DNA damage is that the delivery of NO• and O_2 occurred under conditions not considered to be biologically relevant. For example, Nguyen et al. exposed DNA and TK6 cells to a ~20 mM total bolus (syringe) dose of NO• and found that dX and dI were formed to the extent of 3 and 10 lesions per 10^3 nt, respectively, for isolated DNA, with 3-fold lower levels in cells. Yields of dI and dX in DNA were found to be 15- to 100-times higher, respectively, than those observed with free dA and dG. Similarly, Wink et al. found 5 dU per 10^3 nt in DNA exposed to NO• by bubbling the gas into solution until 1 mol l^{-1} had been absorbed. Caulfield et al. used a delivery system in which Silastic tubing allowed controlled diffusion of NO• into solution (with headspace!) at a rate of 10–20 μM min^{-1} and found that xanthine was formed at twice the rate of uracil and single-stranded DNA oligonucleotides were nearly 10-fold more reactive than double-stranded DNA.

To avoid the anomalous gas-phase chemistry of NO•, Deen and coworkers developed a Silastic tubing-based reactor without headspace. As mentioned earlier, a recent study by Dong et al. employed this reactor to define the spectrum of DNA lesions arising under conditions approaching physiological relevance. While dX, dI and dU were formed at nearly identical rates, dO was not detected in NO•-exposed DNA (<6 lesions per 10^8 nt). Another important observation was the NO•-induced production of abasic sites, which likely arise by nitrosation of the N7 positions of guanine and adenine with subsequent depurination, to the extent of ~10 per 10^6 nt after 12 h of exposure in the NO• reactor. In conjunction with other studies of nitrosatively induced dG–dG cross-links, these results suggest the following spectrum of nitrosative DNA lesions in inflamed tissues: ~2% dG–dG cross-links, 4–6% abasic sites and 25–35% each of dX, dI and dU.

Enzymatic Deamination of Nucleobases

While hydrolysis and nitrosation have been recognized as the major mechanisms of nucleobase deamination for decades, a growing body of literature points to a variety of enzymatic mechanisms with the potential to contribute to the cellular burden of DNA and RNA deamination products.

AID Protein

The most notable recent example of an enzymatic DNA deamination mechanism is the dC deaminase activity termed AID, an enzyme subject to extensive review in the past few years. This enzyme, originally discovered by Honjo and coworkers by subtractive RNA hybridization of transcripts differentially expressed in activated B lymphocytes, performs critical functions in three facets of immunoglobulin diversification: class switch recombination, somatic hypermutation and gene conversion. However, it does not appear to be involved in V(D)J recombination. Whereas class switch recombination requires exchange of heavy chain, class-specific DNA fragments between genes, and thus requires double-stranded DNA cleavage, somatic hypermutation entails generation of numerous point mutations in the variable region exons of Ig heavy and light chain genes to cause combinatorial selection of high affinity antibodies against a novel antigen. As covered in the excellent review by Chaudhuri and Alt, these diverse mechanisms probably require all of the different DNA repair pathways and a host of ancillary proteins in addition to AID. While the biological end-points are clearly defined, the biochemical mechanism underlying these functions are yet to be clearly defined, with evidence pointing to cytidine deamination in both DNA and RNA.

The DNA target hypothesis involves AID-mediated conversion of dC to dU followed, in the case of somatic hypermutation, by mutagenic responses to dU. These include abasic site formation as a result of the action of uracil N-glycosylase, with subsequent polymerase errors at the resulting abasic site; error-prone mismatch repair of the dU:dG pair or polymerase bypass of unrepaired dU. In the case of class switch recombination, the conversion of dC to dU by AID initiates a cascade of repair activities leading to highly controlled, sequence-specific recombination events. The recent claim by Honjo and coworkers that uracil glycosylase is not required for somatic hypermutation is problematic in several regards, the most important of which is that they used DNA double-strand breaks, as inferred from histone H2Ax phosphorylation, as an endpoint for somatic hypermutation. While double-stranded DNA breaks can occur by a statistical coalescence of single-strand breaks, double-strand breaks are not required for somatic hypermutation, so this endpoint seems inappropriate for studying uracil glycosylase involvement in this process. Several other studies have established a role for uracil glycosylase in somatic hypermutation.

The RNA hypothesis, which more narrowly affects class switch recombination and is not supported by experimental evidence, involves the action of AID on one or more hypothetical mRNAs that code for nuclease activities that actually cause the recombination-inducing DNA cleavage. The basis for this hypothesis is the sequence and biochemical similarity of AID to apolipoprotein B mRNA editing catalytic subunit 1 (APOBEC-1). This model does not account for somatic hypermutation, but it is quite possible that multiple mechanisms of AID action exist in light of the multiple physiological functions affected by AID and the evidence for multiple activities present in the single AID molecule.

One of the major obstacles to defining the precise mechanism of action of AID is the highly selective substrate and sequence selectivity of AID. While the earliest studies of AID revealed no activity against nucleic acid substrates, Goodman and coworkers clearly defined the substrate selectivity of AID as involving single-strand DNA, with no apparent activity with double-strand DNA, single-strand RNA or RNA–DNA hybrids. To define sequence selectivity of AID, Goodman and coworkers took the approach of quantifying mutations as an index of AID activity on single-strand DNA substrates and on an actively transcribed circular DNA model.

They observed that mutations initially occurred at hotspot sequence motifs for somatic hypermutation A A/G C, with a 15-fold preference for the non-transcribed over the transcribed strand of DNA, and expanded to neighboring dCs to create larger clusters of mutated regions. These in vitro results with AID are consistent with observed traits of somatic hypermutation, including the sequence selectivity and transcriptional dependence.

Enzymatic Editing of RNA

The identification of DNA deaminase activity was preceded by several decades by the discovery of numerous chemical modifications of nucleobases in tRNA, including N-methylation of rG and rA, 2′-Omethylation, N-isoprentenylation of rA, formation of pseudouridine, trans-glycosylation of guanine with the base analog qucuine and, of course, nucleobase deamination products. The latter phenomenon is now known to involve conversion of both rA to rI and rC to rU.

As reviewed elsewhere, the enzymatic deamination of RNA bases was first described in the South African clawed toad, *Xenopus laevis*, with the conversion of adenosines to inosines within double-stranded regions of RNA. This led to the identification of three recognized adenosine deaminases that act on RNA (ADARs) and are found only in higher eukaryotes. The enzymes act on unspliced transcripts at rA in an exon that is base paired with an adjacent intron, with the resulting rI being read as rG during translation. Currently known genes affected by A to-I editing include the calcium-gated glutamate receptor, the 5-hydroxytryptamine receptor, the potassium channel KCNA1 and several identified by comparative genomics, including filamin A protein (FLNA), bladder cancer-associated protein (BLCAP), insulin-like growth factor binding protein 7 (IGFBP7) and cytoplasmic FMR1 interacting protein 2 (CYFIP2).

The first example of site-specific editing was observed in a pre-mRNA encoding the vertebrate calcium-gated glutamate receptor subunit (GluR-B) of the aminohydroxymethylisoxazole propionate (AMPA) class of glutamate receptors. Editing by ADAR2 converts a glutamine to an arginine within the ion pore of the channel and occurs in virtually all transcripts of the gene under normal conditions. The unedited form of the GluR-B subunit causes the associated AMPA receptor to be more permeable to calcium ions. With glutamate as the major excitatory neurotransmitter in the mammalian brain, it is not surprising that loss of function mutations in ADAR2 causes a variety of neurological symptoms, including death in infancy with seizures and neurodegeneration in the hippocampus. Interestingly, these symptoms only occur when the GluR-B transcript is expressed in its unedited form, since mice with complete deletion of the GluR-B gene are viable due to overlapping function of other subunit genes.

The 5-hydroxytryptamine receptor 2C is a member of the rhodopsin family of G protein-coupled receptors and is the only known G protein-coupled receptor known to undergo *RNA editing*. The editing phenomenon involves positions 157, 158, 159 and 161 in an intracellular loop of the receptor that functions in receptor–G protein coupling in rats and humans. The resulting change from A to I causes conversion of isoleucine to valine, asparagine to glycine, asparagine to serine and isoleucine to valine, respectively, with tissue-specific expression of at least seven 5-HT2C receptor isoforms encoded by eleven different RNA species.

Levanon et al. used a comparative genomics approach to identify other genes subject to RNA editing, including FLNA, BLCAP, the

IGFBP7, CYFIP2. Editing was verified in mice and chickens. Aberrant editing of the transcripts of these genes may account for some of the non-neuronal phenotypes generated by loss of ADARs in mice.

One interesting consequence of ADAR sequence searches in the genomes of yeast and *Drosophila* was the discovery of a family of ADAR-related adenosine deaminases that act on tRNA (ADAT or Tad). To date, four ADATs have been detected in eukaryotic genomes and one ADAT homolog, the Tad1 gene, in *E. coli*. These enzymes deaminate adenosine at position 34 (adjacent to the anticodon) or 37 (within the anticodon) in a variety of tRNAs in prokaryotes and eukaryotes. Based on sequence similarities, O'Connell and coworkers have argued that ADARs in higher eukaryotes evolved from the more widely distributed ADATs.

RNA editing also involves conversion of rC to rU in several genes. There are several features of C-to-U editing that distinguish it from A to-I, including reaction of the involved enzymes with single-strand DNA template and a more complicated (i.e., less predictable) substrate specificity. The first description of C-to-U editing involves the transcript for apolipoprotein B (apoB) in the intestine. The deamination is performed by the apoB mRNA editing catalytic subunit 1 (APOBEC-1), a member of the apobec family of cytidine deaminases and a relative of AID protein discussed earlier, in complex with apobec-1 complementation factor (ACF). The editing involves changing a CAA to a UAA stop codon, which results in truncated protein and affects lipoprotein metabolism and transport. A second physiological example of C-to-U editing involves the neurofibromatosis type 1 gene. This time, the change entails conversion of a CGA to a UGA translation termination codon that is predicted, though not yet proven, to truncate the neurofibromin protein product.

Consequences of Aberrant RNA Editing

It is highly likely that RNA editing by both A-to-I and C-to-U mechanisms will prove to be more widespread than is currently appreciated. This suggests a possible role for aberrant editing in the pathophysiology of many diseases, with genetic polymorphisms affecting genes coding for both the target transcripts (e.g., altered substrate structures) or affecting the deaminases themselves (e.g., alter target recognition or catalytic properties). In addition to the established neurological disorders caused by faulty RNA editing, there is evidence for aberrant editing in several forms of cancer. The possible consequences of inappropriate RNA editing are further complicated by the recent discovery of proteins, the vigilins that bind to promiscuously A-to-I-edited transcripts and target them, or their degradation products, to heterochromatic regions of the nucleus. This suggests the possibility of a gene silencing mechanism for RNA fragments containing inappropriately located rI arising from virtually any mechanism, including inflammation or altered purine metabolism, as discussed next.

Purine Metabolism as a Source of Nucleobase Deamination in DNA and RNA

In addition to hydrolytic, inflammatory and enzymatic mechanisms for nucleobase deamination in DNA and RNA, there may be a role for defects in both pyrimidine and, as we have recently observed for both DNA and RNA, purine metabolism as determinants of the genomic burden of nucleobase deamination products. The relationship between pyrimidine metabolism and levels of dU in DNA is now clear and there is an emerging recognition of an association between defects in pyrimidine metabolism and cancer risk, though some studies suggest that simple defects in folate metabolism cannot account fully for the increased cancer risk. There has been an extensive review of pyrimidine metabolism and cancer risk, so this chapter will address very recent studies of the role of purine metabolism in levels of I and X in DNA and RNA.

Background on Purine Metabolism

The anabolism and catabolism of purine bases and nucleotides is highly conserved in all living organisms with a central role for X and I in all aspects of purine metabolism. The synthesis of purine ribo- and 2′-deoxyribonucleotides occurs by three mechanisms: *de novo* synthesis, salvage of purine bases by attachment to ribosephosphate, and salvage by phosphorylation of nucleosides. The *de novo* pathway is a 10-step reaction that starts with a rate-limiting conversion of phosphoribosylpyrophosphate (PRPP) to 5-phosphoribosylamine and ends in the formation of IMP. IMP is the precursor to both AMP and GMP and is normally present in cells at low micromolar concentrations. Conversion of IMP to AMP is a second rate-limiting process in purine synthesis and involves two steps: (1) displacement of the O^6 of IMP by the amino group of aspartate to form adenylosuccinate (mediated by adenylosuccinate synthase, the product of the *E. coli* purA gene); followed by (2) removal of fumarate to form AMP (mediated by adenylosuccinate lyase, the product of the *E. coli* purB gene). Phosphorylation steps lead to the formation of ADP and ATP, while conversion to dADP occurs by the action of ribonucleotide reductase on ADP. Given the many sources of ATP (e.g., glycolysis; electron transport in mitochondria in higher eukaryotes), it is not surprising that it is present at millimolar concentrations in all cells.

The formation of GMP likewise derives from IMP but through the intermediacy of XMP. Oxidation of IMP by IMP dehydrogenase (*E. coli* GuaB protein) yields XMP that is then converted to GMP by transfer of an amino group from glutamine via GMP synthase (*E. coli* GuaA protein). Again, the appropriate di- and triphosphate and 2′-deoxyribonucleotide arise by analogous kinases and ribonucleotide reductase as with adenosine nucleotides.

One of the central issues here is the potential for formation of ITP, XTP, dITP and dXTP and their subsequent incorporation into RNA and DNA, respectively. We have observed large increases in the DNA content of dI and dX in *E. coli* containing mutations in the purA/rdgB and purA/rdgB/guaA genes, respectively, which suggests that the mutations in purine metabolism lead to increases in the content of dXTP and dITP in the nucleotide pool available to DNA polymerases. The formation of dITP and dXTP likely involves the action of ribonucleotide reductase on IDP and XDP derived from IMP and XMP by phosphorylation (ndk, adk). Even with allowances made for large variations in concentration as a function of cell cycle and stress, ribonucleotides are present at concentrations one to three orders-of-magnitude higher than deoxyribonucleotides (millimolar vs. micromolar), though prokaryotes often have higher concentrations of dNTPs (up to 200 μM).

The DNA precursor pools are maintained at limited concentrations (enough for 15–30 s of DNA synthesis) that are tightly coupled to DNA synthesis, with increases in pool concentration as the cell cycle enters S phase, such that changes in precursor levels can cause large changes in dNTP concentrations. For example, mutations in purine biosynthesis have been observed to increase mutation rates by up to 300-fold in mammalian cells. One explanation for this involves DNA polymerase error rates that are dependent on the relative dNTP concentrations. These observations suggest that even low concentrations of dXTP and dITP could result in significant incorporation of X and I into DNA.

Diseases Associated with Defects in Purine Metabolism in Humans

The relationship between defects in purine metabolism and human disease has long been recognized. As noted earlier, imbalances in dNTP concentrations lead to toxic cellular outcomes such as apoptosis and a mutator phenotype. These and other mechanisms have been proposed to underlie diseases associated with purine metabolism, such as gout, immunodeficiency and neurological disorders such as autism and Lesch–Nyhan syndrome. It is also possible, based on our observations, that altered purine metabolism contributes to the background of endogenous deamination DNA lesions that might increase the risk of cancer and other diseases.

The biochemical basis for these diseases entails loss of activity of key enzymes in the purine metabolic network. For example, Lesch-Nyhan syndrome involves loss of I/G phosphoribosyl transferase (H- or GPT), a key enzyme in the G salvage pathway. Loss of this enzyme leads to an accumulation of X and I and, subsequently, uric acid. While the exact causative agent has not been identified, it is thought that the resulting accumulation of X, I and uric acid, and the associated hyperuricemia, lead to neurological disease during fetal development, including mental and growth retardation. Another example is the role for purine metabolic defects in one form of autism with epilepsy, in which loss of adenylosuccinate lyase activity leads to accumulation of adenylosuccinate detectable in blood of patients.

The observed pathophysiology of defects in purine metabolism raises an important question: would reduced activity in specific steps of purine metabolism lead to an accumulation of X- and I-containing nucleotides that eventually find their way into DNA and RNA? There is evidence for increased levels of ITP in cells from humans lacking inosine triphosphate pyrophosphohydrolase (dITPase; RdgB in *E. coli*), the enzyme that removes ITP, XTP, dITP and, presumably, dXTP from the nucleotide pool. It is reasonable to assume that levels of dITP will also be increased and, given our observations, that levels of dI in DNA will follow suit. Another cell line consists of B-lymphocytes from a patient lacking adenosine deaminase activity. This defect is associated with severe combined immunodeficiency, the basis for which is not clear. Given our observations of elevated levels of dI in DNA when analyses are performed in the absence of adenosine deaminase inhibitors and the precedent for elevated levels of dU in B-lymphocytes expressing a cytidine deaminase (AID protein), loss of which is also associated with immunodeficiency, it is possible that cells lacking adenosine deaminase will have reduced levels of dI in DNA than other B-lymphocyte lines. This model assumes that dI formation in the DNA of B-lymphocytes could serve the same function as dU in immunoglobulin gene recombination.

Repair and Mutagenesis of Nucleobase Deamination Products

Mechanisms Controlling the Levels of dX and dI in DNA

The genetics and biochemistry of processes that ultimately prevent the accumulation of base deamination products in DNA are best understood in *E. coli*. One mechanism to exclude dX and dI from DNA is the removal of their dNTP forms from the DNA precursor pools. An *E. coli* dNTP phosphohydrolase, RdgB protein, was shown to be active on dITP, ITP and XTP, so it can be deduced that dXTP will also be a substrate. Similar enzymes have been purified from *T. maritima* and the cloned human ITPA gene, while the gene encoding it is present in the genomes of almost all organisms for which a complete genome sequence is known.

The role played by this dNTP phosphohydrolase has been defined by studies in *E. coli*. The rdgB gene was originally identified as a gene required for survival of *E. coli* deficient in recombinational repair promoted by RecA protein. The authors of this report suggested that, in the absence of RdgB protein, a lesion was formed in DNA that required recombinational repair. They linked the production of this lesion to purine biosynthesis by showing that over-expression of the PurA protein restored viability to a recA–rdgB double mutant. The identification of the rdgB homolog in yeast, HAM1, as a gene controlling sensitivity to N-6-hydroxylaminopurine further supported the role of the rdgB gene in some aspect of purine metabolism. The biochemical function of RdgB protein as the dNTP phosphohydrolase strongly suggests that the primary lesion arising in DNA may be the presence of X, I and HAP.

Recent work has shown that the *E. coli* chromosome undergoes double-strand breaks in the absence of active RdgB protein, and that these breaks are formed only in the presence of an active endonuclease V. Originally described by Demple and Linn and later as an endonuclease that incises DNA containing inosine, EndoV is a Mg^{2+}-dependent enzyme that cuts the second phosphodiester bond located 3′ to the damaged base. Similar enzymes have been purified from several microorganisms, while genes encoding EndoV homologs have been found in many organisms, including mice and humans, with the exception of *S. cerevisiae*. In addition to dI, EndoV recognizes a variety of lesions including dU, base mismatches, AP sites, hairpins and flap structures and has recently been shown to be the major repair activity for dX in DNA. Recent studies have shown that dO, the other dG deamination product, is also recognized by EndoV. One model posits that EndoV incision at dI, dX or dHAP directly causes double-strand breaks or that replication forks that traverse DNA nicked by EndoV create double-strand breaks. In either case, RecA-mediated recombination is required to repair the breaks.

Biochemical studies have shown that the *E. coli* 3-methyladenine glycosylase (AlkA) reacts with dI. However, the role of AlkA in the *in vivo* repair of dI in *E. coli* is unclear, since genetic analysis is consistent with EndoV as the major dI repair enzyme. Another study has shown that endonuclease VIII (EndoVIII) is active on X and O in DNA. The role of these enzymes *in vivo* has not been studied.

These studies lead to a model for a system to prevent accumulation of non-canonical purines in DNA, including dX, dO and dI. The dNTP forms of purine analogs can arise from (1) salvage of free bases, (2) phosphorylation of naturally occurring (d)IMP and (d)XMP, or (3) deamination of the nucleotide forms of (d)G and (d)A. Whatever the source, RdgB sanitizes the precursor pools of dNTP and rNTP and prevents these species from being incorporated into DNA and RNA. If deamination products do arise in DNA, then a repair event is initiated by incision next to the base by EndoV.

dX and dI Mutagenesis

The deamination products of DNA bases have been implicated in the formation of mutations. Especially important is the high rate of G:C→A:T mutations at CpG sites containing 5′-methylcytosine, which may result from the deamination of 5-methylcytosine to thymine. The deamination of cytosine to uracil also produces G:C→A:T mutations possibly by base pairing of uracil with adenine. On the basis of *in vitro* studies, xanthine represents another possible source of G:C→A:T mutations. However, the assumption of rapid depurination of dX has led to the suggestion that the G:C→A:T mutations arise by insertion of adenine opposite the resulting abasic sites.

In spite of the well-established use of dI in random mutagenesis techniques, there have been relatively few quantitative or mechanistic studies of X and I mutagenesis in cells or under conditions relevant to eukaryotic and prokaryotic organisms. *In vitro* polymerase insertion assays indicate that dITP is inserted most frequently opposite dC by Taq polymerase, most likely due to the greater stability of I:C base pairs over other combinations. Studies with dXTP insertion by Klenow fragment of *E. coli* Pol I also reveal a strong preference for inserting dX opposite C, which contradicts the greater stability of X:T over

X:C. The situation with insertion of dNTP opposite templates containing dX and dI parallels the dXTP and dITP insertion studies. The frequency of insertion of dNTP opposite dX occurs in the order T>C>A~G for *Drosophila* polymerase α and in the order C>T for Klenow fragment.

Substantive evidence for *in vivo* mutagenesis by dX and dI comes from studies of site-specific mutagenesis and of *E. coli* exposed to nitrous acid and NO•. At low pH, formation of nitrous acid from nitrite leads to RNS capable of causing DNA deamination. Weiss and coworkers demonstrated that *E. coli* lacking EndoV (nfi mutants) were more resistant to nitrous acid-induced toxicity and had increased A:T→G:C mutations thought to be due to dI formation, while the G:C→T:A mutations expected for a preponderance of apurinic sites at presumably unstable dX residues represented only 0.2% of the mutations. While the G:C→A:T mutations could arise by deamination of dC or 5-methyl-dC, dX has been shown to cause G:C→A:T mutations *in vitro*. *E. coli* alkA mutants, on the other hand, did not display an increased mutation frequency in the presence of nitrous acid, which suggests that EndoV plays a greater role in dI repair than AlkA. However, these studies were not designed with the specificity or sensitivity needed to assess the contribution of dX. Indeed, Kow and coworkers demonstrated the activity of EndoV on dX-containing substrates that are otherwise resistant to repair by other enzymes.

It is unclear what role abasic sites may play in NO•-induced mutagenesis, given the observation in repair-deficient *E. coli* exposed to nitrous acid that the G:C→T:A mutations expected for AP sites represented only 0.2% of total mutations. The bulk of the mutations consisted of G:C→A:T and A:T→G:C transitions. However, Engelward and coworkers have demonstrated that *E. coli* cells lacking AP endonuclease activity were highly sensitive to NO• exposure, which suggests that, along with base excision repair of nucleobase deamination products, the directly formed abasic sites may contribute to NO•-induced toxicity in cells.

The most direct studies of dI mutagenesis are those performed by Hill-Perkins et al., in which they determined the mutant frequency associated with dI by site-specific mutagenesis in the M13mp9 vector replicated in *E. coli*. As expected, dI was found to pair with dC most frequently, resulting in A→G transitions, and there was an 11% mutation frequency for dI paired with dT (i.e., as if dI had formed from dA). Kamiya and coworkers studied the mutagenicity of dXTP, dITP and dOTP when these nucleotides were transfected into E. coli. They observed that the deamination products did not induce mutations at a higher frequency than control transfections, while 8-oxo-dGTP, 5-OHdCTP and 5-formyl-dUTP all showed significant increases in mutation frequency. These findings were interpreted to mean that X and I as dNTPs are not mutagenic and that they are only mutagenic when formed directly in DNA. A major drawback to these studies is that no accounting was made for deoxynucleotide pyrophosphohydrolase activity. It is quite possible that dITPase/dXTPase (RdgB) is more efficient than MutT (8-oxo-dGTPase) and other dNTPases. It is also possible that the higher mutagenicity of 8-oxo-dGTP, 5-OH-dCTP and 5-formyl-dUTP is the result of more efficient incorporation by DNA polymerase.

This chapter has covered the numerous established and potential mechanisms by which nucleobase deamination products can arise in or enter DNA and RNA. Among all of the types of DNA damage, nucleobase deamination appears to have the most abundant and diverse mechanisms of formation, including nitrosative deamination at sites of inflammation, simple hydrolysis, the actions of several deaminase enzymes on DNA and RNA and defects in purine and pyrimidine metabolism. This level of complexity suggests that nucleobase deamination products could act as biomarkers of several facets of cellular pathophysiology, while their involvement in carcinogenesis and other disease processes could involve both direct mutagenesis and, via the nucleotide pools, disruption of cell signaling, cycling or other facets of cell physiology. The future of research in this area will depend on the development of ultra-sensitive analytical methods to quantify these lesions in small amounts of human tissue, an effort currently underway in several laboratories including ours.

5

DNA ADDUCTS

^{32}P-POSTLABELING ANALYSIS OF DNA ADDUCTS

^{32}P-Postlabeling analysis is an ultrasensitive method for the detection of DNA adducts, such as those formed directly by the covalent binding of carcinogens and mutagens to bases in DNA, as well as other DNA lesions resulting from modification of bases by endogenous or exogenous agents (e.g., oxidative damage). The procedure involves four main steps: enzymatic digestion of a DNA sample; enrichment of the adducts; radiolabeling of the adducts by T4 kinase-catalyzed transference of ^{32}P-orthophosphate from [γ-^{32}P]ATP; and chromatographic separation of labeled adducts and detection and quantification by means of their radioactive decay. Using 10μg or less of DNA, this technique is capable of detecting adduct levels as low as one adduct in 10^{9}–10^{10} normal nucleotides. It is applicable to a wide range of investigations, including monitoring human exposure to environmental or occupational carcinogens, determining whether a chemical has genotoxic properties, analysis of the genotoxicity of complex mixtures, elucidation of the activation pathways of carcinogens, and monitoring of DNA repair.

A common mechanism by which carcinogens initiate the process of malignant transformation is through damaging the DNA in the target organ in such a way that errors in replication can be induced. In many cases, this damage is in the form of a chemical modification of one of the nucleotides in DNA, in which the carcinogen becomes covalently bound to form a stably modified nucleotide (a DNA adduct). When a replication error occurs at a critical site in a gene essential for cell cycle control or genomic integrity, such as a proto-oncogene, tumor suppressor gene, or DNA repair gene, the result can be a progeny cell that lacks the normal growth restraints of that cell's lineage, which can then undergo clonal expansion into a tumor. Thus, the monitoring of DNA adduct formation in human tissues and experimental systems is an important component of studies on the etiology of cancer and on hazard identification for carcinogens and mutagens.

Because of the low levels of DNA adduct formation that can result in tumor initiation, sensitive methods are required for detecting these events. A number of methods are currently available that fulfil some or all of the necessary criteria. These include earlier approaches in which the carcinogen itself was radiolabeled, so that its binding to DNA could be detected by means of its radioactive decay. However, this method was not applicable to monitoring human exposure to carcinogens, nor to any situation in which exposure occurs over a prolonged period, owing to the economic and safety issues of long-term exposure to radioactive substances. In another approach, antibodies have been prepared to a selected range of carcinogen–DNA adducts, and these have been used to detect adducts of various classes in human and animal tissues. Sensitive fluorescence detection methods have also been developed for those classes of carcinogen–DNA adducts that are naturally fluorescent (such as etheno adducts and those formed by polycyclic aromatic hydrocarbons), and mass spectrometry has been applied in a number of instances. The latter method provides the most definitive characterization of adduct structure of all the methods available.

The basis of the ^{32}P-postlabeling method for DNA adduct detection is that the radiolabel is introduced into the adduct after it is formed. This overcomes the problem of radioactive containment during the initial experiment and allows retrospective analysis for DNA adducts, which is particularly important for human studies. Furthermore, the use of ^{32}P as the isotope allows for a level of sensitivity not achievable with longer-lived isotopes. For most applications, the principal stages of the ^{32}P-postlabeling assay are digestion of the DNA to nucleoside 3'-monophosphates, enrichment of the adducts to enhance the sensitivity of the assay, 5'-labeling of the nucleotides with ^{32}P-orthophosphate (catalyzed by T4 polynucleotide kinase); chromatographic and/or electrophoretic separation of the labeled species, and their detection and quantitation.

The method was originally developed for simple alkyl-modified DNA adducts but was then adapted for the detection of bulky aromatic and/or hydrophobic adducts with high sensitivity. One of the two principal enhancement procedures that followed was digestion of the nucleotides with nuclease P_1 prior to labeling, resulting in normal nucleotides, but not many adducts, being converted to nucleosides, not substrates for T4 polynucleotide kinase. The other enhancement method involved extraction of the aromatic/hydrophobic adducts into butanol as a means of separating them from the unadducted normal nucleotides. For these methods, the labeled adducts are resolved and detected as 3',5'-nucleoside bisphosphates. However, alternative digestion strategies, carried out both before and after ^{32}P-postlabeling, can lead to the production of labeled nucleoside 5'-monophosphates. For some applications, the possession of only one charged phosphate group can result in better resolution of carcinogen–DNA adducts and, additionally, improve confidence in the assignment of structures to unknown species on the basis of cochromatography with synthetic standards. Since the earliest days of the assay's use, resolution of DNA adducts has been most commonly performed by multidirectional *thin-layer chromatography* (TLC), using polyethyleneimine (PEI)-cellulose plates. Alternatively, *high-performance liquid chromatography* (HPLC) offers a technique of higher resolution that is being used more frequently. For small DNA lesions, such as those resulting from oxidative damage to DNA, polyacrylamide gel electrophoresis (PAGE) of DNA digests has also proved useful for resolving the ^{32}P-postlabeled species.

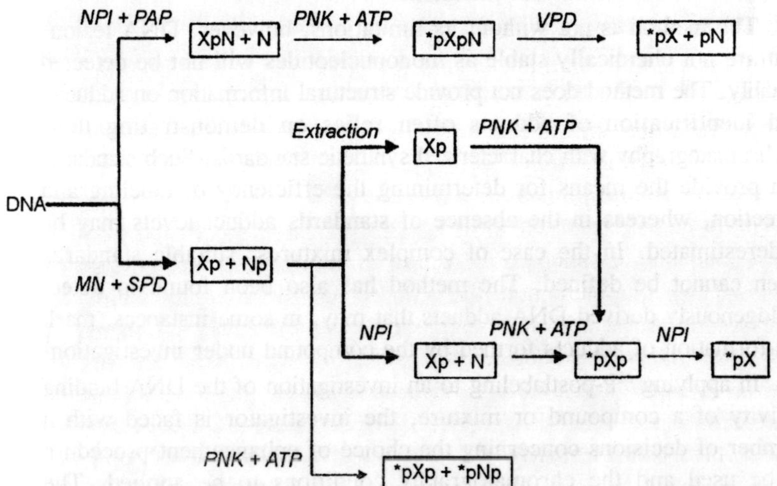

Fig. 5.1. Method of ^{32}P-postlabeling. Protocols are given in this article for procedures indicated by bold arrow.

The ^{32}P-postlabeling assay currently has multiple applications that include monitoring human exposure to environmental carcinogens, mechanistic investigations of carcinogen activation and tumor initiation, monitoring DNA repair, testing new compounds for genotoxicity, investigating endogenous DNA damage and oxidative processes, monitoring marine pollution through measurement of DNA adducts in aquatic species, and assessing patient response to cytotoxic cancer drugs.

There are several advantages of ^{32}P-postlabeling over other methods. It does not require the use of radiolabeled test compounds, making it useful in experiments in which multiple dosing is required, and it is applicable to a wide range of chemicals and types of DNA lesion. Prior structural characterization of adducts is not required, although some assumptions about their likely chromatographic properties may be necessary. It has been used to detect DNA adducts formed by polycyclic aromatic hydrocarbons, aromatic amines, heterocyclic amines (food mutagens), small aromatic compounds (such as benzene, styrene, and alkenylbenzenes), alkylating agents, products of lipid peroxidation, reactive oxygen species, and ultraviolet radiation. It requires only microgram quantities of DNA and is capable of detecting some types of DNA adducts at levels as low as one adduct in 10^{10} normal nucleotides in this amount of material. It can be applied to the assessment of the genotoxic potential of complex mixtures of chemicals, such as environmental airborne combustion products, particulates, and industrial or environmental pollutants.

The method is not without its limitations, however. DNA lesions that are not chemically stable as mononucleotides will not be detected reliably. The method does not provide structural information on adducts, and identification of adducts often relies on demonstrating their cochromatography with characterized synthetic standards. Such standards can provide the means for determining the efficiency of labeling and detection, whereas in the absence of standards adduct levels may be underestimated. In the case of complex mixtures, suitable standards often cannot be defined. The method has also been found to detect endogenously derived DNA adducts that may, in some instances, mask the formation of adducts formed by the compound under investigation.

In applying ^{32}P-postlabeling to an investigation of the DNA binding activity of a compound or mixture, the investigator is faced with a number of decisions concerning the choice of enhancement procedure to be used and the chromatography conditions to be applied. The protocols given here should be regarded as providing guidance for an initial investigation. In many cases it may be necessary to try several different approaches before the best procedure is found.

Following the adoption of ^{32}P-postlabeling by many laboratories and its use for an increasingly diverse number of applications, it became apparent that protocols varied widely from laboratory to laboratory, even for analysis of the same types of carcinogen–DNA adducts. Therefore, an international interlaboratory trial was initiated to establish a set of standardized protocols that would allow comparisons between studies from different laboratories, particularly in the interpretation of human biomonitoring studies. Furthermore, validated modified DNA samples, containing adducts derived from benzo[a]pyrene, from 4-aminobiphenyl, and from 2-amino1-methyl-6-phenylimidazo[4,5-b]pyridine (PhIP) were prepared, as was DNA containing O^6-methylguanine, and these standards have been made available to investigators to enable them to determine the efficiency of the ^{32}P-postlabeling assay in their hands.

The protocols described here can be considered an introductory approach to the method and are based on validated studies of known carcinogen–DNA adducts. When a new or unknown type of DNA adduct is being investigated, it cannot be asserted that these conditions will be optimal for its detection and quantitation. Indeed, different carcinogen–DNA adducts have been shown to be postlabeled with different efficiencies.

Materials

DNA digestion

1. Use double-distilled water or equivalent throughout.
2. Micrococcal nuclease. Dissolve contents in water to give 2 U/μL.
3. Spleen phosphodiesterase. Mix to give final concentrations of 36 mU/μL MN and 6 mU/μL SPD.
4. Digestion buffer: 100 mM sodium succinate, pH 6.0, 50 mM $CaCl_2$.
5. All solutions can be stored at –20°C in small aliquots.

Nuclease P_1 digestion

1. 0.25 M Sodium acetate buffer, pH 5.0.
2. 2.0 mM $ZnCl_2$.
3. 1.25 mg/mL Nuclease P_1.
4. 0.5 M Tris base.
5. All solutions can be stored at –20°C in small aliquots.

Butanol extraction

1. Buffer A: 100 mM ammonium formate, pH 3.5.
2. Buffer B: 10 mM tetrabutylammonium chloride.
3. 1-Butanol (redistilled, water-saturated).
4. 1-mL Syringe with blunt-ended needle.
5. 200 mM Tris-HCl, pH 9.5.
6. All solutions should be stored at 4°C.

DNA postlabeling

1. T4 polynucleotide kinase (with or without 3'-phosphatase activity).
2. Kinase buffer: 200 mM bicine, pH 9.0, 100 mM $MgCl_2$, 100 mM dithiothreitol, 10 mM spermidine.
3. [γ-^{32}P]ATP: >3000 Ci/mmol.
4. All solutions must be stored at –20°C in small aliquots.

Thin-layer chromatography

1. 20 × 20 cm PEI-impregnated cellulose TLC sheet.
2. Whatman no.1 filter sheets.
3. D1: 1 M sodium phosphate, pH 6.0.
4. D2: 3.5 M lithium formate, 8.5 M urea, pH 3.5.
5. D3: 0.8 M lithium chloride, 0.5 M Tris-HCl, 8.5 M urea, pH 8.0.
6. Efficiency solvent: 250 mM ammonium sulfate, 40 mM sodium phosphate.
7. Specific activity solvent: 0.5 M sodium phosphate, pH 6.0.

Detection and quantification

1. 2 pmol/μL 2'-Deoxyadenosine 3'-monophosphate, in distilled water.
2. Autoradiography film or an electronic imaging device.

HPLC cochromatography

1. 4 M Pyridinium formate, pH 4.5.
2. Ammonium buffer: 2 M ammonium formate, pH 4.5.
3. Acetonitrile.
4. Phenyl-modified reversed-phase column (e.g., 250 × 4.6 mm, particle size 5 mm, Zorbax Phenyl).
5. HPLC system with in-line radioactivity monitor.

Methods

DNA digestion

1. Take 4 μg DNA solution in a 1.5-mL tube and evaporate to dryness in a Speedvac evaporator.

2. Add 4 μL MN/SPD mix and 0.8 μL digestion buffer/sample. Vortex and centrifuge to ensure complete mixing.
3. Incubate at 37°C overnight.

Nuclease P_1 digestion

1. To the above digest add 2.4 μL sodium acetate buffer, 1.44 μL $ZnCl_2$, and 0.96 μL nuclease P_1/sample. Incubate at 37°C for 1 h.
2. Stop the reaction by addition of 1.92 μL Tris base.

Butanol extraction

1. Increase volume of DNA digest from 4.8 to 50 μL with water.
2. Premix 15 μL buffer A, 15 μL buffer B, and 70 μL water/sample.
3. Add 100 μL of premix to side of tube.
4. Immediately add 150 μL of butanol and vortex for 60 s at high speed.
5. Microcentrifuge at 8000g for 90 s. Remove upper butanol layer and keep.
6. Repeat steps 4 and 5.
7. To pooled butanol extracts add 400 μL butanol-saturated water. Vortex for 60 s. Microcentrifuge as above.
8. Remove water through the butanol layer using a syringe, being careful not to remove any of the butanol.
9. Repeat step 7 twice, discarding the water each time.
10. Add 3 μL 200 mM Tris-HCI to washed butanol. Vortex briefly.
11. Speedvac to dryness. Redissolve in 50 μL water by vortexing and Speedvac to dryness again.
12. Redissolve in 11.5 μL of water.

Labeling of adducts

1. Premix stock labeling mixture (number of samples + 2) for each sample from: 1.0 μL kinase buffer, 6 U T4 polynucleotide kinase and 50 μCi [γ-^{32}P]ATP/sample. Add appropriate volume to each solution.
2. Incubate at 37°C for 30 min.
3. Staple a 10 $\times$ 12-cm Whatman no.1 paper wick to the top edge of a 10 $\times$ 20 cm PEI-cellulose TLC sheet. Spot the whole of each sample onto the origin of this sheet. Keep tube for efficiency test.
4. Run in D1 overnight with wick hanging outside tank.
5. Cut plates down to 10 $\times$ 10 cm.

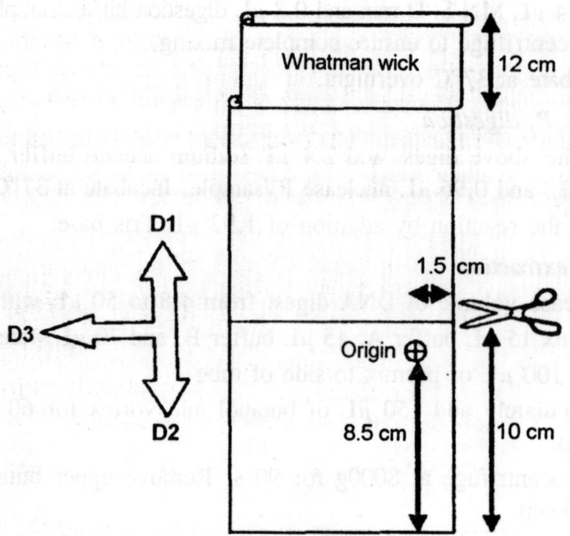

Fig. 5.2. Diagram showing multidirectional thin-layer chromatography procedures for the resolution of ^{32}P-labeled adducts on polyethyleneimine-cellulose.

6. Wash plates twice in water and dry plates with cool air.
7. Run in D2 and D3 in directions. Before each run, dip lower edge of plate in water to give an even solvent front. Lids should be taken off tanks for 15 min at end of run.
8. Wash plates twice in water and cool air-dry between solvents.

Test for efficiency of enrichment techniques

1. Wash bottom of tube with 50 μL water.
2. Vortex and microcentifuge.
3. Spot 5 μL near lower edge of 10 × 20-cm PEI-cellulose TLC sheet.
4. Run in efficiency solvent item 6 to top edge.

Determining the specific activity of [γ- ^{32}P] ATP

1. Take 3 μL of 2'-deoxyadenosine 3'-monophosphate (6 pmol) + premix. Incubate at 37°C for 30 min.
2. Dilute to 1.0 mL. Spot 2 × 5 μL 2 cm from the lower edge of a 10 × 20-cm PEI-cellulose TLC sheet. Run in specific activity solvent, item 7 to top edge.
3. Visualize and count adenosine bisphosphate spot.
4. This will give you dpm/pmol after allowing for dilution and efficiency of counting. Divide by 2.22×10^3 to give Ci/mmol.

Imaging and quantification

1. Adducts can be visualized by placing plates in cassettes with autoradiography film and keeping at -80°C for several h, for up to 4 d. Adduct spots can then be cut from the plate and quantitated in a scintillation counter. Alternatively, an InstantImager can be used, which will give a result in a few minutes.
2. Counts per minute of the adduct should be corrected for efficiency of the counting procedure and divided by the amount of DNA labeled to give dpm/μg. Dividing this by the specific activity figure of dpm/fmol will give fmol of adduct/μg DNA. Results can be expressed in this way or as adducts per 10^8 normal nucleotides. To arrive at this latter figure, divide the number of fmols by 0.03, as 33 adducts per 10^8 nucleotides are equivalent to 1 fmol/μg DNA.

Extraction of adducts for HPLC cochromatography

1. Cut the adduct spot out of the PEI-cellulose TLC sheet and place it in a scintillation vial.
2. Add 500 μL pyridinium formate and shake gently overnight.
3. Microcentrifuge extracts at 8000g for 90 s to remove small particles.
4. Speedvac to dryness. Redissolve in 100 μL water and methanol (mix 1:1).

HPLC cochromatography

1. Analyze aliquots (e.g., 50 μL) of the above extract on a phenyl-modified reversed-phase column with a linear gradient of acetonitrile (from 0 to 35% in 70 min) in aqueous ammonium buffer. Measure the radioactivity eluting from the column by monitoring Cerenkov radiation through a radioactivity detector.

Notes

1. It is necessary to dialyze the MN solution to remove residual oligonucleotides. Use a 10K Slide-A-Lyzer from Pierce suspended in 5 L distilled water at 4°C for 24 h. Change water once. The SPD must also be dialyzed to remove the ammonium salts, which may inhibit the labeling. The enzymes should be stored at -20°C and may be kept for at least 6 mo without loss of enzyme activity.
2. Originally, Roche SPD was used at 2 mU/μL. This product was discontinued in the year 2000, and alternative sources (e.g., bovine phosphodiesterase) have not proved to be as active. It may be

necessary to vary the amount used depending on the type of adducts to be detected.

3. Nuclease P1 solutions (in water) should be stored at –20°C.
4. Plates should be prerun with distilled water and dried to remove a yellow contaminant, which may lead to an increased background.
5. 1 M Sodium phosphate is usually sufficient for many bulky adducts, but smaller or more polar adducts may require higher concentrations (1.7–2.3 M sodium phosphate) to avoid streaking.
6. Use lithium hydroxide to adjust pH to 3.5.
7. D2 and D3 are suitable for many lipophilic bulky adducts, but considerable variation is possible in both concentration and content.
8. Caution: [γ-^{32}P]ATP is a high-energy β-particle emitter and due regard should be given to handling the material. Exposure to ^{32}P should be avoided by working in a confined laboratory area, with protective clothing, shielding, Geiger counters, and body dosimeter. We normally use 1-cm-thick Perspex or glass shielding between the operator and the source material throughout. We routinely wear two pairs of medium-weight rubber gloves and handle the

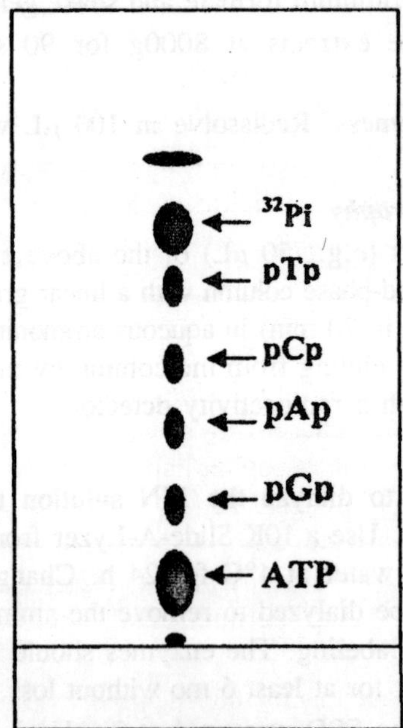

Fig. 5.3. One-dimensional chromatography of ^{32}P-labeled normal nucleotides on polyethyleneimine-cellulose.

tubes with 30-cm forceps. An appropriate Geiger counter should be on during the whole procedure, and working areas should be monitored before and after work. All apparatus should be checked for contamination and cleaned when appropriate by immersion in a suitable decontamination fluid. Waste must be discarded according to appropriate local safety procedures.

9. The top of the tank and the lid should be wrapped around with cling film to avoid contamination with radioactivity.
10. Poor efficiency of either enrichment procedure will be demonstrated by the appearance of the four normal nucleotide spots. If there is no indication of excess ATP, then the sample should be discarded.
11. When quantifying the standard, it is necessary to run a blank using water instead of standard and to subtract the value obtained as background.
12. The origin after D1 can also be cut out of the PEI-cellulose TLC sheet.
13. The extraction can be monitored by measuring Cerenkov radiation in a scintillation counter before and after the extraction procedure.
14. Depending on the adduct type, other HPLC conditions may be more suitable.

Modification of the ^{32}P-Postlabeling Method to Detect a Single Adduct Species as a Single Spot

The original ^{32}P-postlabeling method developed by Randerath and his colleagues has been modified to detect a single type of adduct as a single spot in *thin-layer chromatography* (TLC), because some types of adducts gave multiple adduct spots by the original method. In the remodified methods, DNA is first digested with micrococcal nuclease and phophodiesterase II and then labeled with [γ-^{32}P]ATP under standard or adduct-intensification conditions. Since the labeled digest includes adducted mono-, di-, and/or oligo-deoxynucleotides, it is further treated with phosphatase and phosphodiesterase prior to TLC. The labeled digest is treated with nuclease P1 (NP1) in method I, and with T4 polynucleotide kinase and NP1 in method II, and then with phosphodiesterase I in both cases, and subjected to TLC. The advantage of these methods is that the number of adduct species formed can be estimated by TLC.

The ^{32}P-postlabeling method devised by Randerath and his group is widely used to detect DNA adducts formed in vitro and in vivo with various mutagens and carcinogens. The advantages of this method (and simple modifications like butanol extraction and use of nuclease P1 [NP1] to detect adducts with high efficiency) are introduced previously. The principle is to detect DNA lesions as adducted deoxynucleoside 3', 5'-diphosphate elements. However, with the established methodology, a single type of adduct is not necessarily detected as a single spot owing to incomplete digestion of adducted DNA.

In this section, approaches are introduced that allow for the detection of single adducted forms as single spots, with modifications to the original Randerath method. In these methods, DNA is first digested with *microccocal nuclease* (MN) and phosphodiesterase II (PDE II), and labeled with [γ-^{32}P]ATP under standard or adduct-intensification conditions, the labeled digests obtained are further treated with NP1, T4 polynucleotide kinase (PNK), and phophodiesterase I (PDE I), before analysis of adducted deoxynucleoside 5'-phosphate formation by *thin-layer chromatography* (TLC).

In some cases, the labeled DNA digests include mono-, di-, and/ or oligodeoxynucleotides: [^{32}P]pX(pN)$_n$p, where X is an adducted deoxynucleoside, and N is a normal deoxynucleoside. By treatment with NP1, the 3'-phosphate of [^{32}P]pX(pN)$_n$p can be removed to yield [^{32}P]pX(pN)$_n$, and further treatment with PDE I may then produce [^{32}P]pX and n(pN). Some types of adducted deoxynucleoside 3', 5'-diphosphate are, however, resistant to the phosphatase activity of NP1, although they are sensitive to that of PNK. Thus, in method I, labeled digests are treated with NP1, and in method II, with PNK and NP1 and then treated with PDE I in both cases. It is known that the optimum pH for the 3'-phosphatase activity of PNK is 5.9, whereas that for its kinase activity is 6.5–8.5.

To give a concrete example, when DNA from rats treated with the food-borne mutagenic/carcinogenic heterocyclic amine 2-amino-1-methyl-6-phenylimidazo[4,5-b]pyridine (PhIP) was analyzed by the ^{32}P-

$$^{*}pXp + {}^{*}pX(pN)_nP + {}^{*}pYp + {}^{*}pY(pN)_np \xrightarrow{PNK} {}^{*}pX + {}^{*}pX(pN)_n + {}^{*}pYp + {}^{*}pY(N)_np$$

$$\xrightarrow{NP1} {}^{*}pX + {}^{*}pX(pN)_n + {}^{*}pY + {}^{*}pY(pN)_n$$

$$\xrightarrow{PDEI} {}^{*}pX + {}^{*}pY + pN$$

*Fig. 5.4. Principle of the modified method. *, ^{32}P-label; X and Y, modified deoxynucleosides; N, normal deoxynucleoside.*

postlabeling method under standard or intensification conditions, several adduct spots were detected on TLC, and the spot for authentic N-(deoxyguanosin-8-yl)-2-amino-1-methyl-6-phenylimidazo[4,5-b]pyridine 3', 5'-diphosphate (3', 5'-pdGp-C8-PhIP) coincided with a minor adduct spot, although it has been demonstrated to be the sole adduct of PhIP by *high performance liquid chromatography* (HPLC) analysis using [^{3}H]PhIP. The additional spots were demonstrated to be owing to incomplete digestion of DNA. A similar result was also obtained with a second heterocyclic amine, 2-amino-3,4-dimethylimidazo[4,5-f]quinoline (MeIQ). Single spots thus were generated with DNA from animals treated with PhIP or MeIQ by method I.

In the case of the another heterocyclic amine, 2-amino-3-methylimidazo[4,5-f]quinoline (IQ), five spots were detected on TLC by the standard method, and for two of them their structures were tentatively identified as N-(deoxyguanosin-8-yl)-2-amino-3-methylimidazo[4,5-f]quinoline 3',5'-diphosphate (pdGp-C8-IQ) and 5-(deoxyguanosin-N^2 -yl)-2-amino-3-methylimidazo[4,5-f]quinoline (pdGp-N^2-IQ). However, relatively large amounts of radioactivity were also present in the remaining three spots. When method I was applied for the analysis of IQ-DNA adducts, four spots were detected, and pdGp-N^2-IQ was demonstrated to be resistant to the phosphatase activity of NP1. However, it was converted to pdG-N^2-IQ with PNK, with or without NP1. Thus, for IQ-DNA adducts, method II is appropriate, and by this method, spots of pdG-C8-IQ and pdG-N^2-IQ, as well as a very small radioactive spot representing an unknown form of adduct, could be detected.

Recoveries with the modified methods are very close to those with the standard and intensification methods; in other words, very high after treatment with PNK, NP1, and PDE I. These results indicate that ^{32}P-labeled oligonucleotides have modified bases at the 5'-most position.

A major advantage of these methods is that the number of adduct species formed in vivo and/or under in vitro conditions can be estimated by TLC.

Materials

DNA digestion

1. 0.01X SSC, 0.1 mM EDTA: make as 1X SSC (0.15 M NaCl, 0.015 M Na-citrate), 10 mM EDTA. The solution can be stored at 4°C.
2. MN: dissolve in water to give 4 U/μL.

3. PDE II from bovine spleen: dissolve in water to give 40 mU/μL.
4. Nuclease mixture: mix MN and PDE II solutions at a ratio of 1:1 to give a final concentration of 2 U/μL for MN and 20 mU/μL for PDE II.
5. Digestion buffer: 0.1 M sodium succinate and 0.05 M $CaCl_2$, pH 6.0. This can be stored at 4°C.

Postlabeling

1. [γ-^{32}P]ATP with a specific activity of approx 260 TBq/mmol (~370 MBq/60 μL).
2. 10 U/μL PNK.
3. 10X Kination buffer: 0.3 M Tris-HCl, pH 9.5, 0.1 M dithiothreitol, 0.1 M $MgCl_2$, 0.01 M spermidine.
4. ATP solution: 200 μM ATP.
5. Kination solution A (10 μL used for each tube): 1.5 μL of 10X kination buffer, 1 μL of PNK, 5 μL of [γ-^{32}P] ATP, and 3 μL of ATP solution.
6. Kination solution B (5 μL used for each tube): 1.5 μL of 10X kination buffer, 0.5 μL of PNK, 1.5 μL of [γ- ^{32}P] ATP, and 1.5 μL of water.

Total nucleotide analysis

1. 20 mU/μL Potato apyrase.
2. Polyethyleneimine (PEI)-cellulose TLC sheets.
3. 0.5 M LiCl.
4. Scintillation counter or BioImaging Analyzer.

Digestion of adducted oligonucleotides by method I

1. NP1: dissolve in water to give 1.6 U/μL.
2. PDE I: dissolve in water to give 20 mU/μL.
3. Digestion buffer I: 0.3 M sodium acetate (or 0.13 M sodium citrate), pH 5.3. This can be stored at 4°C.
4. 1 mM $ZnCl_2$. This can be stored at 4°C.
5. 0.3 N HCl. This can be stored at room temperature.
6. 0.5 M Tris-base. This can be stored at 4°C.

Digestion of adducted oligonucleotides by method II

1. NP1.
2. PNK: dissolve in water to give 10 U/μL.
3. PDE I.

4. Digestion buffer II: 0.2 M sodium citrate buffer, pH 5.7. This can be stored at 4°C.
5. 1 mM $ZnCl_2$.
6. 0.3 N HCl.
7. 0.5 M Tris-base.

Thin-layer chromatography of labeled adducts

1. PEI-cellulose TLC sheet, 20 × 20 cm. Keep at 4°C.
2. Whatman no. 1 filter sheets.
3. D1: 2.3 M sodium phosphate buffer, pH 6.0.
4. D2: 3.4 M lithium formate, 6.4 M urea, pH 3.5.
5. D3: 0.7 M NaH_2PO_4, 8.5 M urea, pH 8.0.
6. D4: 1.7 M sodium phosphate buffer, pH 6.0

Methods

DNA digestion

1. Dissolve DNA in 0.01X SSC, 0.1 mM EDTA at a concentration of 2 μg/μL.
2. Transfer 5 μL of the DNA solution, 1.5 μL of water, 1.5 μL of the nuclease mixture, and 2 μL of digestion buffer to a 1.5-mL tube.
3. Incubate at 37°C for 3–3.5 h and centrifuge at 12,000g for 5 min at 4°C. Dilute a 2-μL aliquot of the supernatant with 58 μL of water.

^{32}P-postlabeling by the standard method or adduct-intensification method

1. Standard condition: transfer an aliquot of 5 μL of the diluted DNA digest and 10 μL of kination solution A to a 1.5-mL tube, and incubate at 37°C for 1 h. Spin down in a microcentrifuge at 4°C.
2. Adduct intensification condition: transfer an aliquot of 5 μL of DNA digest, 5 μL of water, and 5 μL of kination solution B to a 1.5-mL tube, and incubate at 37°C for 1 h.

Total nucleotide analysis

1. Transfer an aliquot of 2 μL of the ^{32}P-labeled sample to a 0.5-mL tube, add 5.4 mU (3 μL, 1.8 mU/μL) of apyrase, and incubate at 37°C for 45 min.
2. Add water to make a total of 250 μL.
3. On a PEI-cellulose sheet, draw 1-cm^2 grids, 3 cm from the base.
4. Spot an aliquot of 5 μL on a PEI-cellulose sheet and dry.

5. Develop with LiCl solution to the top edge.
6. Check separation of nucleotides (origin) from phosphate (Rf: approx 0.2) by exposure to an X-ray film for approx 3 min.
7. Carefully cut out the squares containing nucleotides. Place in scintillation vials, add 3 mL toluene cocktail, and count over the entire energy window.

Adduct analysis by method I

1. Adjust the pH of the remaining sample (13 μL) of the incubate to approx 6.0 by adding 1.8 μL of 0.3 N HCl.
2. To the tube, add 1 μL of NP1 solution (1.6 U), 1 μL of $ZnCl_2$ solution, and 1.5 μL of digestion buffer I (pH 5.3) and incubate at 37°C for 10 min.
3. Adjust the pH to 8.0–9.0 by adding 3 μL of 0.5 M Tris-base.
4. Add 1.5 μL of PDE I solution (30 mU) to this tube and incubate at 37°C for 30 min.

Adduct analysis by method II

The 3'-phosphate of some adducts is resistant to NP1 phosphatase activity. In this case, prior PNK treatment is useful.

1. Adjust the pH of the remaining sample (13 μL) of the incubate to approx 6.0 by adding 1.3 μL of 0.3 N HCl.
2. Add 3 μL of PNK solution (30 U) and 1.5 μL of digestion buffer II pH 5.7 (the final concentration of citrate is 16 mM) to the tube and incubate at 37°C for 30 min.
3. Add another 1 μL of PNK solution (10 U) and incubate at 37°C for 30 min.
4. Add 0.7 μL of NP1 solution (1.1 U) and 1 μL of $ZnCl_2$ solution, and incubate at 37°C for 10 min.
5. Adjust the pH to approx 8.0 by adding 3 μL of 0.5 M Tris-base.
6. Add 1.5 μL of PDE I solution (30 mU), and incubate at 37°C for 30 min.

TLC analysis

Almost the same TLC conditions as those described previously are applicable, although migration distances differ from the adducted deoxynucleoside diphosphate case. Run D3 twice. Run D4 in the same direction as D3 after attaching a 35-mm Whatman filter paper to the top edge of the TLC sheet.

Imaging and quantification

1. Visualize and quantify adduct spots as described above.

2. Under standard conditions, calculate relative adduct labeling (RAL) according to the following equation:

$$RAL = \frac{\text{adduct radioactivity (cpm)}}{\text{radioactivity of total deoxynucleotide (cpm)} \times \text{fold dilution}}$$

3. For analysis under intensification conditions, calculate intensification factor (IF) according to the following equation:

$$IF = \frac{RAL_{int}}{RAL_{std}}$$

where RAL_{int} is RAL under intensification conditions, and RAL_{std} is RAL under standard conditions.

Notes

1. Ultrapure water prepared by passing through Milli-Q spUF is used.
2. All solutions should be stored at –20°C, except where otherwise stated.
3. To ensure thorough mixing, it is recommended that all tubes containing different components be vortexed and spun down in a microcentrifuge.
4. Protection from radioactivity during handling of radioactive samples is crucially important.
5. Sheets can be stored at 4°C. Plates should be prerun with water overnight after attachment of a 12-cm filter paper wick and dried at room temperature.
6. The solvent used for IQ-DNA adduct analysis is indicated as an example. For D2, 4.5 M lithium formate, 8.5 M urea, pH 3.5 is prepared and diluted appropriately. For MeIQadducts 60% and for PhIP-adducts 80% solutions were used. For D3, 1.0 M LiCl, 0.5 M Tris-HCl, 8.5 M urea, pH 8.0, was used for MeIQ and PhIP.
7. When analysis is performed under intensification conditions, it is also necessary to perform the procedure outlined above, to determine the IF value of each adduct.
8. After incubation in a tube, the contents should be spun down at 4°C.
9. Potato apyrase (20 mU/μL) is diluted with water to give a concentration of 1.8 mU/μL.
10. When BIA is used for quantification, a 500X dilution for the standard method (and a 50X dilution for the adduct intensification method), and exposure to X-ray film for approx 30 min are recommended.

For BIA analysis, total and adduct analyses should be made on the same imaging plates.

11. This condition is appropriate for PhIP and MeIQ adducts, but the optimum pH may differ depending on specific adducts and it is necessary to check the optimum pH, which should be between 5.3 and 7.0.
12. The background usually becomes clean by running twice. Running once is enough in some cases.

DNA Isolation and Sample Preparation for Quantification of Adduct Levels by Accelerator Mass Spectrometry

A protocol is described for the isolation of DNA and subsequent preparation of samples for the measurement of adduct levels by *accelerator mass spectrometry* (AMS). AMS is a highly sensitive technique used for the quantification of adducts following exposure to carbon-14- or tritium-labeled chemicals, with detection limits in the range of one adduct per 10^{11}–10^{12} nucleotides. However, special precautions must be taken to avoid cross-contamination of isotope between samples and to produce a sample that is compatible with AMS. The DNA isolation method described is based on digestion of tissue with proteinase K, followed by extraction of DNA using Qiagen DNA isolation columns. DNA is then precipitated with isopropanol, washed repeatedly with 70% ethanol to remove salt, and then dissolved in water. This method has been used to generate reliably good yields of uncontaminated, pure DNA from animal and human tissues for analysis of adduct levels. For quantification of adduct levels from ^{14}C-labeled compounds, DNA samples are then converted to graphite, and the ^{14}C content is measured by AMS.

Most known chemical carcinogens form reactive intermediates that are capable of reacting with DNA, forming covalent adducts. This damage may lead to mutations and ultimately cancer. Consequently, for risk assessment it is important to establish whether drugs and toxicants are capable of forming DNA adducts, particularly following doses that are encountered in everyday life. Traditional methods used to monitor DNA adducts include ^{32}P-postlabeling, fluorescence techniques, gas chromatography/mass spectroscopy (GC/MS), and immunoassays, with detection limits typically in the range of one adduct/10^7–10^9 nucleotides. *Accelerator mass spectrometry* (AMS) allows one to establish whether chemicals form DNA adducts at even lower levels (10^{-10}–10^{-12} nucleotides range) through the use of carbon-14 (^{14}C)- or tritium (^3H)-labeled compounds. Thus, DNA adduct levels can be established following low chemical doses or using compounds that have a low covalent binding index. Because the amounts of chemicals and radioactivity required are low, such studies can be conducted safely in humans.

AMS is a nuclear physics technique that can measure isotopes with a low natural abundance and a long half-life (e.g., ^{14}C and ^3H) with high sensitivity and precision. It was originally developed for use in the earth sciences but has now found widespread use in biology, with applications in areas such as cancer, nutrition, and pharmaceutical research. However, as AMS is so sensitive, cross-contamination of samples by isotope from equipment and laboratory supplies can be a major problem. Therefore, certain methods have been chosen to avoid contamination. For example, we have found that phenol/chloroform extraction, a process that is used frequently in DNA isolations, can be a major source of ^{14}C contamination. All gloves, tubes, forceps, and containers for buffers and other substances used in sample preparation must be disposable. Furthermore, before analysis by AMS, samples must be converted to graphite (for ^{14}C analysis) or titanium hydride (for ^3H analysis). Therefore, the samples must be compatible with this process. For example, this necessitates the complete removal of sodium salts from the extracted DNA samples by repeated washing with 70% ethanol.

This section describes a protocol for extracting DNA from tissues for analysis of ^{14}C or ^3H content by AMS. The method is based on the use of Qiagen columns. Procedures for contamination avoidance in samples are included throughout. After the section on DNA isolation, a description of the process for conversion of the biological material to graphite for ^{14}C analysis is presented. AMS is then used to quantitate the amount of ^{14}C in the graphite samples. Owing to the size and cost of an AMS instrument, this technique is not yet a routine tool in many laboratories. However, there are several facilities in the United States where samples can be sent for analysis. One such facility, The Center for Accelerator Mass Spectrometry at Lawrence Livermore National Laboratory, has a compact AMS system for the analysis of biological samples.

Materials

Tissue homogenization and protein digestion

1. Plastic wrap.
2. Aluminum foil.

3. Parafilm.
4. 50-mL Polypropylene tubes.
5. Hammer and plastic bag to cover.
6. Disposable scalpels.
7. Disposable forceps.
8. Lysis buffer: 4 M urea, 1% Triton X-100, 10 mM EDTA, 100 mM NaCl, 10 mM Tris-HCl, pH 8.0, 10 mM dithiothreitol.
9. 40 mg/mL Proteinase K in double-distilled water.
10. Shaking water bath or other mixer that will incubate at 37°C.

RNA digestion

1. RNAse T1: 100 μg/mL in double-distilled water.
2. RNAse A (DNAse-free): 10 mg/mL in double-distilled water.

Column purification

1. Qiagen Genomic tip 500 columns.
2. 5 M Sodium chloride.
3. 1 M 3-Morpholinopropanesulfonic acid (MOPS), pH 7.0.
4. Buffer B: 750 mM NaCl, 50 mM MOPS, 15% ethanol, 0.15% Triton X-100, pH 7.0.
5. Buffer C: 1 M NaCl, 50 mM MOPS, 15% ethanol, pH 7.0.
6. Buffer λ: 1.25 M NaCl, 50 mM MOPS, 15% ethanol, pH 8.0.
7. 50-mL Polypropylene tubes.
8. Holders for 50-mL polypropylene tubes.

DNA precipitation, washing, redissolution, concentration, and purity

1. Isopropanol.
2. Ice-cold 70% ethanol.
3. Double-distilled water.
4. UV spectrophotometer.

Conversion to graphite

1. 4 (Inner dimension) × 50-mm quartz sample tube.
2. Copper oxide (wire form).
3. 7 (Inner dimension) × 155-mm quartz combustion tube with breakable tip.
4. 9 (Outer dimension) × 155-mm borosilicate tube with dimple 2 cm from the sealed end.
5. 6 × 50-mm Borosilicate culture tube.
6. Tributyrin.

7. Zinc (powder).
8. Titanium hydride (powder).
9. Cobalt (powder).
10. Vacuum source.
11. Disposable vacuum manifold made from 5/16-inch plastic Y-connector and 1/2-inch outer dimension × 5/16-inch inner dimension plastic tubing.
12. Torch for tube sealing (oxyacetylene-type preferred).
13. Muffle furnace.
14. Vacuum concentrator.
15. Liquid nitrogen bath (consisting of liquid nitrogen in a Dewar flask).
16. Dry ice/isopropanol bath (consisting of a slurry made of dry ice and isopropanol).

Methods

Tissue homogenization and protein digestion

1. Place 400 mg of fresh tissue in the middle of a piece of the plastic wrap and fold the top half of the plastic wrap over the bottom half. Cover the wrapped tissue in a layer of aluminum foil.
2. Cover hammer with a plastic bag or plastic wrap. Pound tissue with the hammer until tissue is well homogenized. Scrape homogenized tissue into a 50-mL polypropylene tube using a clean, disposable scalpel.
3. Add 25 mL fresh lysis buffer.
4. Add 500 μL proteinase K. Mix by vortexing for 5 s.
5. Wrap the top of the tubes with parafilm to prevent leakage and contamination.
6. Place tubes in a 37°C shaking water bath overnight, or until tissue appears to be fully digested (i.e., there are no visible lumps of tissue).
7. Centrifuge at 20°C, 2000g, 20 min to remove any undigested tissue.
8. Pour supernatant into a clean 50-mL polypropylene tube. Discard pellet.

RNA digestion

1. Add 1.25 mL RNAse A and 1.25 mL RNAse T1 to sample.
2. Mix by vortexing for 5 s.
3. Incubate for 30–60 min at room temperature.

Column purification

1. Add 1.25 mL 1 M MOPS and 4.5 mL 5 M NaCl to the sample.
2. Mix by vortexing for 5 s.
3. Stand the required number of Qiagen columns in a rack, with a disposable 50-mL polypropylene tube under each one.
4. Add 25 mL buffer B to each of the columns.
5. Let the buffer run through the column completely and then discard the buffer.
6. Pour the samples into the columns. Discard the eluate. If column becomes clogged.
7. Add 25 mL buffer C to each of the columns. Discard the eluate. Repeat and discard the eluate.
8. Add 25 mL buffer λ to each of the columns. Collect the eluate in a clean, new 50-mL polypropylene tube. Keep the eluate, as this will contain the DNA.

DNA precipitation

1. Add 25 mL of ice-cold 100% isopropanol to the eluate containing the DNA.
2. Mix by vortexing for 5 s.
3. Wrap the lid in parafilm and place at –20°C overnight to precipitate the DNA.
4. Centrifuge at –4°C, 2000g for 3 h.
5. Carefully pour off supernatant. Save the pelleted DNA, and discard the supernatant.

Sample washing and redissolving

1. Add 5 mL 70% ethanol to the pellet.
2. Mix by vortexing for 5 s.
3. Centrifuge at 4°C, 2000g for 10 min.
4. Save the pellet, and discard the supernatant.
5. Repeat wash step with 70% ethanol and centrifuge.
6. Carefully pour off the supernatant, taking care not to dislodge the pellet. If the pellet becomes loose, recentrifuge.
7. Carefully invert the tube on laboratory bench paper to drain excess solvent. Leave the tube inverted for 10–15 min.
8. Add double-distilled water to the pellet.

DNA concentration and purity

1. Dilute an aliquot of the DNA with double-distilled water.

2. Measure and record the UV absorbance of the diluted DNA at 260 and 280 nm.
3. A 50 μg/mL solution of DNA has a UV absorbance of 1 at 260 nm. Therefore, DNA concentration in μg/mL = absorbance at 260 nm × 50 × dilution factor.
4. DNA purity = absorbance at 260 nm/absorbance at 280 nm. Pure DNA should have a ratio of 1.7–1.9.
5. DNA should be prepared for AMS analysis as soon as possible to prevent contamination.

AMS sample preparation

1. Place all quartz components into muffle furnace and heat to 900°C for 2 h. Remove components after they have cooled; handle 6 × 50-mm tubes with disposable forceps only (to prevent contamination).
2. Pipet known amount of DNA into clean, uncontaminated quartz sample tube, and add tributyrin if necessary. The quartz tube should then be placed within a test tube to protect the sample during vacuum concentration.
3. Remove all volatile components by completely drying with vacuum concentration.
4. Remove quartz sample tube from test tube using disposable forceps. Add 150–200 mg of copper oxide to dried DNA.
5. Place quartz sample tube in larger quartz combustion tube and evacuate. Seal evacuated combustion tube with torch.
6. Place combustion tube in muffle furnace at 900°C for 2 h. Remove after it has cooled.
7. Place all borosilicate components in the muffle furnace and heat to 500°C for 2 h. Remove components after they have cooled; handle 6 × 50-mm tubes with disposable forceps only (to prevent contamination).
8. Place 100–150 mg zinc powder and 10–20 mg titanium hydride powder into larger borosilicate tube.
9. Place 5–8 mg cobalt powder into 6 × 50 mm borosilicate tube.
10. Drop smaller tube into larger tube so that smaller tube rests on dimple in larger tube, thereby suspending it above the zinc and titanium hydride levels.
11. Place disposable vacuum manifold on vacuum source with the arms of the Y hanging down.

12. Push the breakable tip end of the quartz tube into one arm of the Y and push the open end of the borosilicate tube onto the other arm.
13. Evacuate the manifold with the tubes attached.
14. Place the quartz tube into the dry ice/isopropanol bath.
15. Keeping the quartz tube in the dry ice/isopropanol bath, place the borosilicate tube into the liquid nitrogen bath.
16. Isolate the manifold from the vacuum source (do not remove from the vacuum source).
17. Crack the breakable tip of the quartz tube, allowing the carbon dioxide inside to transfer to the borosilicate tube.
18. Evacuate the manifold again without removing the tubes from either bath.
19. Using the torch, seal off the borosilicate tube above level of the top of the 6 × 50-mm tube, trapping the carbon dioxide in the larger borosilicate tube with its other contents.
20. Place the sealed tube in the furnace and heat to 500°C for 4 h. Remove after cooling.
21. Break open the larger borosilicate tube to remove the smaller tube. The black powder in the small tube is the graphite, which can be analyzed by AMS.
22. AMS will establish the $^{14}C/^{12}C$ ratio of the sample. This is then used to calculate the adduct level.

Notes

1. The protocol described is for isolation of up to 400 μg DNA using Qiagen Genomic tip 500 DNA isolation columns. This is approximately equivalent to the amount of DNA obtained from 400 mg wet tissue. Other column sizes are Qiagen Genomic tip 20 for up to 20 μg DNA and tip 100 for up to 90 μg DNA. The protocol can be scaled down for the smaller columns.
2. When handling samples, it is essential to avoid cross-contamination of isotope by the use of disposable plastic ware, scalpels, forceps, and gloves. These should be changed in between samples. Liquid samples should be pipeted using filter tips and clean pipets. When homogenizing the tissue, there should be disposable barriers (plastic wrap and foil) in between the sample and hammer.
3. The flow rate of the column will depend on the viscosity of the sample. If the column exhibits a very slow flow rate or becomes completely clogged, the flow can be assisted by attaching a small

amount of tubing to the bottom of the column and withdrawing eluate slowly with a syringe.

4. The volume of water required will depend on the amount of DNA extracted. Typically in this procedure, 300 μL of water will result in well-dissolved DNA with a concentration of 1–2 mg/mL. A 1:20 dilution of this solution should then be within the range suitable for DNA concentration determination by UV spectrophotometry. The AMS sample tubes used in our laboratory have a sample capacity of about 400 μL, so larger samples may need to be concentrated prior to AMS preparation.
5. If A260/A280-nm absorbance ratios are not within the range of 1.7 to 1.9, this is probably because of incomplete removal of protein or RNA. The DNA should be repurified prior to analysis by AMS.
6. We try to submit DNA for analysis by AMS within 24 h of extraction. This reduces the chance of cross-contamination of samples with radioisotope. However, if this is not possible, samples should be stored in a refrigerator or freezer that is not used for storage of high levels of radioisotope.
7. Tributyrin is a nonvolatile hydrocarbon that contains depleted levels of carbon-14. It is used in AMS to increase the size of small samples for efficient graphitization. Typically, using this method, samples that contain less than 0.5 mg carbon require the addition of carrier. For DNA (29% carbon), this would be equal to 1.7 mg. A 40 mg/mL solution of tributyrin in methanol is made, and then 50 μL is added to each DNA sample. Carrier controls should be prepared at the same time.
8. The isotope ratios determined by AMS are converted to adduct levels first by subtracting the natural radiocarbon content of the sample and the radiocarbon contributed from addition of any carrier. The natural radiocarbon content of the DNA is determined using control DNA samples from subjects or rodents not given the [^{14}C]-labeled compound. Adduct levels (ratio of moles of compound/moles nucleotide) are then calculated based on the percent carbon of DNA (29%) and the compound specific activity.

Fluoroimaging-Based Immunoassay of DNA Photoproducts

Sensitive and accurate measurement of photoproducts induced in DNA by natural or artificial ultraviolet-B (UVB; and UVC) light is essential to evaluate the toxic and mutagenic effects of this radiation. Monoclonal antibodies specific for the two major classes of photoproducts—cyclobutane pyrimidine dimers (CPDs) and pyrimidine-[6-4]- pyrimidinone photoproducts ([6-4]PPs)—have made possible highly specific and sensitive assays. Described here is the use of these primary antibodies with fluorescent secondary antibodies to generate 96-spot arrays. Stable fluorescence signals are rapidly and sensitively scored by fluoroimaging and computer analysis of peak-and-valley traces. CPD levels in a series of calibration standards are determined by acid hydrolysis/thinlayer chromatography analyses of radiolabeled bacterial DNA, UV-irradiated to known high fluences, and linear extrapolation to known lower fluences. The nonlinear fluorescence vs CPD curve reflects the effect of photoproduct concentration on single vs double binding by divalent antibody proteins. This technique is applied to photoproducts in whole inbred *Xenopus laevis* tadpoles, chronically irradiated at a series of UVB fluences that reach a lethality threshold when in vivo steady-state photoproduct levels are still quite low. As few as 0.01–0.02 CPDs per DNA kbp can be reliably detected, at signal/ noise ratios of roughly 3:1.

Sensitive and accurate detection of photoproducts induced in cellular DNA by *ultraviolet* (UV) light is essential to interpretation of viability and survival data. Most studies have used cultures of prokaryotic or eukaryotic cells, because of their uniformity and amenability to statistical analyses. Notable exceptions are analyses of photoproduct accumulation and "*sunburn*" response in outer layers of mammalian skin, as well as measurements of photoproducts in thin leaves of alfalfa and *Arabidopsis* seedlings. To analyze quantitatively ultraviolet-B (UVB) effects on amphibians, whose drastic global population declines have been linked in some cases with solar UVB radiation, we have employed cohorts of inbred *Xenopus leavis* tadpoles. Their genetic and chronological homogeneity maximizes biological uniformity, and their small size and semitransparency make even interior organs vulnerable to UV light. When parallel tadpole subpopulations are exposed to UVB light regimes of increasing chronic intensity, survival decreases abruptly at fluences that still induce relatively low levels of photoproducts in DNA. Thus, photoproduct assays that are sensitive, accurate, and reasonably reproducible from one animal to another are needed to evaluate lethal UVB thresholds.

Assays that depend on cleavage of DNA strands at photoproduct sites and analysis of the size distributions of the resulting fragments can be highly sensitive. Size distributions are typically measured by alkaline sedimentation of DNA previously radiolabeled in vivo, or alkaline gel electrophoresis and electronic imaging. Radiolabeling of tadpole DNA in vivo is not practical, since the animals are grown in 1-gallon tanks, and the electrophoresis video-imaging technique requires highly specialized apparatus. Furthermore, extraction of DNA by all but the gentlest techniques breaks DNA, thus distorting size distributions. In any case, determinations of average photoproduct levels from fragment analyses typically involve assumptions about the randomness of photoproduct distribution that may not be warranted for thicker tissues. Lastly, efficient and highly specific incising enzymes are available only for one major class of UV photoproducts, cyclobutane pyrimidine dimers (CPDs); for the other major class, pyrimidine-[6-4']-pyrimidinone photoproducts ([6-4]PPs), precise and efficient incision is difficult to achieve.

In the past few years, polyclonal and monoclonal antibodies specific for CPDs and [6-4]PPs have been used for photoproduct-specific immunoassays. Radioimmune dilution and enzyme-linked immunosorbent assay techniques have been employed with considerable success, but the relatively large variability in such measurements has limited sensitivity. More recently, secondary antibodies, able to bind tightly and specifically to photoproduct-specific primary antibodies and themselves linked to signal-generating moieties, have been used for sensitive and reproducible assays. Antibody-linked horseradish peroxidase can directly generate a color signal on a membrane, which may then be quantitated by densitometry, or can generate a chemiluminescent signal from a proprietary peracid/luminol/enhancer cocktail that registers on film. Disadvantages of the chemiluminescence-film technique are limited linear response and the requirement that membranes must be exposed to film immediately after reactions; the signals slowly decline with time, limiting reproducibility at low signal levels. All these techniques yield signals that can be used for more or less sensitive and reproducible direct comparisons among samples, but absolute determinations of photoproduct frequencies (per DNA bp) require calibration against irradiated DNA standards in which absolute numbers of photoproducts can be determined.

Here we describe a modified photoproduct-immunoassay approach that addresses both sensitivity/reproducibility and calibration issues. DNA is vigorously extracted from irradiated tadpoles so as to minimize contaminants that might engender spurious fluorescence, and aliquots quantitatively spotted onto membranes, to which anti-CPD or anti-[6-4]PP primary antibodies and fluorescent secondary antibodies are bound. Fluorescence intensities are determined by fluoroimaging of washed membranes, and sample and background signals are analyzed with computer software. CPD signals are calibrated against DNA standards whose CPD contents can be chromatographically determined.

Materials

Isolation of total DNA from whole tadpoles

1. Frog tranquilizer (0.1% tricane).
2. Liquid N_2.
3. GenomicPrep Cells and Tissue DNA isolation kit.
4. 20 mg/mL Proteinase K.
5. Phaselock Gel.
6. Phenol/chloroform/isoamyl-alcohol, 25:24:1.
7. Chloroform/isoamyl-alcohol, 24:1.
8. 3 M Sodium acetate.
9. Absolute ethanol.
10. TE buffer: 10 mM Tris-HCl, pH 7.5, 1 mM Na_2EDTA.
11. Filter paper.
12. Mortar and pestle.
13. 1.5-mL Microcentrifuge tubes.
14. Tabletop microcentrifuge.

Photoproduct immunoassay

1. Irradiated [^{3}H]DNA standards:
   (a) DNA is extracted from thymine-requiring *E. coli* (*thy*–, *deo*–) cells grown in broth plus [^{3}H]thymidine and then irradiated with UVC light fluences from 15 to 120 J/m^2.
   (b) Frequencies of T-T cyclobutane dimers (T[CPD]Ts) are determined by acid hydrolysis and thin-layer chromatography, as previously described, and total numbers of CPDs are estimated from known or estimated relative frequencies of T[CPD]T, T[CPD]C, C[CPD]T, and C[CPD]C photoproducts. The same methods are used to measure sample and standard DNA concentrations.
   (c) Standards for [6-4]PPs require a more complicated approach. Treatment of UV-irradiated plasmids with purified CPD-photolyase will leave only [6-4]PPs, whose average density (per plasmid or per DNA bp) can be estimated by transfection of completely repair-incompetent (uvr–, phr–, recA–) *E. coli*, or by quantitative polymerase chain reaction (PCR) amplification.
   (d) In each case, comparison with unirradiated controls yields the fraction of irradiated targets with no [6-4]PPs, and the

Poisson distribution yields the average number per plasmid or per bp.

2. 20X SSPE buffer: 3.6 M NaCl, 2 M $NaH_2PO_4 \cdot H_2O$, 0.02 M $Na_2EDTA \cdot 2H_2O$, pH 7.4 (174 g NaCl, 27.6 g NaH_2PO_4, and 7.4 g Na_2EDTA, dissolved in 800 mL H_2O); pH adjusted to 7.4 with 10 N NaOH; volume made up to 1000 mL.
3. 0.4 M NaOH.
4. 10X PBS buffer: 1.4 M NaCl, 26 mM KCl, 10 mM Na_2HPO_4, 17.6 mM KH_2PO_4, pH 7.4 (80 g NaCl, 2 g KCl, 14.48 g Na_2HPO_4, 2.4 g KH_2PO_4); pH adjusted to 7.4; volume made up to 1000 mL.
5. Tween-20 detergent.
6. PBS-T buffer: 0.2% Tween-20 in PBS buffer (1000 mL volume).
7. Nonfat dried milk.
8. Primary monoclonal anti-CPD or anti-[6-4]PP antibody, diluted respectively to 1:2000 or 1:1000 in sterile PBS (1X).
9. Fluorescently labeled secondary antibody, Alexa 568 goat anti-mouse. The excitation and emission capabilities of the fluoroimager must be taken into account.
10. Microcentrifuge tubes or PCR tubes.
11. Vortex mixer.
12. Slot-blot apparatus.
13. Hybond N^+ membrane.
14. Cellulose filter paper for gel blots, Island Scientific grade 238 or equivalent.
15. Shallow rectangular plastic containers, with lids: two 10-oz containers for soaking of nitrocellulose membrane and for reactions with primary and secondary antibodies; one 48-oz container for incubation with blocking solution.
16. Rocking platform(s) (used at both room temperature and at 4°C, i.e., in the cold room).

Detection and quantification of fluorescent signal from bound secondary antibody

1. Fluoroimager, with software.
2. Software for data analysis.

Methods

Isolation of total DNA from whole tadpoles

1. Anesthetize tadpole in 0.1% Tricane.
2. Place tadpole on a filter paper to drain excess water.

3. Add liquid N_2 to a mortar to chill it, then add more liquid N_2 and submerge tadpole.
4. Grind tadpole to a fine powder and transfer into microcentrifuge tube. At this point the sample can be stored at -80°C until further processing.
5. Isolate DNA using GenomicPrep Cells and Tissue DNA isolation kit, supplemented with proteinase K, according to the manufacturer's instructions, beginning with 20–50 mg of frozen sample. Resuspend DNA in 200 μL of TE buffer.
6. Centrifuge samples for 1 min. If a pellet is formed, transfer the supernatant into a fresh tube and discard the pellet.
7. Add an equal volume of phenol/chloroform/isoamyl-alcohol, and vigorously invert tube 10 times (if using Phase-Lock Gel, add roughly 200 μL to each tube).
8. Centrifuge for 5 min in microcentrifuge at 12,000–14,000 rpm (~12,000g).
9. To the supernatant add an equal volume of chloroform/isoamyl-alcohol, and vigorously invert tube 10 times to remove residual phenol from the sample.
10. Centrifuge for 5 min in microcentrifuge at 12,000–14,000 rpm (~12,000g).
11. Transfer the supernatant to a fresh tube.
12. Add 0.05 vol of 3 M sodium acetate and 2.5 vol of absolute ethanol. Mix well.
13. Centrifuge 1 min in microcentrifuge at 12,000–14,000 rpm (~12,000g).
14. Discard the supernatant. Resuspend pellet in 50–100 μL TE buffer.
15. Vortex vigorously and pipet several times up and down with an automatic pipet to shear the DNA. Alternatively, digest DNA with restriction enzyme. Store samples at 4°C.
16. Determine DNA concentration of each sample.

Photoproduct immunoassay

Sample preparation and blotting

1. Make dilutions so as to place 100 ng of sample or standard DNA in each tube in a volume of 200 μL or less (if using PCR tubes, 100 μL or less); for [6-4]PP assays, use 1 μg.
2. Boil tubes with samples or standards for 5 min. Use PCR thermocycler, if possible, to avoid condensation and sample contamination.

3. Chill on ice for 5 min.
4. Add equal volumes of 20X SSPE buffer and vortex. Microcentrifuge (1 min at 12,000–14,000 rpm [~ 12,000g]) to remove any particulate matter.
5. Saturate membrane with deionized water and then with 20X SSPE buffer.
6. Place membrane on a plastic gasket and cut one corner for orientation. Set up slot-blot apparatus according to the manufacturer's instructions.
7. Add 200 μL of 20X SSPE buffer to each well, and pull through with a vacuum.
8. Add samples and standards (maximum volume 400 μL to each well) and let stand for 15 min. Pull through with vacuum; adjusted to slow flow.
9. Add 200 μL 20X SSPE buffer to rinse wells, and pull through with vacuum.

Fixing and probing of membrane with antibody

10. Soak filter paper in 0.4 M NaOH and pour off excess.
11. Place membrane on NaOH-soaked filter paper for 15 min.
12. Rinse membrane briefly with 5X SSPE buffer.
13. Block membrane by covering with 5% nonfat milk solution in PBS-T buffer (100 mL), in shallow rectangular plastic container with lid.
14. Rock gently at room temperature for at least 2 h, or overnight, at 4°C.
15. Rinse off the milk with PBS-T buffer quickly twice and then for 15 min with rocking.
16. React with primary CPD antibody: place washed membrane in 10 mL of primary antibody solution diluted with PBS buffer, typically 1:2000 for CPDs and 1:1000 for [6-4]PPs (test solutions beforehand with irradiated DNA standards); incubate for 2 h at room temperature in 10-oz plastic container, rocking gently. Remove and store antibody solution at 4°C; solution can be used once more within 2 wk.
17. Wash membrane in PBS-T buffer twice quickly and then once with 20 min of rocking, and twice with 5 min of rocking.
18. React membrane with secondary antibody, diluted 1:2500 in PBS buffer: place washed membrane in 10 mL of secondary antibody

solution. Incubate for 1 h at room temperature, rocking gently. Remove secondary antibody solution and discard.

19. Wash membrane as in step 17, but increase the number of 5-min washes (with rocking) to six.
20. Cover membrane with plastic wrap to keep from drying and with foil to prevent photobleaching.

Detection and quantification of photoproducts

1. For detection of the fluorescent signal from bound secondary antibody use excitation and emission settings recommended by the antibody supplier and compatible with the fluorimager. Commonly used lasers excite at 405 nm, 488 nm, 543 nm, and 633 nm, with tunability offering some flexibility around each line. Separation between excitation and emission maxima should be maximal, consistent with filtering characteristics of the instrument. Extinction coefficients and quantum yields should be high enough to generate adequate signals. Obviously, the immunospecificity of the secondary must match the primary antibody.
2. Membrane must be wet and flattened out on a glass plate. All bubbles must be removed.
3. Place second glass plate on top of the membrane. Scan according to instructions for fluoroimager.
4. For analysis, scan must first be opened using attached FMBIO Analysis V.6.0.11 software. Invert image under "Mode" drop-down menu and select "*Reverse Analysis*" option to return to light spots on dark background. Next, "Save Copy As" choosing a unique file name, and change file format to TIFF (Tagged Image File Format). This TIFF file can then be analyzed using ImageQuant software, which gives better control of background and is easier to use. Analyze spots using ImageQuant software. It is usually best to generate a peak and valley trace using a line scan, because backgrounds are determined unambiguously. Comparison of box scans of spots and background (no spot) regions is less reliable.

Calculations

1. Construct a standard curve of fluorescence (arbitrary units) vs known amounts of CPDs, using irradiated DNA standards.
2. Use a standard (nonlinear) calibration to determine the CPD amounts from relative fluorescence values of samples. To determine relative sample fluorescence values, multiple the ratio (observed absolute sample fluorescence)/(observed absolute standard

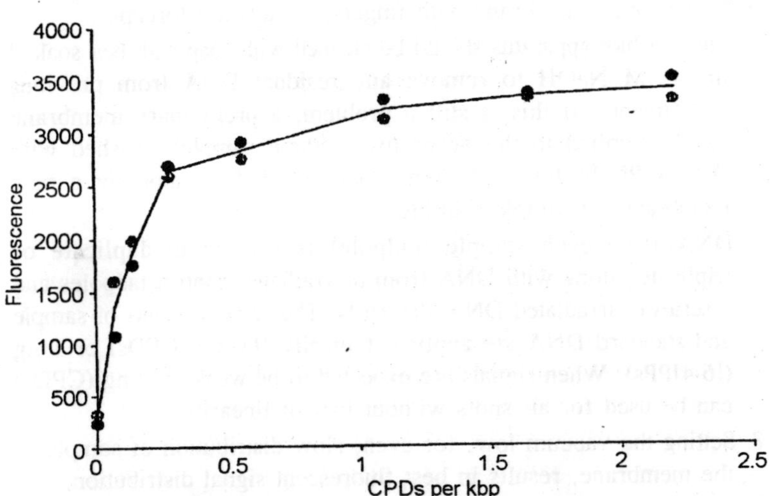

Fig. 5.5. Fluorescence vs CPD-density calibration.

fluorescence) by the appropriate relative standard fluorescence from the standard calibration curve. For example, values would be 1.0 for 0.14 CPD/kb and 0.57 for 0.07 CPD/kb. Then read the corresponding CPD values from the calibration curve. Alternatively, use an equation fitted to the curve, $y = 2.56\ x/(0.199 + x)$, where y is relative fluorescence intensity and x is a photoproduct density (CPD/kb), to obtain x for a given y.

Notes

1. Linearity between photoproduct induction and UVC or UVB light fluence is well known. Typically only the highest fluences induce enough photoproducts to be measured quantitatively by the acid hydrolysis/TLC technique. Photoproduct levels in lower fluence DNA standards are estimated by linear extrapolation.
2. DNA fragmented to average lengths of 10 kbp or less works best with the slot-blot apparatus.
3. For dsDNA, we use PicoGreen dye, with a microplate fluorescence reader. Samples and DNA standards are measured in duplicate or triplicate. Dilute at least 5 μL of sample into a final volume of 200 μL. If DNA concentration is too high, make successive dilutions, always using at least 5 μL.
4. If particulate matter is observed, pipet off the top 80% (as much as can be cleanly removed from the pellet) of the supernatant and transfer to a clean tube for subsequent processing. Particulate matter to some extent is typical, so this may be done routinely.

5. Never touch membrane with fingers; always use forceps.
6. The slot-blot apparatus should be cleaned with soap and then soaked in 0.4 M NaOH to remove any residual DNA from previous experiments. If this is still a problem, a preliminary membrane can be applied to the apparatus (without sample), washed with 20X SSPE buffer, and then discarded, before applying a new membrane for sample spotting.
7. DNA from each sample (tadpole) is spotted in duplicate or triplicate, along with DNA from unirradiated control tadpoles and a series of irradiated DNA standards. The same amounts of sample and standard DNA are applied, typically 100 ng (CPDs) or 1 μg ([6-4]PPs). When signals are expected to be weak, 150 ng (CPDs) can be used for all spots without loss of linearity.
8. Setting the vacuum low, for even, slow distribution of sample to the membrane, results in best fluorescent signal distribution.
9. To decrease background, dilute secondary antibody more. (This also decreases signal.)
10. The number of 5-min washes can be increased further, with additional rinses after each wash, to reduce nonspecific binding of secondary antibody further.
11. It is important to check the fluorimager filter, laser, and mirror periodically for obstruction by dust particle or spilled samples from previous users. Soft lens tissue or air can be used to clean these instruments; if necessary, use 70% ethanol.
12. To minimize air bubbles, sparingly wet the membrane on the first glass plate and then sandwich the membrane with the second glass plate. To remove trapped air bubbles on the other side of the membrane, remove the second glass plate.
13. The appropriate fluoroimager channel should be used. Depending on the amount of fluorescence signal, the sensitivity should be adjusted. Results are typically best with 15–25% sensitivity.
14. It is very important to turn the auto focus off and to adjust the focus manually. Manual focus is done by scanning a small area (which includes the fluorescence signal), then changing the focus setting up or down in 0.2-mm increments (until the fluorescence signal reaches a maximum and then starts to decline) and then using the setting for maximum signal.
15. Antibody signals show a linear response only at low photoproduct levels, at which presumably one (divalent) primary antibody reacts

with one photoproduct. The curvature at higher levels is thought to reflect binding of two neighboring photoproducts by one antibody. For this reason, apparently linear calibration curves obtained by diluting a single heavily irradiated sample (even with unirradiated DNA added to keep total concentrations the same) are spurious.

16. We have routinely determined CPD levels as low as 0.01–0.02 per kbp, at a signal/noise level of roughly 3:1.

Analysis of DNA Strand Cleavage at Abasic Sites

Abasic sites in DNA arise under a variety of circumstances, including destabilization of bases through oxidative stress, as an intermediate in base excision repair, and through spontaneous loss. Their persistence can yield a blockade to RNA transcription and DNA synthesis and can be a source of mutations. Organisms have developed an enzymatic means of repairing abasic sites in DNA that generally involves a DNA repair pathway that is initiated by a repair protein creating a phosphodiester break ("*nick*") adjacent to the site of base loss. Here we describe a method for analyzing the manner in which repair endonucleases differ in the way they create nicks in DNA and how to distinguish between them using cellular crude extracts.

Apurinic/apyrimidinic (AP) abasic sites arise in DNA under a variety of circumstances that, taken together, make them one of the more common lesions found in DNA. For example, free radicals can interact with DNA bases leading to their destabilization and ultimate loss. Free radical attack on DNA can also lead to DNA base modifications, some of which are known to be removed by *N*-glycosylases, resulting in the formation of an AP site as part of the *base excision repair* (BER) pathway. Even in the absence of environmental factors, DNA bases are known to be spontaneously lost, leaving behind abasic lesions that, if left unrepaired, can be mutagenic and can also form a blockade to RNA transcription.

To illustrate the importance of abasic sites, all organisms that have thus far been tested have the ability to repair these sites by creating an incision adjacent to the AP site to initiate the repair process. The major class of AP endonuclease, at least quantitatively, is one that hydrolytically cleaves 5' and adjacent to an abasic site, producing nucleotide 3'-hydroxyl and 5'-deoxyribose-5-phophate termini.

Another kind of activity that acts on abasic sites is part of the BER pathway that is initiated by *N*-glycosylases directed toward a modified or nonconventional base in DNA. Often, these *N*-glycosylases also possess AP lyase activity that cleaves DNA 3' to an abasic site via a β-elimination reaction to leave a 3' 4-hydroxy-2-pentenal-5-phosphate. An example of this type of activity is that possessed by *E. coli* endonuclease III (endo III), a broad-specificity *N*-glycosylase/AP lyase used for the repair of oxidative damage to DNA. In some cases, *N*-glycosylases/AP lyases not only cleave DNA via a β-elimination reaction but also are capable of carrying out a second ∂-elimination incision. This results in the removal of the AP site and the formation of a one-nucleotide gap bordered by 3'- and 5'-phosphate termini. The β, ∂-elimination reaction can be concerted, as appears to be the case for the *E. coli* formamidopyrimidine glycosylase (Fpg), which repairs oxidative DNA damage, primarily in the form of 8-oxoguanine (8oxoG). On the other hand, repair of 8oxoG by the *Drosophila* S3 *N*-glycosylase/AP lyase activity has been concluded to occur in two distinct steps, catalyzing a ∂-elimination reaction on a second encounter with the lesion after first dissociating from the AP substrate when the β-elimination reaction was completed.

There are several ways to monitor enzyme activity on abasic sites present in naturally occurring or synthesized DNA substrates. Originally, we utilized a [^{3}H]-labeled supercoiled phage DNA in a filter-binding assay that accurately measured DNA nuclease activity, but this technique was hampered by the tedious and time-consuming preparation of the substrate DNA. Moreover, this assay could only quantify the cleavage of a preprepared abasic DNA substrate, not identify the type of cleavage event unless it was followed up by DNA synthesis to determine whether the incision created a productive 3'-OH terminus. Recently, we have turned to an assay that utilizes a 5'-end-labeled DNA duplex oligonucleotide containing a single abasic site. After reaction with an AP endonuclease or AP lyase, the products of the reaction are separated on a polyacrylamide gel. Based on the migration of the cleaved product, one can easily visualize the type of strand cleavage possessed by a DNA repair endonuclease by autoradiography. Quantitation of the product(s) formed can be performed either by video densitometric analysis of autoradiograms, or by Phosphorimager analysis and scanning of dried gels. Importantly in this assay, different types of cleavage events generate unique visual images of the products formed by autoradiography; the assay is also adaptable in most cases to the use of both highly purified enzymes as well as cruder preparations.

For the assay described here, a synthetic oligonucleotide is utilized that is 37 bp in length (37-mer). Within the 37-mer is a single uracil

(U) residue placed at position 21 during the synthesis of the oligonucleotide. After 5'-end-labeling and gel purification of the single-stranded U-containing oligonucleotide, the complementary strand is annealed to create a duplex 37-mer. This forms a substrate for uracil-DNA glycosylase, which liberates the nonconventional base and forms an abasic site in its place.

Alternatively, tetrahydrofuran can be placed at position 21 within the 37-mer. Tetrahydrofuran is an analog of an abasic site and represents a productive substrate for a hydrolytic AP endonuclease. It is, however, refractive to cleavage by AP lyases, therefore making it a convenient substrate for measuring hydrolytic AP endonuclease activity in crude preparations that would ordinarily be compromised by AP lyase activity.

To demonstrate the utility of the oligonucleotide assay, the products of three different AP lyases acting on an abasic oligonucleotide DNA substrate are presented. In each case, the migration pattern of the reaction products provides direct information on the type of DNA termini produced by each enzyme. The hot alkali control (HA) provides a landmark for the production of a β, ∂-elimination reaction that reflects the production of a 5'- and 3'-phosphoryl terminus. DNA fragments containing a terminal phosphoryl group migrate faster than those of the same length that lack a terminal phosphate. As can be seen, the reaction products are completely distinct for each of the enzymes tested. Endonuclease III produces a β-elimination product, regardless of the amount of protein added to the assay, where the substrate is totally consumed yet yields only a single product. For *Drosophila* S3, a β-elimination product is also evident at low protein concentrations, yet higher amounts of protein yield what is clearly a ∂-elimination product as well. This suggests that S3 is dissociating from the abasic substrate once the original β-elimination reaction is completed and on a second encounter is then cleaving the remaining AP site via a ∂-elimination reaction. This is in contrast to what is observed for *E. coli* Fpg, which produces equal amounts of β- and ∂-elimination products, regardless of protein concentration or time of incubation. This indicates that Fpg is remaining bound to the AP substrate as it carries out both incision activities.

Another utility of the oligonucleotide assay is that it is amendable to analyzing 5'-acting AP endonucleases in crude extracts without concern over the contribution of contaminating AP lyases that could make interpretation of the actual products formed difficult. This is accomplished by switching from an authentic AP site created in the oligonucleotide substrate by U incorporation to a tetrahydrofuran analog of an AP site that is refractive to cleavage to AP lyases. The 5'-acting hydrolytic human APE/ref-1 is clearly capable of acting on a 37-mer synthetic DNA substrate with a tetrahydrofuran spacer, yet the same substrate is totally refractive to cleavage by the AP lyase activity possessed by *Drosophila* S3. The same preparation of *Drosophila* S3 is, however, active on a DNA substrate containing a single 8oxoG residue.

Materials

All solutions should be made using molecular biology-grade reagents and sterile distilled water.

5'-End-labeling and purification of oligonucleotides containing a single tetrahydofuran or U residue

The oligonucleotides used in our studies are commercially prepared to our specifications and contain the nonconventional bases U or 8oxoG or the abasic spacer tetrahydrofuran. The single-stranded oligos are deprotected and purified by spin-column chromatography. The individual single-stranded and purified oligonucleotides are then resuspended in distilled water to 10 pmol/μL.

1. 10 U/μL T4 polynucleotide kinase.
2. 10X T4 polynucleotide kinase buffer: 700 mM Tris-HCl, pH 7.6, 100 mM $MgCl_2$, 50 mM dithiothereitol (DTT), 1 mM spermidine-HCl.
3. [γ-^{32}P] ATP, 10 mCi/mL, 6000 Ci/mmol.
4. 10X Annealing buffer: 100 mM Tris-HCl, pH 7.6, 100 mM $MgCl_2$, 10 mM EDTA.
5. Loading buffer: 50% glycerol, 0.5% bromophenol blue, 0.5% xylene cynanol.
6. Phenol, molecular biology grade, neutralized, and equilibrated with 10 mM Tris-HCl, pH 8.0, 1 mM EDTA.
7. Phenol/chloroform/isoamyl alcohol mixture (25:24:1 by volume).
8. 40% Acrylamide stock: 38:2 acrylamide/bis-acrylamide in 100 mL of distilled water.
9. 10X TBE: 890 mM Tris-borate, 20 mM EDTA, pH 8.0.
10. Nondenaturing 20% polyacrylamide gel (per 100 mL): 50 mL 40% acrylamide stock, 10 mL 10X TBE, 500 μL 10% ammonium persulfate, 60 μL TEMED, distilled H_2O to 100 mL final volume.
11. Centrex MF-0.4 microcentrifuge tubes.
12. 35 mM HEPES-KOH, pH 7.4.

Cleavage of uracil-containing oligonucleotides

1. Uracil-DNA glycosylase.
2. 10X Uracil-DNA glycosylase buffer: 200 mM Tris-HCl, pH 8.0, 10 mM EDTA, 10 mM DTT, 100 μg/mL bovine serum albumin (BSA).
3. 10 mM HEPES-KOH, pH 7.4.

Enzymatic reactions and electrophoresis

1. Abasic oligonucleotides.
2. Purified AP endonuclease or AP lyase.
3. 10X *Drosophila* S3 (dS3) buffer: 300 mM HEPES, pH 7.4, 500 mM KCl, 10 mg/mL BSA, 0.5% Triton X-100, 10 mM DTT, 5 mM EDTA.
4. 10X *E. coli* Endo III buffer: 150 mM KH_2PO_4, pH 6.8, 100 mM EDTA, 100 mM β-mercaptoethanol, 400 mM KCl.
5. 10X *E. coli* Fpg buffer: 150 mM HEPES, pH 7.5, 500 mM KCl, 10 mM β-mercaptoethanol, 5 mM EDTA.
6. 10X human APE/ref-1 buffer: 500 mM HEPES, pH 7.5, 500 mM KCl, 10 μg/mL BSA, 100 mM $MgCl_2$, 0.5% Triton X-100.
7. 1 M Piperidine.
8. Denaturing polyacrylamide gel: 16% polyacrylamide solution, 7 mM urea, 1X TBE.
9. Formamide loading buffer: 96% formamide, 0.05% xylene cyanol, 0.05% bromophenol blue, 10 mM EDTA.
10. 15% methanol: 10% acetic acid solution.
11. Whatman 3MM paper.
12. X-ray film or Phosphorimager.

Methods

Characterization of endonucleases that act at abasic sites existing in DNA can be divided into several parts: first, a 5'-radiolabeled synthetic oligonucleotide containing either a single tetrahydrofuron residue, or one containing a single deoxyU residue, is prepared. Single-stranded oligos are then annealed to their nonradioactive complementary oligonucleotide. The duplexes are then purified and subsequently further processed by a uracil-DNA glycosylase so as to form an abasic site if necessary. This, or the tetrahydrofuran-containing oligonucleotide, is then employed as a substrate for enzyme reactions using proteins known, or suspected, to act on abasic sites. Upon completion of the enzymatic assays, the reaction products are then separated on a DNA sequencing gel.

5' End-labeling and purification of oligonucleotides

Bacteriophage T4 polynucleotide kinase is used to catalyze the transfer of the γ-phosphate of ATP to the 5'-hydroxyl terminus of the oligonucleotide. The following procedure produces sufficient quantities of 5'-end-labeled duplex oligonucleotides for several enzymatic reactions.

1. Prepare 5'-end labeling reaction mixtures in a 0.5-mL microcentrifuge tube containing the following: 3 μL [^{32}P]ATP, 4 μL 10X kinase buffer, 2 μL oligonucleotide, 2 μL (2U) of polynucleotide kinase, and 2 μL distilled water.
2. Incubate the reaction mixture for 30 min at 37°C.
3. Extract the reaction mixture once with phenol/chloroform/isoamyl alcohol.
4. Mix for 1 min, and then centrifuge at 12,000g for 3 min at room temperature in a microcentrifuge. Transfer the aqueous supernatant to a new tube. Add 2.5 vol of ethanol, mix, and store the tube at -20°C for 1 h.
5. Recover the oligos by centrifugation at 12,000g for 15 min at 4°C in a microcentrifuge. Remove the supernatant, and leave the tube open at room temperature until all the ethanol has evaporated.
6. Dissolve the pellet in 20 μL of distilled water.

Annealing reaction

1. Mix together in a microcentrifuge tube the following: 20 μL labeled oligos (1 pmol/mL), 4 μL complementary strand, 4 μL 10X annealing buffer, and 4 μL distilled water to 40 μL final volume.
2. Incubate the annealing mixture at 75°C for 10 min.
3. Slowly cool to room temperature.
4. Add 10 μL loading buffer and mix well.
5. Separate the labeled duplex oligonucleotides on a 20% non-denaturing polyacrylamide gel and then subject to autoradiography.
6. Excise the band corresponding to the labeled duplex oligos from the gel, and transfer to a Centrex MF-0.4 microcentrifuge tube.
7. Crush the acrylamide gel into small pieces against the wall of the tube, add 200 μL 35 mM HEPES-KOH, pH 7.4, to the tube, and incubate for 5 h to overnight at 4°C to elute the labeled oligos from the gel. (Typically, < 95% of labeled oligo is eluted.)
8. Collect the duplex oligos by centrifugation at 4000g for 3 min in a microcentrifuge.

Uracil excision

1. Uracil-DNA glycosylases are used to hydrolyze the *N*-glycosidic bond between the deoxyribose sugar and uracil base. The reaction mixture is as follows: 10 pmol labeled uracilcontaining duplex oligo, 4 μL 10X uracil-DNA glycosylase buffer, 1 μL uracil-DNA glycosylase (1 U/μL), and distilled water to 40 μL final volume.
2. Incubate the reaction for 20 min at 37°C. Extract the reaction mixture once with phenol/chloroform/isoamyl alcohol and precipitate the DNA as described above.
3. Dissolve the purified labeled duplex oligonucleotide in 10 mM HEPES-KOH, pH 7.4. It can be stored at 4°C for up to 1 wk.

Enzymatic reaction

1. Mix together in a microcentrifuge tube: approx 1 pmol of γ-^{32}P abasic oligonucleotide (typically 10,000 cpm), 1 μL 10 X reaction buffer, X μL enzyme, and distilled water to 10 μL final volume. Incubate at 37°C for the desired time.
2. Stop the reactions by heating at 75°C for 10 min. Add 2 μL of formamide loading buffer, heat for 4 min at 90°C, cool on ice, and then load immediately on a denaturing polyacrylamide gel.

Hot alkali treatment

1. Add 90 μL of 1 M piperidine to 10 μL of 5'-end-labeled abasic oligonucleotide, and incubate for 30 min at 90°C.
2. Lyophilize to dryness using a Speed Vac, and redissolve the pellet in 20 μL of distilled water.
3. Repeat lyophilization step twice more in order to remove all the piperidine.
4. Dissolve the remaining pellet in 50 μL of formamide loading buffer, heat for 4 min at 90°C, cool on ice, and then load immediately on a denaturing polyacrylamide gel.

Analysis of endonuclease activity by denaturing gels

1. Load an equal amount of radioactivity (about 5000 cpm) per lane on a pre-electrophoresed 16% denaturing polyacrylamide gel.
2. Electrophorese in 1X TBE buffer at 45-W constant power until the bromophenol dye front is near the bottom of the gel.
3. Remove the gel plates, pry apart, and transfer the gel to a bath containing 15% methanol and 10% acetic acid for 20 min.
4. With the gel still attached to the glass plate, place a similar sized piece of Whatman 3MM paper on top of the gel, and then carefully peel off the 3MM paper with the gel attached to it.

5. Cover the gel with plastic wrap, and dry under vacuum at 80°C for 45 min.
6. Expose the dried gel to X-ray film at 70°C for 12–16 h with an intensifying screen. Alternatively, PhosphorImager cassettes can be used for the same length of time, but at room temperature.

Notes

1. One advantage of the oligonucleotide assay is that the sequence can be manipulated so as to determine whether enzyme activity is affected by surrounding DNA bases either adjacent to, or opposite, the target site.
2. Caution should be taken in the preparation of ^{32}P-labeled oligonucleotides when planning assays over a sustained period. We have found that regardless of the method of storage of prepared oligos, degradation products begin to appear in our controls that are presumably owing to radioactive decay that splinters the oligos into smaller fragments. Generally, after 2 wk unused oligos are of little use because of such fragmentation.
3. We have used gels containing 20% polyacrylamide, but to maximize the separation of a β- and ∂-elimination product, 16% gels are preferred.

6

DNA Repair

Microsatellite Instability

The DNA *mismatch repair* (MMR) pathway plays a prominent role in the correction of errors made during DNA replication and genetic recombination and in the repair of small deletions and loops in DNA. Mismatched nucleotides can occur by replication error, damage to nucleotide precursors, damage to DNA, or during heteroduplex formation between two homologous DNA molecules in the process of genetic recombination. Defects in MMR can precipitate instability in *simple sequence repeats* (SSRs), also referred to as *microsatellite instability* (MSI), which appears to be important in certain types of cancers, both spontaneous and hereditary. Variation in the highly polymorphic alleles of specific microsatellite repeats can be identified using PCR with primers derived from the unique flanking sequences.

These PCR products are analyzed on denaturing polyacrylamide gels to resolve differences in allele sizes of more than 2 bp. Although $(CA)_n$ repeats are the most abundant class among dinucleotide SSRs, trinucleotide and tetranucleotide repeats are also frequent. These polymorphic repeats have the advantage of producing band patterns that are easy to analyze and can be used as an indication of a possible MMR defect in a cell. The presumed association between such allelic variation and an MMR defect should be confirmed by molecular analysis of the structure and/or expression of MMR genes.

DNA repair is present in all organisms as a major defense against damage to cellular DNA. It is involved in processes that minimize cell killing, mutations, replication errors, persistence of DNA damage, and genomic instability. DNA *mismatch repair* (MMR) has a prominent role in the correction of errors made during DNA replication and genetic recombination.

The MMR pathway is responsible for detecting and repair ing short segments of mismatched base pairs, such as T opposite G, or an addition of extra nucleotides, resulting in unpaired bases within the DNA. Thus, MMR recognizes normal nucleotides that are either unpaired or paired with a noncomplementary nucleotide. The formation of mismatched nucleotides can occur by polymerase misincorporations (i.e., replication error), damage to nucleotide precursors, damage to DNA, or heteroduplex formation between two homologous DNA molecules during genetic recombination. Rapid repair of replicative errors provides the genome with a protection against mutation and guards the genome by preventing recombination between nonhomologous regions of DNA.

In *E. coli*, methyl-directed MMR involves the products of the mutator genes mutS, mutL, mutH, and uvrD. In vitro, MutS is a DNA mismatch-binding protein, UvrD is a DNA helicase II, and MutH is an endonuclease that incises at the transiently unmethylated DNA strand. In eukaryotes, the mismatch repair system is more complex. Genetic studies have demonstrated that the major DNA mismatch repair pathway in *Streptomyces cerevisiae* requires three bacterial MutS homologs, MSH2, MSH3, and MSH6, and two bacterial MutL homologs, MLH1 and PMS1. Human homologs of the yeast mismatch repair genes hMSH2, hMLH1, and hPMS2 have been identified and have been shown to be mutated in patients and their kindred with *hereditary nonpolyposis colon cancer* (HNPCC).

The first clue that an MMR defect might be responsible for HNPCC came from the observation of a previously unrecognized phenomenon in colon cancer cells from patients with HNPCC. These tumors often exhibited "*ladders*" of new microsatellite alleles created by insertion and deletion of multiples of the repeat length in tumor DNA compared with nonneoplastic DNA. The addition of novel microsatellite alleles in the tumor was called *microsatellite instability* (MSI). In HNPCC, MSI was discovered to be the result of germline mutations in the MMR genes.

MSI occurs mainly because of DNA biosynthetic errors that are generated by DNA polymerase and escape the proofreading mechanism. Strand slippages result in misaligned intermediates in repetitive sequences, creating the potential for insertion and deletion mutations if they are not corrected prior to replication in the subsequent cell cycle, as in MMR-deficient cells. Because microsatellite repeats fall into this category, tumors from patients with HNPCC have elevated mutation rates in microsatellite sequences, and monitoring of MSI has become an indirect, semiquantitative tool to characterize MMR. Experiments demonstrating how certain DNAdamaging agents can transiently inactivate the MMR system by saturating its repair capacity, creating a temporary "*mutator*" phenotype with MSI, have reinforced the ability of MSI to assess the MMR status of a cell.

As the list of MMR proteins grows, studies are beginning to identify many ways that these proteins can mix and match to generate distinct complexes with specificities for different substrates involved in meiotic recombination, base mismatch repair, and the repair of small deletions and loops in DNA. Biochemical studies have demonstrated that mismatch recognition is mediated primarily by a heterodimer of hMSH2 and hMSH6. Interestingly, although mutations in the hMSH2 gene are shown to segregate frequently with HNPCC, hMSH6 has been shown to be mutated to date in only a few atypical HNPCC families, as well as in a few sporadic colon tumors.

Moreover, there are significant differences between the mutator phenotypes of cell lines lacking hMSH2 or hMSH6, inasmuch as both are deficient in the correction of base/base mismatches, but only the former is also deficient in the repair of insertion/ deletion loops, resulting in MSI. The hMSH2/6 heterodimer has been shown to recognize base/base mispairs efficiently, but its affinity for loops of more than one extra helical nucleotide is relatively low, depending on flanking sequence context. In later studies, it was shown that a third MutS homolog, hMSH3, could form a heterodimer with hMSH2 and that this latter complex efficiently recognizes loops of two or more extrahelical nucleotides. Thus, the two MSH heterodimers, hMSH2/6 and hMSH2/3, are functionally complementary in the correction of slippage products in insertion/deletion loops.

Defective MMR results in abnormalities in the processes of DNA repair that have been implicated in carcinogenesis and aging. It has been suggested that MMR defects are themselves procarcinogenic and may also be involved in the development of resistance to cancer chemotherapy. This chapter describes gel-based radioactive and nonradioactive methods to detect an MMR defect indirectly by analyzing microsatellite sequence variation in matched samples of tumor and nontumor DNA.

Materials

Genomic DNA isolation

1. Lysis buffer: 0.32 M sucrose (autoclaved), 5 mM $MgCl_2$, 0.01 M Tris-HCl, pH 8.0, 1% Triton X-100. Store at room temperature.
2. Digestion buffer: 100 mM NaCl, 25 mM EDTA, 0.5% sodium dodecyl sulfate (SDS), 10 mM Tris-HCl, pH 8.0.
3. Phenol equilibrated with 0.1 M Tris-HCl, pH 8.0. Use gloves and store at 4°C.
4. Chloroform.
5. Isoamyl alcohol.
6. 3 M Sodium acetate, pH 5.2.
7. Absolute ethanol.
8. TE buffer: 10 mM Tris-HCl, pH 8.0, 1 mM EDTA, pH 8.0.
9. Gel loading dye: 0.25% bromophenol blue, 0.25% xylene cyanol, 0.25% and 30% glycerol. Use gloves and store at 4°C.
10. TBE buffer: 80 mM Tris-base, 40 mM boric acid, 2 mM EDTA. Make as 10X stock solution, and store at room temperature.
11. Ethidium bromide: 10 mg/mL stock solution in autoclaved distilled water. Use gloves, protect from direct light, and store at 4°C.
12. 1% Agarose in 1X TBE buffer.
13. Genomic DNA diluted in autoclaved distilled water from test samples to be analyzed. Store at 4°C.

Polymerase chain reaction

Use gloves to handle

1. Sterile PCR tubes.
2. PCR kit: reaction buffer, enzyme, dNTP mix, [α ^{32}P]dCTP. Store at –20°C.
3. Primers for microsatellite region. Store at –20°C until use and after.
4. Mineral oil. Store at room temperature.
5. Thermal cycler.

Preparation of polyacrylamide gel and gel electrophoresis

1. Autoclaved distilled water.
2. Sequencing gel apparatus.
3. Sigmacoat (Sigma). Store at 4°C.
4. 29:1 Acrylamide/bis-acrylamide stock. Store at 4°C.
5. Urea.

6. 10X TBE running buffer: 0.8 M Tris-base, 0.4 M boric acid, 20 mM EDTA.
7. Stop buffer or loading dye: 0.25% bromophenol blue, 0.25% xylene cyanole, 1 mM EDTA, 95% formamide, 5% 1X TBE. Store at 4°C.
8. Sequencing gel apparatus.
9. Power pack.

Processing of denaturing acrylamide gel data for analysis

1. Phosphorimager (e.g., Shimmazdu) or, alternatively, X-ray film and X-ray film developing solutions.

Agarose purification of DNA bands

1. Agarose, molecular biology grade.
2. Tris-saturated phenol, pH 8.0. Store at 4°C.
3. 3 M Sodium acetate, pH 5.2. Store at room temperature.
4. Absolute ethanol.

Ligation of DNA bands for sequencing

1. PCR product ligation kit.
2. Insert DNA.

Transformation of ligated product and screening of positive clones

1. Competent bacterial cells (e.g., DH5α).
2. Sterile culture plates.
3. Luria broth medium.
4. Ampicillin. Store at –20°C.

Sequencing reactions for confirming and determining microsatellite allele sizes

1. PCR tubes.
2. Primers for sequencing the allele.
3. Sequenase-dye termination kit.
4. Mineral oil.
5. Thermal cycler.

Preparation of polyacrylamide gel for nonradioactive microsatellite marker analysis

1. Autoclaved distilled water.
2. Acrylamide/bis-acrylamide stock (19:1).
3. Ammonium persulfate (APS; 10%) and TEMED.
4. 1X TBE buffer: 80 mM Tris-base, 40 mM boric acid, and 2 mM EDTA. Make as a 10X stock solution.

5. Gel loading dye: 98% formamide, 10 mM EDTA, 0.05% bromophenol blue, 0.05% xylene cyanole.

Methods

Preparation of template

Set up all reactions on ice.

1. Isolate total genomic DNA from blood samples using a standard genomic DNA isolation protocol.
2. Check the quality of DNA by running an 0.8% agarose gel at a low voltage of 40–50 V. Mix the genomic DNA with 1/6 volume of gel loading dye and load onto the wells. Visualize the high-quality genomic DNA on a UV transilluminator; it should be seen as a single band without shearing.
3. Quantify the DNA by taking the optical density (OD_{260}) spectrophotometrically, dilute the samples at a concentration of 25 ng/μL in autoclaved distal water, and store at –20°C until analysis.

Polymerase chain reaction for amplification of microsatellite markers

1. 12.5 μL vol for polymerase chain reaction (PCR) reaction of each sample includes a microsatellite marker primer set: 6.25 pM of each primer, 10 ng target DNA, 100 nM dNTPs, 1X PCR reaction buffer, 0.5 U Taq polymerase and [α^{32}P]dCTP.
2. Process the PCR reaction for 25 cycles with denaturation at 94°C for 2 min, annealing at 55–65°C for 30 s, and extension at 72°C for 1 min and a final extension at 72°C for 5 min.
3. Stop the PCR by adding 3 μL of stop buffer containing formamide.

Preparation of denaturing polyacrylamide gel for microsatellite marker analysis

1. Clean the sequencing gel plates very well with distilled water.
2. Wipe the plates with absolute ethanol.
3. Coat one of the sequencing gel plates with fresh Sigmacoat.
4. Clean spacers with absolute ethanol and place securely on the bottom plate. Secure the plates properly with clamps.
5. Clean the shark-tooth comb with absolute ethanol, and keep it ready to be inserted between the two plates after pouring the gel mix.
6. Prepare the gel mix (8%) by adding 5.7 g of acrylamide, 0.3 g of bis-acrylamide, 31.5 g of urea (8 M), 7.5 mL of 10X TBE, 300 μL of 10% APS, and 20 μL of TEMED. Mix all the constituents properly, and pour between the two plates.
7. Leave the assembly undisturbed until the gel is polymerized.

8. Denature the samples at 95°C for 5 min, and chill immediately on ice for 5 min prior to loading.
9. Load around 3 μL vol of each reaction into the appropriate well of the denaturing gel, and electrophorese at a high temperature of 40–45°C at constant watt (45 W) for 2–4 h.

Processing of denaturing acrylamide gels for microsatellite analysis

1. After completion of the gel run, fix the gel in 10% methanol, 10% acetic acid for 15–20 min, and wash the urea; then carefully transfer it onto a 3MM Whatman sheet and dry in a gel dryer.
2. Use phosphorimager intensifying plates to expose the dried gel, and analyze the results in a phosphorimager. Alternatively, expose the gel to X-ray film and develop.

Agarose purification of DNA bands from samples, which differ in mobility shift in denaturing gel

1. Excise the PCR-amplified product from the agarose gel, and put gel fragment in a 1.5-mL microcentrifuge tube.
2. Add 1 mL of saturated phenol, pH 8.0, to the tube and freeze it at –80°C. Take out the frozen tube, and thaw it completely.
3. Repeat the freeze-thaw steps three times.
4. Take out the frozen tube containing the agarose piece, and centrifuge at a high speed of 16,000g for 20 min at room temperature.
5. Take out the aqueous phase, and transfer to a fresh tube. Add an equal volume of chloroform to the tube, mix, and centrifuge again at 13,500g for 10 min.
6. Transfer the aqueous phase, add 1/10 vol of 3 M sodium acetate, pH 5.2, and make up to 1 mL with absolute ethanol. Allow the DNA to precipitate for 30–45 min at –20°C.
7. Centrifuge at 16,000g at 4°C for 20 min to precipitate the DNA.
8. Wash the DNA pellet with chilled 70% ethanol for 10 min at 4°C.
9. Dry the pellet and finally dissolve it in 10 μL of autoclaved distilled water.
10. Check the quality of the DNA by running on an agarose gel, and quantitate concentration.

Ligation of gel-eluted product for determination of allele size or repeats

1. Mix 2X reaction buffer, T-tailed Vector (e.g., pGEM-T), enzyme (ligase), and DNA insert (gel-eluted product) in a 0.5-mL

microcentrifuge tube. Mix well, and make up the volume to 10 μL (per instructions given in, e.g., Promega PCR ligation kit. Determine the quantity of insert required for carrying out ligation according to kit instructions.)

2. Incubate at 16°C for 4–6 h, followed by an overnight incubation at 4°C.

Transformation of ligated product and screening of positive clones

1. Carry out the transformation using competent cells of *E. coli* strain (e.g., DH5α, XL-1).
2. Rescreen for positive clones through colony PCR using the same set of primers as was used for amplifying the genomic DNA, under the same PCR conditions.

Recombinant plasmid isolation from positive clones for sequencing of insert (amplified microsatellite region)

1. Grow positive clones overnight in 5 mL of LB medium.
2. Isolate the plasmid as described in the plasmid isolation kit.

Sequencing of plasmid with microsatellite insert

1. For each template, label four 0.5-mL PCR tubes "G," "A," "T," and "C," respectively.
2. Aliquot 2 μL each of ddGTP mix, ddATP mix, ddTTP mix, and ddCTP mix into the corresponding microcentrifuge tubes.
3. For each template (containing set of four tubes: G, A, T, C), prepare a master mix consisting of 7.2 μL of 3.5X reaction buffer, template (plasmid with insert DNA), 0.7 μL of 15 pmols/μL sequencing primer, 0.5 μL of labeled dNTP (^{32}P-dCTP/dATP), 1.0 of enzyme, and water to make up the volume to 17 μL.
4. Gently vortex the mix, then briefly spin down the tube containing the master mix.
5. Dispense 4 μL of the master mix in each of tube containing ddGTP mix, ddATP mix, ddTTP mix, and ddCTP mix. Mix them by pipeting up and down a few times, and finally, overlay the reaction mix with mineral oil.
6. Carry out sequencing reactions in a thermal cycler using the following conditions: denaturation at 95°C for 30 s, annealing at 42°C for 30 s, extension at 72°C for 1 min; repeat the cycle 30 times, followed by a final extension for 10 min at 72°C.
7. Stop each reaction by adding 2 μL of stop buffer provided with the sequencing kit.

Preparation of polyacrylamide gel for sequencing of microsatellite product

1. Prepare and run the gel as described above.
2. Fix and process the gel as described above.
3. Develop the gel to read the microsatellite sequence.

Preparation of polyacrylamide gel (10–12%) for nonradioactive microsatellite marker study

1. Prepare the gel apparatus as described above.
2. Prepare (20%) acrylamide stock of 19:1 acrylamide/bis-acrylamide, and filter it, and store it at 4°C. Prepare the required gel concentration from the stock solution when required as described above.
3. Leave the assembly undisturbed until the gel is polymerized.
4. Prepare the samples by adding appropriate amplicons and 2 μL of dye (98% formamide, 10 mM EDTA, 0.05% bromophenol blue, and 0.05% xylene cyanol) in each sample. Make up the volume to 10 μL.
5. Load the full volume of each reaction into the appropriate well of the nondenaturing gel, and electrophorese at room temperature at 120 V for different time periods depending on the length of the amplicon.

Processing of nondenaturing acrylamide gels for MSI analysis

1. After completion of the gel run, stain the gel in ethidium bromide stain and visualize on a UV transilluminator.
2. For storage of the gels and further processing, fix the gel in 10% ethanol/0.5% acetic acid for 15–20 min.
3. Stain the gel in 0.1% silver nitrate solution for 30 min.
4. Wash the gel properly three times with distilled water.
5. Develop in 1.5% sodium hydroxide solution in the presence of 400 μL of formaldehyde until the bands appear.
6. Finally, when bands start appearing, replace the solution with 0.75% sodium bicarbonate solution until the bands become intense.
7. Stop, and store the gels in 2% acetic acid.

Notes

1. While isolating genomic DNA, handle with care to minimize the shearing of DNA.
2. DNA is better purified with phenol/chloroform.

3. Target template should be well-quantified because PCR sensitivity and product amplification are directly correlated.
4. For all PCR reactions, use fresh sterile tips, tubes, and aseptic bench area.
5. The protocol describes the analysis of MSI through *simple sequence length polymorphism* (SSLP) analysis. The primers used should flank the microsatellite loci of interest and be specific to avoid amplification of any undesirable region in the genome.
6. High-proofreading-activity polymerase is preferred to other polymerases.
7. The PCR conditions should be standardized for each microsatellite marker under study. Optimization or standardization of cycling conditions may be required for specific PCR product apart from other factors, e.g., $MgCl_2$, target concentration, annealing temperature, and so on.
8. For microsatellite PCR primer standardization, three-step touch-down PCR is preferred (three different annealing temperatures to obtain specific product and to avoid short size products).
9. APS should be freshly prepared.
10. Filter the gel mix before adding APS and TEMED.
11. While polymerizing the gel, avoid air bubbles in the gel matrix.
12. Wash the wells properly to remove traces of urea prior to sample loading, using a syringe and a needle; otherwise smiling and distortion of bands may occur.
13. While analyzing the results of microsatellite marker study, the most intense band should be considered the authentic band, as there may be "*stutter*" bands.
14. Any indecision in band shifts can be removed by repeating the PCR either fresh or by reamplifying the eluted variant band.

UNSCHEDULED DNA SYNTHESIS

The unscheduled DNA synthesis (UDS) assay measures a cell's ability to perform global genomic *nucleotide excision repair* (NER). This section provides instructions for the application of this technique in living cells by creating 6-4 photoproducts and pyrimidine dimers using UVC irradiation, then allowing for their repair. Repair is quantified by the amount of radioactive thymidine incorporated after this insult, and the length of time allowed for this incorporation is specific for repair of particular lesions. Radioactivity is evaluated by grain counting after autoradiography. The results are used to diagnosis repair-deficient disorders clinically and provide a basis for investigation of repair deficiency in human tissues or tumors. At the present time, no other functional assay is available that directly measures the capacity to perform NER on the entire genome without the use of specific antibodies. Since live cells are required for this assay, explant culture techniques must be previously established. Host cell reactivation is not an equivalent technique, as it specifically measures transcription-coupled repair at active genes, a subset of total NER.

Long patch, or *nucleotide excision repair* (NER), is the primary process by which cyclobutane pyrimidine dimers, 6-4 photoproducts, and DNA crosslinks are removed from DNA. Ultraviolet $(UV)_{254}$ nm light (UVC), as well as UV mimetic drugs, induces DNA lesions that are corrected by this pathway. Damage lesions caused by agents that act as inter- and intrastrand crosslinkers, such as cisplatin, covalently bind to DNA, creating "bulky" adducts such as N-acetoxyaminoacetyl-fluorene (AAAF) and, perhaps, alkylating agents such as cyclophosphamide are also remediated by this pathway. NER is a complicated process requiring the protein products of 25–30 genes. NER involves the recognition of a damage lesion causing distortion of the DNA helix, incisions flanking the lesion on the damaged strand, excision of 27–29 bases including the damage lesion, and replication and ligation to replace the excised information and seal the strand breaks at each end of the newly synthesized region. This pathway can also be recruited for other types of DNA damage lesions that have not been corrected by base excision and other single-stranded DNA repair mechanisms. In effect, the NER pathway provides redundancy for these other repair systems should they be overwhelmed by a genotoxic exposure.

Human cells perform NER at two levels: the rapid and efficient removal of lesions that block ongoing transcription and thus need to be eliminated quickly, also known as *transcription-coupled repair* (TCR), and the slower, less efficient repair of bulk DNA, including the nontranscribed strand of active genes, also referred to as *global genomic repair* (GGR). In addition, the sense strand of the actively transcribed gene is repaired before the antisense strand.

NER of the overall genome can be measured quantitatively using the unscheduled DNA synthesis assay (UDS). The UDS assay involves the measurement of labeled base incorporation into the DNA after in vitro exposure to UV light or certain chemicals. The UDS assay is a cell-autonomous, functional assay, in that it allows one to look at the

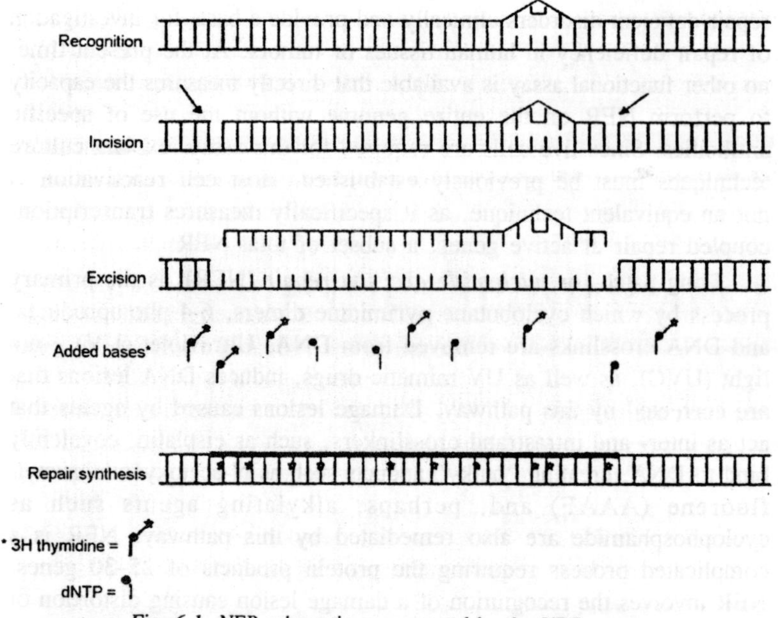

Fig. 6.1. NER schematic as measured by the UDS assay.

complex process of NER as a whole, at least as it is expressed in a particular cell type. As applied in our laboratory, this assay predominantly quantifies the repair of UV-induced DNA 6-4 photoproducts, and elements of both the GGR as well as the TCR components of NER contribute to the results.

The autoradiographic UDS assay requires the analysis of living cells. It has previously been applied primarily to skin fibroblasts and *peripheral blood lymphocytes* (PBLs) for diagnosis of xeroderma pigmentosum (XP) and other DNA repair diseases impacting specifically on the NER pathway. Classical NER deficiency disorders are characterized by UV sensitivity manifesting mainly in the skin and cornea.

Studies involving functional assays in general, and specifically functional assays of DNA repair capacity, have been hampered by a technical lack of ability to perform primary explant culture on all cell types. The one notable exception is that of rat hepatocyte primary cultures, which have been used extensively in UDS assays for evaluation of the carcinogenic potential of chemicals. Although repair assays can be performed on established, transformed cell lines, the generation of cell lines from normal adult tissue has proved to be a technical challenge. In addition, during the process of passaging, established cell lines undergo clonal evolution that may alter or extinguish many of the original characteristics of the cells, including their intrinsic repair capacity.

Until recently, cell culture techniques have not existed to support primary culture explants of most human tissues. These tissues require attachment to a substratum of some sort of extracellular matrix. Our laboratory has developed methods for primary culture of various cell types.

The UDS assay was first described by Rassmussen and Painter. Its name stems from the fact that the assay evaluates the DNA repair mechanisms of cells in all stages of replication except synthesis or S phase, when "scheduled" DNA synthesis of the entire genome takes place. (We know of no technique that will measure NER during S phase.) There are two methods of quantifying data from the assay: autoradiography and scintillation counting. Autoradiography is the preferred method and is described in this chapter. Although it is labor-intensive, software packages have been designed in an attempt to remove the human subjectivity of this aspect of data analysis. However, our laboratory still performs grain counting with two to three independent counters on each slide, because the current software is still inadequate for appreciating the differences between, for example, darkly stained nucleoli and silver grains in some cases. An additional problem with the automated counting system is the fact that emulsion is more than one focal-length thick; i.e., one has to focus up and down to see all of the silver grains over a nucleaus. Finding rare cells can also be difficult without integrating control of an automated stage into the grain counting software program. The greatest strength of software-based grain counting is the evaluation of background, as this is the area in which individual reader subjectivity is greatest.

Scintillation counting is a simplified form of the autoradiographic assay that was popularized in industry for the hepatocyte evaluation of mutagenic chemicals. In order for it to be accurate, all the S-phase cells have to be eliminated. from the analysis, because radiolabel incorporation during replicative synthesis is orders of magnitude greater than during repair synthesis. In an attempt to achieve this, the use of hydroxyurea was incorporated into the original UDS protocol. However, we have found that up to 40% of S phase cells can still persist in the presence of hydroxyurea, which would significantly affect the results and render them inaccurate. Indeed, because S-phase nuclei incorporate hundreds of times more radioactive label than non-S-phase cells, only a few cells that happen to be in synthesis mode would render these experiments quite inaccurate. We therefore recommend the autoradiographic form of this assay over the scintillation counting form, which probably should only be used to determine rough trends. Autoradiography has the added benefit of allowing the counter to determine different cell types present on each slide and evaluate each type for NER.

Controls for use in combination with this assay can include commercially available, repair-deficient XP cell lines. Our laboratory usually utilizes *foreskin fibroblasts* (FF) as a positive standard for comparison. These cells can reliably be used as extended explants up to passage 13. Explants beyond 13 passages show a decreasing repair capacity relative to the earliest passages. We have recently demonstrated considerable tissue variation in NER capacity, suggesting that a tissue-matched control should also be used. For lymphocyte studies, we recommend the lymphoblastoid cell line TK6, although transformed cell lines do not always accurately reflect the NER capacity of their progenitor tissue.

Published doses of UV· irradiation utilized for UDS experiments range from 5–50 J/M^2 . It is recommended that a dose–response curve be performed to determine the optimal dose of UVC for a given cell type.

Materials

Cell irradiation, labeling, and fixation

1. Viable experimental samples.
2. Positive (and, if appropriate, negative) controls, including "tester" slides.
3. Two-chamber chamber slides, two to four slides per sample; controls, four slides minimum.
4. 10-cm^2 Round cell tissue culture dish (one per chamber slide).
5. Whatman filter paper (3-mm CHR in 35 × 45-cm sheets) cut into 2.5 × 5-cm strips, wrapped in tinfoil and autoclaved (one strip per chamber slide).
6. Appropriate growth medium for each type of cell that will be analyzed.
7. Fetal bovine serum (FBS).
8. Sterile tissue culture hood.
9. Tissue culture incubator with 5% CO_2.

10. Vortex mixer.
11. UV delivery device.
12. Short-wave UV meter.
13. 80 Ci/mmol [^{3}H]thymidine. Thaw and allow to warm to room temperature before use.
14. Hot thymidine incubation medium: 10 μCi [^{3}H]thymidine label (80 Ci/mmol) per mL of appropriate medium for each cell type, including serum and 1X penicillin-streptomycin (10,000 U/mL penicillin G sodium, 100,000 μg/mL streptomycin sulfate in 85% saline). For example, for 20 slides, in a total volume of 20 mL of medium with serum, 200 μL of label are added. Add [^{3}H]thymidine to the medium immediately before use.
15. Cold thymidine chase medium: medium of choice supplemented with 10^{-3} M thymidine nucleoside. Add 10% serum just prior to use and filter through a 0.4-μm filter.
16. 1X Salt sodium citrate (SSC).
17. 100 mL 70% Ethanol (made fresh to prevent evaporation; AAPER, Shelbyville, KY).
18. 33% Acetic acid (Fisher) in ethanol (made fresh), total 100 mL.
19. Scalpel.
20. Two hemostats.
21. Vertical glass slide Copeland jars. Each holds five slides, so the number needed depends on the size of the experiment.
22. 4% Perchloric acid (diluted from stock 60% perchloric acid). *Caution*: store in a fume hood; can be explosive. Need about 60 mL per Copeland jar.

Slide processing I: Dipping in emulsion

1. Rectangular glass slide jars with glass slide holders. Each holds 10 slides.
2. Distilled water.
3. Paper towels.
4. Sealed darkroom.
5. Kodak Radiography Emulsion NTB-2, approx 4.0 oz, stored at 4°C.
6. 48°C Water bath in the darkroom.
7. Lab tape.
8. 50-, 400-, and 1000-mL beakers.
9. Amersham dipping chamber.
10. Darkroom drying box.

11. Light-tight slide boxes containing desiccant at one end behind a glass slide.
12. Regular and heavy-duty aluminum foil.
13. Refrigerator.

Slide processing II: Developing emulsion

1. Four rectangular glass slide dishes.
2. Three lab timers.
3. Tap water and ice.
4. Medium-sized plastic developing tray.
5. Thermometer.
6. Kodak D-19 Developer, stored at 4°C.
7. Kodak fixer, stored at 4°C.
8. Two glass staining dishes for slides.
9. 0.5 g Giemsa powder.
10. Glycerol.
11. 60°C Water bath.
12. Methanol.
13. Stirring plate.
14. Parafilm.
15. Whatman filter paper (3-mm CHR) and funnel.
16. 100-mL Brown glass bottle.
17. Giemsa stock solution.
18. 0.1 M Citric acid.
19. 0.2 M Na_2HPO_4.
20. Staining solution: 0.015% (w/v) Giemsa, 0.6 M methanol, 7 mM citric acid, 0.02 M Na_2HPO_4, pH 5.75. For 100 mL: 2 mL Giemsa stock solution, 2.4 mL methanol, 6.8 mL 0.1 M citric acid, 9.2 mL 0.2 M Na_2HPO_4, and 80 mL distilled H_2O.
21. Rinse buffer: 7 mM citric acid, 0.02 M Na_2HPO_4. For 100 mL: 6.8 mL 0.1 M citric acid and 9.2 mL 0.2 M Na_2HPO_4. Bring up to 100 mL with distilled H_2O.
22. Upright microscope with oil immersion 100× objective.

Grain counting and normalization

1. Create a standardized counting sheet, with columns for grains over nuclei and background (grains over a nucleus-sized area of the acellular field). Several other pieces of data that we suggest should be recorded include: total number of cells in the microscope field

(countable nuclei and S-phase cells), S-phase cells, and morphology of the cells. These parameters may be correlated with NER, or may define differential cell populations.

2. Grain counts can be processed with any suitable statistical software, such as StatView or the statistical package included in the Excel spreadsheet program.

Methods

Cell irradiation, labeling, and fixation

1. All cells should be placed into culture at least 2 d before the performance of the UDS assay. Ideally, cells on the final slides should be easy to find, but not identifiable as clumps or clones (i.e., the slides should be less than semiconfluent on the day of the assay). Therefore, seed appropriate numbers of each experimental and control cell population into both chambers of four two-chamber slides (total volume of 1 mL, free of dimethylsulfoxide, trypsin, and so on).
2. Place each chamber slide into a 10-cm^2 round cell culture dish with a piece of dampened sterilized filter paper.
3. Incubate at 37°C in a standard humidified tissue culture incubator with 5% CO_2 for 2 d.
4. Turn on UV bulbs on the UV delivery device, and allow them to warm up for at least 1 h. Test the dose-delivery rate under experimental conditions with a short-wave (254-nm) UV meter, and adjust if necessary (time of exposure and/or distance from bulbs).
5. Thaw radioactive label, and allow to warm to room temperature.
6. Feed all cells (replace with fresh medium) 1 h before UV exposure. Label all slides in pencil.
7. Thoroughly mix the [^{3}H]thymidine label by vigorous vortexing. For up to 20 slides, add 200 μL label to 20 mL medium with serum to create "*hot incubation media*" with a final concentration of 10 μCi/mL. Vortex until foam appears.
8. Remove regular medium from all chamber slides. Divide experimental and control chamber slides into groups of four, ensuring there is a positive control slide (and a negative control slide [un-irradiated control], if necessary) in each group.
9. Leave the chamber of each slide closest to the ground glass label covered with the plastic lid, and uncover the other chambers.

10. Start the turntable (set at "mid" speed) to equalize exposure. Expose slides in sets of four, as determined in step 8.
11. Immediately after irradiation, add 0.5 mL of "*hot incubation medium*" to each chamber of each chamber slide, for a total of 1 mL of media per slide. Ten to 12 slides should be handled at a time to prevent the cells from drying out, with a maximum of 40 slides per experiment.
12. Incubate slides for 2 h at 37°C in tissue culture incubator. (You may wish to designate a "*radioactive*" incubator and/or a "*radioactive*" shelf).
13. Add FCS to the "*cold chase medium.*"
14. After 2 h, using the radioactive hood, remove the "*hot incubation medium*" from all chamber slides by pipeting, and replace with 0.5 mL of "*cold chase media.*"
15. Incubate slides for 2 h at 37°C in a tissue culture incubator.
16. Prepare fresh 70% ethanol and fixative solutions (33% acetic acid in 100% ethanol).
17. In the radioactive hood, remove the "*cold chase medium*" by aspiration, and gently rinse each side of the chamber slides with 1 mL of 1X SSC.
18. Remove the 1X SSC immediately by aspiration, and replace it with 0.5 mL fixative solution in each chamber. Leave at room temperature for 15 min.
19. Remove fixative by aspiration and leave slides to dry partially for 5 min. Add 0.5 mL of 70% ethanol to each chamber, and leave at room temperature for 15 min.
20. Remove the ethanol by aspiration. Remove the chambers and rubber gaskets from the slides, using a sharp scalpel to loosen one corner of the rubber gasket. Once the corner is free, use a pair of hemostats to pull the remaining gasket away from the slide. Any remaining gasket can be lightly scraped off with the scalpel. All traces of the gasket must be removed, or it will cause the emulsion to be too thick on the edges of the slide.
21. Place slides in radioactively labeled Copeland jars with 4% perchloric acid. Then place the jars in a refrigerator overnight.

Slide processing I: Dipping in emulsion

Caution: all steps in the dipping process must be done in complete darkness (with no safe lights) until the slides are dry, packaged, and wrapped three times in foil.

1. Remove slides from Copeland jars and rinse by letting them sit in distilled H_2O for 3–4 min. Then allow the slides to dry in the hood for 24 h in glass slide holders sitting on paper towels.
2. Melt emulsion, and heat to 48°C in a water bath in the darkroom. First, place the emulsion in a 1000-mL beaker with 400 mL of water, and then place the beaker into the water bath for 1.5 h. To keep the emulsion container from floating, fill a 50-mL beaker, and place it on top of the emulsion container. Swirl the emulsion container every 30 min, to ensure complete thawing.
3. Prepare a drying box in which to hang and dry the slides.
4. Before taking the slides into the darkroom, place a triangular piece of lab tape on the upper right corner of each slide on the ground glass. This is to allow the slides to be oriented by touch in the dark while dipping. At this time, select one slide of each type of control to be "*tester*" slides. These slides will be placed in a separate drying box and will be developed first to determine when the emulsion on the slides from the entire experiment have exposed sufficiently for scoring.
5. Place an Amersham slide-dipping container in a beaker half full of 48°C water. In the darkroom, with all the lights off including the red ("safe") light, carefully pour the emulsion into the dipping container. Use your ungloved little finger to ensure that the emulsion has filled the dipping container to the top. (The emulsion is nontoxic.)
6. Orienting the slides using the piece of tape from step 4, take each slide and slide it into the dipping container. (Lightly tap the slide on both sides of the container to ensure it is fully immersed in the dipping container.)
7. Allow each slide to drip for a few seconds after removing it from the dipping container, and then hang the slide in the box with the bulldog clips clamped onto the ground glass labeling portion of the slide in the mouth of the slip.
8. The "*tester*" slides should be hung exclusively on the first string and all subsequent slides hung on the other three pieces of string. The emulsion will have to be refilled every 15– 20 slides.
9. After all slides have been dipped, the lid should be placed over the box. Allow the slides to dry in the box in complete darkness for 1 h.
10. Preparation of plastic slide boxes.

(a) Place a clean glass slide at one end of the box. Tape the edges of the slide to prevent its removal.

(b) In the space behind the slide, add desiccant to the end of the box.

(c) Place a piece of tape on the lid of the slide box to orient the front of the box in the dark.

(d) For each box, have three layers of aluminum foil ready to wrap the boxes in the dark after the slides have been placed in them (two regular layers and one heavy duty).

11. Place the tester slides only in the first slide box, close the lid, wrap it in foil, and mark it with a "T" (for testers) on the foil, with the date.
12. Remove the remaining slides from the drying box, and place them in the other slide boxes, wrapping them in foil and marking them "E" (for experimental) and dating them.
13. Place the emulsion back in its original box and wrap it with foil three times as well. The emulsion is very light-sensitive, so any measures that are taken to lessen the exposure to light will prolong the useful lifetime of the emulsion and maintain low background on the slides.
14. Place the slide boxes in a refrigerator until developing.

Slide processing II: Developing emulsion

1. Develop the tester slides 12 d after dipping.
2. Take all slide boxes out of the refrigerator, and allow to warm to room temperature for a minimum of 5 h.
3. In the darkroom, create a 15°C water bath using cold water and a small amount of ice in a medium-sized developing tray. Use a thermometer to verify the temperature.
4. Place four slide dishes into the 15°C water bath. In the first dish, place D19 developer (1:1 mixed with dH_2O), distilled H_2O in the second dish, fixer in the third dish, and distilled water in the fourth dish (each slide dish holds 250 mL of liquid). The red light may be on while these solutions come to temperature.
5. Set three timers (one for 4 min and two for 5 min) before you enter the darkroom. It helps if the timers beep when the start button is pressed as well as when the time has expired.
6. In complete darkness, place the tester slides in a glass slide holder, and attach the wire holder. Lower the slide holder into the first dish (developer), and start the timer set for 4 min.

7. After 4 min, dip the slides into the second dish (water) for a count of 10 s, and then dip them into the third dish for 5 min.
8. After 5 min dip the slides into the fourth dish (water again), and start the second timer set for 5 min. The lights can then be turned back on, as long as there are no other open slide boxes or unexposed slides.
9. After 5 min dry the tester slides for at least 1 h on the bench at room temperature.
10. Giemsa-stain the slides for 7 min in Copeland jars.
11. Rinse the slides in rinse buffer for 3 min, and allow to air-dry in a dust-free environment for 2–3 h.
12. Score the tester slides. If the emulsion on the slides is determined to have been exposed long enough, develop the experimental slides in batches of 5–10 as described above, steps 1–9. The experimental slides can dry overnight in a dust-free environment, to be stained the following day. If exposure is not sufficient, return the experimental slides to the refrigerator, and allow the emulsion to be exposed longer.

Grain counting and normalization

Once all the slides have been stained, the nuclei of the cells can be counted. There should be at least two slides per type of cell. Two criteria must be met for both the controls and the experimental slides for a successful experiment:

1. There must be a reasonable number of grains per nucleus, particularly with regard to the background (25–50 for the irradiated chamber, and 1–5 in the unirradiated chamber).
2. There must be sufficient cells (or nuclei) on at least two slides (100 scorable nuclei is ideal, and less than 20 is insufficient).

The counting procedure is as follows:

1. Orient the slide to be counted on the microscope stand so that the ground glass is to the left. (The unirradiated side of the slide will now always be to the left and the irradiated to the right.)
2. Scan both sides of the slide with a low-power objective before counting, to ensure there are at least 20 cells on both sides. If less than 20 cells are visible in each chamber, then it will be necessary to pool multiple slides of the same exposure time to obtain 20 unirradiated nuclei and 20 irradiated nuclei. If multiple slides do not exist, then this specimen cannot be evaluated for repair capacity. It is best to count a minimum of 100 cells on

both sides of a slide. There should be some nuclei that are black with grains indicating cells that are in S phase. The number of these cells can be tallied in a separate column on the counting sheets but it is impossible to score them for silver grains.

3. If the slide is scorable, view it under oil immersion at a total magnification of 1000× (10× eyepiece × 100× objective) to resolve individual silver grains.
4. The Giemsa stain should provide three shades of purple at high magnification. The lightest purple is the cytoplasm of the cells. There should be few to no grains in this area. The nuclei are the second darkest purple. The silver grains in this area represent the [^{3}H]thymidine incorporated into the cell's DNA. The number of grains in the nuclei is proportional to the amount of repair. These are the grains that are counted. For the positive control and the experimental slides, if the positive control is appropriate, the average number of grains per nuclei should be approx 50 on the irradiated side of the slide. The third, deeper purple, is often manifested in the nucleolus of the cell nucleus.
5. To determine the background grain count outside the nuclei, the counter should define an acellular area that is about the same size as the nuclei in that field; count the number of grains in that area. Background counts should be usually 5 grains or less.
6. For each experiment, two slides should be counted for each type of cell, and two individuals should count each slide. Slides of the same cell type analyzed in the same experiment and developed on the same day should have a coefficient of variance of 10–15%. Counters on the same slide should have results that are within 10–15% as well.
7. After the unirradiated and irradiated sides of a slide are counted, statistical analysis may be completed. To arrive at the corrected value for the individual nuclei, take the counts per nucleus and subtract the background for that field for both the unirradiated and irradiated counts. To find the mean number of grains for each slide, take the corrected value for the unirradiated cells and divide by the total number of nuclei counted (not including S-phase cells). Do the same for the irradiated cells, then take the average number of grains per nucleus for the unirradiated nuclei, and subtract it from the average number of grains for the irradiated nuclei.
8. To compare the experimental slides with the control, take the average number of grains per nucleus for the experimental slide,

and divide by the average number of grains per nucleus for the control. Multiply this number by 100 to arrive at the percent repair for the experimental slide compared with the control.

9. To compare the experimental slides with a population of controls, take the percent repair compared with the concurrent control (run in the same experiment), and multiply this by the ratio of the concurrent control divided by the average repair for the population. Multiply this number by 100 to arrive at the percent repair for the experimental slide compared with the average of the control population.

Notes

1. There is a perception that the *host cell reactivation* (HCR) assay is specific for the *transcription coupled repair* (TCR) component of NER, whereas the UDS assay is specific for *global genomic repair* (GGR). The specificity of the HCR assay comes from the fact that repair is detected through repair of a reporter gene (although it is a foreign gene in an unnatural context). However, to be specific for TCR, the GGR machinery would also have to specifically avoid or exclude repairing damage in transcribed sequences, and there is no evidence that GGR has such specificity. Indeed, it has been estimated that approx 10% of the repair measured in the HCR assay occurs through the incidental activity of GGR on the reporter gene. The specificity of the UDS assay, if it has any, comes simply from the fact that the vast majority of the genome is either noncoding, or nontranscribed in any particular cell type. Indeed, given the faster kinetics of TCR, the UDS assay probably quantitates a greater proportion of this type of repair than actual GGR; however, how much this contributes to the final result is unknown.
2. The UDS assay has traditionally been performed on monolayer cell cultures, such as skin fibroblasts, transformed fibroblastic cell lines, or hepatocytes. The stable attachment of such cells to glass slides (generally coated with some sort of substratum) allows the entire assay to be performed as described, on cells cultured on chamber slides. However, irradiation and labeling can be done prior to the attachment of the cells to a slide for quantification if such attachment is impossible. Indeed, with cells such as lymphocytes that have a weaker attachment to the slides themselves, we see a significant attrition in scorable cells through slide processing. Thus, we have coated the slides to enhance their

attachment. Similarly, we have attached single-layer sheets of cells to slides for processing, or even isolated labeled nuclei and attached them to the slide. We have also found that 3D cellular structures can be analyzed, as long as only the outer layer of cells is scored, since they are the only ones that receive an unattenuated dose of UV and that are directly exposed to the emulsion.

3. Since the UDS assay is affected by the strength of the radiolabel as well as the number of times the emulsion has been thawed, it cannot be considered an absolute assay of DNA repair, and raw grain counts in and of themselves are relatively meaningless (although they are often reported). Instead, repair capacity should be reported relative to a standardized positive control, analyzed concurrently in each experiment. *Foreskin fibroblasts* (FFs) have traditionally been used as the positive control for the UDS assay. Besides being relatively easy to acquire, FFs under 13 passages are described as having relatively high levels of repair, suggesting that NER declines with age, which some studies have observed, but not our own. The positive control should ideally provide two different, but related, references: first, it should provide a baseline measure of the "normal" level of NER for the experimental samples to be compared against, and second, it should provide a guide as to when the experiment, specifically the exposure of the emulsion, can be successfully concluded. FFs have long been considered to provide both references, both for analyses of cell lines and for fibroblast samples taken from patients for diagnosis. However, it is significant that diagnostic studies of PBLs have used normal PBLs as controls; we have recently shown that there is a 20-fold difference in the baseline NER capacity of these two cell types. In addition, a single "normal" sample, often randomly acquired, usually serves as the control, whereas we have also shown that there is considerable interindividual variability in NER capacity in the "normal" population. Mixtures of FFs from several babies have sometimes been used to attempt to account for possible interindividual differences. Instead, we suggest that a population of normal samples should first be analyzed, with the "concurrent" control included.

If lymphocytes are being run in the experiment, an appropriate control appears to be the lymphoblastoid cell line TK6 (although transformed cells, in general, cannot be assumed to have "normal" repair). Lymphocytes need to be developed for a longer period because of their low repair, usually 15–18 d instead of 12. The accuracy of the final determination is based on the number of grains scored, not the number of cells. Thus, if the slides are developed too early (which would be the case if lymphocyte slides were developed on a timetable based on FF controls), they have very few grains, making it difficult to establish unambiguously a difference between the irradiated and unirradiated populations. In general, grain counts of 50–100 should be projected prior to emulsion development, and we regularly count 200–300 nuclei per slide.

4. Tester slides are extra positive control slides that must be designed into an experiment to determine the optimal exposure time for the emulsion. The freshness of the label and of the emulsion, as well as the changing conditions of the darkroom, can all be variables in terms of the length of time autoradiographic slides should be developed for maximal signal-to-noise ratio. Generally two extra FFs (or other control) slides are made for this purpose and are packaged separately for development at 12 d, to be grain counted before the slides from the rest of the experiment have been developed. If the rest of the experimental slides are developed on the same day as the tester slides, then the tester slides can be used as additional positive control slides in the experiment. If the tester slides are developed on a day other than the experimental slides, they may not be included (as positive standards of comparison) in the analysis of the experimental slides.
5. If the experiment is designed to document repair deficiency, "negative" controls, i.e., repair-deficient cells, may be included, in addition to the standardized positive controls. Indeed, a second set of slides may be prepared and developed using the negative controls slides as guides, although these will not in any way replace the unirradiated chamber controls. Three human diseases have been found to be associated with defects in the NER genes: XP, with seven complementation groups, Cockayne's syndrome, with five complementation groups, three of which overlap with those of XP, and trichothiodystrophy, with three complementation groups, two of which overlap with XP. UDS has historically been used to diagnose XP in skin fibroblasts or in PBLs, since these patients are more or less deficient in NER depending on their complementation group. Cockayne's syndrome affects TCR. There is a considerable range of residual activity amongt patients in these various complementation groups (<10% in groups A, B,

and G, up to 50% in groups D and E), with none exhibiting complete deficiency. Complete NER deficiency may be a prenatal lethal condition; mutations in ERCC1, the first NER gene cloned, have never been identified in a patient, perhaps because they are inviable at the organismal level. XP cell lines (immortalized both with and without the use of exogenous agents) can be purchased from the American Type Culture Collection or Coriell Cell Repositories for negative control use.

6. Date the label when it arrives, and discard 1 mo from the arrival date, owing to chemical deterioration. Label should be stored at –20°C.
7. Cold thymidine media should be stored without the presence of serum, which can bind and effectively lower the bioavailable thymidine. For 100 mL of medium, add 24.2 mg of thymidine. (This solution can be stored at 4°C for a period of 3 mo as long as it lacks serum.)
8. This portion of the assay is extremely light-sensitive. All light sources must be covered or removed, including lights on water baths, temperature control for the room, light leaks from doorways and light fixtures, and any other sources in the darkroom including fluorescent watches. Spend 20 min in the room with all the lights off to identify light sources, and cover them before the procedure is begun if you are uncertain of the integrity of your darkroom. The assay can also be affected by static electricity from gloves and clothing during the winter months.
9. Reuse of previously melted emulsion can cause higher background in sequential experiments, owing to factors like static electricity that expose it with each use. Use the same emulsion at most three times to avoid increasing spurious background grains.
10. Giemsa stock solution: 0.8% (w/v) Giemsa in 1:1 glycerol/methanol. Warm glycerol in a 60°C water bath, add 0.5 g Giemsa powder to 33 mL glycerol, and place it on a stir plate overnight without heat. The following morning, add 33 mL methanol and cover with Parafilm and Saran Wrap. The next day, filter the solution using Whatman filter paper, and store in a dark bottle at room temperature. The filtration step takes several hours.
11. The Petri dish also provides an extra layer of protection against air-borne contamination. The moistened filter paper creates an additional humidity chamber for the cells growing in chamber slides.

12. The recommended dosage of UVC light at 254 nm is 14 J/m^2 to produce the desired amount of DNA damage, although a dose-dependence curve should be performed at the start of any study of NER. For a desired dose of 14 J/m^2 , with a mean fluence of 1.2 J/m^2/s from the UV bulbs, a 12-s exposure of the cells is generally used by our laboratory (dose in J/m^2 = fluence [read from the meter] × number of seconds). The readout from the Spectroline meter will be μW/cm^2 (e.g., 210 μW/cm^2 = 2.1 J m^{-2} sec^{-1})
13. This allows sufficient time for the cells to repair the 6-4 photoproducts that were created by the UVC light but not the pyrimidine dimers. (To effectively quantitate the repair of pyrimidine dimers would require an 8-h incubation).
14. Slides may be stained as many times as needed in order to view the nuclei clearly. Alternatively, methanol can be used to lighten the stain if it is too heavy. Some cells such as CHO cells only need to be stained for 2 min instead of 7 min.
15. For the tester slides, once the slides have dried, view under an oil immersion lens at a total magnification of 1000×, and count 25 nuclei on both the irradiated and unirradiated sides of the slide. This will allow a decision to be made as to whether or not the experimental slides should be developed that same day. If no grains are observed, then the radioactive label was not added to the incubation mixture, and the experiment is unusable. If an average of approx 50 grains/nucleus or more above background are observed in the irradiated chamber of the positive control, the experimental slides are ready to be developed. However, a set of controls and the experimental slides must be counted and developed at the same time under the same conditions in order to perform the normalization. S-phase cells should be visible on both sides of the slide (in approximately equal numbers). If the controls do not exhibit the required number of grains/nucleus, the remaining control and experimental slides should be developed 24–72 h later. If longer development seems necessary, it is likely that the signal-to-noise (background) ratio will be too high to determine NER capacity accurately. If background grains appear to be unevenly distributed, or distributed in a pattern, there is probably a light leak in the slide boxes used to store the dipped slides. Background counts of 8–10 or above are too high for accurate analysis.
16. If the cytoplasm is covered with grains and the nucleus is relatively uncovered, it is most likely a result of Mycoplasma contamination.

These slides are not scorable, and the cell population will have to be reacquired or rendered free of contamination in order to be assayed.

17. If the tester slides have been used correctly and the experimental slides average about 50 grains/nucleus, nuclei with more than approx 90 grains should be considered to be in S phase.
18. FFs can be generated in large quantities from a single foreskin by finely mincing the tissue and stirring it in trypsin for 5 h at room temperature, followed by repeated trituration with a 25-mL pipet and subsequent plating in tissue culture dishes. The first few passages should be performed to remove cell clumps and create even monolayers of fibroblasts. Then these early-explant passages can be frozen in 10% dimethylsulfoxide for use in many UDS experiments. FF repair capacity is stable for about 18 passages, so we recommend the use of FFs only up to passage 13 to retain consistency.

Analysis of DNA Repair Using Transfection-Based Host Cell Reactivation

Host cell reactivation (HCR) is a transfection-based assay in which intact cells repair damage localized to exogenous DNA. This section provides instructions for the application of this technique using UV irradiation as a source of damage to a luciferase reporter plasmid. Through measurement of the activity of a reporter enzyme, the amount of damaged plasmid that a cell can "reactivate" or repair and express can be quantitated. Different DNA repair pathways can be analyzed by this technique by damaging the reporter plasmid in different ways. Because it involves repair of a transcriptionally active gene, when applied to UV damage the HCR assay measures the capacity of the host cells to perform *transcription-coupled repair* (TCR), a subset of the overall nucleotide excision repair pathway that specifically targets transcribed gene sequences.

The term *host cell reactivation* (HCR) was first used to describe the survival of ultraviolet (UV)-irradiated bacteriophages in host cells that had been pretreated with UV irradiation. Survival of phages was increased in pretreated host cells compared with untreated hosts. Researchers first hypothesized that the mechanism that accounted for this "*reactivation*" of the phage involved homologous recombination between the phage and the bacterial genome. This hypothesis was later replaced by the idea of enzymatic repair. In an adaptation of the use of viral DNA to measure inherent cellular repair capabilities, transient expression plasmid DNA vectors were used by Protic-Sabljic and Kraemer on SV40 transformed human fibroblasts in 1985 and by Athas et al. on human lymphocytes in 1991.

The plasmid reactivation assay indirectly monitors cellular repair of transcriptional activity by measuring activity associated with a transfected enzymatic marker gene. In brief, cells are transfected with the damaged plasmid, allowed time to express the reporter enzyme, harvested for protein, and then assayed for the enzymatic activity of the reporter. Two levels of controls are utilized for the HCR assay. The first involves the use of damaged and undamaged versions of the same expression vector to determine the ratio of expression of the damaged (and repaired) plasmid divided by the expression of the undamaged vector. In addition, a plasmid distinguishable from the experimental plasmids is also necessary to control for transfection efficiency. To make the results of individual experiments comparable to each other, we also recommend that the absolute numbers expressed by the ratio of damaged (and repaired) over undamaged plasmid be divided by similar results derived from a standard cell line run in every experiment. The experimental reporter used is firefly luciferase, and the control is bacterial β-galactosidase. Other reporter systems such as bacterial chloramphenicol acetyltransferase can and have also been used.

The host repair system interrogated in the HCR assay depends entirely on the type of transcription-inhibiting damage introduced into the plasmid. In practice, the vast majority of studies of this type have involved repair of UV-induced DNA damage via the *nucleotide excision repair* (NER) pathway.

NER is one of a number of types of DNA repair acting to maintain the integrity of the genome. It is a particularly complex pathway, however, which can remediate many types of DNA damage. Indeed, unlike other DNA repair pathways, it is not the specific damage itself that activates NER, but the resulting distortion in the DNA helix, making it applicable to a broad spectrum of genotoxic insults. Human cells perform NER at two distinct levels. First, the rapid and efficient removal of lesions that block ongoing transcription and thus need to be eliminated quickly, also known as *transcription-coupled repair* (TCR), and second, the slower, less efficient, repair of bulk DNA, including the nontranscribed strand of active genes, also referred to as *global genome repair* (GGR). The former process links NER to transcription, and the latter process links it to replication. TCR therefore represents a subset of the overall repair that occurs in NER.

The HCR assay specifically provides researchers with a method of investigating the ability of a cell to perform TCR. It is presumed that some of the damaged reporter plasmid makes its way into the nucleus, where repair occurs, and then gene transcription and translation occur via normal cellular trafficking.

The plasmid vectors used in this experiment include pGL3, used as the experimental vector, and pCH110, used as the control plasmid. pGL3 codes for a luciferase gene derived from the firefly. It allows for high levels of expression because of the presence of an SV40 promoter upstream of the luciferase gene and a downstream SV40 enhancer and polyadenylation signal. The sensitivity of this system is generally 100-fold greater than that based on the chloramphenicol acetyltransferase (CAT) gene. pCH110 codes for the β-galactosidase enzyme derived from the *E. coli* lacZ gene under the control of the SV40 early promoter.

In our hands, the pGL3 vector is irradiated using 700 J/m^2 of UV light to induce DNA damage in the form of 6-4 photoproducts and pyrimidine dimers that block transcription and cannot produce an active luciferase enzyme until it is repaired. The pCH110 plasmid, with lacZ as an internal reporter gene to control for transfection efficiency, remains undamaged.

Published doses of UV irradiation utilized for HCR experiments in mammalian cells can range from 56 to 800 J/m^2. Protic-Sabljic and Kraemer demonstrated that a dose as low as 56 J/m^2 was enough to inactivate a CAT reporter plasmid in repairdeficient xeroderma pigmentosum complementation group A (XPA) and XPD fibroblasts, whereas a dose of 680 J/m^2 was required to inactivate the same vector in normal human fibroblasts. Athas et al. used incremental doses of 0, 200, 400, 600, and 800 J/m^2 in their field test of HCR on human lymphocytes. Their results showed a significant, 11-fold difference in repair capacities between normal peripheral blood lymphocytes and XPA and XPD lymphoblastoid cell lines at a UV dose of 200 J/m^2.

The ability of cells to repair UV-induced DNA damage is expressed as the percentage of the reactivated luciferase activity of damaged relative to the activity of undamaged (baseline expression) genes after a period of gene repair and expression.

A major advantage of this technique is that it minimizes the cytotoxic effects of damaging agents that might indirectly compromise the repair mechanisms of the cell. Damage takes place *in vitro* and can be adapted to investigate specific damaging agents. Concerns arise

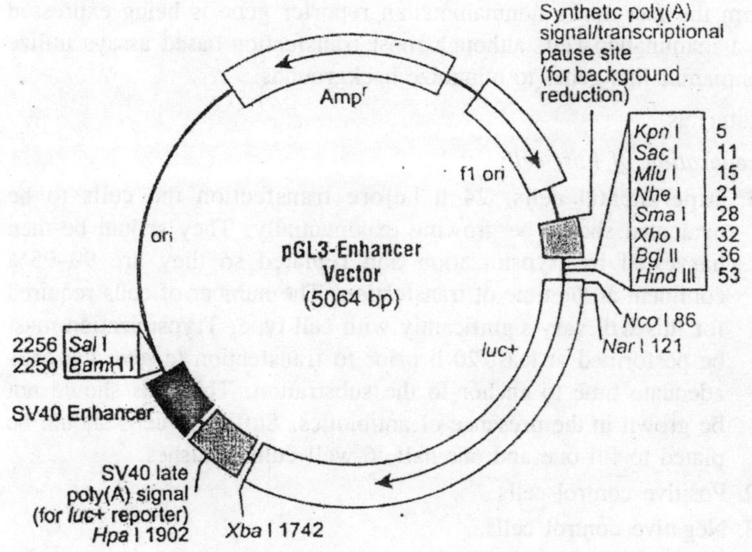

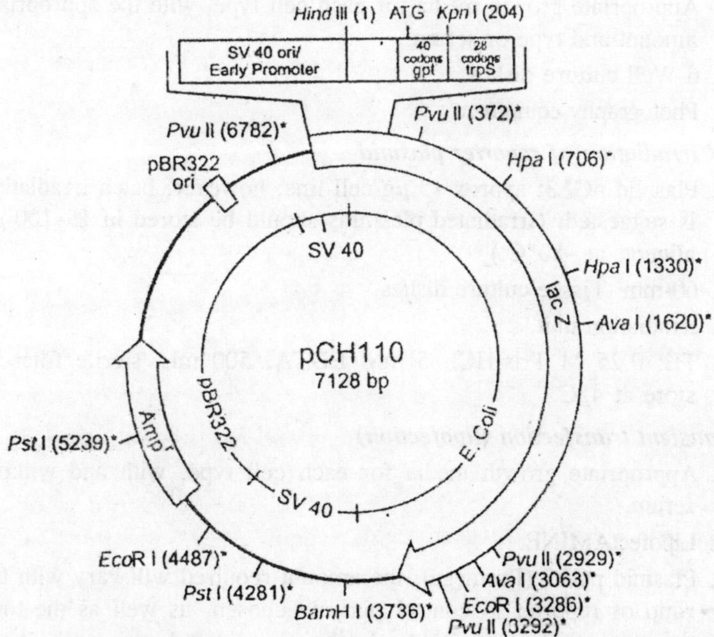

Fig. 6.2. The (top) pGL3 and (bottom) pCH110 vectors.

from the fact that a nonmammalian reporter gene is being expressed in a mammalian cell, although most transfection-based assays utilize nonmammalian genes to minimize backgrounds.

Materials

Preparation of host cells

1. Experimental cells: 24 h before transfection the cells to be evaluated should be growing exponentially. They should be then harvested by trypsinization and replated so they are 90–95% confluent at the time of transfection. The number of cells required for this will vary significantly with cell type. Trypsinization must be performed at least 20 h prior to transfection to give the cells adequate time to anchor to the substratum. The cells should not be grown in the presence of antibiotics. Sufficient cells should be plated to fill one and one-half, 6-well culture dishes.
2. Positive control cells.
3. Negative control cells.
4. Cell culture incubator.
5. Appropriate growth media for each cell type, with the appropriate amount and type of serum.
6. 6-Well culture dishes.
7. Photography equipment.

UV irradiation of reporter plasmid

1. Plasmid pGL3: approx 15 μg/cell line; however, batch irradiation is suggested. (Irradiated plasmids should be stored in 15–100-μg aliquots at –80°C.)
2. 60-mm^2 Tissue culture dishes.
3. Irradiation unit.
4. TE: 0.25 M Tris-HCl, 5 mM EDTA, 500 mL, sterile filtered; store at 4°C.

Transient transfection (lipofection)

1. Appropriate growth media for each cell type, with and without serum.
2. LipofectAMINE.
3. Plasmid pGL3 (Promega): the amount required will vary with the ratio of reporter to control plasmid chosen, as well as the total amount of plasmid DNA chosen to be used per well. As a guideline, approx 30 μg of this reporter plasmid DNA per cell

line should be prepared if one is using a total of 5 μg per well and a ratio of 5:1 reporter/ control plasmid.

4. Plasmid pGH110. As a guideline, approx 5 μg of this plasmid DNA per cell line should be prepared if one is using a total of 5 μg per well and a ratio of 5:1 reporter/control plasmid.
5. UV-irradiated plasmid pGL3.

Protein isolation

1. 1X Reporter lysis buffer (RLB). Prepare in bulk by dilution of 5X RLB (Promega; stored at –20°C) with 4 vol of dH_2O and mixing. Each well will require 500 μL. The 1X buffer should be equilibrated to room temperature prior to use.
2. Phosphate-buffered saline (PBS), Ca^{2+}/Mg^{2+}-free.
3. Rocking platform or orbital shaker.
4. Rubber policeman (one each for each well).
5. 1-mL Microcentrifuge tubes.
6. 1-mL Micropipetor and tips.
7. Refrigerated microcentrifuge.

Protein quantification

1. BCA Protein Assay Kit: one kit will provide more than 50 assays.
2. Centrifuge tubes (1.5-mL).
3. TE: 0.25 M Tris-HCl, 5 mM EDTA, 500 mL, sterile filtered; store at 4°C.
4. Bovine serum albumin (BSA) stock (included in the BCA kit).
5. Micropipetors (200 and 20 μL) and appropriate tips.
6. Reagents A and B (included in the BCA kit).
7. 96-Well tissue culture plastic plates: 18 wells are needed for the control + 36 wells for each cell line analyzed.
8. Rocking platform or orbital shaker.
9. Incubator: could be same as cell culture incubator, although it does not need to be humidified or in the presence of CO_2.
10. Microplate reader.

Quantification of luciferase expression

1. Luciferase Assay System.
2. Luciferase assay reagent (LAR): resuspend the lyophilized luciferase assay substrate in 10 mL of luciferase assay buffer (both provided in the kit). The reagent should be green. The optimum temperature for luciferase activity is 20–25°C (approximately room temperature).

Allow LAR to equilibrate fully to room temperature before using. Also ensure that samples to be measured are at room temperature.

3. 1X RLB.
4. Luminometer tubes (e.g., Sarstedt 5 mL, 75 × 12 mm).
5. Luminometer.

Quantification of β-galactosidase expression

1. Breaking buffer: 0.2 M Tris-HCl, 0.2 M NaCl, 0.01 M Mg acetate, 0.01 M 2-mercaptoethanol, 5% glycerol, pH 7.6. Need approx 2.5 mL per cell line.
2. Z buffer: 0.06 M Na_2HPO_4, 0.04 M NaH_2PO_4, 0.01 M KCl, 0.001 M $MgSO_4$, 0.05 M 2-mercaptoethanol, pH 7.0 (all constituents from Sigma). Need approx 10 mL per cell line.
3. 4 mg/mL o-Nitrophenyl-β-D-galactosidase (ONPG) in dH_2O.
4. 1 M Na_2CO_3.

Methods

Preparation of host cells

1. One day before transfection, trypsinize and count all cells to be transfected.
2. Replate cells in 6-well culture dishes so they will be 90–95% confluent on the day of transfection. (Best results are achieved when the cells are transfected at this high cell density). The number of cells required to achieve this will be different for each cell type or cell line. For each well, the appropriate number of cells should be resuspended in 2 mL of normal growth media containing serum and no antibiotics. For each experimental cell line, nine wells (1.5 dishes) will be required.

UV irradiation of reporter plasmid

1. For each cell line, 15 μg of reporter plasmid is necessary; however, batch irradiation can be performed (i.e., irradiation of reporter plasmid for the evaluation of a number of target cell populations can be performed at the same time).
2. Immediately before irradiation, dilute pGL3 DNA to 50 μg/mL in cold (4°C) distilled, sterile filtered water.
3. Pipet dilute plasmid solution into a 60-mm² tissue culture dish on ice. Four mL of diluted DNA solution is used per dish.
4. Irradiate with a dose of 700 J/m² of UVC light at 254 nm. The turn-table should turn during the entire irradiation.
5. After exposure, cover the plate and keep on ice.

6. The damaged plasmid should be aliquoted and stored at –80°C. To ensure that additional damage is not done to the plasmid DNA, make sure aliquots are small enough so that each one is sufficient for a standardized experiment, with only a small volume remaining (i.e., aliquots of 15–100 μg). Aliquots should not be refrozen after use because refreezing will cause nicking of the plasmid.

Transient transfection (lipofection)

The following protocol is adapted from Invitrogen Life Technologies Lipofectamine 2000 CD Reagent instructions.

1. Every experiment and control is done in triplicate, i.e., in three wells. A minimum of nine wells is therefore required for each host cell type to be assayed.
2. Several types of controls are used in these experiments. As an internal control of transfection efficiency, each well is transfected with undamaged pCH110 plasmid, which expresses β-galactosidase. As another control for transfection, wells are mock transfected, not by withholding plasmid, as has been done traditionally, but by omitting the lipofectamine agent.
3. On the day of transfection, feed each well of cells normal growth media complete with serum. It may be useful to capture an image of the cells prior to transfection as a reference for evaluating their condition later in the experiment.
4. A total of 5.0 μg of DNA (which includes a 10:1 ratio of experimental [pGL3] to control plasmid [pCH110]) is required for every well, in 250 μL of medium without serum per well. (Charged proteins and lipids in serum may interfere with the formation of DNA–cationic lipid complexes.) These solutions can be prepared in bulk. For each experimental point, six wells will need a 10:1 ratio of undamaged pGL3 to pCH110, and three wells will need a 10:1 ratio of damaged pGL3 to (undamaged) pCH110.
5. Mix the Lipofectamine 2000 reagent (LF2000) gently before use. Do not vortex. Dilute 15 μL of LF2000 into 250 μL of medium (without serum) per well, and incubate for 3 min at room temperature. This dilution can also be prepared in bulk for multiple wells. For each experimental point, six wells will receive LF2000 and three wells will receive only medium. The LF2000 should sit no longer than 5 min after dilution in medium, as inactivation can occur.
6. Immediately mix the lipofectamine and plasmid solutions 1:1 in the following combinations:

(a) Plasmid-only row

3 wells: medium – LF2000 undamaged pGL3 + undamaged pCH110

(b) Undamaged row

3 wells: medium + LF2000 undamaged pGL3 + undamaged pCH110

(c) Damaged row

3 wells: medium + LF2000 damaged pGL3 + undamaged pCH110

Incubate at room temperature for 20 min to allow DNA–LF2000 complexes to form. The solutions may begin to appear cloudy as the complexes form. These complexes are stable for at least 6 h at room temperature.

7. After the 20-min incubation, remove the media from each of the cell wells. Add 500 μL of the appropriate plasmid solution to each well, and mix gently by rocking the plate back and forth. Incubate the cells at 37°C in a CO_2 incubator for 1 h.
8. After the 1-h incubation, add 1.5 mL media with serum to each well. There will be no need to change the media again after this point.
9. At 24 h after transfection, observe and (if necessary) capture images of the cells. Transfected cells should appear damaged and unhealthy.

Protein harvest and quantification

The following protocol was adapted from Promega's Technical Manual No. 040, Dual Luciferase Reporter Assay System, and Pierce's BCA Protein Assay Reagent Kit manual.

1. At 44 h after transfection, remove the growth media from each well of cultured cells and gently rinse each well with approx 500 μL of PBS to remove dead cells. To add the PBS, place the pipet tip on the side of the well, and allow the PBS to trickle down the side of the well and spread out across it. Completely remove this rinse solution by placing a pipet into the corner of each well and aspirating off the PBS.
2. Add 500 μL of prepared 1X RLB to each well. Place the plate on a rocking platform or orbital shaker with gentle rocking/shaking for 10 min (or longer if culture is overgrown) at room temperature.
3. After about 10 min, you should see a white clump forming in the middle of each well as the cells lyse. At this point, take a rubber policeman and scrape the cells from the bottom of the wells.

Scrape in both the vertical and horizontal directions, paying special attention to the sides of the wells.

4. After scraping, return the plates to the orbital shaker for an additional 10 min. Check the plates under a microscope to verify that there are no whole cells remaining attached to the bottom of the wells.
5. Using a 1-mL micropipetor, transfer the lysate to the appropriate microcentrifuge tube. Disperse the white clump by pipeting up and down.
6. Clear the lysate by centrifuging for 30 s at the top speed of a refrigerated microcentrifuge.
7. Transfer cleared lysates to a fresh tube for further handling and storage. Proteins may be stored at this point at –80°C before continuing further.

Protein quantification

1. Begin by preparing a standard consisting of a small set of serial dilutions of BSA. Label four centrifuge tubes with the following standardized concentrations: 1, 0.5, 0.25, and 0.125 μg/μL. Add 100 μL of TE to each tube. Add 100 μL of BSA stock to the "1-mg/ mL" tube and mix. Transfer 100 μL of this solution to the "0.5-mg/mL" tube, and mix. Continue until serial dilutions are complete. Standards remain good for 1 week at 4°C.
2. Next, prepare "*working reagent*" by combining 50 parts reagent A with 1 part reagent B The working reagent will be green.
3. Pipet 10 μL of each BSA standard (including the 2 mg/mL stock and the blank, 10 μL of buffer) into appropriate 96-well microtiter plate wells, changing tips each time. Perform these standards in triplicate.
4. Pipette 10-μL samples of each lysate into fresh wells, in duplicate.
5. For 1:2 dilutions, pipet 5 μL of each lysate and 5 μL TE buffer into fresh wells, in duplicate.
6. Make a map showing where each standard and sample were placed.
7. Add 200 μL of working reagent to each well.
8. Cover the microtiter plate and shake at 200 rpm at room temperature for 30 s on an orbital shaker.
9. Incubate at 37°C for 30 min.
10. Using a plate reader, read the absorbance of each well at 562 nm. Average the absorbances of the three replicates of each

standard, and create a standard curve for each plate using the controls by directly connecting the dots. (This curve should reflect the actual data, rather than relying on an idealized, computer-generated curve fit.) Average the absorbances of the two undiluted samples with the average of the two 1:2 dilutions multiplied by 2, and then determine the concentration of protein based on the absorbance vs concentration curve. Calculate the volume of each sample necessary to yield 26.0 ng of total protein.

Quantification of luciferase expression

The following protocol was adapted from Promega's Technical Manual No. 281, Luciferase Assay System.

1. If a manual luminometer is being used, proceed directly to step 2. If the luminometer being used has an automatic injector, place pump tubing into the reagent reservoir. Prime the injector with sufficient reagent before beginning. Settings for the automated luminometer should be as follows: measuring time: 10 s; delay: 3 s; injection delay: 1 s; injection volume: 100 μL.
2. To measure background (all measurements in relative light units [RLUs]), pipet 50-μL aliquots of 1X RLB into three luminometer tubes, and measure the luminescence. This background reading will automatically be subtracted from all subsequent readings.
3. To measure samples, pipet the amount of each calculated to give 26 ng of total protein into each of three luminometer tubes. Add sufficient 1X RLB to each tube to give a total volume of 50 μL.
4. For each sample, first pipet 100 μL of LAR into a luminometer tube. Then, add the amount of each sample calculated to give 26 ng of total protein, and mix by pipeting two or three times. Do not vortex. Vortexing will coat the sides of the sample tube with the luminescent mixture. After 10 s of reading, remove the tube and record the reading.

Quantification of β-galactosidase expression

1. For each sample, pipet the amount calculated to give 26 ng of total protein into a 15-mL conical tube, and add sufficient 1X RLB to provide a final volume of 50 μL.
2. Dilute this sample 1:100 in breaking buffer.
3. Add 50 μL of this dilution to 1 mL Z buffer in a disposable cuvet, and equilibrate at 28°C.
4. Prepare a blank of breaking buffer in Z buffer as a control for spontaneous hydrolysis of ONPG.

5. To all samples and blank, add 0.2 mL ONPG solution, also equilibrated to 28°C.
6. Incubate samples for at least 10 min at 28°C, watching for a yellow color to develop.
7. As each sample becomes noticeably yellow, stop the reaction by adding 0.5 mL 1 M Na_2CO_3, and record the length of time required for the color change.
8. Read the OD_{420} against the negative control for spontaneous hydrolysis of ONPG control, and calculate the specific activity of each sample.
9. Subtract the average specific activity of the three mock-transfected wells from those of both the "damaged" and "undamaged" wells. This will control for the endogenous β-galactosidase activity present in some cell types.

Calculating relative TCR capacities

1. For each sample, divide the luciferase RLU by the β-galactosidase specific activity to correct for transfection efficiency.
2. Find the average of the mock-transfected wells, the wells transfected with undamaged plasmid, and the wells transfected with damaged plasmid for each sample.
3. Subtract the average of the mock-transfected wells from the average of the undamaged and the average of the damaged wells.
4. The ratio of damaged to undamaged wells is a measure of TCR.
5. If desired, divide again by positive control to express as % normal.
6. If normal control has been evaluated in the context of a population of normals, normalize again by the ratio of the experimental normal to the average of the normal population to express your experimental data relative to the normal population.

Notes

1. Next to UV, X-irradiation is the most common damaging agent used in the HCR assay. Under most conditions, this treatment results in a mixture of DNA double-strand breaks and lesions caused by ionization of the medium, followed by its interaction with the DNA target. In this simple system, DSB repair probably involves mostly nonhomologous end joining, although more complicated HCR assays specific for homologous recombinational repair have also been developed. UV damage creates primarily pyrimidine dimers and 6-4 photoproducts, both of which involve covalent binding of adjacent bases from the same DNA strand

and result in an obvious constriction of the DNA helix. A number of other agents have been used to generate such *intrastrand crosslinks* (ICL) in the plasmid target of an HCR assay, including cis-platinum, L-phenylalanine mustard (L-PAM), and mechlorethane. Like 8-methoxypsoralen, however, some of these agents also cause interstrand crosslinks, which in turn block replication at S phase or cause double-strand breaks during mitotic chromosome segregation.

NER also repairs so-called *bulky adducts*, such as those induced by 2-amino-1-methyl-6-phenylimidazole[4,5]pyridine (PhIP) and N-acetyl-2-aminofluorene (AAF), and these have also been used to damage plasmids for HCR analysis of repair. 4-Hydroxyamino-quinoline-1-oxide, the proximate form of 4-nitroquinoline-1-oxide (4NQO) has also been used to study NER by HCR, as has benzo[a]pyrene diol epoxide, a derivative of the tobacco smoke mutagen benzo[a]pyrene. These compounds illustrate the fact that since the plasmid is exposed outside of a biological system, chemicals that require metabolic activation are not operative in this assay. If the carcinogenic derivatives of a chemical are known, however, as in the above examples, they can be studied instead of the parental species; there is also no reason why pretreatment of the parental chemical with microsomal S9 couldn't be used, although this would be expected to produce a mixed exposure. Plasmid treatment with monofunctional alkylating reagents such as 2-chloroethyl ethyl sulfide would also be expected to generate bulky adducts. Finally, rather than simply expose the plasmid to a damaging agent, an altered base can also be specifically incorporated during its synthesis, such as the free-radical–induced bulky adduct 8,5'-(S)-cyclo-2'-deoxyadenosine, or even a simple fluorescein label.

Base excision repair (BER) has also been analyzed by HCR, using either nonspecific methylating agents such as N-methyl-N'-nitro-N-nitrosoguanidine (MNNG) or very specific methylating agents known to produce substrates for specific BER glycosylases, such as 5-(3-methyl-1-triazeno)imidazole-4-carboxamide (MTIC). BER is also known to remediate some of the damage caused by exposure of DNA to oxidative agents, such as ozone and sources of singlet oxygen. The steps in BER beyond the initial glycosylation can be analyzed by acid/heat treatment of the plasmid to produce apurinic sites, or apurinic sites can be specifically introduced.

A specific modification of the HCR assay has been developed to allow for analysis of DNA mismatch repair via generation of microsatellite instability following exposure of the reporter plasmid to etoposide or fotemustine. This is not a very quantitative assay, however, and it seems strange that HCR plasmids have not simply been generated with single or multiple base mismatches by isolation of heteroduplexes. Further guidance in the creation of site-specifically modified templates can be found in Perlow et al.

2. Appropriate positive control cells would include: fibroblasts or lymphocytes derived from healthy adult patients, or skin fibroblast cultures derived from patients with xeroderma pigmentosum complementation group C (XPC). These cell types are all known to be competent in TCR. (The deficiency in XPC cells is specific to GGR.) It is important to consider the fact that NER has been shown to be tissue-specific and that the choice of a positive control should reflect this tissue specificity, if possible. In addition, when a putative disease specimen is being tested, this sample should be placed into the context of the normal range. This can be accomplished by running several normal controls for comparison or by comparing with a previously established range of normal. "Normal" human fibroblasts or lymphocytes can be obtained from the Coriell Cell Repositories. It should be noted, however, that some of these cell lines have been immortalized using exogenous agents and that several of these agents have been shown to alter the original DNA repair capacity of the cells. Several cell lines that have not been treated with exogenous agents are available.
3. The most appropriate negative controls for this experiment are fibroblasts or lymphocytes that have been derived from *Cockayne syndrome* (CS) patients, either type I or type II. Patients with deficiencies in XP complementation groups A, D, F, and G share their inability to perform TCR. Explant cultures as well as immortalized cell lines of fibroblasts and lymphocytes derived from patients with these inborn diseases can be obtained from Coriell Cell Repositories.
4. A specialized machine has been created to deliver the damaging dosage of UVC light (or any UV-based light) accurately. The machine consists of a turntable, an electronically timed shutter, and three Wistam bulbs placed above the turntable behind the shutter. An issue that has arisen involves the length of time required to irradiate the plasmids: it is too long to use on the electrically timed shutter, making it necessary to turn the light sources on and off manually. The company that produced this instrument is

being consulted for an alternate timer that encompasses a longer time period.

5. The amount of DNA used in each well, the ratio of experimental to control plasmid, and the amount of Lipofectamine 2000 reagent may be different for every cell type. Cell lines may vary by several orders of magnitude in their ability to take up DNA. Experiments to optimize these amounts can be carried out per recommendations by Invitrogen. Ratios of 10:1 to 50:1 experimental-to-control vector are recommended by Promega, as they minimize potential trans effects between promoter elements.
6. The reconstituted LAR can be frozen at –80°C for 1 mo. The components are heat-labile, and frozen aliquots should be thawed in a water bath at room temperature. Mix thawed reagent prior to use by inverting several times or gently vortexing.
7. UV bulbs should be turned on 2 h prior to use and tested with a Spectroline short-wave (252 nm) UV meter. After determining fluence, use the formula fluence × time = dose to determine the amount of time needed for irradiation. The readout from the Spectroline meter will be in $\mu W/cm^2$ (e.g., 210 $\mu W/cm^2$ = 2.1 J m^{-2} sec^{-1}).
8. For 700 J/m^2 with a mean fluence of 2.1 J/m^2 s from the UV bulbs, a 333-s exposure of the plasmid is required. In order for such a long exposure time to be undertaken with the machine described above, the latch on the shutter must be unhooked and the lights themselves turned on and off for timing.
9. For example, if the assay was conducted for 10 min and the OD_{420} was 0.500, the specific activity would be:

$$\frac{0.500 \times 380}{10.0 \times 0.026} = 730 \text{ units / mg.}$$

7

Optimization of Amplification

PCR-VNTRs are important markers for questions of identification, individualization, and discrimination. They already form an integral part of forensic DNA analysis. They can be subdivided into the systems of *short tandem repeats* (STR) with fragment lengths ranging between approx 100 and 300 bp and amplified fragment length polymorphisms with fragment lengths between 350,000 bp. Several hundred thousand STR loci are interspersed throughout the mammalian genome, and thousands have been further developed and mapped for the human genome.

STR loci are useful to forensic science are characterized by their small range of alleles, their high sensitivity and suitability if the DNA is degraded. Furthermore, they show discontinuous allele distributions with consecutive alleles differing by 2 bp. Among STRs, dinucleotide polymorphisms suffer from the disadvantage of quite intensive slippage, or stutter, bands leading to patterns that are difficult to interpret in stain work. Tetranucleotide polymorphisms are more suitable for two major reasons: They have negligible or no slippage effects, and consecutive alleles can be more easily resolved. Because of their polymorphic character and the aforementioned reasons, tetra-and pentanucleotide polymorphisms have revolutionized forensic case work.

Validation Studies

For their application in forensic casework, extensive validation studies have to be carried out. This would include population studies, investigation of a great number of meioses to determine mutation rates, and analysis of experimental stains. Studies of stains must include effects of the stain substrate, storage time, mixtures, and sensitivity studies.

Population Studies

A minimum of 200 unrelated individuals and/or 500 meioses have to be investigated for each STR system to study allele frequencies, the mendelian inheritance, and whether significant numbers of mutations exist. Only STRs with a high forensic efficiency are suitable for application in forensic science at present approx 30 such systems have been characterized. Besides the sensitivity, forensic efficiency values comprise a high discrimination index (DI) within populations and mutation rates, which should be <1% if the loci are to be used in parentage testing. The DI of individual STR systems varies in the range between 0.82 and 0.99. The combination of seven STR systems results in a combined DI of approx 1:100,000,000. The mutation rates are below 1% for all STR systems investigated so far. If mutations are observed, insertions or deletions of single repeats are the predominant type.

Stain Analysis

Before an STR system can be applied to casework, extensive validation is necessary. This must include the examination of a series of different stain substrates, a series of various storage conditions and times, and unequal mixtures of samples from different persons. It is necessary that the PCR system resolves DNA mixtures from different sources up to a proportion of 1:10 with no allelic dropout. Microbloodstains and different sources of the stain material, e.g., mixtures of vaginal cells/semen, hair roots, saliva from stamps, and bones should be typeable. The success rate in stain analysis depends both on the quality and the quantity of DNA. Because of the heterogeneity of the stain material, it is necessary to establish different extraction procedures and make an individual decision for each case. Several extraction methods for different applications have been validated:

1. Organic extraction,
2. Inorganic extraction, and
3. Extraction by boiling.

The most common method depends on the lysis of the cell membrane and the denaturation of proteins in the presence of proteinase K, EDTA, and detergents. Removal of the proteins and purification of the DNA is achieved by the organic phenol/chloroform extraction. An alternative procedure is to use 6 M NaCl and to remove the proteins by precipitation instead of organic extraction. These procedures should be applied in cases where the co-extraction of PCR inhibitors is to be expected, e.g., tissue samples, hair shafts, and bone material.

A simpler and faster method of DNA extraction is the Chelex 100 extraction. Chelex 100 is a chelating resin and has the ability to bind metal ions. The basic procedure consists of boiling the sample in a 5% Chelex solution. The addition of proteinase K increases the efficiency of lysis. This procedure has the disadvantage that PCR amplification of longer fragments (>500 bp) can fail. In consequence, the AmpFLPs with fragment lengths between 350 and 1000 bp cannot be analyzed. Nevertheless, this method can be applied in cases with blood-stains on different stain substrates, saliva on cigarette butts, and hair roots. In the case of vaginal/sperm mixtures, a modification of the common proteinase K treatment in combination with the phenol/chloroform extraction is well established: preferential or mild preferential lysis. The basic principle is the lysis of the vaginal cells in the absence of DTT in a first step, and in a second step, lysis of the sperm cells in the presence of DTT.

The method of micromanipulation of single spermatozoa is another important application in forensic casework, even in mixtures of several

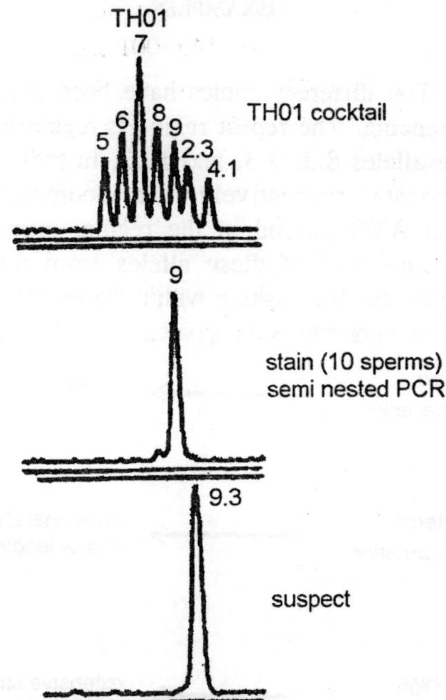

Fig. 7.1. Amplification pattern of the STR system HumTH01 from a casework slide: DNA from single sperms were extracted using the method of micromanipulation and amplification using seminested PCR for the TH01 locus.

hundred vaginal cells and only very few spermatozoa. The spermatozoa are selectively scratched off from a microscope slide and after complete lysis are directly amplified.

Sequence Variability in STR Systems

According to the ISFH recommendations, the allele nomenclature should be based on the sequence structure. Therefore, an essential part of research in legal medicine is the determination of the extent of sequence variability in each individual STR system, the exact allele definition according to the number of repeats, and the construction of system-specific allelic ladders.

Several STR systems have been elaborated:

1. HumACTBP2; HumFES/FPS, HumVWA,
2. HumD21Sll; HumF13B

HumTHOl; HumF13Al; HumCD4. The systems investigated so far show different extents of sequence variability and can accordingly be subdivided in three system categories.

Examples

Category (I)

HumTHOl: Ten different alleles have been observed so far and verified by sequencing. The repeat region is regularly spaced with the exception of the alleles 8.3, 9.3, and 10.3. In these alleles, the sixth and seventh repeats, respectively, are incomplete and have the trinucleotide unit ATG instead of the regular tetranucleotide repeat AATG. Sequencing data of these alleles from different unrelated individuals confirm that the position within the repeat region is constant. This system therefore constitutes an apparently regular STR polymorphism.

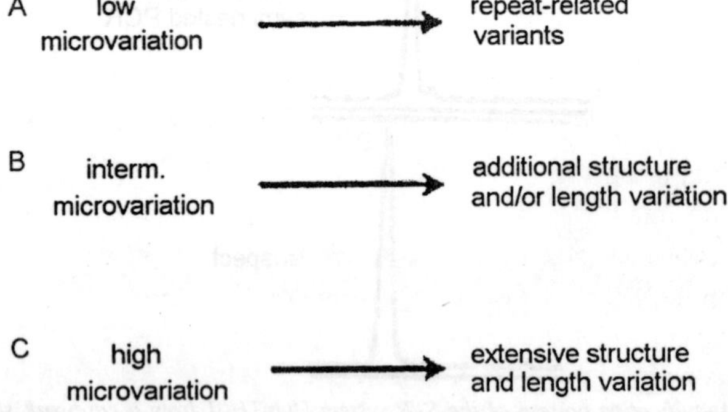

Fig. 7.2. Different types of microvariation. (a) STRs with low microvariation; (b) STRs with intermediate microvariation; (c) STRs with high microvariation.

HumCD4: CD4 is a system of the first category with pentameric repeat units as basic motifs. From allele 9 onward, the fourth repeat unit shows a T to C transition, which is the only minor variation in this system. Eleven consecutive alleles have been observed.

Category (II)

HumVWA: This system shows a more complex sequence structure with two tetranucleotide units (TCTA and TCTG) in combination. Two allele types were found that differ fundamentally from each other. The consensus allele has a composite repetitive structure starting with one TCTA, continuing with three to five TCTGs and ending with the proper variable TCTA part. Allele 14 is unique and has a different structure at three sites leading to a slight electrophoretic shift under high-resolution/nondenaturing conditions.

Category (III)

HumACTBP2: HumACTBP2 (SE33) has a large number of alleles and is therefore the most informative, but is also the most complex STR system characterized for forensic work to date. More than 250 alleles have been sequenced and analyzed, and three different types of structure variation have been observed. Sequence variability in the repeat region is further increased by the existence of deletion/insertion mutations and/or point mutations in both flanking regions. Because of this high complexity there have been warnings regarding reproducibility, especially under different gel conditions: alleles with the same fragment length but different sequence structures can exhibit various electrophoretic mobilities in a high resolution/nondenaturing gel system. A better reproducibility was obtained using a denaturing gel system in combination with automatic fragment analysis and fluorescence detection.

Methodologies for STR Analysis

For the demonstration of structure and/or length variation different methods have been established: discontinuous, horizontal, nondenaturing PAGE; vertical, nondenaturing PAGE; and vertical, denaturing PAGE.

Visualization of the bands can be achieved either by silver staining or by the much more sensitive fluorescence detection, which is often used in combination with automatic fragment analysis.

For PCR systems with a low or an intermediate extent of microvariation (e.g., TH01, vWA, FES/FPS, etc.) the horizontal/nondenaturing gel system is the method of choice even in laboratories with a high sample throughput. The advantages of this gel system are ease of handling and low costs of reagents.

Microvariant alleles occurring in systems like FES/FPS and F13B can be easily detected using native gels. Their detection increases the extent of individualization and the chance of exclusion.

For the analysis of systems with an expressed microvariation such as ACTBP2 it is not generally advisable to use native gels because of the great number of "*interalleles.*" The ACTBP2 system needs a high level of standardization and good laboratory skill to achieve the necessary reproducibility. Therefore, especially in collaborative exercises, the use of a vertical, denaturing gel system in combination with fluorescence detection is the methodology of choice. The use of fluorescence labeled primers avoids the occurrence of double bands that could make the interpretation of amplification patterns difficult. Extensive studies have been carried out within and between laboratories to validate this highly complex STR system. It could be shown that reproducible results were obtained when typing the sample DNA against an allelic ladder for the system and with fluorescence detection. "*Interalleles,*" i.e., alleles with the same lengths but different mobilities, did not occur, because the electrophoretic mobilities depend only on the fragment length and not on the sequence structure.

The possibility of coamplification of several STR systems ("*multiplexing*") offers the possibility to achieve a high sample throughput in a very short time. The term "*multiplexing*" is not well-defined and there exist different approaches: independent amplification of each system and mixing before loading, coamplification of two systems ("*duplex*") and mixing before loading, and coamplification of several systems and direct loading.

Our experience shows that coamplification of several systems is disadvantageous in stain cases, especially if only a small stain quantity is available. Simultaneous amplification of several systems reduces the sensitivity (a minimum of 1 ng human genomic DNA is necessary) and increases the susceptibility to artefact bands. However, if enough template DNA is available, the simultaneous co-amplification of several STR systems is an efficient method to quickly establish a convincing population database.

Optimization of Amplification Reactions

PCR optimization is usually performed in order to obtain maximum *specificity* and *yield.* In some applications for which the amount of template may be limiting, or when there is a large amount of nontarget sequences, the *sensitivity* is maximized. Nonoptimized conditions promote artifactual bands resulting from primer dimerization and mispriming, broad bands containing a mixture of correct and incomplete products, and, generally speaking, a poor signal-tonoise ratio. Poorly designed PCR protocols also lack robustness. Such situations can occur in which the PCR is challenged with less than pristine DNAs or when the ingredients of the reaction are not added in the exact amounts as described by the authors of the protocol. Thus, a well-optimized PCR should be *reliable* in the hands of a coworker or in the laboratory of another institute.

Since the original description of the PCR, many techniques have been described for the amplification of a wide variety of templates. Ways were found to coamplify more than one target in a single reaction (i.e., multiplex PCR), to analyze genes of a single cell, to amplify several hundred samples at a time, to rapidly cycle so that the PCR will take only approx 15 min, and to amplify many-kilobase-long stretches of DNA in a reproducible manner. Perhaps the widest use of the PCR is in genome screening. Obviously, a short chapter cannot cover all of these techniques. Instead, we shall focus on the optimization of two different PCR methods used in analyzing DNA polymorphism, which can be used to identify individuals and to discover gene locations. The principles described here can be adapted to the development of any PCR protocol.

Conventional (target-specific) PCR uses locus-specific primers that flank the region of the polymorphism. This type of PCR requires prior knowledge of the target sequence, so that perfectly complementary primers can be designed. In addition, different techniques have been developed for situations in which the sequence around a gene or polymorphic site of interest is unknown. These methods are called variously, *randomly amplified polymorphic DNA* (RAPDs), arbitrarily primed PCR (AP-PCR), *differentially amplified fragments* (DAFs), and *amplified fragment length polymorphisms* (AFLPs). Although each of these techniques has unique aspects, all rely on a principle of genome-wide screening in an arbitrary, or non-targeted, fashion, and use non-locus-specific primers. The goal is to find a maximal number of useful polymorphisms that can be applied to the construction of a map, or ifrecombinant inbred or similar genetic stocks are being used, finding closely linked markers to a gene of interest. Once the markers are found, they can be developed into *sequence-confirmed amplified fragments* (SCARs), which allow specific primers to be synthesized that can specify the analysis for a particular locus. A final refinement, bulked segregant analysis, obviates the need for tedious generations of backcrossing in the field of plant molecular genetics, for example, or the need to develop specialized genetic materials in order to target the region around a gene of interest for marker discovery.

An important aspect of molecular-marker screening techniques is to perform many assays quickly, in order to allow only those systems that provide useful results to be retained for development. Thus, other goals of optimization of a PCR technique are speed and simplicity, and the aim is to provide these without sacrificing reliability.

Primer Selection

The first two partial reactions of the PCR involve denaturation of the template and hybridization of the primers to specific sites on the opposing strands of the matrix. Then, in the third partial reaction of the PCR, the DNA polymerase extends the primer from its 3' end. It is important to realize that only the 3' terminus of the primer needs to hybridize perfectly with the template for initiation of the polymerization to occur. This feature can result in the generation of a mixture of desired and unrelated PCR products if annealing conditions are permissive with respect to the entire primer sequence.

There are guidelines, as reported by numerous authors, that may be useful in designing effective primers. The suggestions for primer design are based on empirical observations from a limited number of primers and should not be considered as general rules. More important for a successful PCR are comparable T_ms for the primers.

Sometimes, the DNA sequence of the target allows little or no latitude in primer selection. However, visual inspection of the template annealing sites and careful selection of the primer sequences will often minimize the time required to optimize the PCR. For example, avoid potential hairpin-forming sequences in the primer binding site of the template that may limit the accessibility of the primer. Computer programs can also be used for predicting template secondary-structure effects on primer binding efficiency. Despite a gallant attempt at optimization of the PCR and primer design, poor sensitivity might only be relieved when new primer pairs are tried.

Primers Designed to Provide Specificity

When the target sequence is known, specific primers can be designed for amplifying the region between the annealing sites of the two oligonucleotides. An optimized, target-specific PCR has good yield with a minimum number of amplification cycles. When an adequate signal requires very many cycles, the noise will generally be high as well. With good primers, there is a better chance that the desired signal will appear early in the PCR relative to the undesired signals from misprimed sites. Thus, the goal is to have the highest yield of desired product without having nonspecific products.

Primers Designed to Exploit Target Degeneracy

When the sequence of the target is unknown, randomly primed or arbitrarily primed PCR (e.g., RAPDs) can be utilized to generate patterns of fragments at sufficiently high concentration to be readily visualized. As in the case of conventional PCR, attention to the principles of primer design can lead to oligonucleotides, the majority of which will give satisfactory results under one or two PCR conditions. Here, in contrast to targeting a specific sequence, a reproducible pattern is the goal, rather than one unique product. The more complex the PCR fingerprint, the more reproducible it seems to be. Primers yielding fewer than ten distinct products should be avoided.

Another type of genome-wide arbitrary screen can be accomplished using the AFLP technology. Here, the genomic DNA is restricted with appropriate endonucleases, and the PCR target sequences are ligated to the sticky ends so generated. The design of these "*adapters*" should follow the guidelines for designing any good primer, including the lack of duplex formation between or within the adapters. Several adapter pairs have been optimized, and there are commercial kits available as well. Following modification of the fragmented DNA by adapter ligation, subsets are amplified using primers complementary to the adapter sequence and the restriction endonuclease recognition site. The primers are designed at the 3' end so there can be complementarity to only one internal nucleotide of the genomic DNA, to obtain a reduction of the complexity of the fragment pattern (so-called "*preselective*" amplification). The process can be repeated with another specific primer to reduce the complexity of the product mixture still further (''*selective*" amplification). The final result is a highly reproducible fragment pattern, which may be used as finger prints for identification or as the basis for a search for polymorphisms between related individuals in the construction of genetic maps.

Touchdown PCR is often used when many sets of primers are being evaluated. Initially, a Tanneal about 10° higher than the highest estimated T_m is selected and the T_{anneal} is reduced by 1° in successive rounds of amplification. In this protocol, mispriming is reduced, because the primers anneal at the most stable site early in the amplification process.

Optimal Annealing Temperature

Since the second step of the PCR is duplex formation between the primers and template, it is obviously helpful to have an estimate of the temperature (T_m) at which 50% of the template-annealing site is in a duplex with the primer. Of the several methods available to estimate T_m, the one considered to be most reliable is the nearest neighbor algorithm, which is tedious to calculate manually and is best used in commercial software. If software is unavailable, then it is recommended to compare the results obtained from using one of the empirical formulas for T_m that is based on AT and GC content of the primers. The PCR yield will be greatest when the T_m values of the primers match, and even a rough estimate is better than none at all. In addition, mispriming can occur if there is a significant difference between the T_ms of the two primers. For example, if one primer, *b*, has a higher T_m than the other primer, a, there may be mispriming by b at the lower temperature required for adequate annealing of *a*. This scenario may lead to a considerable fraction of the product being something other than the desired target. Thus, once the primer sequences are chosen, take the time to estimate the T_m values of all primers to be used in the PCR and change the sequences as necessary to match T_m values. Once the primers are available, they must be tested in the PCR to empirically determine the optimal temperature for annealing, T_{anneal}. One tries to find the T_{anneal} that provides a balance between maximum yield and minimum mispriming. The dissociation rate of the primer from the template and the initial elongation rate will affect the value obtained.

Regard data from computer programs with healthy skepticism. One reason for this is that the T_m values may be calculated for conditions of membrane hybridization (i.e., equilibrium without elongation) and high salts not exactly what one uses in the PCR). If the condition of 50 mM Na^+ (K^+) is included, the T_m values are lower than those obtained in 1 M salt. The algorithms also neglect the contribution of Mg^{2+} in stabilizing the duplex. The empirically derived T_{anneal} for a PCR is usually higher than the value calculated for 50 mM salt. In spite of the shortcomings of the algorithms, the experimentally derived, optimal annealing temperature can be very close to the estimated T_m values obtained by a variety of methods. If the values do match, it is probably by chance, because there are many factors left out of the calculations. Algorithms for obtaining T_m cannot substitute for an experimentally derived temperature optimum, but they do provide help in matching the primers during the design stage.

The optimal multiplex system will have primers with matching T_m values. However, there are cases when one wants to use sets of primers developed by someone else or by a commercial supplier that do not have matching T_ms. When coamplifying such sets of primers, it may be necessary to operate at less than the optimal T_{anneal} for some of them, if there are primers that have a lower optimal T_{anneal} present in the mixture. For example, the primers have an empirically derived optimal T_{anneal} of 64°C when used alone, but work best in a multiplex at 60°C when combined with two other primer sets. This conclusion was derived from a systematic test of a variety of reaction conditions.

When there is no sequence information available and arbitrary primers must be used, a low T_{anneal} is chosen. It is important to realize that increasing the stringency does not increase the reliability of a fingerprint in arbitrary PCR; indeed, the reverse has been observed. This result is probably caused by the competition among annealing sites that occurs in these complex PCRs.

Once primers have been designed properly, it is also important to keep in mind adverse-reaction conditions that could lead to a poor PCR result. One situation that can occur is polymorphism in the primer annealing site. This will lead to a weaker interaction of the primer with the template, resulting in low yield in the PCR, and could even prevent primer extension, if it is in the very important 3' region of the primer binding site. Another factor to consider is the purity of the primers themselves. Unpurified primer preparations may contain sequences that are truncated, oligonucleotides with base modifications that prevent hybridization, and fragments that are incomplete chains. In a PCR that is not operating with stringency (i.e., not well optimized), these oligonucleotides could lead to weak signals and irreproducible banding patterns. The best primer preparations are those purified by reversed-phase HPLC, but this option may not always be available. If purity is suspect, perform a preparative polyacrylamide-gel purification. When hundreds of primers are to be screened, they will probably be purchased, and it is important to choose a vendor that provides pure primers. "*Cheap*" oligonucleotides cost a lot, if time and template are lost. Finally, it is good practice to personally measure the optical density of the primer preparation.

PCR Artifact Bands

Two types of artifactual banding patterns may be observed even from a PCR working at high stringency, when sites of sequence polymorphism are amplified. In one, there is a mixture of two bands that differ in length by the addition of a single nucleotide to the expected size of the single-stranded DNA fragment. This PCR artifact is not restricted to amplification of polymorphic loci and is dependent on the concentration of free Mg^{2+}. In the other pattern, observed only in the amplification of microsatellite loci, shadow, or stutter, bands are observed. These bands are usually less than the size of the main band by an integral of one or more repeat lengths. A stutter band may be observed as well at one repeat integral larger than the main band. The propensity to form stutter bands increases as the repeat size decreases (i.e., tetranucleotide <trinucleotide <dinucleotide). Artifactual bands resulting from nontemplated nucleotide addition can be eliminated, as suggested earlier, whereas the stutter artifacts are more difficult to control.

One of the activities of DNA polymerases is to make nontemplated additions to the 3' end of a primer extension product, called *terminal transferase* like activity, thus producing a mixture of blunt and non-blunt-ended molecules. The efficiency of the addition seems to be a function of the sequence at the 5' end. We have confirmed that when the 5' end of a primer terminates with a pyrimidine, there is much less addition to the 3' terminus of the complementary strand. However, it has seldom been possible to obtain 100% blunt ends by this tactic; there is always some non-templated addition. We have been more successful in obtaining single bands by using a primer with a purine at the 5' terminus and aiming for complete addition. If the template sequence does not have a complementary pyrimidine base for the 5' terminal purine of the primer, one can add an artificial sequence to the 5' end of the primer. The added sequence will be non-templated only in the first round of thermal cycling. As long as the primer has sufficient complementarity at the 3' end, there is a wide latitude for adding mismatched "*tags*" of different lengths at the 5' end.

The process of nontemplate nucleotide addition can be considered to occur when "the *engine idles*". What is meant by this metaphor is that the reaction will proceed in a forward direction when the binding of the DNA polymerase to the blunt-ended PCR products is favored. The forward reaction is favored when the PCR protocol includes a long extension step at the end of thermal cycling. Also, since nucleotide addition does not occur when ends are opened by breathing, a low temperature and a high Mg^{2+} concentration will increase the yield of the extra nucleotide addition. Stutter bands are more difficult to manage. In discussions among persons performing the PCR on microsatellites, one hears that this or that primer leads to shadow (or stutter) bands. However, it is not the primer selected, but rather the *locus* chosen for amplification that results in the observance of these bands. Stutter bands are a cause for concern, if they have an intensity close to that of the main band, because homozygotes may be mistyped in family studies of linkage analysis using dinucleotide tandem repeats. In forensics, the evidence sample is often a mixture of DNA from more than one human source, and stutter bands will make the analysis more difficult.

TEMPLATE PREPARATION

The importance of a good template is often overlooked during the development of a PCR protocol: It is generally considered that organically extracted DNA is sufficiently clean. However, after establishing a protocol with a control DNA, there may be difficulties with DNA obtained from samples of origins different from the control. Examples of refractory amplifications have been reported for DNA obtained postmortem, from fresh blood and stains, from cells isolated from urine, degraded human tissue, bones, and plant tissue, to list just a few. Before optimizing a PCR protocol with a commercially available DNA or a control DNA obtained from cells grown in culture, consider the sample preparation that will be used to isolate the template. Obviously, an optimized PCR protocol will not work satisfactorily, if the test sample contains an effective concentration of inhibitors or unwanted templates that will also bind the primers (e.g., AP-PCR). Another important feature is a good estimation of the input amount of the specific template. Features specific for forensic and plant templates are worth considering in more detail.

Templates for Forensic DNA Analysis

A robust PCR protocol should work well with DNA isolated by either of the two popular extraction methods, since laboratories differ in their preference. Organically extracted DNA is double-stranded and can be used for analysis by both restriction digestion and the PCR. The organically extracted DNA is obtained in a small volume. DNA extracted by the Chelex method is singlestranded, so it can only be used for analysis by the PCR. The DNA obtained from the Chelex extraction method may be recovered in a rather large volume.

DNA quantification should be carried out on templates for PCR analysis of DNA in forensic applications. The concern is that, although the PCR systems are specific for human templates, the signal obtained from the PCR may be too low if the extracted DNA contains templates from nonhuman sources. The amount of template estimated from spectroscopic measurements of DNA extracted from biological evidence could lead to little or no human DNA. Thus, the quantitation assay must be able to exclude DNA from bacteria, yeast, dog, rodent, and so on. Specificity for human DNA can be obtained by utilizing a primatespecific probe in a slot-blot assay, and commercial kits are available. One compares the signal of the sample with that observed for a series of standards.

Templates for Plant-Genome Analysis

Plant DNA is too variable in its manifestations to give a comprehensive list of the purification protocols that have been successfully used in particular instances. A rigorous CTAB procedure with at least two rounds of chloroform extraction and three rounds of successive CTAB precipitation and selective resolubilization of the DNA, followed by a high-salt precipitation, have given sufficient purity and yield of DNA for all of the PCR procedures. A final RNase treatment with a phenol-chloroform extraction has been helpful in reducing PCR artifacts and in the quantification of yield.

In AP-PCR analysis of plant genomes, two independently purified DNA preparations must be used for each sample, in particular if one wishes to compare field samples. Independent samples are desirable, because other DNAs may be present from molds, mildews, and so on, and the copurified DNA may contribute a signal that can be mistaken for a polymorphism in the plant DNA. It must be remembered that if DNA is purified from plant tissue, mitochondrial and chloroplast DNAs are present, and the short primers used in the assays for polymorphisms may well bind and give rise to a PCR product. Another important control in plant-genome analysis by AP-PCR is to use at least two concentrations of DNA template for each primer, in order to eliminate many false positives. For example, with barley DNA, we use 10 and 50 ng DNA per PCR analysis, of sample obtained from axenically grown plants. In AFLP analysis, it is unnecessary to use two concentrations of DNA, but it is still necessary to consider impurities from field samples and organellar genomes.

Detection of PCR Products

PCR optimization is responsive to the means of detecting the reaction products: The method chosen must be simple, reliable, and sensitive. PCR products may be separated on either an agarose gel or an acrylamide minigel, denaturing or native, and detected after staining with either ethidium bromide or silver. In the denaturing system, many more bands can be seen, and more products will appear to be polymorphic, thanks to strand separation. Detection can be supplemented by photographic recording of the stained fragments, or the intensity can be digitized and recorded with the Eagle Eye followed by densitometry using an instrument such as the LKB Ultrascan XL and analysis with software such as the Gelscan XL. The primers can be radioactively labeled for autoradiography with subsequent densitometry or scanning with a PhosphorImager, followed by analysis with the accompanying software. Automated methods for analysis of PCR products with database-management possibilities exist for the DNA sequencer employing laser-induced fluorescence detection. Primers labeled with dyes at the 5'-end can be used in the PCR, since they do not inhibit the Taq DNA polymerase, and the sensitivity is greater than that obtained with silver staining of short amplicons (<400 nt). This approach allows automation of genomewide screening.

OPTIMIZING THE PCR

A set of primers with similar T_m, values, a sensitive detection method, and an understanding of the template limitations, provide the tools for the optimization endeavor. Examination of the PCR literature reveals that many amplifications work well under a standard set of buffer conditions composed of 1.5 mM Mg^{2+} low salt (50 mM KCl), 0.2 mM of each dNTP and 0.2 μM each primer. Optimization experiments can be started by looking for "*windows*" around these established values. Many researchers regard optimization as the process, which defines conditions that give the maximum yield in a reaction. However, that concept is limited and can be compared with the act of only seeing the trees and not the forest. What one should strive for is finding those conditions under which similar yields are obtained even when the constituents vary somewhat. For example, in an optimized PCR, a 10% variation in Mg^{2+} concentration should not make much difference in the yields. The reason for this requirement is that inorganic analytical assays can have an inherent variation associated with them, generally about 10%. Variations in pipetting and weighing the reagents is generally only a few percent. Finally, as the careful analyst knows, material is often left clinging to the inside of a pipet tip after ejection of the buffer stock solution. Some people will rinse the tip by pulsing solution in and out of the pipet tip before they withdraw the tip from the mix in order to get all the material into the solution. This practice is impractical when hundreds of solutions are being pipetted. Thus, the goal should be to determine a concentration range at which similar results will be obtained in the PCR, rather than a concentration at which a maximum yield is obtained. The concentration range will be fairly flat, but when the limits are known, it will be possible to chose conditions within the plateau to compensate for performance variables.

Prevention of Pre-PCR Artifacts

Taq DNA polymerase has significant activity at 0.5°C to give rise to multiple bands resulting from mispriming and especially primer dimers (primer oligomerization) in some PCR systems. Even the practice of mixing the reagents and holding the tubes on ice until they are placed in the thermal cycler block may not prevent these PCR artifacts from emerging. There is a solution to the problem. "*Hot-start*" PCR involves the practice of leaving a critical reaction component out of the master mix and then adding it when the solution reaches 70.4°C. In this temperature range, primers involved in weak annealing interactions will have dissociated. The elimination of pre-PCR mispriming and primer dimerization may be the most important feature of the PCR protocol, especially when sets of primers are being co-amplified. The yield will increase, and there will be fewer artifact bands. It is difficult to design multiple primer sets that exclude intermolecular interactions; whereas the hot start is fairly simple.

Wax can be used to separate an incomplete master mix from the missing component. When the tubes are placed in the thermal cycler, the wax will melt at a temperature sufficiently high that weak primer interactions will no longer survive, and the aqueous layer above the wax will blend with the master mix by thermal convection. After the PCR, the wax acts as a barrier to prevent evaporation and contamination, but it must be penetrated to withdraw a sample for analysis. Commercially available, chemically modified wax beads used with small reaction volumes (5000 μL) are easily penetrated.

Another way to perform hot-start PCR is to pipet the missing component through an oil layer once the tubes are in the thermal cycler and at the elevated temperature. This procedure is simple, but there are a number of precautions. Heated air in the pipet tip can push out the volume containing the missing component, so one must not linger in the oil layer too long, or the reaction mix might receive only a portion of the missing component (the rest will be above the oil layer). The template preparation room normally does not have a thermal cycler, so care must be taken not to introduce contaminants. Adding the missing component through an oil layer would be very tedious when screening hundreds of primers. Advances in enzymology also provide solutions for eliminating pre-PCR artifacts. Recently, a modified version of recombinant AmpliTaq DNA Polymerase, which is inactive until it reaches temperatures around the normal T_{den} (92.5°C), has become available for "*invisible*" hot-start. Since the polymerase is activated in a pre-PCR heating step at high temperature, mispriming events will have dissociated before the enzyme has become activated. A similar stratagem utilizes a monoclonal antibody to Taq DNA polymerase, which deactivates the polymerase at 25°C. When the PCR is started, the deactivation is reversed as the temperature rises during the denaturation step. By these two approaches, all of the reaction components can be added to one PCR solution, and there are no extra steps. The enzymatic-activation approach provides a method for hot-start in capillary PCR, since the tubes cannot be opened to add the missing component at high temperature.

Finding the Optimal Reaction Components of the PCR

Defining the optimal magnesium ion concentration

Magnesium ion stabilizes the DNA duplex and has been regarded as the single most important constituent in the PCR. Exhaustive experiments in variations of the salt, pH, primer, and dNTP concentrations often lead to very little effect on the yield of the PCR. However, high Mg^{2+} concentrations can promote incorrect annealing of the primer to its intended binding site, resulting in extraneous bands, and may make it more difficult to melt internal template hairpins, reducing the yield. A too low Mg^{2+} concentration will increase the stringency, but could decrease the activity of Taq DNA polymerase, resulting in lower yields. Commercially available "*PCR optimization*" kits can be used to help find the optimal Mg^{2+} concentration window. These kits can save time required for optimization.

Adjusting reaction components other than the magnesium ion

Instead of "*binning*" primers in sets to be coamplified according to their estimated T_ms, it is possible to adjust the ionic conditions so that a series of primers can work optimally at one temperature. Different series of primers would require different buffers for optimal performance. Thus, the primers are "grouped" according to the optimal buffer, making primer screening amenable to automation. The pH of the buffer may effect the PCR efficiency, especially in multiplex PCR, when many primers are present. Other components to evaluate are the salts. KC1 and $MgCl_2$ may be less effective than $(NH_4)_2SO_4$ and $MgCl_2$.

Optimization for Nonstringent PCR

Many descriptions exist for the optimization of RAPDs, including systematic variations in the magnesium ion and primer concentrations, the effect of additives such as detergents, formamide, glycerol, and so on. However, two of the advantages in using molecular marker screening techniques are simplicity and speed. Perhaps for that reason, researchers using the RAPD/AP-PCR/DAF techniques choose the standard PCR buffer containing 1.5 mM $MgCl_2$ Tris-HCl buffer, and 50 mM KCl. However, the recommended primer concentration depends on the specific technique being used.

The AFLP technique, which combines the accuracy and reliability of the RFLP technique with the power of PCR, needs much less optimization. The increase in reliability derives from the ligation of oligonucleotides to restricted DNA, allowing the use of longer PCR primers and thus more stringent annealing conditions. By adding "*selective bases*" to the 3' end of the PCR primer sites, the method can be "tuned" to amplify from one to thousands of restriction fragments simultaneously in a highly reproducible way, without having to carry out a lengthy optimization procedure.

Finding the Right Thermal Cycler Parameters

In the optimization process, it is important to examine the temperature windows, the duration of the holding times, and the ramping speed between the denaturation, annealing, and extension steps. These experiments should be done in order to arrive at consensus parameters. For example, a particular temperature for denaturation (T_{den}), or the time spent at T_{den}, might give the best yields in one thermal cycler, but a slightly different temperature, or duration, may be optimal for the same PCR with a different thermal cycler. Thus, if the PCR protocol is to be utilized in other laboratories or with other thermal cyclers within the same laboratory, then the best protocol would be to utilize a T_{den} or duration at T_{den}, that lies in the middle of the range that gives satisfactory yields.

One paper often cited compares rapid cycling in capillaries with conventional cycling in a heat block, where it is shown that clean reactions are obtained only in the rapid system. This comparison is a bit unfair, because the reactions were performed at 3 mM Mg^{2+} concentration: One will invariably get spurious bands at this magnesium-ion concentration in conventional thermal cyclers! A 2 min ramp-down time from 94 to 54°C at 1.5 mM Mg^{2+} concentration resulted in no spurious bands at 1.5 mM Mg^{2+} in a four-loci multiplex system. In fact, the slow ramping results in greater yield than one can obtain with rapid ramping in this system. In arbitrarily primed PCR, the ramping time from T_{den} to T_{anneal} has been reported to be one of the factors leading to variability between laboratories. The number of polymorphisms increased as the ramping time interval was prolonged, suggesting that differences among laboratories using the same primers and template might be because of the ramping-speed differences among the various thermal cyclers.

Amplifying Regions of High GC Content

When Taq DNA polymerase must amplify a segment having a high proportion of G + C nucleotides, it may encounter undissociated template, because the local T_m of these regions is high. These templates may be refractory to the PCR. To increase the efficiency of amplification through such regions, a number of techniques has been employed. Upon PCR optimization, the amplification of GC-rich regions will often be successful. An initial denaturation at alkaline pH, followed by neutralization and precipitation of the single-stranded DNA may provide the solution for refractive templates containing high GC content.

Prevention of Contamination

Optimization will come to naught if one does not guard against contamination. In forensic DNA analysis, the issue is not whether such-and-such PCR technique can be used to analyze crime-scene mixtures containing template from more than one source. The issue that should concern forensic scientists, or any researcher who is contemplating the PCR for DNA analysis, is how to avoid contamination of samples by either the PCR products of previous experiments or by other templates at the workbench. The supreme PCR protocol will be worthless if the laboratory is not set up to avoid potential contamination. We cannot discuss in detail ways to control contamination in this chapter, but we shall give some suggestions for good laboratory practice.

Materials

The items listed in this section were used by the authors with repeated success. Similar materials from manufacturers or suppliers other than those listed (i.e., with a similar degree of quality control) may also work satisfactorily.

PCR Protocols

PCR with primers to provide specificity

1. GeneAmp PCR Reagent Kit with AmpliTaq DNA Polymerase containing buffer and dNTPs.

2. Molecular-biology-grade water, 18 Megaohm.
3. Light mineral oil.

PCR with primers to exploit target degeneracy

RAPDs protocol

1. AmpliTaq DNA Polymerase, Stoffel Fragment, with 10X PCR buffer and 25 mM $MgCl_2$.
2. Formamide.
3. GENESCAN 2500-ROX Size Standard.
4. Long Ranger.

AFLP protocol

1. AFLP Plant Mapping Kits: AFLP Amplification Core Mix Module, AFLP Ligation and Preselective Amplification Module, and AFLP Selective Amplification Start-Up Module.
2. TE (10^{-4} : 0.1 mM EDTA, 10 mM Tris-HCl, pH 8.3. Dissolve 121 mg Tris-HCl in 80 mL 0.1 mM EDTA, solution, adjust pH to 8.3 with 0.2 NHCl and bring volume up to 100 mL. For 0.1 mM EDTA, make a 1 mM solution and dilute 1:10. For 1 mM EDTA, dissolve 93 mg EDTA, disodium salt, in 100 mL molecular-biology-grade water.

Establishing the T_{anneal}

Tubes for the PCR: 0.5 mL thin-walled tubes for the GeneAmp PCR System 9600 or DNA Thermal Cycler 480; 0.2 mL MicroAmp Reaction Tubes for the GeneAmp PCR System 9600.

PCR Artifact Bands

1. T4 DNA Polymerase, 3000 U/mL.
2. 2 mM EDTA: dissolve 74 mg EDTA, disodium salt, in 90 mL molecular-biology-grade water, adjust the pH to 8.0, and bring the volume to 100 mL.
3. 7.5 M ammonium acetate: dissolve 58 g anhydrous salt in molecular-biologygrade water to give a final volume of 100 mL.

Template Preparation

Quick Pre-PCR template purification

Microcon-100 ultrafiltration device.

Rapid DNA quantitation

1. PicoGreen dye.
2. TE: 1 mM EDTA, 10 mM Tris-HCl, pH 8.3. Dissolve 121 mg Tris-HCl and 93 mg EDTA, disodium salt, in 80 mL water, adjust

the pH to 8.3 with 0.2 N HCl and bring up the volume to 100 mL.

Detection of PCR Products

1. Loading buffer: make 2 mL blue dextran solution, 50 mg/mL, filtered through a Gelman Acrodisc. Mix with 2 mL 10X TBE and 8.8 mL deionized water.
2. 10X TBE buffer.
3. Sizing ladder: GENESCAN 2500-ROX, or GENESCAN 350-ROX Size Standards.

PCR Optimization

Prevention of pre-PCR artifacts

Using wax as a barrier in hot-start PCR

AmpliWax PCR Gem 100.

Using DNA polymerase activation to avoid pre-PCR artifacts

AmpliTaq Gold, 5 U/μ-L.

Adjusting the reaction components of the PCR

Defining the optimal magnesium ion concentration

1. 25 mM $MgCl_2$ stock solution.
2. dNTP stock solution: Set ofdATP, dCTP, dGTP, dATP, 100 mM. Add 12.5 μL of each dNTP to 450 μL molecular-biology-grade water.
3. Enzyme solution: use AmpliTaq DNA Polymerase, 5 U/μL. Dilute 16 μL stock enzyme with 64 μL molecular-biology-grade water and dispense immediately.
4. PCR optimization kits are available from commercial sources: PCR Optimizer Kit; Opti-Prime PCR Optimization Kit.

Finding the Best Thermal Cycler Parameters

GeneAmp PCR System 9600 or DNA Thermal Cycler 480.

Primers and Remedies for Amplifying Regions of High GC Content

1. 7-Deaza-dGTP, Li-salt, 10 mmol/L, pH 7.0.
2. DMSO: methyl sulfoxide, stored with molecular sieves at room temperature in the dark.
3. UlTma DNA polymerase, 6U/μL.
4. Vent exo- DNA Polymerase.

Guidelines for Prevention of Contamination

ART Tips.

Methods

Guidelines for Primer Design

Primers designed to provide specificity

1. Target-specific PCR primers are generally from 17 to 25 nucleotides in length. Primers can be much longer or even shorter and still provide Specificity. The length of the two primers does not need to be identical.
2. The G + C content is usually between 40 and 60% and is similar between the primers. When this procedure is limited by the template sequence, one of the primers is lengthened or shortened to compensate for the difference in G + C content.
3. Primers with a GC "*clamp*" at the 3' end may increase the sensitivity, but mispriming may be observed in multiplex PCR with primers having runs of more than two GCs at the 3' end.
4. Pick 3' sequences that are non-complementary with sequences in the other primer, since primer dimer amplification can occur and reduce the concentration of substrates available for producing the desired product. When incorporating sets of primers that worked well in singleplex PCR into a multiplex PCR protocol, re-examine the primer complementarity.
5. Avoid palindromes and hairpin loops that are sufficiently stable to compete with the target sequence and therefore reduce the sensitivity.
6. If the length and %GC of the region of primer complementarity are minimal, then the primer/primer duplex should not be a cause of concern with regard to primer/template formation.
7. Avoid stretches of sequences at the 3' end that are complementary to repetitive motifs, unless degeneracy is desired.

Conventional PCR protocol

1. Program the thermal cycler. Start with 5 min at 94°C for one cycle. Link to a regime of 1 min at 94°C, 1 min at the T_m, 1 min at 72°C for 30 cycles. Link to 10 min at 72°C for one cycle and then to a holding step at either 4 or 25°C. The number of cycles necessary to obtain a signal will depend on the amount and quality of the template. If insufficient signal is obtained with 30 cycles, try 35 and 40 cycles.
2. On ice, prepare a cocktail containing the proportion of PCR buffer recommended by the supplier of the DNA polymerase. If Mg^{2+} is to be added to the buffer, choose 1.5 mM in the initial experiments.

Add primers to a final concentration of 0.25 μM each, dNTPs to 0.2 mM each, and use 100 ng template. Bring the volume to 45 μL with molecular-biology-grade purified water. Add 5 μL solution containing 2.5 U thermal-stable DNA polymerase. Mix gently and pulse spin to bring the contents of the tube to the bottom.

3. Layer a drop of light mineral oil over the mixture if a thermal cycler without a heated lid is to be used.
4. Start the thermal cycler and when the temperature reaches 94°C, place the reaction tube in the block.
5. When analyzed, if the signal from amplified products is a smear, or if the product is produced in too high an amount, reduce the number of cycles or the amount of template.

Primers designed to exploit target degeneracy

1. DNA amplification fingerprinting in the arbitrarily primed mode uses primers of length 6-8 nt.
2. Most primers are minimally 50% GC, with no obvious dimer-forming characteristics. One can tailor the primers to the genome, if some information is available for the overall GC composition and on any structural motifs, such as diand trinucleotide repeats and Alu-repeats.
3. It has been shown that primers having a "*core*" of arbitrary sequence and a stable mini-hairpin at the 5' terminus (GCGAAGC) can increase detection of polymorphic DNA. However, in some situations, it can be helpful to use pairs of unstructured primers, as they lead to products that do not have complementary ends, which may form poorly amplified "*panhandles*".
4. In detecting a "*consensus*" sequence or a group of related sequences, primers with deoxyinosine can be helpful. Primers with deoxyinosine can pair with all four nucleotides at positions of complete degeneracy. The deoxyinosine is placed in the primers at sites of potential sequence ambiguity.
5. The concentration of the arbitrary primers can be used to complement the structure in generating bands. For example, in the DAF approach, the primers are present in a high concentration (3 μM), which leads to a large number of bands. However, the RAPD system uses a more conventional concentration of primers (0.3μM), so that fewer products result.

Rapds protocol

Use from 2 mM $MgCl_2$, 0.075-0.1 U/μL Taq DNA polymerase or 0.2-0.4 U/μL AmpliTaq DNA Polymerase, Stoffel Fragment (which is reported to give up to twice as many fragments, although of smaller size), and 0.1-0.2 mM dNTPs. The template concentration should be at least 5 ng/μL DNA for plasmid, 1 ng/μL DNA for low-complexity genomes and 0.1 ng/μL for high-complexity genomes. Restriction digestion of the template DNA, either before or after the PCR reaction, will also increase the detection of polymorphisms. It is probably easier to standardize the restriction of the post-PCR product than of the starting DNA sample, because the large number of cycles in these experiments causes a plateau to be reached and the same volume of PCR sample will give a very reproducible amount of signal. An example of a RAPD protocol follows.

1. Make a PCR cocktail (for 50 reactions, the volume will be 1 mL): 100 μL 10X PCR buffer (no $MgCl_2$), 30 μL $MgCl_2$, stock (25 mM), 3 μL 0.1 mM primer, 50 U Taq DNA polymerase, 607 μL molecular-biology-grade water.
2. Dispense 15 μL per tube.
3. Add 5 μL template DNA at 10 ng/μL.
4. Thermal cycling conditions vary, but the conditions recommended here are 72°C, 2 min (once); 94°C, 30 s; 36°C, 1 min; 72°C, 2 min (25 cycles). Ramping times are not faster than 2°C/s. There is a final incubation at 72°C for 7 min.
5. Analyze 10 μL of the PCR sample on an agarose gel or 5 μL on an acrylamide gel. If fluorescent-dye labeled oligonucleotides were used in the PCR, the products can be analyzed on the ABI Prism DNA Sequencer. Dilute the sample with formamide either to 1:50, or to 1:150, and load 1 μL of the dilution with a dye-labeled size standard after denaturation at 95 μC for 3 min. With the 373 DNA Sequencer, analyze the samples on a 6% polyacrylamide gel (29:1 acrylamide/bis) containing 6 M urea in IX TBE at 1800 V for 11 h. With the 377 DNA Sequencer, use a 5% Long Ranger gel in IX TBE with 4M urea and run for 7 h at 3 kV. Use of the internal-lane size standard and GeneScan Analysis software allows a high level of sensitivity and precision in identifying the bands.

AFLP protocol

Prior to the PCR, AFLP reactions require biochemical steps, which involve restriction of the genomic DNA with endonucleases followed by ligation of adapter molecules. This technology has been licensed by Keygene, N.V., the inventor of the technique, to Life Technologies and Perkin-Elmer. These companies supply AFLP kits that include the adapters, PCR primer sets, and protocols with detailed instructions. An example of an ALFP protocol follows.

1. Amplification of target sequences: Combine the following materials in a thin-walled 0.2 mL PCR tube: 4.0 μL diluted DNA from a restriction-ligation reaction, 1.0 μL pre-selective primer pairs (have two sets per DNA sample: one with EcoRI + A and MseI + C; one with EcoRI and MseI + C), 15.0 μL AFLP mix (which includes IX PCR buffer) 0.1 mM dNTPs, 0.5 U Taq DNA polymerase in amounts appropriate for 20 μL reaction volume. If using a thermal cycler without a heated lid, overlay the sample with 20 μL light mineral oil.
2. Cycling the preselective amplification reaction: Thermal cycling conditions are 65°, 2 min (once); 94°, 10 s; 56°, 30 s; 72°, 2 min (20 cycles). Ramping times should not be faster than 2°/s. At the end, the reactions are brought to 4°. If the reactions were successful, then there should be a smear of product from 150,000 bp visible on a 1.5% agarose gel.
3. AFLP reaction: Combine the following in a thin-walled 0.2 mL PCR tube: 3 μL diluted preselective amplification reaction product (10 μL preselective amplification reaction product diluted with 190 μL TE 10 -4 buffer), 1 μL MseI[primer + CXX] at 5 μM, 1 μL EcoRI[labeled primer + AXX] at 1 μM, 15 μL AFLP PCR mix. If using a thermal cycler without a heated lid, add 20 μL light mineral oil to each tube.

Guidelines for Establishing T_{anneal}

1. Test the PCR at various T_{anneal}, using 2°C intervals and starting 4°C below the estimated T_m, working up to 10°C above it. If the product yield does not significantly decrease at the higher temperatures, choose a higher temperature for the PCR. If the yield decreases, drop back to the plateau area. Stringency becomes important, when the target is contaminated with other genomic DNA, so operate close to the high value if possible.
2. To screen for the best T_{anneal} of a multiplex system, start 4°C lower than the lowest primer T_m and perform the PCR at various T_{anneal}, increasing the value by 2°C intervals to the point at which the first locus fails to amplify. Cut back to a temperature at which all loci yield strong signal-to-noise ratios.
3. When arbitrary primers are used, the choice of the temperature depends on whether the primers are structured or not. For example,

use 35 cycles of 94°(30 s), 30°(30 s), 72°(30 s) for primers with minihairpins at the 5'-terminus and 45 cycles at 94°(1 min), 35°(1 min), 72°(2 min) for unstructured primers.

4. When adopting a PCR protocol optimized in another laboratory with a different thermal cycler, the optimal T_{anneal} or the time at the T_{anneal} may need to be adjusted. Amplify a low and medium amount of template at the temperatures described in the protocol, performing the assays in duplicate. If pattern changes are observed, raise the T_{anneal} in 1° increments or the time at T_{anneal} by 10-5 s. If the yield drops, increasing the denaturation temperature or holding times may improve the yield. If the pattern is identical, but the yield is low, it may be helpful to consider the following: Try a tube with a thin wall, check the temperature at which the clock starts counting, and verify that the instrument is still calibrated using the manufacturer's recommended procedure.

Reduction or Elimination of PCR Artifact Bands

Removing a non-templated nucleotide addition with T4 DNA polymerase

The nonuniform end of a primer-extended PCR product can be "*polished*" with either T4 DNA polymerase or with Pfu DNA polymerase. The following procedure is a simple and cheap way to polish the ends of PCR products. The treatment is a post-PCR one, so do not perform this assay in the template preparation area. Even though using a thermal stable DNA polymerase that has 3' to 5' exonuclease activity in the PCR, such as UITma (Perkin-Elmer) will help somewhat in removing non-templated nucleotide additions, this type of polymerase is still sufficiently active in non-templated nucleotide addition that one obtains a mixture of blunt and 3'-overhanging ends.

1. Generally, this procedure is performed as a group of a series of samples obtained from different PCRs that have been stored at -20°C. Thaw the samples, vortex, and pulse-spin the tubes to collect the solution before opening the tube.
2. Remove 10 μL PCR solution and place in a 0.5 mL microfuge tube with cap. Heat 2 min at 98°C.
3. Add 5 U of T4 DNA polymerase and incubate at 25°C in a thermal cycler blo`ck for 30 min. Additional dNTPs do not need to be added if the PCR was carried out with 0.2 mM of each dNTP.
4. Add 1.3 μL 2 mM EDTA to quench the reaction or heat-inactivate at 80°C for 10 min.

5. The amplicons (i.e., PCR products) may be precipitated after adding 0.5 vol of 7.5 M ammonium acetate and 2.5 vol 95% ethanol. The pellet is washed with 70% ethanol and dried.

Adjusting the thermal cycling protocol to effect blunt-end addition

After all the thermal cycles have been completed, there is a one-time incubation at 72°C in most protocols. Change this incubation step to 30 min at 60°C to convert most of the blunt ends to +1 additions at Mg^{2+} concentrations of 1.25 mM or above.

Reducing shadow (stutter) band signals

1. Keep the template concentration as low as possible, preferably below 10 ng, and do not overamplify. As the main band reaches the plateau state, the stutter band appears to increase in proportion to it.
2. Since stutter tends to increase at higher Mg^{2+} concentration, using a concentration toward the low end of the Mg^{+2} window may be beneficial.
3. Change the locus. If there is a large amount of stutter with the chosen locus, look for another one that provides a similar discriminatory power but does not produce intense stutter bands.
4. Perform the PCR with different DNA polymerases to find one that is more processive.

Template Preparation for the PCR

Quick pre-PCR purification of the template

DNA extracted from forensic samples by the organic extraction method still may contain inhibitors of the PCR. We have found that further purification by ultrafiltration may improve the success rate of amplification of compromised samples. Perform these operations in the template preparation room (if available) to avoid contamination with amplicons, but spin the samples in a different area to avoid problems associated with aerosols.

1. Label both the filter and reservoir with a marking pen.
2. Place 500 μL dH_2O on top of the membrane of a Microcon-100, being careful not to touch the membrane with the pipet tip. To see if it leaks and to remove the moisturizer from the membrane, let the apparatus sit vertically for 15 min, or pulse centrifuge at 500 g. If the membrane seal is not tight, a large volume of water will pass quickly through the device. Throw away leaky spin columns.
3. Force the water through the membrane by centrifuging at 500g for 15 min, discard the ultrafiltrate from the reservoir, and reattach the filter.

4. Place a known volume of DNA sample without chloroform residue on the membrane. We use up to 100 μL and rinse the walls of the apparatus with another 100 μL dH_2O. Cap the column. Work with one uncapped column at a time in order to avoid cross-contamination.
5. Centrifuge according to the manufacturer's recommendations (500g), then remove and measure the volume of the ultrafiltrate. Since the membrane was prewet, there should be approx 200 μL. If not, spin longer.
6. Rinse the walls of the filter with 200 μL dH_2O, working with one apparatus at a time to avoid cross-contamination, and spin again. This step may be repeated.
7. Finally, collect the retentate containing the purified template according to the manufacturer's recommendations.
8. Measure the volume: in our hands, it varies from about 10 to 50 μL. Reconstitute to the original volume of the sample applied to the membrane and store in a 0.5 mL capped tube.
9. If an inhibitor is suspected, include a positive control in the PCR (i.e., primers and template that give a characteristic band) to insure that the purification was successful.

Protocol for rapid DNA quantification

DNA can be quantified accurately with a fluorescence method that distinguishes between double-and single-stranded nucleic acids. An example that has worked well is presented here.

1. Make a 1:400 dilution of PicoGreen in TE buffer.
2. Dispense 100 μL per well of a 96-well microtiter dish for reading on the fluorometer LS-50B or an equivalent instrument.
3. Add 1 0 μL of sample or standard to wells.
4. Read on the LS50B using the "WPR" software. Use the following settings for detection and quantification: Excitation Wavelength, 480 nm; Excitation Slit Width, 5 nm; Emission Wavelength, 520 nm; Emission Slit Width, 4 nm; Emission Filter, 515 nm.
5. Use the Generic WPR Macro and template for generating a spread sheet that displays the concentrations in μg/mL.

Detection of PCR Products

Manual detection methods

1. For arbitrarily primed PCR: in the stage of doing the initial screen for useful primers, 10 5 μL PCR product commonly is run on a

1.5% agarose gel in IX TBE buffer at 4 V/cm for 3 h, stained with ethidium bromide, and visualized on a UV trans-illuminator.

2. The products may also be separated on a 6% acrylamide minigel, denaturing or native, and stained with either ethidium bromide or silver.
3. For AFLP, the samples must be radioactive.

Automated analysis on a DNA sequencer with fluorescence detection

1. If converting from manual detection methods to automated fluorescence detection methods, initially try 0.1 μM concentration of both primers in the PCR and cut the number of cycles of amplification by 2 rounds. Increase the concentration of primers in 0.5 μL increments as necessary to obtain sufficient signal.
2. Dispense 1.5 μL PCR solution and 0.5 μL dye-labeled sizing ladder into a 1.5 mL microfuge tube, dry on a heat block at 90°C for 3 min, and add 6 μL loading buffer. Denature 2 min at 95°C and load onto the proper polyacrylamide gel containing urea as suggested in the chemistry guide of the manufacturer for the particular DNA sequencer being utilized. Perform electrophoresis as recommended by the manufacturer for the size plates selected.
3. For AFLP, mix 0.3 μL ROX sizing ladder, 0.2 μL loading buffer, 0.7 μL deionized formamide, 0.4 μL FAM-or JOE-labeled PCR products, and 0.8 μL TAMRA-labeled PCR products in a 0.5 mL tube with cap. Denature for 3 min at 95°C and snap-cool. Load immediately onto a 5% Long Ranger gel with 6% urea and IX TBE. Perform the electrophoresis as recommended by the manufacturer.

Procedures for PCR Optimization

Prevention of pre-PCR artifacts

Using wax as a barrier in hot-start PCR

Perform the following steps in the template preparation room or special area clear of amplicons.

1. Dispense 200 μL reaction mix that lacks one or more components such as the DNA polymerase and the template in the PCR tube. Pulse spin to bring the liquid to the bottom of the tube.
2. Place a wax bead over the reaction mix, put the tube in a heat block set at 80°C for 5 min to melt the wax, then remove the tube so the wax will solidify and seal off the master mix. A large number of tubes can be prepared in advance and stored at 4°C, but do not store frozen.

3. Carefully dispense 300 μL of a solution containing the missing component, usually combined with the test sample, on the wax surface (without disturbing the barrier and), cap the tube.
4. Load the tubes in the thermal cycler and perform the amplification as normally done without the wax barrier.

Using DNA polymerase activation to avoid pre-PCR artifacts

1. Program the thermal cycler with a one-time incubation at 95°C for 11 min as the initial step before initiation of the thermal-cycling regime and increase the normal number of cycles by one round.
2. When preparing the reaction cocktail, add 2.5 U AmpliTaq Gold for 10 ng template. Add oil to tubes if the thermal cycler does not have a heated lid.
3. Place the capped tubes in the thermal cycler and initiate the pre-PCR heating step.

Adjusting the reaction components of the PCR

Defining the optimal magnesium ion concentration

In the following protocol, the samples are assayed in duplicate.

1. Obtain mixes of (a) the buffer without Mg^{2+}, (b) a dilution of Taq DNA polymerase, (c) $MgCl_2$, (d) dNTPs, and (e) primers.
2. On ice, make cocktails from these reagents for the optimization experiments, instead of pipeting each constituent in each individual reaction. This practice will save time and reduce variations that arise in pipetting concentrated solutions. Use molecular-biology-grade water (various suppliers) if there is no laboratory means of obtaining high-purity water lacking ions and organic substances.
3. Dispense 100 ng of two different DNA preparations (in water) in a total volume of 20 μL into the four PCR tubes on ice for each magnesium ion concentration (4 × 6 = 24 reactions). Keep all tubes capped except for the one you are working with in order to avoid crosscontamination. Immediately add 30 μL of the respective cocktail containing the buffer and other reaction components. The amount of DNA to choose depends on the sensitivity of your detection system.
4. Set the thermal cycler for 93°C, 3 min (once) and a three-step PCR format of 94°C, 30 s; T_m 30 s; 72°C, 30-20 s (30 cycles), followed by 60°C, 30 min; and then 15°C (hold).
5. Repeat the experiment at 4°C below and 8°C above the estimated T_m (24 × 3 = 72 reactions per complete experiment).

6. Plot the results and note where the plateau begins. Choose a Mg^{2+} concentration for your PCR near the middle of the plateau. If the yield does not level off (as might occur under rapid PCR conditions in capillaries), continue the experiment up to 4 mM Mg^{2+} concentration.

Adjusting the other reaction components of the PCR

1. Two components worth investigating in the optimization endeavor are the primer concentration and the optimal amount of Taq DNA polymerase. Perform the experiment with 0.1, 0.2, 0.5, and 0.8 μM primer (i.e., both primers are at these concentrations) with 1.25,5, and 10 U Taq DNA polymerase (12 reactions). If the primer is limiting, there will not be much effect from an increase in the amount of enzyme. Use that primer concentration at which there is a significant increase in yield when the enzyme concentration is higher. If stringency is required in the PCR, then cut back the primer concentration to the level at which no extraneous bands are detected.
2. Taq DNA polymerase is inactive in buffers of high KCl. To investigate the effect of KCl at the optimal Mg^{2+} concentration, run the PCR at 40, 50, 55, 60, and 70 mM concentrations.
3. Investigate the effect of pH on the system by increments of 0.2-pH unit from 8.1 to 8.9. Test at least ten DNA samples extracted by the same procedure.

Finding the Best Thermal Cycler Parameters

Establishing windows for T_{den}, T_{anneal}, and $T_{>ext}$

To establish the range, perform the thermal cycling with denaturation at 92, 93, 94, 95, and 96°C, keeping T_{anneal} constant. Perform the experiment with duplicate samples and use a 1 min duration at T_{den}. When the optimal T_{den} is established, investigate the variation around the $T_{optimum}$ for annealing in the same way (i.e., with 0.5°C increments). The temperature of the extension step, T_{ext}, can be examined too, but it does not affect the results as critically as T_{den} and T_{anneal}. Repeat the testing at a duration of 30 s for T_{den}.

Adjusting ramping times for stringency and degeneracy

To test the effect of ramp-down time on the yield and stringency, examine 60-, 80-, 100-, 120-, and 160-s time intervals from T_{den} to T_{anneal}. Keep the default settings for the time intervals between T_{anneal} and T_{anneal} and T_{ext} and T_{ext} and T_{den}, and do not change T_{den}, T_{anneal}, and T_{ext}.

Primers and Remedies for Amplifying Regions of High GC Content

1. Extend the primer at a temperature high enough to reduce or eliminate the template GC hybridization. Design high-melting primers with T_m values between 70 and 74°C and use them with a combined annealing and extension step between 70 and 80°C as a two-step PCR to amplify regions of > 70% GC.
2. Partially replace the dG with either 7-deaza-2'-deoxy-guanosine: try 150 μM 7-deaza-dGTP with 50 μM dGTP for long stretches of G/C nucleotides. Deoxyinosine has also been used with dGTP for amplifying recalcitrant GC-rich templates.
3. Employ an additive in the PCR, such as formamide (up to 5%) or DMSO, to reduce the melting temperature of the GC-rich regions. Test the effect of 2, 5, 10, and 15% DMSO and try the PCR at a T_{anneal} 5, 10, 15, and 20°C lower than that used without the additive. The DMSO should be the purest available and should be reserved for molecular-biology work only.
4. Perform the PCR at the highest T_{den} possible. Use a short time at very high T_{den}; only a few seconds are needed. Addition of glycerol to the PCR buffer (up to 20%) may help stabilize the Taq DNA polymerase at high temperatures and improve the yield. Use a DNA polymerase such as UlTma or Vent(exo-) that has a higher thermal stability than Taq, which has a half-life of only 10 min at 97.5°C. Be aware that the hyperthermostable DNA polymerases may have an intrinsic 3' to -5' exonuclease activity, which can shorten the primers from the 3' end.

Guidelines for Prevention of Contamination

1. Establish a separate room for template preparation and PCR setup if the laboratory budget permits. If a separate room is impossible, then devote a "*clean*" space in the laboratory for these two functions that is far removed from the bench where the thermal cycler is located and where amplicons are to be handled for analysis.
2. Purchase a set of pipetters for the clean-work area and leave them there. Use either positive-displacement pipeters (various suppliers) that work with a disposable barrel and plunger, or use standard pipetters with aerosol-resistant tips. The object is to prevent template deposited in the pipetter via aerosols from the first sample from being injected into the second sample.
3. Work with one glove instead of two. Use the gloved hand to handle tubes with reagents and samples and the other hand to handle the

pipeter, fixtures (i.e., door knobs, faucets, drawer pulls), utensils, and appliances. If the equipment becomes contaminated with template or amplicons, it will not be transferred to the reagents and samples so easily, since the gloved hand is used for these tubes. Change gloves often, since they can become contaminated too. The object of using gloves is not to protect your hands, but rather to control contamination.

4. Run a reagent-only control (i.e., template blank) in each PCR in order to detect contamination as early as possible. If a work area becomes contaminated with amplicons due to poor laboratory practice, it is important to discover the problem before it gets out of hand.
5. Dispense stock reagents and control template solutions in small portions into "one-use" tubes, and discard material not used in setting-up the PCR. This practice is time-consuming, but it will prevent contamination of the stock solutions.
6. Pulse-spin tubes containing reagents and template before opening them to control for aerosols. This operation should be performed outside of the clean area in order to avoid aerosols associated with centrifugation.
7. If many samples are to be treated, open only one tube at a time, keeping the other tubes capped (i.e., closed) when not in immediate use.
8. Dispose of solutions of amplicons and used gel-electrophoresis buffers with caution. Amplicon-containing liquids can almost be considered hazardous materials!
9. Clean the work areas and pipetter barrels with a weak solution of bleach on a regular basis, which is determined by the usage.

Notes

1. Zabeau, M. and Vos, P. (1993) European Patent Application, pub. no. EP 0534858.
2. A discussion of salt effects on the T_m can be found. Another factor of importance for the PCR is the dependency of the T_m on the concentration of the primer. Primers are in a high concentration under the conditions of the PCR and do not change significantly during the PCR.
3. On a few occasions, HPLC-purified primers have been reported to yield "*ladder*" bands in the PCR of tetranucleotide repeats. In one case, this gross stuttering could be traced to an inhibitor of

Taq that passed through the laboratory water-filtration unit. Commercially available purified, sterile water may be the best choice for a primer stock solution.

4. Suppose the upper primer (A_5 C_5 G_4 T_4, n = 18 nt) was obtained as a dry pellet from a core facility, and the amount was reported to be 3.2 OD units. It was resuspended in 0.5 mL molecular-biology-grade water with 20 mM Tris-HCl, pH 8.0, and 50 mM NaCl; 50 μL of the stock was diluted in 1 mL of the same for measuring the absorbance at 260 nm. An optical density of 0.26 was obtained. This is lower than expected, and the concentration of the stock is 27 μM instead of 33 μM. One may obtain the molar concentration of the stock solution: When the primer has one fluorescein or rhodamine derivative attached, one should add 26,662 to the denominator.
5. There are many speculations on the origin of stutter bands, but there is no proof. A currently popular idea is that stutter is thought to occur during pausing of the DNA polymerase because of the incorporation of a wrong nucleotide, the difficulty of extending the primer through a region of substantial single-stranded secondary structure, or encountering a region of the template that is not fully dissociated. After pausing, the polymerase could dissociate from the template, although there is experimental evidence against such a scenario. The polymerization enzyme-template complex could become destabilized during the pause and enter into a secondary state that has a lower binding constant for the polymerase and the template and allows the less tightly bound strand to partially dissociate from the active site. When the strand rejoins, it may do so one repeat out of register (or by an integral multiple of repeats). This event would lead to a loss of a repeat (or a multiple of repeats) in primer extension if the template loops out. The mechanism is similar to slipped-strand mispairing, and it has been suggested to be a likely cause of stutter bands. We have found that stutter is not reduced when UlTma DNA polymerase, which has an inherent 3' to 5' exonuclease activity, is substituted for Taq DNA polymerase. This result appears to be inconsistent with the idea that stutter occurs when the polymerase is paused as a result of misincorporated nucleotides, because the 3' exonuclease activity should quickly correct such a situation. We also observed no reliable decrease in stutter band formation as a result of experiments with additives such as DMSO and formamide (i.e., denaturants that should melt regions of single-stranded secondary

structure). Until the biochemical understanding of the PCR is available, predictions on the cause of stuttering will remain intuitive.

6. For example, in one paper, five different methods of pathogen DNA-sample preparation are compared, and the template isolation is presented as an important pre-PCR step.
7. A number of methods were examined for removal of inhibitory substances from a stubborn substrate, and a chromatographic cellulose purification step proved to be a simple way to obtain amplifiable template at low copy number.
8. A rapid method for removal of inhibitors of the PCR from urine involved the use of either polyethylene glycol precipitation or glass-powder extraction.
9. Pathogens can be purified even from sewage for examination by the PCR.
10. CTAB: hexadecyltrimethyl ammonium bromide.
11. Axenically grown plants will obviate the need for this precaution, if they are available.
12. Before screening a F2 population with a given primer, the PCR was repeated at least twice on different days and with the two DNA concentrations. If the polymorphic band still appeared (i.e., if it were consistently present), a test sample of DNA from the F2 generation was used to assess whether or not the marker segre gated in a Mendelian fashion.
13. Depending upon the inherent level of polymorphism in the cross and the degree of marker saturation required, the researcher must decide whether to invest extra effort. The barley lines we examined had been back-crossed for seventeen generations, and the level of polymorphism was extremely low. Out of 1600 10-mer primers screened, only ten gave reproducible polymorphisms, and of those only half were detectable in a native gel system.
14. Primer dimers and mispriming are often observed in DNA analysis by multiplex PCR, long-range PCR, and when the target is at low copy number and in the presence of a high amount of non-target DNA, to mention a few cases. A good example of the latter situation is HIV-1 DNA (or cDNA) analysis from whole blood samples. Also, in forensics, the human-target template may be contaminated with an excess of bacterial DNA. Mispriming can occur to single-stranded DNA present in the preparation. It is not unusual to have single-stranded DNA if one uses a heat

denaturation step during the template-preparation procedure. An example is heat denaturation of protease K. Chelex extraction utilizes a boiling step and leads to single-stranded DNA.

15. We suggest that before one invests a lot of time running a battery of tests, a control template should be assayed in duplicate. Use the kit components to run the PCR under the standard conditions of 1.5 mM Mg^{2+}, 50 mM KC1, and at a concentration of 0.2 mM each dNTP and 0.2 μM of each primer.
16. Panhandles: The 10-mers used as RAPD primers can anneal at the ends. They are as complementary as the primers and compete, so they are inefficiently amplified.
17. The PCR was performed in the GeneAmp PCR System 9600 thermal cycler with 100 ng DNA.
18. Spinning 200 μL in a microcentrifuge at 500g. Ten minutes is sufficient.
19. A good standard is salmon sperm DNA from Gibco-BRL supplied at a concentration of 10 mg/mL.
20. The Taq DNA polymerase should be diluted to 1 U/μL in order to avoid errors in pipetting viscous solutions. The enzyme may be diluted in 1X PCR buffer without Mg^{2+} if it is to be used immediately.
21. Make a solution containing each primer at a concentration of 5 μM. One may wish to screen primers for a number of loci by coamplification. Choose primers of similar T_m, ones that will yield amplicons in discrete size ranges, so they do not overlap. Check via computer or visually that the chosen primers will not anneal to each other, especially at the 3'-end.
22. Some precaution may be necessary, since the detection of 7-deazaguanine-containing PCR products with ethidium bromide is more difficult: The fluorescence is less with these duplex DNAs. There is no reduction in the signal when deoxyinosine is used.

8

GENOTOXICITY

Phenols are ubiquitous substances that exert a broad spectrum of biological activities. Vitamin E and naturally occurring polyphenols in fruits and vegetables are known for their antioxidant activity through scavenging *reactive oxygen species* (ROS). This property is thought to be beneficial to human health and contribute to the protection against cardiovascular disease and cancer. However, other phenols may display deleterious prooxidant activities and generate ROS that contribute to aging and disease. There is increasing evidence that the prooxidant properties of phenols proceed through a radical pathway initiated by phenoxyl radical formation, and the development of antioxidants for clinical use includes strategies to minimize prooxidant activity. Bioactivation of certain phenols, including hydroquinones and catechols, can also generate benzoquinone and quinone methide electrophiles that are Michael acceptors and react covalently with proteins and nucleic acids. Covalent reactions of these electrophiles with nucleic acids to generate DNA adducts may initiate mutagenesis and carcinogenicity.

Efforts have been made to categorize phenol toxicity using *quantitative structure activity relationships* (QSAR). Phenols that act as oxidative uncouplers inhibit oxidative phosphorylation in mitochondria by inhibition of mitochondrial ATP production. Phenols in this category include hydrophobic, electron-deficient phenols with weakly acidic phenolic groups (pKa 3.8–8.5). Electron-withdrawing substituents also increase phenol electrophilicity that may lead to a covalent interaction with proteins and nucleic acids. This electrophilic mode of toxic action can also take place after initial biotransformation, in which case the phenols are classified as proelectrophiles. Another mode of toxic action by phenols in aquatic organisms is polar narcosis, which is a membrane irritation caused by noncovalent interactions of phenol accumulation in lipid tissue. Phenols that are good hydrogen bond donors tend to act as polar narcotics. In view of the various types of interactions that may occur between phenols and membranes, proteins, and nucleic acids, the toxicity of a given phenol is likely caused by the superposition of effects from different mechanisms. This has made it difficult to equate a certain mode of action with the overall hazardous effect of phenols in biological systems.

Chlorophenols and Ochratoxin A

Within the family of phenolic toxins, man-made chlorophenols (CPs) along with the natural chlorophenol mycotoxin *ochratoxin A* (OTA) have attracted considerable interest. Man-made CPs are widely distributed in the environment due to their agricultural and industrial uses as insecticides, herbicides, fungicides, and wood preservatives. The US Environmental Protection Agency (EPA) has designated 11 phenolic compounds as major priority pollutants and four CPs (e.g., 2-CP, 2,4-DCP, 2,4,6-TCP, and pentachlorophenol (PCP)) are classified into the most toxic and carcinogenic class. The fungal toxin OTA is a potent renal carcinogen in rodents and has been implicated in human kidney and testicular carcinogenesis. OTA contaminates a wide range of human and animal foodstuffs making total avoidance of OTA consumption practically impossible. Thus, the ubiquitous nature of these substances coupled with their carcinogenicity in animal models has raised public awareness of the potential health risks posed by CPs and OTA.

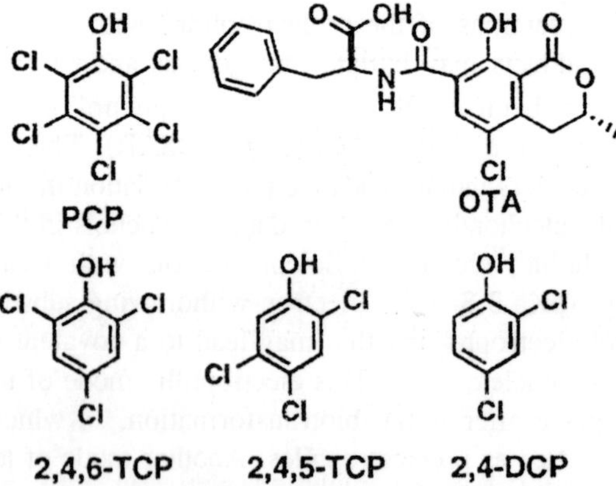

Fig. 8.1. Chemical structures of CPs and OTA.

For simple CPs, it is known that toxicity depends on the number and position of chlorine substitutions. Some CPs such as PCP, are regarded as classic examples of oxidative uncoupling agents due to their hydrophobic and weakly acidic nature. OTA is also known to inhibit mitochondrial ATP production. However, both OTA and PCP are classified as Group 2B (possible carcinogenic to humans) by the International Agency for Research on Cancer (IARC) and one hypothesis for their carcinogenicity is based on their genotoxic properties following metabolic activation. PCP is known to undergo bioactivation by cytochrome P450 (CYP450) enzymes to generate benzoquinone electrophiles through oxidative dechlorination pathways. The resulting quinone electrophiles are known to react covalently with DNA to form DNA adducts. On the basis of the ^{32}P-postlabeling assay, OTA has also been shown to form DNA adducts in vivo. However, mutagenicity assays for OTA and CPs have not provided definitive answers. The direct genotoxicity of OTA is also a hotly debated topic, as some laboratories have been unable to detect OTA-mediated DNA adducts following in vitro and in vivo studies. The goals of this review are to present the currently available information and opinions on CP- and OTA-mediated genotoxicity and outline opportunities for future research that should help elucidate the mechanisms of CP and OTA carcinogenicity, which is critical in assessing human health risk and determining tolerable levels of dietary intake.

CHLOROPHENOLS

Production and Properties of Chlorophenols

CPs are toxic chemicals that are persistent in the environment. They have found wide use in pesticides, disinfectants, wood preservatives, personal care formulations, and are substantial by-products of wood pulp bleaching with chlorine. PCP has been produced and used in the largest quantities. Annual production of PCP all over the world was estimated to be 25,000–90,000 tons at its peak. Today, PCP is still used to protect timber from fungal rot and wood-boring insects. PCP concentrations in groundwater can be 3–23 μg/L in wood-treatment areas and concentrations in milligram per liter can be found near industrial discharges. The general population is exposed to PCP through the ingestion of water (0.01–0.1 μg/L), food (up to 405 μg/L), and through inhalation of indoor air where concentrations up to 25 μg/m^3 have been found.

CP toxicity and bioaccumulation increases with the degree of chlorine substitution. The pKa values of CPs decrease with the number of chlorine substitutions. Ortho CPs (2-CP) are more acidic than other isomers because of the large inductive effect of chlorine on the hydroxyl group in close proximity. Increased chlorine substitution also increases the octanol–water partition coefficient (K_{ow}), which is positively correlated to the bioaccumulation potential of CPs. Thus, PCP with the largest K_{ow} value is the most hydrophobic CP, which allows it to diffuse through cellular membranes. At pH 12, standard reduction potentials (E^{o}_{red}) for the phenoxyl radical/ phenolate ion couples are similar for the CPs showing a range of 0.85–0.99 V vs. the normal hydrogen electrode (NHE). At pH > pKa, E^{o}_{red} tends to increase with increased chlorination. However, at pH < pKa, E^{o}_{red} increases with increasing acidity. Thus, at physiological pH 7, PhOH has an E^{o}_{red} value ~1.03 V, which is higher than E^{o}_{red} for PCP at pH 7 (0.99 V), because PCP remains deprotonated at physiological pH. Thus, highly substituted acidic CPs undergo oxidation into the phenoxyl radical readily at physiological pH, because the oxidation step involves the concerted loss of an electron and a proton and these CPs exist as the phenolate.

In terms of radical stabilization through resonance, it has been observed that remote substituent effects of phenoxyl radicals exhibit a linear correlation with Brown σ^+ constants, because of the through-resonance between the electron-deficient phenoxyl radical and the ring substituent. A high value of σ^+ suggests that the radical is localized on the oxygen atom and for the mono-substituted analogs, a chlorine substituent in the *meta* position (3-CP) has a higher σ^+ value (0.40) than the other isomers. The fully substituted analog PCP has the highest σ^+ value (1.1) followed by 2,4,5-TCP > 3-CP > 2,4,6-TCP > 2,4-DCP > 4-CP > 2-CP.

Carcinogenesis of Chlorophenols

Case reports suggest an association between CPs and Hodgkin's disease, soft-tissue sarcoma, and acute leukemia. Carcinogenicity of orally administered PCP has been tested in rats and mice. The purity of PCP is an important factor, since PCP is usually contaminated with chlorinated dibenzo-p-dioxins, some of which are animal carcinogens. The National Toxicology Program (NTP) tested technical-grade PCP (90% pure PCP) in mice. Groups of male and female B6C3F1 mice were given diets that contained 0, 100, or 200 ppm PCP. Male mice displayed a significant increase over the male control incidence in tumors of the adrenal medulla and liver (adenomas and carcinomas combined). Treated females displayed a significant increase over female controls with regard to the incidence of hemangiosarcomas of the spleen and liver. Although this study was limited because of the unusually low survival in the male control group, the occurrence of rare hemangiosarcomas was considered a carcinogenic response due to PCP exposure.

NTP also tested pure PCP (~99%) for carcinogenicity in rats. Groups of male and female F344 rats were given diets that contained 0, 200, 400, or 600 ppm PCP for 105 days. In 2 years, some evidence that purified PCP is carcinogenic to rats was detected with malignant mesotheliomas and nasal squamous cell carcinomas being noted in some of the rats being treated with high dose regimes that actually exceed the maximum tolerable dose. However, unlike the study with mice, hepatocellular adenomas and carcinomas were not detected. Overall, these choric animal bioassays suggested that the liver is a target organ for carcinogenesis in mice, but not in the rat. On the basis of the NTP studies on PCP carcinogenesis, EPA has classified PCP as a Group B2 substance (probable human carcinogen). A cancer potency factor of 0.12 mg/kg/day was calculated by the Integrated Risk Information Systems (IRIS) based on the NTP data, which translates to an upper-bound unit risk level of 9×10^{-3} mg/kg/day for a cancer risk of 1 in 1000.

Metabolism of Chlorophenols

Results from animal and human studies indicate that PCP is not completely metabolized, as evidenced by a large portion of the administered dose being excreted in urine unchanged in all species studied. Approximately 74% of PCP ingested by humans is eliminated in urine as PCP, while fecal elimination accounts for only 4%. Metabolism of PCP does occur in the liver, and the major pathways involve conjugation to form the glucuronide and oxidative dechlorination

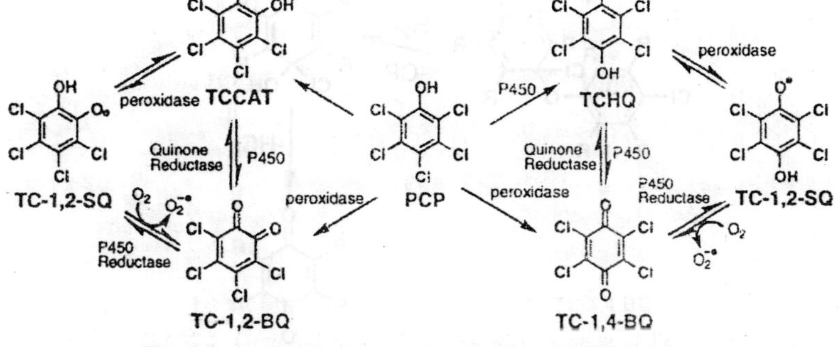

Fig. 8.2. Proposed pathways for the bioactivation of PCP.

to generate hydroquinone, catechol, and benzoquinone metabolites. Two distinct pathways have been proposed for conversion of PCP into its benzoquinone metabolites. One involves CYP450-mediated dechlorination of PCP to produce tetrachlorohydroquinone (TCHQ) and tetrachlorocatechol (TCCAT), which are subsequently oxidized to the corresponding quinones, tetrachloro-1,4-benzoquinone (TC-1,4-BQ) and tetrachloro-1,2-benzoquinone (TC-1,2-BQ).

The second pathway involves direct CYP450-mediated oxidation of PCP (accompanied by loss of chlorine anion) to the TC-1,4-BQ metabolite without the obligatory intermediacy of the hydroquinones which are generated from reduction of the benzoquinone. Consistent with the pathways 2,4,6-TCP has been shown to undergo oxidation by Aroclor 1254-induced rat liver microsomes to yield 2,6-dichloro-1,4-benzoquinone (2,6-DC-1,4-BQ).

Horseradish peroxidase (HRP)/H_2O_2 also catalyzes the oxidation of PCP and 2,4,6-TCP into their respective 1,4-BQ metabolites. However, unlike metabolism of CPs by CYP450 enzymes, phenoxyl radical intermediates are generated. As outlined in Scheme for HRP/H_2O_2 oxidation of PCP, the TC-1,4-BQ product may arise by elimination of HCl from a gem-chlorohydrin intermediate that would form through HRP oxidation of the phenoxyl radical to yield a carbocation

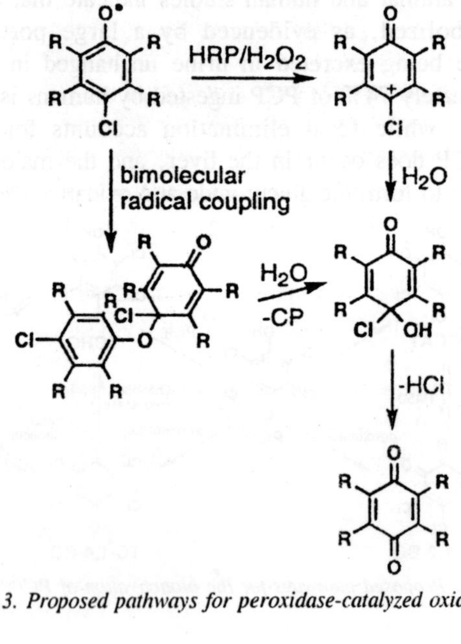

Fig. 8.3. Proposed pathways for peroxidase-catalyzed oxidation of CP.

intermediate that reacts with water. Alternatively, the gem-chlorohydrin could arise by hydrolysis of the ether 2,3,4,5,6-pentachloro-4-pentachlorophenoxy-2,5-cyclohexadienone formed by pentachlorophenoxyl radical coupling. Kazunga and co-workers presented evidence that the final TC-1,4-BQ product is in fact an artifact of extraction and analytical methods and that the principal product is the ether 2,3,4,5,6-pentachloro-4-pentachlorophenoxy-2,5-cyclohexadienone formed by pentachlorophenoxyl radical coupling. This suggests a common mechanism for HRP/H_2O_2-mediated oxidation of a CP involving bimolecular radical coupling for 1,4-BQ formation. This is a potential *in vivo* metabolic step that could be catalyzed by mammalian peroxidases, including prostaglandin H synthase, myeloperoxidase (MPO), salivary peroxidase, lactoperoxidase, or uterine peroxidase.

Zhu and co-workers have shown that the TCHQ metabolite of PCP is also capable of reacting with H_2O_2 to yield the hydroxyl radical ($HO^{\bullet}$) in a metal-independent organic Fenton reaction. From an electron spin resonance (ESR) spin-trapping study, it was concluded that the semiquinone anion radical ($TCSQ^{\bullet -}$) directly reacts with H_2O_2 and reduces it to $HO^{\bullet}$ with concomitant formation of TC-1,4-BQ. This type of reaction has been proposed previously by Koppenol and Butler, who suggested that if a quinone/semiquinone couple has a one-electron reduction potential between –330 and +460 mV vs. NHE, it can theoretically bring about a Fenton reaction that is thermodynamically feasible and does not require a metal ion for catalysis. Structure-activity relationships demonstrated that 2-chloro-, 2,5-dichloro-, tetrafluoro-, tetrabromo-, and TC-1,4-BQ were capable of generating $HO^{\bullet}$ from H_2O_2. In contrast, no $HO^{\bullet}$ formation could be detected from reactions of H_2O_2 with BQ itself, 2,6-dimethyl-, and tetramethyl-1,4-BQ, which possess reduction potentials outside the range stipulated by Koppenol and Butler.

An assay developed by the Rappaport laboratory has been used to simultaneously quantitate protein adducts of quinones and semiquinones following PCP administration to rats and mice. These efforts have shown that the benzoquinone metabolite (TC-1,4-BQ) of PCP is a Michael acceptor and forms adducts with cysteinyl residues (CySH) of proteins both *in vitro* and *in vivo*. As shown in Scheme, TC-1,4-BQ retains its oxidized quinone structure following covalent attachment of CySH with chloride displacement. The product (monoadduct) continues to react with additional sulfhydryls leading to disubstituted and trisubstituted adducts. The assay employs Raney nickel to selectively cleave the cysteinyl adducts, which generates quinones or tetrachlorophenols from semiquinone-derived adducts; the latter products were only detected *in vivo*. Thus, this assay can be used to measure the extent of quinone vs. semiquinone adduct formation during the metabolism of PCP. In this regard, administration of a single oral dose of PCP to Sprague–Dawley rats and B6C3F_1 mice generated proportionally greater amounts of TC-1,2-SQ adducts in the livers of the rodents at low doses of PCP (<4–10 mg/kg body weight) that was 40-fold greater in rats than mice. Production of TC-1,4-BQ adducts was proportionally greater at high doses of PCP (>60–230 mg/kg body weight) and was 2- to 11-fold greater in mice than in rats over the entire range of doses. These results suggested that species differences in the metabolism of PCP to semiquinones and quinones were, in part, responsible for the production of liver tumors in mice but not in rats.

TC-1,4-BQ also undergoes displacement of chloride by hydroxide in strong alkaline solution to yield chloranilic acid (2,5-dichloro-3,6-dihydroxy-1,4-BQ) through initial formation of trichlorohydroxyquinone. It also reacts directly with H_2O_2 in a pH-dependent manner with chloride displacement. On the basis of this reactivity, Zhu et al. have speculated that the O–O bond of such a hydroperoxide adduct would undergo homolytic fission to yield HO$^{\bullet}$ and a resonance-stabilized phenoxyl-like radical. Such a pathway could contribute to HO$^{\bullet}$ production by TC-1,4-BQ/H_2O_2 in the absence of redox-active transition metals, suggesting that peroxide-dependent decomposition pathways of TC-1,4-BQ may be important in biological systems where peroxide is either used or produced, as in the peroxidase-catalyzed oxidation of PCP.

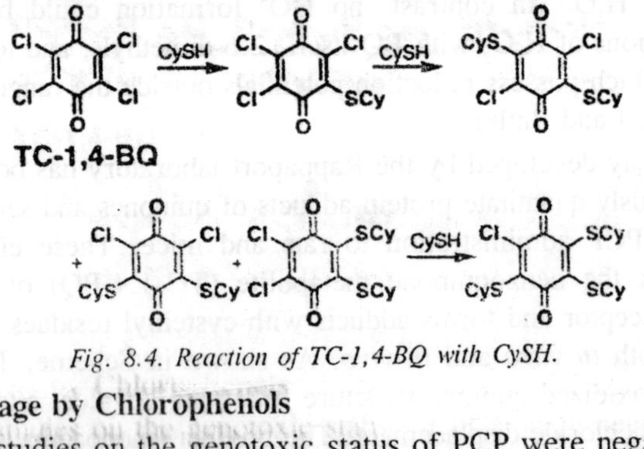

TC-1,4-BQ

CySH

CySH

Fig. 8.4. Reaction of TC-1,4-BQ with CySH.

DNA Damage by Chlorophenols

Early studies on the genotoxic status of PCP were negative. The toxin is non-mutagenic in the Ames test, it did not induce DNA damage in Chinese hamster ovary (CHO) cells, and occupational exposure to

PCP did not induce sister chromatid exchange or chromosomal breakage. In contrast, the genotoxicity of TCHQ has been well established. TCHQ undergoes autoxidation to form superoxide radical anion ($O_2^{\bullet -}$) and subsequently H_2O_2, which is activated by transition metals to cause oxidative DNA damage. TCHQ was found to induce single-stranded breaks in isolated DNA, in human fibroblasts, V79 cells, CHO cells, and the liver of mice. TCHQ also induced micronuclei and mutations at the hypoxanthine–guanine phosphoribosyltransferase (HPRT) locus of V79 cells and cause formation of 8oxo-dG in V79 cells and B6C3F$_1$ mice. Glutathione depletion, p53 protein accumulation, and cellular transformation were also observed in mice treated with TCHQ. Because TCHQ is a major metabolite of PCP and can stimulate oxidative stress, TCHQ is thought to play a key role in PCP-mediated carcinogenicity.

While one notion suggests that TCHQ induces genotoxicity by initiating a flux of ROS that promotes oxidative DNA damage and oxidative stress, the Witte laboratory has examined the genotoxicity of TCHQ and has concluded that its autoxidation intermediate, the semiquinone anion radical (TCSQ$^{\bullet -}$), is responsible for the observed cytoand genotoxicity of TCHQ. This conclusion was based on the demonstrated ability of desferrioxamine (DFO) to inhibit TCHQ-induced single-strand breaks in isolated DNA by its efficient scavenging of TCSQ$^{\bullet -}$. Extension of these experiments to human fibroblasts showed that DFO provided marked protection against TCHQ-induced genotoxicity, while the HO$^{\bullet}$ scavenger dimethyl sulfoxide (DMSO) was ineffective. UV–visible spectroscopic experiments showed that 50 μM TCHQ readily autoxidizes at physiological pH to generate TCSQ – with λ_{max} at 455 nm and an ESR signal at g = 2.0056. The visible absorption for TCSQ$^{\bullet -}$ reaches maximum intensity at about 10 min and then it is gradually replaced by an absorbance at 292 nm for TCBQ, and finally (several hours) a peak at 332 nm for chloroanilic acid. In the presence of DFO, or other hydroxamic acids, the maximal concentration and life span of the signal for TCSQ$^{\bullet -}$ was markedly reduced, while the signal for chloroanilic acid at 332 nm was markedly enhanced with 90% conversion of TCHQ into chloroanilic acid following 30 min reaction time. Comparison of the genotoxicity of TCHQ to H_2O_2 in human fibroblasts also revealed a greater genotoxic potential for TCHQ than for H_2O_2. DNA damage was determined after 1 h treatment with H_2O_2 or TCHQ by the comet assay. Here, a distinct tail moment was noted for TCHQ at concentrations < 10 μM, whereas 60 μM H_2O_2 was required to produce the same extent of DNA damage.

By monitoring the incorporation of [^{3}H]-thymidine into DNA of non-replicating cells (UDS), the extent of DNA repair was measured and 25 μM TCHQ was found to inhibit repair, while H_2O_2 continuously induced DNA repair up to 60 μM. In contrast to H_2O_2, TCHQ was also mutagenic in the HPRT locus of V79 cells with a mutant frequency of 75 and 151 mutants per 10^6 clonable cells at non-toxic concentrations of 5 and 7 μM. Witte and coworkers suggested that the $TCSQ^{\bullet-}$ may react with DNA directly and cause apurinic/apyrimidinic (AP) sites which are transformed to strand breaks either by endonucleases or under the alkaline conditions of the comet assay. This would explain the ineffectiveness of DMSO to quench TCHQ-induced damage in cellular DNA. However, an alternative explanation may stem from TCHQ-induced $HO^{\bullet}$ production by a metal-independent process that takes place close to the DNA surface, precluding effective $HO^{\bullet}$ scavenging by DMSO. That TCHQ also inhibits DNA repair enzymes would provide a rationale for its potent genotoxicity and mutagenicity. In contrast, DNA damage by H_2O_2 would require metal ions for catalysis and DNA repair enzymes are not inhibited by H_2O_2.

While little is known about direct interactions of $TCSQ^{\bullet-}$ with DNA, the fully oxidized TC-1,4-BQ metabolite of PCP is known to react covalently with DNA to generate DNA adducts, as evidenced by the ^{32}P-postlabeling assay. Treatment of calf thymus DNA with 5 mM TC-1,4-BQ generated four major and several minor adducts (3.5 adducts per 10^5 total nucleotides). These adducts were chemically stable and do not generate AP sites. In addition, increases in 8oxo-dG and AP sites were observed that were ascribed to oxidative damage. These results demonstrated that PCP quinone and hydroquinone metabolites induce direct and oxidative base modifications as well as the formation of 5´-cleaved AP sites in genomic DNA.

Cell culture and *in vivo* studies have now shown that PCP itself shows direct genotoxicity under certain conditions. Treatment of rat hepatocytes with a single dose of PCP (50 μM) generated 17 adducts per 10^9 total nucleotides. Chronic (60 mg/kg/day for 27 weeks), but not acute (60 mg/kg/day for 1 or 5 days), exposure of rat to PCP induced a twofold increase in 8oxo-dG (1.8 vs. 0.91 $\times 10^{-6}$ in controls) and generated two major adducts, one derived from TC-1,4-BQ, with relative ^{32}P-postlabeling of 0.78 adducts per 10^7 total nucleotides. The TC-1,4-BQ-derived DNA adduct was also detected in mouse liver DNA following exposure to PCP at 8 adducts per 10^7 nucleotides which is 10-fold greater compared with the rat.

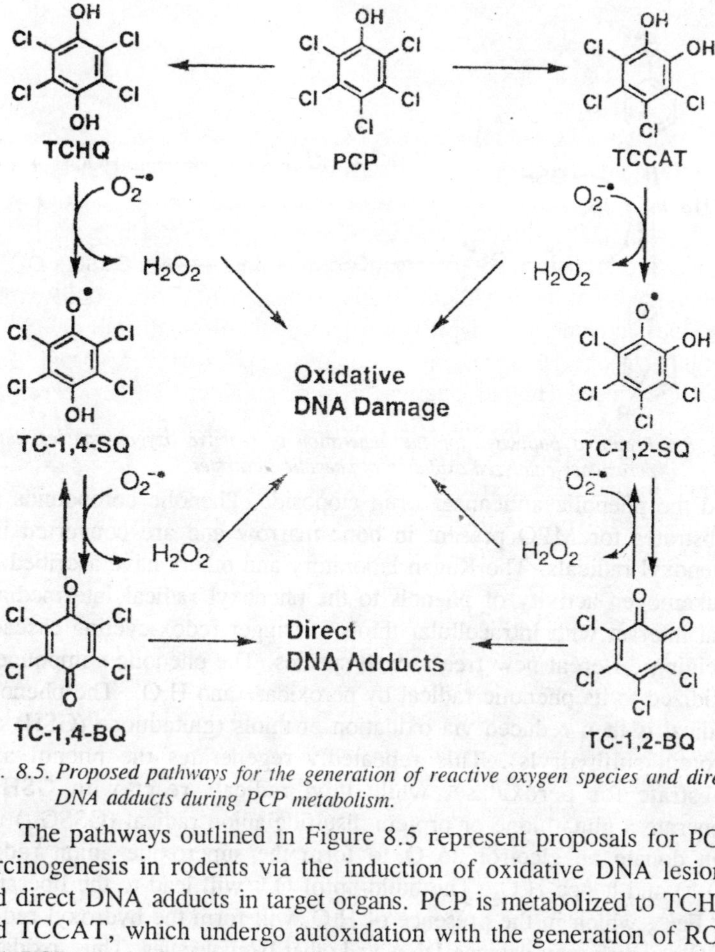

OH Cl Cl Cl Cl OH TCHQ
OH Cl Cl Cl Cl Cl PCP
OH Cl OH Cl Cl Cl TCCAT
$O_2^{-\bullet}$ H_2O_2
TC-1,4-SQ
TC-1,2-SQ
Oxidative DNA Damage
TC-1,4-BQ
TC-1,2-BQ
Direct DNA Adducts

Fig. 8.5. Proposed pathways for the generation of reactive oxygen species and direct DNA adducts during PCP metabolism.

The pathways outlined in Figure 8.5 represent proposals for PCP carcinogenesis in rodents via the induction of oxidative DNA lesions and direct DNA adducts in target organs. PCP is metabolized to TCHQ and TCCAT, which undergo autoxidation with the generation of ROS and PCP semiquinone and quinone metabolites that cause oxidative DNA damage and direct DNA adducts, respectively. The Swenberg laboratory suggested that the pathways in fig. 8.5 might provide a rationale for PCP-mediated hepatic carcinogenesis in mouse. The greater amounts of both oxidative and direct DNA damage, together with increased hepatotoxicity and cell proliferation, may provide the critical events necessary for hepatic carcinogenesis in the mouse. In contrast, the decreased amount of DNA damage and the lack of hepatotoxicity and cell proliferation in the rat do not result in such critical changes.

The association of CPs to incidences of leukemia is also consistent with the leukemogen activity of phenolic xenobiotics including phenol

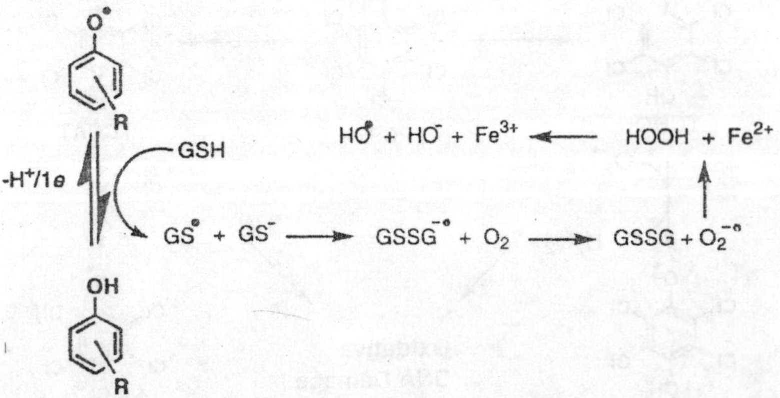

Fig. 8.6. *Proposed pathways for the generation of reactive oxygen species during peroxidase-catalyzed oxidation of phenolic substrates.*

and the phenolic anticancer drug etoposide. Phenolic compounds are substrates for MPO present in bone marrow and are converted into phenoxyl radicals. The Kagan laboratory and others have ascribed the leukemogen activity of phenols to the phenoxyl radical intermediates that interact with intracellular thiols to trigger redox-cycling cascades yielding different new free radical species. The phenolic compound is oxidized to its phenolic radical by peroxidase and H_2O_2. The phenoxyl radical is then reduced via oxidation of thiols (glutathione (GSH) and protein sulfhydryls). This repeatedly regenerates the phenol as a substrate for peroxidase, while thiyl radicals react with GSH to generate a glutathione or protein disulfide anion radical ($GSSG^{\bullet -}$) that can donate an electron to O_2 to form the superoxide anion radical ($O_2^{\bullet -}$) and hence H_2O_2. The build-up of $O_2^{\bullet -}$ will lead to the liberation of Fe^{2+}, which in the presence of H_2O_2 will form the hydroxyl radical ($HO^{\bullet}$), which may damage DNA and other biomolecules. Thus, oxidative stress is induced and oxidative modifications of proteins as well as oxidative and mutagenic modifications of DNA occur, ultimately leading potentially to carcinogenesis. Direct reactions of phenoxyl radicals and thiyl radicals with biomolecules could also contribute to peroxidase-driven toxic effects of phenolic xenobiotics.

With regard to direct reactions of phenoxyl radicals with DNA, an *in vitro* study by the Turesky laboratory demonstrated that adduct levels ($36 \pm 9/10^5$ nucleotides) by 100 μM PCP following activation by HRP/H_2O_2 are 30-fold higher than levels induced by microsomes that contain CYP450 and 10-fold higher than levels induced by 5 mM TC-1,4-BQ itself. This suggested the possibility that the pentachlorophenoxyl

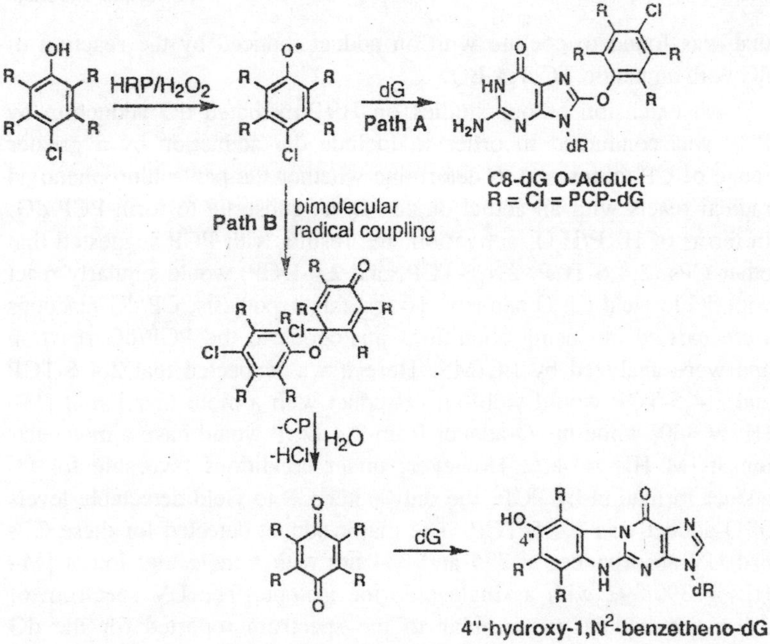

Fig. 8.7. Summary of peroxidase-mediated reactions of a CP with dG.

radical generated by HRP/H_2O_2 oxidation of PCP contributes to DNA adduction. Thus, we examined the reaction of PCP (100 μM) with DNA nucleosides (2 mM) using HRP/H_2O_2 as oxidation catalyst and liquid chromatography/mass spectrometry (LC/MS). Interestingly, these conditions yielded a single DNA adduct that had the five-chlorine isotope pattern of PCP and had a molecular ion at $[M-H]^- = 528$, suggesting attachment of dG with loss of two protons (i.e., PCP(264)+dG(267) - 2H = 529). Isolation and nuclear magnetic resonance (NMR) (^1H and ^{13}C) analysis confirmed C8 attachment by the O-site of PCP to yield the adduct PCP-dG.

Additional experiments were carried out to determine whether PCPdG could be formed by additional enzyme systems, and whether other DNA bases could react with PCP following HRP/H_2O_2 activation. These experiments showed the reaction to be absolutely specific for dG; no detectable adduct(s) was observed from HRP/H_2O_2 and PCP in the presence of dA, dC, or T. It was also found that PCP-dG could be generated by the treatment of PCP/dG with MPO. However, treatment of PCP/dG with rat liver microsomes that contain CYP450 failed to yield PCP-dG and instead an adduct with $[M-H]^- = 440$ was detected that was found to coelute with an adduct induced by the reaction of dG with authentic TC-1,4-BQ.

An extension of our studies on HRP-mediated dG adduction by PCP was conducted in order to include dG adduction by a greater range of CP toxins and to determine whether the pentachlorophenoxyl radical reacts with an actual duplex DNA substrate to form PCP-dG. In terms of HRP/H_2O_2 activation, the results with PCP suggested that other CPs (2,4,6-TCP, 2,4,5-TCP, and 2,4-DCP) would similarly react with dG to yield C8 O-adducts. To test this hypothesis, CP/dG reactions were carried out using conditions analogous to the PCP/dG reaction and were analyzed by LC/MS. Here it was expected that 2,4,6-TCP and 2,4,5-TCP would yield an O-adduct with a molecular ion at $[M-H]^- = 460$, while the O-adduct from 2,4-DCP would have a molecular ion at $[M-H]^- = 426$. However, under conditions favorable for O-adduct formation by PCP, the only other CP to yield detectable levels of O-adduct was 2,4,5-TCP. The major adduct detected for these CPs had UV absorbances at 275 and 334 nm with a molecular ion at $[M-H]^- = 390/392$ with a single chlorine isotope. The UV spectrum of the major adduct was similar to the spectrum reported for the dG adduct generated from 1,4-benzoquinone (BQ)/dG, suggesting that bioactivation by HRP/H_2O_2 for these CP substrates (100 μM) yielded a BQ electrophile.

As outlined, 1,4-BQ could arise from a gem-chlorohydrin generated by the hydrolysis of the ether formed by C–O coupling of two chlorophenoxyl radicals. This suggested the possibility that lowering the concentration of the CP to retard radical coupling would favor C8-dG O-adduct formation for 2,4,6-TCP, 2,4,5-TCP, and 2,4-DCP. Thus, the CP/dG reactions were repeated at 10 μM CP and now all CPs generated the anticipated C8-dG O-adduct as the major lesion; for 2,4,5-TCP, the O-adduct was the only observable adduct, while 2,4,6-TCP and 2,4-DCP still formed detectable levels of BQ-adduct.

To determine whether a C8-dG O-adduct forms with a duplex DNA substrate, calf thymus DNA (1 mg/mL) was treated with PCP (100 μM) in phosphate buffer (100 mM, pH 7.4) at 37°C for 24 h in the presence of HRP (Type VI, 25 units/mL)/H_2O_2(1 mM). The reacted DNA was precipitated, enzymatically digested, and analyzed by LC/MS using an authentic sample of PCP-dG for comparison. These studies showed that the major DNA lesion formed from PCP activation by HRP/H_2O_2 had high-performance liquid chromatography (HPLC) retention time, MS/MS fragmentation, and parent ion identical to those of the authentic adduct standard. This implied that the pentachlorophenoxyl radical reacted with the duplex DNA substrate to form the O-bonded C8 PCP-dG adduct highlighting the *in vitro* relevance of C8-dG adducts of phenolic toxins.

The results from our studies on CP-mediated DNA adduction by peroxidase activation allowed us to propose the mechanism. The reaction is initiated by the production of the chlorophenoxyl radical that may either react directly with dG to furnish the C8-dG O-adduct in an irreversible process or self-couple to yield the 1,4-BQ electrophile that reacts with dG to give 4"-hydroxy1,N^2-benzetheno-dG. Formation of the benzetheno-dG adduct in Path B may involve initial Schiff base formation from the exocyclic N^2 atom of dG and the carbonyl carbon of the BQ and subsequent nucleophilic attack of the endocyclic N^1 on the vinyl carbon. An alternative pathway, as originally proposed by Jowa et al., would involve initial reaction of N^2 at the vinyl carbon of BQ followed by N^1 attachment to the carbonyl carbon atom to yield 3"-hydroxy-1,N^2-benzetheno-dG. However, the ^{1}H NMR chemical shifts and reaction chemistry for this family of cyclic adducts favor 4"-hydroxy-1,N^2-benzetheno-dG adduct assignment.

Differences in CP reactivity may be ascribed to differences in the rate constants for the phenoxyl radical bimolecular self-reaction. If the bimolecular self-reaction is favorable, then Path B competes effectively with Path A at 100 μM CP substrate, while if the self-reaction is not favorable, then Path A dominates. Increased Cl substitution would be expected to inhibit the bimolecular self-reaction due to steric and/or electronic repulsion. In this regard, the bimolecular self-reaction rate constant for phenoxyl radical in H_2O is 2.6×10^9/M/s and it has a half-life of $\sim$60 μs in CCl_4. In contrast, the pentachlorophenoxyl radical has a half-life of 30–45 min in aqueous buffer, as determined from direct detection by EPR spectroscopy. Clearly, Cl substitution increases phenoxyl radical lifetime and this factor would be expected to contribute to phenoxyl radical reactivity in a biological system by allowing the radical time to diffuse away from its site of formation and react with biopolymers.

Conclusions and Future Research

CP toxins, especially PCP, are known to cause carcinomas in mouse liver. A DNA-reactive mechanism that includes both direct genotoxic DNA damage and oxidative stress-induced indirect DNA damage are proposed to initiate PCP-mediated hepatic carcinogenesis in mice. These events depend on the metabolism of PCP into TCBQ/

TCHQ/TCCAT redox couples. The TC-1,4-BQ metabolite reacts covalently with DNA and with cysteinyl residues of proteins to form di- and trisubstituted adducts. Hence, chlorinated benzoquinones are bi- and tri-functional alkylating agents and it is expected that TC-1,4-BQ participates in the formation of both protein–protein cross-links and/or protein–GSH moieties.

In terms of DNA adduction by TC-1,4-BQ, none of the adducts have been structurally characterized. However, it is anticipated that benzethenotype adducts and cross-linked DNA would contribute to TC-1,4-BQ-induced DNA adduction. Future studies aimed at characterizing the nature of DNA adducts formed by TC-1,4-BQ would be informative, as such adducts are potentially useful markers of chronic exposure to PCP. Structural assignment of the adducts would also permit strategies for the incorporation of TC-1,4-BQ adducts into oligonucleotides to determine the fate of these adducts (repair, mutation, persistence).

The metabolism of CP toxins also generates semiquinone and phenoxyl radical electrophiles. Our work has demonstrated that CP phenoxyl radicals react covalently with the C8-site of dG to form O-bound adducts *in vitro*. If these adducts form in peroxidase-rich tissues, then the fate of C8-dG adducts of CP toxins should be established. Overall, such efforts would increase our understanding of CP-mediated genotoxicity and the contribution that DNA adduction makes to CP-mediated carcinogenesis. This knowledge would be used to establish safe human exposure levels to CP pollutants.

Ochratoxin A

Production and Properties of Ochratoxin A

OTA is a mycotoxin produced by fungi in cool temperate (*Penicillium* spp. including *P. verrucosum*, *P. aurantiogriseum*, *P. citrinum* and *P. expansum*) and tropical latitudes (*Aspergillus* spp. such as *A. ochraceus*, *A. carbonarius*, *A. niger*). The toxin consists of a para-chlorophenolic moiety containing a dihydroisocoumarin group that is amide-linked to L-phenylalanine. In alcoholic solution, fully protonated OTA shows a UV–vis spectrum with an absorption band that peaks at 332 nm (molar absorptivity (ε) ~6650/M/cm). The pKas of the carboxylic group and the phenolic moiety are ~4 and ~7, respectively. Upon deprotonation of the phenolic moiety, ε increases substantially up to 10,970/M/cm and the absorption band shifts to 380 nm. OTA also exhibits strong fluorescence, and as such, HPLC with fluorescence detection for quantitation of low OTA levels in food is common.

Cereals are the main contributor of OTA intake, although other food products such as coffee, cocoa, grape fruits, beans, nuts, dried fruit, and meat can be contaminated with OTA. While OTA exposure is mainly due to ingestion of contaminated food, exposure by inhalation of dust containing OTA is possible. Di Paolo et al. have described a case of acute intoxication in a man with oliguria and tubulonecrosis, which might have been due to inhalation of *A. ochraceus*. It has recently been demonstrated that OTA is present in spores and airborne dust particles, thus supporting this hypothesis. Brera et al. and Iavicoli et al. have demonstrated that exposure to OTA occurs in the workplace from inhalation of dust, which correlates with OTA levels found in plasma. Similarly, we have collected dust "*in silo*" and have isolated *Penicillia* and *Aspergillii*, which are capable of producing OTA.

OTA is very toxic to numerous animal species with the kidney being the main target organ. The toxin is regarded as a major causal determinant of mycotoxin porcine nephropathy as well as being the main etiological agent responsible for Balkan endemic nephropathy (BEN) in humans. Ultrastructural and toxicological investigations in spontaneous cases of porcine nephropathy have been carried out. These studies show striking similarities between the described OTA-induced porcine nephropathy in pigs and BEN. Both diseases are characterized by degeneration of epithelial cells of the proximal tubules and interstitial fibrosis resulting in polyuria and various changes in hematological and biochemical parameters. From the spontaneous cases of porcine nephropathy, OTA was found in 100% of investigated serum samples collected from the diseased pigs (48.34±.6.7–84.2±41.17 ng/mL). Stoev et al. have also induced porcine nephropathy in six pigs by providing a diet containing 800 μg/kg of OTA over a 1-year period. The characteristic renal lesions found in the pigs were similar to the classic Danish porcine nephropathy, highlighting the role for OTA.

In rodent studies, pre-treatment of mice with phenobarbital (PB), an inducer of CYP450 2C, 2B, 3A, and glutathione-S-transferase (GST), decreased nephrotoxicity, but increased hepatic tumor formation. This suggests that biotransformation of OTA by enzymes modulated by PB generated OTA metabolites which are less nephrotoxic than the parent OTA, but are genotoxic. Because urinary tract tumors are associated with BEN and exposure to OTA, the genotoxicity of OTA is thought to play a key role in OTA-mediated tumor formation. While the carcinogenicity of OTA is beyond doubt and is endorsed by IARC, Lyon, there is as yet no clear mechanism for the occurrence of OTA-mediated tumors in rat renal parenchyma. In general, tumor development is a multifactorial process, implicating alteration of DNA after metabolic activation of carcinogens and subsequent mutations that can alter proto-oncogen function or tumor suppression. For renal carcinogenesis in rodents, three mechanisms have been proposed: direct genotoxic DNA damage, oxidative stress-induced indirect DNA damage, or inappropriate stimulation of cell proliferation by accumulation of α-2u-globulin in the kidney of male rats. The latter mechanism does not appear to be involved in the carcinogenicity of OTA, suggesting that DNA damage may make an important contribution to OTA-mediated tumor formation.

Carcinogenicity of Ochratoxin A

OTA is carcinogenic in rodents. The first studies of OTA carcinogenicity were performed on rats, trout, and mice by oral or intraperitoneal administration. Only after oral administration were tumors induced in the kidney of mice and rats, and liver of trout. When these studies were evaluated by IARC, it was considered that the evidence for carcinogenicity was either inconclusive or limited. The results of the mouse carcinogenicity study were subsequently confirmed by a second study by the same group, which also demonstrated a synergistic effect by the mycotoxin citrinin when it was administered simultaneously.

The carcinogenic potency of OTA to mice was confirmed by Bendele et al. Groups of $B6C3F_1$ mice (50 males and 50 females) were given feed containing 40 μg OTA for 24 months. In treated male mice, 31 were affected (14/49 had renal carcinomas and 26/49 renal adenomas). All males showed nephropathy but only a small number of females. None of the females had renal carcinoma or adenoma. A small number of both males and females had hepatocellular neoplasm.

In a study by NTP, three doses of OTA (210, 70, and 21 μg/kg body weight) were administered to male and female F344N rats. At 210 μg/kg body weight, renal tubular adenomas and carcinomas were observed (72% for males and 16% for females) after 2 years. At 70 μg/kg body weight, 39% of the males and 4% of the females developed renal adenomas or carcinomas. The females were less susceptible than the males to OTA carcinogenicity. In addition, non-neoplastic renal modifications (hyperplasia, cell proliferation, cytoplasmic alteration, and karyomegalies) were observed. All animals treated with 70 or 210 μg/kg body weight presented karyomegalies. In view of these results, IARC evaluated the experimental evidence for carcinogenicity as sufficient and classified OTA as Group 2B, "*possible human carcinogen*". The NTP results in rats were confirmed by a study at IARC using Lewis and Dark Agouti (DA) rats. Male DA rats were very sensitive and female DA rats were resistant. Male DA rats were also much more sensitive than either male or female Lewis rats; a factor ascribed to superior biotransformation capacity of OTA in male DA rats. Since 2-mercaptoethane sulfonate (MESNA) protects rats against nephrotoxicity and carcinogenicity induced by oxidative stress by increasing free thiol groups in kidney, the potential protective effect of MESNA on renal toxicity and carcinogenicity induced by OTA was examined in a long-term rat study. MESNA significantly decreased karyomegalies in the kidney of all OTA-treated animals, but had no beneficial effect on renal tumor incidence. In fact, a significant increase in renal tumor formation was observed in male DA rats.

Metabolism of Ochratoxin A

During the past 25 years, the metabolism of OTA has been extensively studied by Stormer and co-workers using *in vitro* and *in vivo* assays in the liver of different animals. These efforts led to the isolation and identification of the hydroxylated derivatives 4(R)-, 4(S)-, and 10-OH-OTA along with OTa, which stems from cleavage of the peptide bond by α-chymotrypsine and carboxypeptidase. It was also established that the metabolism of OTA is organ- and species-specific. For example, 4(R)-OH-OTA was mainly formed after incubation in the presence of human and rat liver microsomes, whereas 4(S)-OH-OTA was essentially formed via pig microsomes [145]. 10-OH-OTA was produced after *in vitro* incubation with rabbit liver microsomes. Furthermore, in vivo studies indicated that the cleavage of the peptide bond in OTA to yield OTα occurs by homogenates from pancreas and small intestine, but not by liver.

Other authors have more recently studied the biotransformation of OTA. *In vitro* incubation in the presence of microsomes or treatment of cell lines with OTA leads to the formation of at least 20 derivatives. We have demonstrated that after *in vitro* incubation in the presence of microsomes, the formation of OTA metabolites is time- and concentration-dependent. For incubation in the presence of pig liver microsomes, the kinetics is linear during the first 10 min and then reaches a plateau at 25 min. At least 10 different derivatives have been separated by HPLC from cell culture (human bronchial epithelial cell, opposum renal cells) and *in vitro* incubation (pig kidney microsomes). Co-elution of these derivatives with synthetic OTA metabolites established that the opened lactone derivative (OP-OA) was formed exclusively with cortex microsomes. Pig liver microsomes (male and female) and female cortex and medulla microsomes induced formation of 4(R)-OH-OTA, but not 4(S)-OH-OTA. In contrast, male pig microsomes from cortex and medulla generated both 4-OH-OTA stereoisomers. The relative quantity of metabolites was dependent on both the origin of the microsomes (male or female, liver or kidney) and on the co-factors used: nicotinamide adenine dinucleotide phosphate (NADPH) and arachidonic acid (AA).

The metabolism of OTA also generates the nonchlorinated OTB analog shown in Scheme. This metabolite is formed from OTA-incubation of rabbit kidney microsomes pre-treated with PB and in monkey kidney cell culture. OTB is also present in the kidney of pigs fed OTA. While little is known about the mechanism of OTB formation in vivo, it is also generated from OTA photochemically. Under photochemical conditions, it is expected that OTA interacts with a solvated electron, which initiates C–Cl bond homolysis to afford an OTA carbon-centered radical and chloride; H-atom abstraction by the radical provides a route to OTB. This reaction is akin to reductive dehalogenation of alkyl- and aryl-halides that are catalyzed by CYP450s. As suggested by Guengerich, ferrous CYP450 should be a good one-electron-reducing agent and that transfer of an electron to a substrate may be competitive with oxidation even in the presence of O_2. OTA also stimulates production of $O_2^{\bullet-}$ that will lead to the liberation of free Fe^{2+}; a co-factor in cells that may also cause reductive dehalogenation of OTA to generate OTB.

The other nonchlorinated metabolite of OTA shown in Scheme is the hydroquinone derivative hydroquinone OTA (OTHQ). Recent biological studies confirm the presence of OTHQ in the urine of rat following the administration of OTA by gavage. On the basis of analogy to the metabolism of PCP, which generates TC-1,4-BQ by oxidative dechlorination pathways, it is expected that a two-electron reduction of the quinone species, quinone OTA (OTQ), by action of NAD(P)H:quinone reductase generates OTHQ. Four observations provide indirect evidence for the intermediacy of OTQ in OTA oxidation. These are: (1) electrochemical methods; (2) treatment of OTA with a biomimetic iron-oxo system; (3) treatment of OTA with redox active transition metals; and (4) the characterization and identification of a OTA-GSH conjugate that is produced from the treatment of OTA with GSH following incubation with rat liver microsomes.

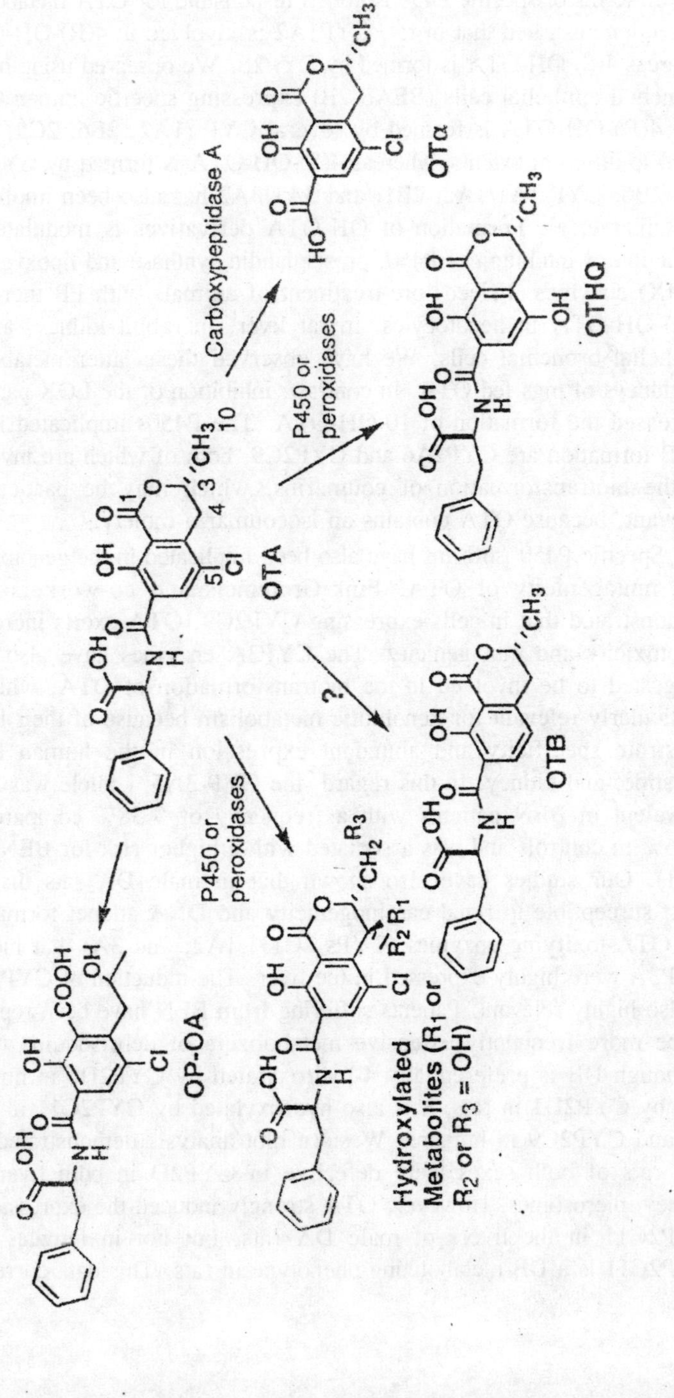

Fig. 8.8. Metabolism of OTA

In terms of specific P450 isoforms responsible for OTA metabolism, Ueno demonstrated that in rat, CYP1A2 is involved in 4(R)-OH-OTA, whereas 4(S)-OH-OTA is formed by CYP2B. We observed using human bronchial epithelial cells (BEAS-2B) expressing specific human CYPs that 4(R)-OH-OTA is formed by several CYP (1A2, 2B6, 2C9, 2D6, 2A6) to different extents, whereas 4(S)-OH-OTA is formed by CYP2D6 and 2B6. CYP 1A1/1A2, 2B1, and 3A1/3A2 has also been implicated by Omar et al. Formation of OH-OTA derivatives is modulated by induction or inhibition of P450, prostaglandin synthase and lipoxygenase (LOX) enzymes. Indeed, pre-treatment of animals with PB increased 4(R)-OH-OTA in hepatocytes, in rat liver, in rabbit kidney, and in epithelial bronchial cells. We have observed these latter metabolites in kidneys of pigs fed OTA. In contrast, inhibition of the LOX pathway increased the formation of 10-OH-OTA. The P450s implicated in the OTB formation are CYP2A6 and CYP2C9, both of which are involved in the biotransformation of coumarins, which may be particularly relevant, because OTA contains an isocoumarin moiety.

Specific P450 isoforms have also been implicated in the genotoxicity and mutagenicity of OTA. Fink-Gremmels and co-workers have demonstrated that in cells expressing CYP2C9, OTA exerts increased cytotoxicity and mutagenicity. The CYP3A enzymes have also been suggested to be involved in the biotransformation of OTA, which is particularly relevant for xenobiotic metabolism because of their broad substrate specificity and abundant expression in the human liver, intestine, and kidney. In this regard, the CYP 3A5*1 allele was more prevalent in BEN patients with a frequency of 9.38% compared to 5.36% in controls and was associated with a higher risk for BEN (OR 2.41). Our studies have also shown that in male DA rats that are most susceptible to renal carcinogenicity and DNA adduct formation, the OTA-toxifying enzymes (CYPs 2C11, 1A2, and 3A) that include CYP3A were highly expressed in the liver. The induction of CYP2C11 is also highly relevant. Patients suffering from BEN have been reported to be more frequently extensive metabolizers of debrisoquine (DB). Although DB is preferentially 4-hydroxylated by CYP2D6 in humans and by CYP2D1 in rats, it is also hydroxylated by CYP2C11 in male rat and CYP2C9 in humans. Western blot analysis demonstrated that DA rats of both sexes were defective in CYP2D in both liver and kidney microsomes. However, OTA strongly induced the expression of CYP2C11 in the livers of male DA rats, but not in females, and CYP2C11 is a DB-metabolizing phenotype in rats. This data correlates with DB-metabolizing phenotypes being important in BEN and is in keeping with the greater susceptibility of males than females to OTA-induced renal carcinogenicity.

A typical HPLC profile with spectrofluorometry detection highlighting the separation of OTA metabolites following extraction with chloroform. Relatively large amounts of OTB and another dechlorinated derivative of OTA are formed in opossum kidney (OK) cells pre-treated with acivicin (α amino-3-chloro-4,5-dihydro-5-isoxazole acetic acid), an inhibitor of gamma glutamyl transpeptidase (GGT) which blocks the cytotoxicity of hydroquinone-S-conjugates. Figure shows the modulation of OTA metabolites by the inhibitors of the GSH pathway that include: MESNA, which protects rats against nephrotoxicity and carcinogenicity induced by oxidative stress by increasing free thiol groups in the kidney, N-acetylcysteine (NAC), a precursor of intracellular CySH and GSH, and an ROS scavenger, buthionine sulfoximine oxide (BSO), an inhibitor of glutathione synthase, and acivicin. The structures of several of these derivatives (OP-OA, OTB, 4R-OH-OTA) were identified by cochromatography and they have also been confirmed by MS.

P450s are primarily responsible for the oxidation of most xenobiotics in liver, whereas much lower P450 activities are expressed in other tissues. In the kidney, lung, and brain, several xenobiotics are cooxidized by COX or LOX. Because OTA induces renal tumors in rats and catalyzes ROS formation and lipid peroxidation in the kidney of rat, its biotransformation could be due to cooxidation by several enzymes, notably those implicated in the metabolism of AA, such as COX, LOX, and epoxygenase; the latter enzyme is related to CYP2C11. Systems that we have used to study OTA metabolism, such as pig seminal vesicle microsomes and BEAS-2B cells express high levels of COX and LOX enzymes, as well as CYP450-epoxygenases that are also found in the cortex and outer medulla of kidney and bladder cells. Pre-treatment of bronchial epithelial cells (WI) with indomethacin (0.1 μM), which inhibits COX enzymes but enhances LOX activity, or nordihydroguaiaretic acid (NDGA), which inhibits LOX enzymes, prior to OTA treatment modified the profile of OTA derivatives, as studied by HPLC with spectrofluorometry detection. Treatment of cells with indomethacin (0.1 μM) generated new OTA metabolites that could not be identified using OTa, 4-(R,S)-OH-OTA and OTB as authentic standards. These metabolites of unknown structure appeared to be formed by LOX enzymes, as they disappeared upon pre-treatment of cells with NDGA. Comparison of the metabolite studies with OTA-mediated DNA adduction suggested that these new metabolites may play a role in OTA-mediated genotoxicity and that LOX enzymes are important in the biotransformation of OTA into genotoxic metabolites.

Hoehler et al. have also shown that OTA still causes generation of ROS in bacteria that have very low CYP450 or peroxidases. They propose that OTA increases the permeability of the cell to Ca^{2+} and the presence of the pro-oxidant OTA uncouples oxidative phosphorylation resulting in the increased leakage of electrons from the respiratory chain producing $O_2^{\bullet-}$ and free Fe^{2+}. Thus, perturbation of Ca^{2+} homeostasis by OTA results in enhanced ROS production in a manner analogous to those proposed with other pro-oxidants, such as t-butyl hydroperoxide and does not involve enzymatic bioactivation of OTA. Interestingly, this non-enzymatic pathway for ROS production by OTA is expected to liberate free Fe^{2+}, may play an important role in reductive dehalogenation of OTA to yield the nonchlorinated OTB metabolite.

The method of metabolite extraction is also of critical importance. As a case in point, Zepnick et al. did not find any OTA metabolites aside from OTα in tissue and urine of rat treated orally with a single OTA dose of 0.5 mg/kg body weight, while under the similar conditions, Castegnaro et al. observed the excretion of OTA and 4-OH-OTA with the amount of 4-OH-OTA excretion related to the dose of OTA administered. A reason for this discrepancy is exemplified by the HPLC data that were obtained from extraction of OTA and its metabolites from rat liver and kidney of male pigs fed 18 days with OTA (18 μg/kg body weight/day). The HPLC was obtained following extraction using chloroform after acidification and treatment with $MgCl_2$, while the HPLC profile was obtained following extraction based on ethanol protein precipitation, as utilized by Zepnick et al. With chloroform extraction, OTA and compounds corresponding to the elution time of 4(R)- and 4(S)-OH-OTA are found in the medulla and to lower extent in the cortex of pig, and in the liver of rats. Compounds with retention times similar to OTB, OTα, OTβ (OTB lacking the phenylalanine moiety), and OP-OA were also detected, as were compounds of unknown nature. In sharp contrast, ethanol extraction only yields OTA. This suggests that the OTA obtained by ethanol extraction is free OTA (that from spiking), which is not proteinbound and is thus easily extracted. To extract protein-bound OTA and its metabolites, acidic conditions and $MgCl_2$ is required to remove OTA from protein. It is well known that OTA binds strongly to proteins with recent studies showing that OTA binding to *human serum albumin* (HAS) occurs preferentially within domain IIA (K_b = 5.2 × 10^6/M); this binding lowers the pKa of the phenolic group, thereby facilitating the formation of an ion pair between the phenoxide group and protonated R257. Studies *in vivo* reveal that the lifetime of OTA in living systems is dependent on the presence of HSA (which increases the lifetime of OTA) and that this binding is species- and sex-dependent.

The studies dealing with the biotransformation of OTA, a chlorinated compound, show that it is a complex system and involves several enżymes such as P450s, but also GSTs and LOX. The metabolites conjugated to GSH and/or uridine diphosphate (UDP) are excreted in bile and in kidney. At least 20 different metabolites of OTA including OTB, OTC, OH-OTA, OP-OTA, OTα, OTβ, and OTHQ, and metabolites of unknown structure have been detected. On the basis of all the available data, known and hypothetical pathways for OTA metabolism are summarized.

One of the important enzymes in the genotoxicity of OTA is leukotriene C4 synthase (LTC4). This enzyme is a member of the group of non-heme Fe-containing enzymes capable of oxidizing GSH to GSSG and simultaneously generating $O_2^{\bullet-}$, which may contribute to oxidative stress in cells, but also participate in GSH conjugation of xenobiotics. In general, GSTs are involved in detoxifying pathways, but in some cases they contribute to the reactivity and toxicity of xenobiotics, notably by the formation of thiyl radicals, which react with macromolecules and yield peroxyl radicals. Conversion of OTA into the quinone OTQ by redox cycling generates ROS that can lead to DNA breaks and lipid peroxidation (LPO)-derived exocyclic adducts. OTQ can either undergo a two-electron reduction by action of the NAD(P)H:quinone reductase to form OTHQ, or it can undergo a one-electron reduction to yield a semiquinone, which in turn could induce DNA breaks, LPO, and exocyclic adducts. OTA was shown to induce oxidative damage due to the generation of hydroxyl radicals ($HO^{\bullet}$) by microsomes in the presence of NADPH as a microsomal reductant and O_2 not requiring exogenous Fe. Pathway 2 is thus inhibited by ROS scavengers, such as MESNA and NAC and explains OTA-induced karyomegalies, which are also reduced after MESNA treatment. OTHQ could be formed directly from OTA by GST and it can be oxidized into OTQ. Indeed, GSTs are involved in dehalogenation: the first step is the formation of an epoxide and in the second step the epoxide is converted into phenol, which can lead to OTHQ and/or OTB.

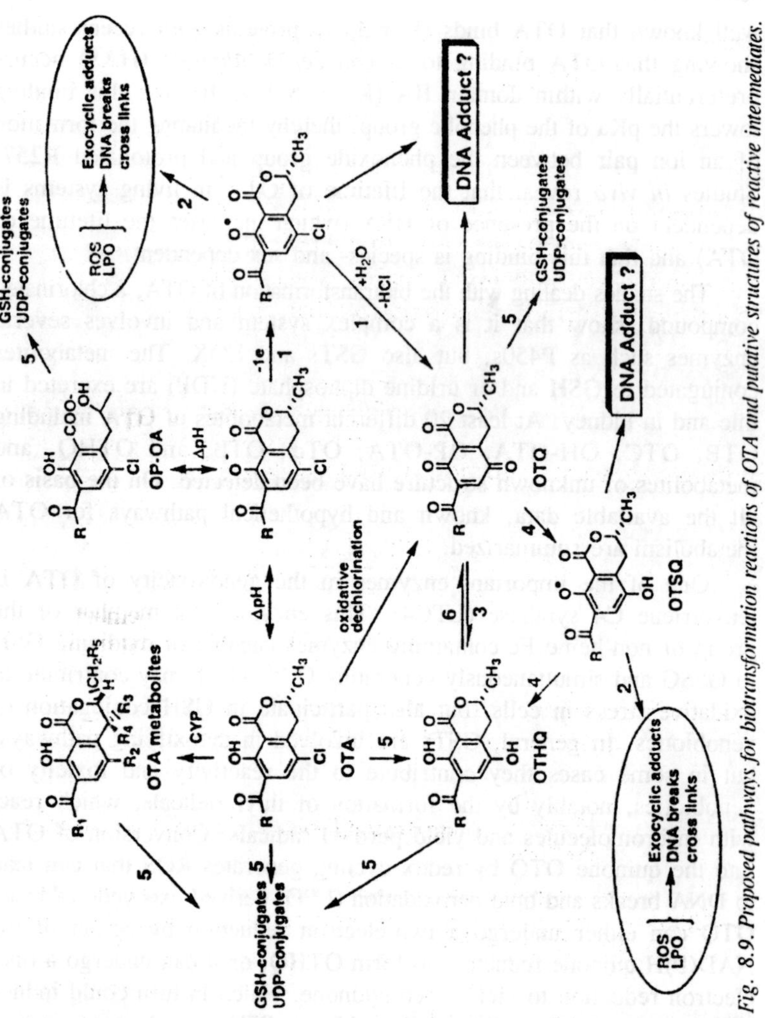

Fig. 8.9. Proposed pathways for biotransformation reactions of OTA and putative structures of reactive intermediates.

DNA Damage by Ochratoxin A

OTA has long been considered non-genotoxic, as various standard tests using prokaryotes are generally negative or very slightly positive. Ames tests carried out in different strains of *Salmonella typhimurium* (TA 98, 102) were negative. No induction of growth inhibition of various strains of *Bacillus subtilis* occurs after OTA treatment and no recombination was observed in OTA-treated *Saccharomyces cerevisiae* D3. At doses of 5 and 10 μg/mL, OTA did not induce 8-azaguanine-resistant mutation in mammary cells of C3H mice. In the absence of metabolic activation, no mutations were detected in cells from FM3A mice exposed to OTA [206].

However, more recent data shows that OTA induces a potent mutagenic effect in *S. typhimurium* TA 1535, 1538, and 100 exposed to supernatant of rat hepatocytes pre-treated with OTA and also in the presence of kidney microsomes in *S. typhimurium* TA 1535, 1538 and 98. Mutagenic potency has been demonstrated in other mammalian cells. OTA-induced unscheduled DNA synthesis has been noted in rat and mouse hepatocytes, in urinary bladder epithelial cells from pig and in primary human urothelial cells. The effect of OTA on DNA repair and induction of DNA damage was further investigated by detecting the occurrence of DNA damage by the comet assay. In MDCK cells, OTA induced single-strand breaks in a concentration-dependent manner. When an external metabolizing system (S9-mix from rat liver) was added, the genotoxic effect was significantly stronger, thus implying a role for metabolism. In the same study, it was demonstrated that OTA-induced DNA damage is increased by blocking repair mechanisms. OTA also slightly increased the response in the SOS–spot test. In the absence of metabolic activation, 4 μM OTA induced SOS repair in Escherichia coli PQ37. OTA also induces chromosomal mitotic recombination in *Drosophila*. A small but dose-dependent increase in sister chromatid exchanges were induced in CHO cells treated with OTA. Sister chromatid exchanges were also induced in human lymphocytes in the presence of hepatocytes and in cultured isolated porcine urinary bladder epithelial cells treated with OTA. In another study, a statistical increase of structural chromosomal aberration and sister chromatid exchanges associated with a decrease in the mitotic index has been observed in bovine lymphocytes. OTA induced micronuclei in ovine seminal vesicle cell cultures, in Syrian hamster fibroblast, and in human hepatic (HepG2) cells; all in a dose-dependent manner. Significant dose-dependent increases in the frequency of DNA single-strand breaks and alkalilabile sites, as measured by the comet assay, and in micronuclei frequency, were obtained in primary kidney cells from both male rats and humans of both genders with OTA from 0.015 to 1.215 μM. Single-strand DNA breaks have been observed in kidney, liver, and spleen DNA of BALB/c mice treated orally with OTA. Manolova et al. demonstrated the presence of chromosomal aberrations on chromosome X from human lymphocytes cultivated in the presence of OTA. Similar aberrations have been detected in BEN patients.

On the basis of structure–activity relationships, Malaveille and co-workers proposed that the presence of the C-5 chlorine atom in OTA is one determinant of its genotoxic action. Xiao et al. also demonstrated that the phenylalanine moiety and the para-chlorophenolic group are important for *in vitro* and *in vivo* toxicity by OTA. In contrast to the proposal by Rahimtula that Fe-chelation may be linked to OTA-toxicity, Xiao and co-workers showed that an O-methylated phenolic derivative of OTA, that lacks metal chelation properties, was equally efficient in generating ROS production, suggesting that the toxicity of OTA is not linked to its chelation of Fe^{2+}. Xiao and co-workers concluded that the phenylalanine group is important for genotoxicity and demonstrated that some OTA derivatives, notably OP-OTA bind macromolecules (protein and DNA).

The genotoxicity of OTA has also been established by the detection of OTA-mediated DNA adduct formation. It has been shown that rats and mice treated with OTA show numerous DNA adducts. The highest levels have been found in kidney DNA where some adducts persist for more than 16 days, while adducts are repaired in liver and spleen after 5 days. Similar adduct patterns have been found in kidney and bladder tumors of BEN patients. Single doses of OTA administered to mice and rat by gavages or in feed induced DNA adducts in kidney in a dose- and time-dependent manner. In cell culture (OK cells or in human bronchial cells), and after *in vitro* incubation in presence of pig and rat kidney microsomes, doseand time-dependent DNA adducts were also observed. Petkova-Bocharova et al. demonstrated that administration of OTA to pregnant mothers at day 9 of gestation induced DNA adduction in fetuses and pups that were detectable several months after birth. Moreover, some of them developed renal carcinoma 2 years later.

In order to elucidate the metabolic pathway leading to adduct formation, a series of in vitro experiments have been undertaken. Only kidney microsomes were capable of inducing adduct formation. OTA alone does not yield DNA adducts by interacting directly with DNA and no adducts can be formed by *in vitro* incubations using hepatic microsomes. This aspect has been confirmed by other researchers, notably Gross-Steinmeyer et al. using ^{3}H-OTA did not find adducts in hepatocytes and Gautier et al. found no evidence for OTA-mediated DNA adduction using liver microsomes for bioactivation. Because kidney is rich in peroxidases, the implication of an oxidative metabolic pathway was investigated. Administration of superoxide dismutase and catalase prior to OTA treatment inhibited DNA adduction in mice kidneys. Protection from OTA-mediated genotoxicity by indomethacin and aspirin (inhibitors of COX and LOX enzymes) in the urinary bladder and kidney of mice was also observed. DNA adduction was also partially prevented by antioxidant vitamins, supporting the implication of a peroxidase pathway. Induction of LOX by vitamin A increases the formation of the main OTA-DNA adduct in the kidney of mice treated by OTA. The implication of the LOX pathways in OTA-mediated genotoxicity was also reinforced by the absence of OTA–DNA adducts when cells were pre-treated with NDGA and a higher dose of indomethacin (10 μM), which inhibits all the AA biotransformation pathways.

Microsomes from transgenic mice demonstrate that formation of OTA–DNA adducts are under control of several biotransformation enzymes such as 1B1, 2C9, LOX, and COX. Moreover, induction of NADPH–quinone-reductase regulated by the AH receptor, decreases OTA genotoxicity, which reinforces the hypothesis for involvement of a quinone pathway in OTA-mediated genotoxicity. In a carcinogenic study, we demonstrated that the susceptibility of male DA rat is due to CYP2C11, corresponding to human CYP2C9, which is able to metabolize DB. Several other experiments implicate CYP2C. For example, BEAS-2B cells expressing specific human CYP isoforms demonstrate that CYPs 1A2, 3A4, 2D6, and 2C9 are responsible for the formation of several OTA–DNA adducts, whereas CYPs 2A6 and 2E1 decrease OTA genotoxicity.

These experiments suggest strongly that OTA forms covalent DNA adducts *in vivo* and have been used to gain mechanistic insight into OTA-mediated genotoxicity. For example, MESNA modified the DNA adduct patterns in kidney of both male rat strains leading to a reduction in spot number and total adduct level, but did not prevent formation of all adduct spots. After acivicin treatment, only one adduct persisted whose formation appeared to involve OTA biotransformation by LOX, as this adduct is the major adduct in OTA-treated cells when the LOX pathway is enhanced, and also in the kidney of mice pretreated by vitamin A, a known LOX inducer. These results suggested different mechanisms for OTA-induced karyomegalies, renal carcinogenicity, and DNA adduction. It is also highly relevant that the OTA–DNA adducts which persisted in kidney of OTA-treated rats had similar chromatographic properties with adducts found in renal tumors from Bulgarian patients suffering from BEN/UTT (urothelial tract tumour) and in a

French patient with kidney tumors. These adducts were also detected in pigs, which had developed OTA-related nephropathy and persisted in the kidney of OTA-treated mice and rats.

The Manderville laboratory has recently used the photochemistry of OTA to isolate and characterize the deoxyguanosine (dG) OTA–DNA adduct standards. This effort was prompted by the work carried out by Obrecht-Pflumio and Dirheimer, who demonstrated using ^{32}P-post-labeling that OTA reacts preferentially with dG. Figure 8.9 shows ^{32}P-postlabeling analysis of DNA extracted from the kidney of rat treated chronically with OTA and from pig following sub-acute exposure to the toxin with the adduct standards for comparison. The ^{32}P-post-labeling analysis show that both adducts comigrate with OTA–DNA adducts formed in the kidney of rats developing tumors. The amount of adduct comigrating with the carbon-bonded C-C8-dG-OTA adduct was 16 adducts per 10^9 nucleotides; this adduct is also formed in the kidney of pigs fed OTA. These data suggest that OTA undergoes bioactivation to selectively attach to the C8-site of dG *in vivo* to form the covalent adducts; a likely intermediate is the phenoxyl radical, as phenoxyl radicals are known to form adducts at the C8-site of dG.

Despite evidence for the direct genotoxicity of OTA, other researchers have been unable to detect direct DNA damage by OTA and favor an indirect mechanism for OTA-mediated carcinogenicity that involves oxidative stress and OTA-mediated cytotoxicity. A recent perspective by Turesky summarizes the argument against direct genotoxicity by OTA.

One reason that an interlaboratory analysis of DNA samples from OTA-treated rats has failed to reach a consensus regarding the nature of spots in OTA-mediated DNA adduction is due to differences in

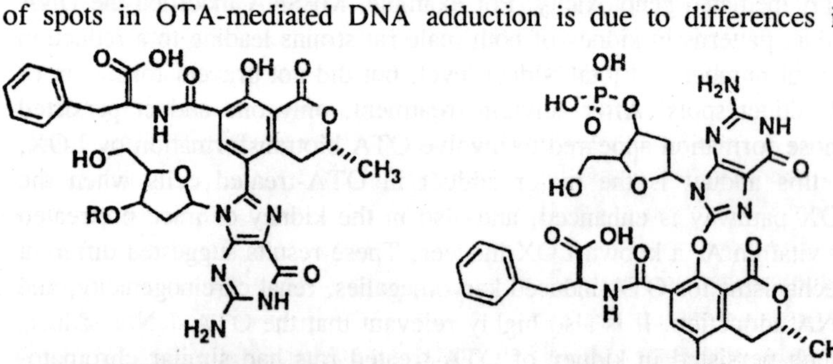

R = H = OTA-dG
R = H_2PO_3 = C-OTA-3'-dGMP

O-OTA-3'-dGMP

Fig. 8.10. Chemical structures of authentic OTA-DNA adduct standards.

methodology. For example, for ^{32}P-postlabeling analysis, Mally and co-workers used phosphodiesterase (SPD) in a ratio of 1 mU/μg DNA, which will lead to incomplete DNA hydrolysis. Indeed, the activity of Calbiochem SPD is such that ~10–15 times more should have been added for complete hydrolysis of the OTA-treated DNA. The authors also used Nucleobond columns for DNA clean-up, which leads to DNA of variable quality with contamination by protein and RNA; DNA of high purity is critical for reliable DNA adduction results. The chromatographic pH conditions for ^{32}P-postlabeling analyses, with D1 at pH 6.8 and D3 at pH 3.5, also do not conform to standard published procedures, where D1 is run at pH below 6.0 and D3 is run at pH 6.4. For generation of OTA–DNA adduct standards, the photoreaction was carried out with OTA at 500 mM and dG at 20 mM; concentrations that are exceedingly high. It also appears that no purification of the photoreaction was carried out and so the solution would be a mixture of C-C8 and O-C8 adduct standards. In the work described by Gautier et al., Qiagen tip-2500 columns were used to isolate DNA and commercial plates from Macherey Nagel were used to separate adducts using conditions described by us, but solvent concentrations were not adjusted to the specific plates, probably due to lack of reference material for proper control. In fact, we have shown that migration of OTA–DNA adducts on MN plates is completely different from that on home-made plates. As specified earlier, the quality of the plates is vital for the analysis of OTA–DNA adducts by the sensitive ^{32}P-postlabeling technique.

Future Research

The mycotoxin and food contaminant OTA is one of the most potent renal carcinogens studied by NCI (National Cancer Institute) and NTP to date. In general, only weak genotoxic effects have been observed and the contribution of genotoxicity to renal tumor formation by OTA remains unknown. However, OTA-mediated DNA adduction has been implied using the ^{32}P-postlabeling technique and given that a strong correlation exists between DNA adduction and tumorigenesis, the direct genotoxicity of OTA cannot, at present, be ruled out as a viable mechanism for OTA-mediated carcinogenesis. The current model for direct genotoxicity by OTA requires oxidative bioactivation for covalent reactions with DNA. The oxidative chemistries of OTA are related to the CPs discussed in this chapter with phenoxyl radicals and quinone/semi-quinone intermediates being generated through bioactivation by CYP450 and enzymes with peroxidase activities. While the ^{32}P-post-labeling results suggest the biological significance of OTA–DNA adducts, the data is not proof of OTA–DNA adduct formation, as the ^{32}P-postlabeling technique does not provide structural evidence. LC/ESI–MS/MS data for OTA–DNA adducts in kidney of rat would provide unambiguous evidence for OTA-mediated DNA adduction and efforts are being made to identify OTA–DNA adducts using MS. The identification of OTHQ as a metabolite of OTA also warrants the investigation of the role played by OTQ/OTHQ in OTA-mediated genotoxicity given that the corresponding hydroquinone/quinone redox couple of PCP is proposed to play a key role in PCP-mediated carcinogenicity.

9

BIOACTIVATION

Recently, the National Toxicology Program of NIEHS declared that steroidal estrogens, both of endogenous nature and as components of *hormone replacement therapy* (HRT) formulations, are "known to be *human carcinogens*", causing breast and endometrial cancers. In July 2002, the Data and Safety Monitoring Board prematurely terminated a major clinical Women's Health Initiative trial on the long-term risks and benefits of estrogen plus progestin therapy, a form of HRT for postmenopausal women that have an intact uterus. This decision was based, in part, on the significantly increased risk (24%) of invasive breast cancer, as well as a higher incidence of heart disease and stroke in women undergoing estrogen replacement therapy as compared to those receiving placebos. Even those without tumors were often found to have more abnormal mammograms than those on placebo. Indeed, it has been known for some time that estrogens and estrogens plus progestin can contribute significantly to the development of cancers, especially of the breast and other hormone-sensitive tissues such as the ovary and uterus. These are some of the major types of cancers that afflict women in the United States.

Nevertheless, there are also significant benefits since estrogen replacement therapy relieves symptoms of menopause such as sleeplessness, hot flashes, and mood swings, protection against early menopausal bone loss, and a lower risk of colon cancer. For these reasons, women continue to use hormone replacement formulations in spite of the well-recognized risk. Although, the sales of standard dose Premarin prescriptions (0.625 mg/day) have decreased by 33%, since the NHLBI terminated the clinical trial on the long-term risks and benefits of estrogen plus progestin therapy in July 2002, the sales of low-dose Premarin preparations (0.45 mg/day) have been rising.

Mechanisms of Estrogen Carcinogenesis

The molecular mechanisms of steroidal estrogen carcinogenesis are still not well understood. Malignant phenotypes arise as a result of a series of mutations, most likely in genes associated with tumor suppressor, oncogene, DNA repair, or endocrine functions. At least two major pathways are being considered to be important and include the extensively studied hormonal pathway, by which estrogen stimulates cell proliferation through *estrogen receptor* (ER)-mediated signaling pathways, thus resulting in an increased risk of genomic mutations during DNA replication (*hormonal mechanism*). The second pathway involves estrogen metabolism, mediated by cytochrome P450, which generates reactive electrophilic estrogen o-quinones and *reactive oxygen species* (ROS) through redox cycling of these o-quinones. Studies have shown that a constitutive and TCDD-inducible P450 isozyme, P4501B1 selectively catalyzes hydroxylation at the 4-position of estrone and 17β-estradiol suggesting that excessive exposure to environmental pollutants could lead to enhanced production of this metabolite. This is particularly significant, since only 4-hydroxyestrone was found to be carcinogenic in the male Syrian golden hamster kidney tumor model, whereas, 2-hydroxyestrone was without activity. Similarly, Newbold and Liehr have shown that 4-hydroxyestradiol induced uterine tumors in 66% of CD-1 mice, whereas, mice treated with 2-hydroxyestradiol or 17β-estradiol had a total uterine tumor incidence of 12% and 7%, respectively. Finally, epidemiological studies have suggested a link between genetic polymorphism in the estrogen 4-hydroxylase (P4501B1

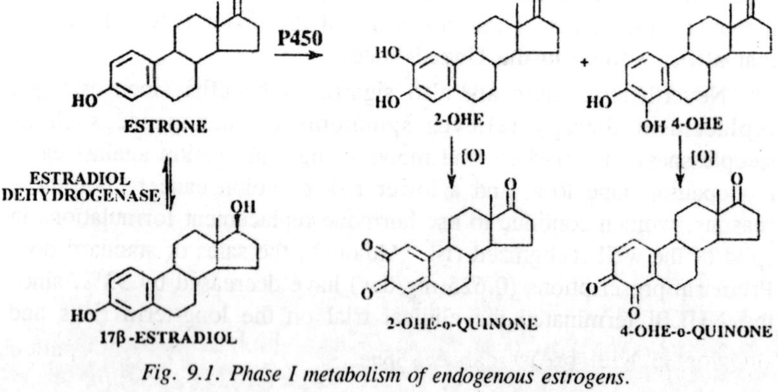

Fig. 9.1. Phase I metabolism of endogenous estrogens.

and/or 1A1) and a risk for developing breast cancer. These data suggest that metabolism of estrogens is required for the development of cancer.

Most of the epidemiological studies on estrogen replacement therapy and cancer risk have been conducted with Premarin (Wyeth-Ayerest) which remains the estrogen replacement treatment of choice and one of the most widely prescribed drugs in North America. Since Premarin was approved by the Food and Drug Administration in the 1940s, very little is known about the metabolism and potential toxic metabolites that could be produced from the various equine estrogens which make up ~50% of the estrogens in Premarin. It is known that treating hamsters for 9 months with either estrone, equilin+equilenin, or sulfatase-treated Premarin, resulted in 100% kidney tumor incidences and abundant tumor foci. We have shown that a major phase I metabolite of both equilenin and equilin (4-hydroxyequilenin, 4-OHEN) can act as a complete carcinogen and tumor promotor *in vitro*, whereas the endogenous catechol estrogen metabolite, 4-hydroxyestrone was much less effective. As a result, it is quite possible that the B-ring unsaturated equine estrogens have very different biological properties *in vivo* compared to the endogenous catechol estrogens.

Interestingly, increasing unsaturation in the B-ring leads to a change in metabolism from predominately 2-hydroxylation for estrone to mainly 4-hydroxylation for equilin and exclusively 4-hydroxylation for equilenin. This could be problematic, since 2-hydroxylation of endogenous estrogens is regarded as a benign metabolic pathway, whereas 4-hydroxylation could lead to carcinogenic metabolites. In fact, based on our progress to date, it is our strong belief that metabolism of equilenin or equilin (and their 17β-hydroxylated metabolites) to 4-OHEN and 4,17β-

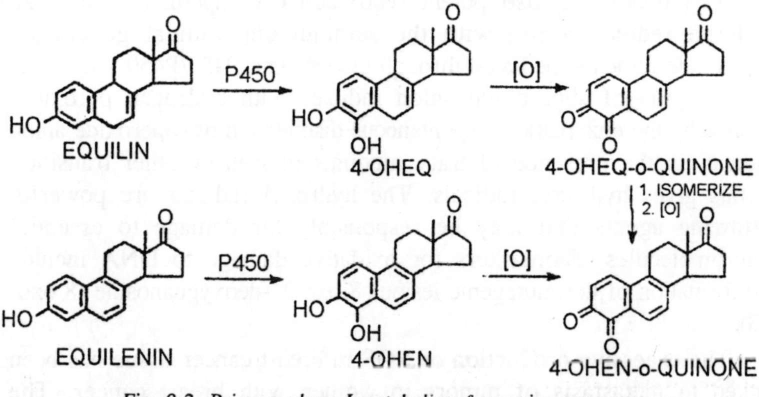

Fig. 9.2. Primary phase I metabolism for equine estrogens.

dihydroxyequilenin represents a major carcinogenic pathway for equine estrogens.

Oxidation of Catechol Estrogens to o-Quinones

Once formed, the endogenous catechol estrogens can be oxidized by virtually any oxidative enzyme and/or metal ion giving o-quinones. The o-quinone formed from 2-hydroxyestrone has a half-life of 47 s, whereas the 4-hydroxyestrone-o-quinone is considerably longer lived ($t_{1/2}$ = 12 min). Interestingly, the 4-hydroxylated equine catechol estrogens (4-OHEN and 4-OHEQ) both autoxidize to o-quinones without the need for enzymatic or metal ion catalysis. The o-quinone formed from 4-OHEN is much more stable than the endogenous catechol estrogens ($t_{1/2}$ = 2.3 h). It appears that the adjacent aromatic ring stabilizes 4-OHEN-o-quinone through extended π-conjugation. In support of this it has been shown that the catechol metabolite of benzo[a]pyrene rapidly undergoes air oxidation to yield a very stable o-quinone, benzo[a]pyrene-7,8-dione. The 4-OHEQ-o-quinone readily isomerizes to 4-OHEN-o-quinone. As a result, most of the biological effects caused by catechol metabolites of equilin are likely due to 4-OHEN-o-quinone formation. Finally, although 2-hydroxylation does occur with equilin producing 2-hyroxyequilin, which will isomerize to 2-hydroxyequilenin, the latter catechol does not autoxidize to an o-quinone at any appreciable rate. This suggests that similar to what has been observed with endogenous catechol estrogens, 2-hydroxylation is likely a benign metabolic pathway for equilin.

DNA Damage Induced by Catechol Estrogens

Oxidative Damage

o-Quinones are also potent redox-active compounds. They can undergo redox cycling with the semiquinone radical generating superoxide radicals mediated through cytochrome P450/P450 reductase. The reaction of superoxide anion radicals with hydrogen peroxide, formed by the enzymatic or spontaneous dismutation of superoxide anion radical, in the presence of trace amounts of iron or other transition metals gives hydroxyl radicals. The hydroxyl radicals are powerful oxidizing agents that may be responsible for damage to essential macromolecules. Biomarkers for oxidative damage to DNA include the formation of the mutagenic lesion, 8-oxo-2′-deoxyguanosine (8-oxo-dG).

The excessive production of ROS in breast cancer tissue has been linked to metastasis of tumors in women with breast cancer. The source of ROS has been suggested to be the result of redox cycling between the o-quinones and their semiquinone radicals generating superoxide, hydrogen peroxide, and ultimately reactive hydroxyl radicals, which cause oxidative cleavage of the phosphate–sugar backbone as well as oxidation of the purine/pyrimidine residues of DNA. In support of this mechanism, various free radical toxicities have been reported in hamsters treated with 17β-estradiol including DNA single-strand breaks, 8-oxo-dG formation, and chromosomal abnormalities. Recently, it has also been shown that 4-hydroxyestradiol also induces oxidative stress and apoptosis in human mammary epithelial cells (MCF-10A), although the concentrations used in this study (25 μM) have questionable physiological relevance. We have shown that 4-OHEN is also capable of causing DNA single-strand breaks and oxidative damage to DNA bases both in breast cancer cells as well as in the rat mammary gland after treatment with 4-OHEN. Treating λ phage DNA with 4-OHEN resulted in extensive single-strand breaks that were due to concentration and time dependence. By including scavengers of ROS in the incubations, DNA could be completely protected from 4-OHEN-mediated damage. In contrast, nicotinamide adenine dinucleotide (NADH) and $CuCl_2$ enhanced the ability of 4-OHEN to cause DNA single-strand breaks presumably due to redox cycling between 4-OHEN and the semiquinone radical generating hydrogen peroxide, and ultimately copper peroxide complexes. It was confirmed that 4-OHEN could oxidize DNA bases, because hydrolysis of 4-OHEN treated calf thymus DNA and high-performance liquid chromatography (HPLC) separation with electrospray *mass spectroscopy* (MS) detection revealed oxidized deoxynucleosides including 8-oxo-dG and 8-oxo-dA. 4-OHEN also caused a dose-dependent increase in the mutagenic lesion 8-oxo-dG in breast cancer cells as determined by LC–MS–MS. In support of this, previous reports have shown that incubations with 4-OHEN-o-quinone, DNA, and hamster liver microsomes also enhanced 8-oxo-dG formation. Using the single cell gel electrophoresis assay (Comet assay) to measure DNA damage, we found that 4-OHEN causes concentration-dependent DNA single-strand cleavage in breast cancer cell lines and this effect could be enhanced by NADH or diethyl maleate. Finally, we have shown that injection of 4-OHEN into the mammary fat pads of Sprague–Dawley rats resulted in dose-dependent increase in single-strand breaks and oxidized bases as analyzed by the Comet assay. In addition, extraction of mammary tissue DNA, hydrolysis to deoxynucleosides, and analysis by LC-MS-MS showed the formation of 8-oxo-dG as well as 8-oxo-dA.

These and other data are evidence for a mechanism of estrogen-induced tumor initiation/promotion by redox cycling of estrogen metabolites generating ROS, which damage DNA.

Formation of Catechol Estrogen DNA Adducts

Some of these metabolites, especially the 3,4-catechols of endogeneous and equine estrogens lead to direct genotoxic effects by damaging cellular DNA. Cavalieri's group has shown that the major DNA adducts produced from 4-hydroxyestradiol-o-quinone are depurinating N7-guanine and N3-adenine adducts both *in vitro* and *in vivo*. Interestingly, they have recently concluded that only the N3-adenine adduct is likely to induce mutations since this adduct depurinates instantaneously, whereas the N7-guanine adduct takes hours to hydrolyze. Similarly, our *in vivo* experiments with rats treated with 4-OHEN as described above, showed the formation of an alkylated depurinating guanine adduct following LC-MS-MS analysis of extracted mammary tissue. However, extraction of mammary tissue DNA, hydrolysis to deoxynucleosides, and analysis by LC-MS- MS also showed the formation of stable cyclic deoxyguanosine and deoxyadenosine adducts as well as the above-mentioned oxidized bases. Interesting, the ratio of the diasteriomeric adducts detected *in vivo* differs from *in vitro* experiments suggesting that there are differences in the response of these stereoisomeric lesions to DNA replication and repair enzymes. This is the first report showing that 4-OHEN is capable of causing DNA damage *in vivo*. In addition, the data showed that 4-OHEN induced four different types of DNA damage that must be repaired by different mechanisms. This is in contrast to the endogenous estrogen 4-hydroxyestrone where only depurinating adducts have been detected in vivo. Finally, in a recent report, highly sensitive nano liquid chromatography–nano electrospray tandem mass spectrometry techniques

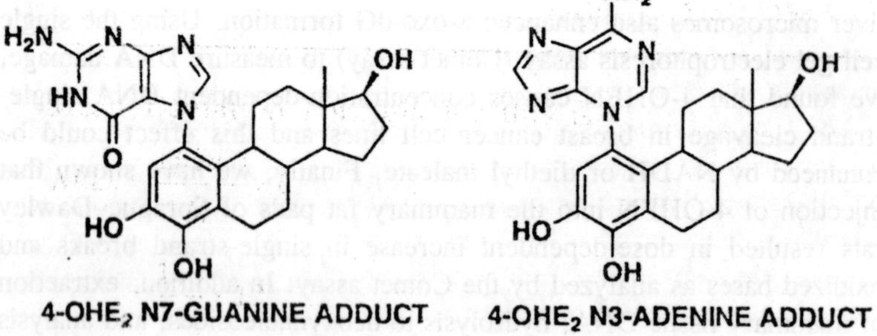

Fig. 9.3. Structures of the DNA adducts of 4-OHE$_2$.

were used to analyze the DNA in five human breast tumor and five adjacent tissue samples, including samples from donors with a known history of Premarin-based HRT. While the sample size is small, and the history of the patients is not fully known, cyclic 4-OHEN-dC, -dG, and -dA stable adducts were detected for the first time in four out of the 10 samples. These results suggest that 4-OHEN has the potential to be a potent carcinogen through the formation of variety of DNA lesions *in vivo*.

Protein Damage Induced by Catechol Estrogens

Glutathione S-Transferase

In addition to DNA damage, it is quite likely that targets for catechol estrogen o-quinones could be crucial cellular proteins. Modification of cysteine sulfhydryl groups either through akylation or oxidation is most likely; however, reaction of o-quinones with nitrogen nucleophiles on proteins has also been reported. For example, Michael-type nucleophilic reactions of quinones with amines and thiols have been implicated in the antitumor activity of ellipticines and some substituted catechols, the neurotoxicity of serotonine, and the hypersensitivity reaction of poison ivy. With estrogens, chemical or enzymatic activation of estrone or 17β-estradiol and their catechol metabolites leads to protein alkylation, which may be responsible for the toxic effects of estrogen o-quinones. For the equine estrogens, we have found that both 4-OHEN and 4-hydroxyequilin (4-OHEQ) are potent irreversible inactivators of glutathione S-transferase. This could be particularly significant to the mechanism of estrogen carcinogenesis, since GST polymorphisms have been associated with increased breast cancer risk. to investigate the role of cysteine residues in the 4-OHEN-mediated inactivation of this enzyme, one or a combination of cysteine residues was replaced by alanine residues (C47A, C101A, C47A/C101A, C14A/C47A/C101A, and C47A/C101A/ C169A mutants). Electrospray ionization mass spectrometric analyses of wild-type and mutant enzymes treated with 4-OHEN showed that a single molecule of 4-OHEN-o-quinone attached to the proteins, with the exception of the C14A/ C47A/C101A mutant where no covalent adduct was detected. 4-OHEN also caused oxidative damage as demonstrated by the appearance of disulfide-bonded species on non-reducing SDS–PAGE and protection of 4-OHEN-mediated enzyme inhibition by free radical scavengers. The studies of thiol group titration and irreversible kinetic experiments indicated that the different cysteines have distinct reactivity for 4-OHEN; Cys 47 was the most reactive thiol group, whereas Cys 169 was resistant to modification. These results demonstrate that hGST P1-1 is inactivated by 4-OHEN through two possible mechanisms: (1) covalent modification of cysteine residues and (2) oxidative damage leading to proteins inactivated by disulfide bond formation. Kinetic inhibition experiments with 4-OHEN showed that GST P1-1 had a lower K_i value (20.8 μM) compared to glyceraldehyde-3-phosphate dehydrogenase (52.4 μM), P450 reductase (77.4 μM), pyruvate kinase (159 μM), glutathione reductase (230 μM), superoxide dismutase (448 μM), catalase (562 μM), GST M1-1 (620 μM), thioredoxin reductase (694 μM), and glutathione peroxidase (1410 μM). We also found that 4-OHEN significantly decreased GSH levels and the activity of GST within minutes in both ER-negative (MDA-MB-231) and ER-positive (S30) human breast cancer cells. In addition, 4-OHEN caused significant decreases in GST activity in non-transformed human breast epithelial cells (MCF-10A), but not in the human hepatoma HepG2 cells, which lack GST P1-1. We also showed that GSH partially protected the inactivation of GST P1-1 by 4-OHEN *in vitro*, and depletion of cellular GSH enhanced the 4-OHEN-induced inhibition of GST activity. In contrast to the significant inhibition of total GST activity in these human breast cancer cells, the other cellular enzymes including P450 reductase, pyruvate kinase, glutathione reductase, superoxide dismutase, catalase, thioredoxin reductase, and glutathione peroxidase were resistant to 4-OHEN-induced inhibition. These data suggest that GST P1-1 may be a preferred protein target for catechol estrogens in vivo. It is possible that the reason for the specificity for GST P1-1 over other cellular enzyme targets is that 4-OHEN could be a substrate for this enzyme; however, to date the rapid kinetic experiments necessary to provide evidence for this hypothesis have not been done and it is unclear that the already very rapid non-enzymatic reaction of the catechol estrogen o-quinones with GSH would be enhanced by enzymatic catalysis *in vivo*.

The inhibition of GST activity in cells may be associated with early events that trigger apoptosis. Not only is GST a detoxification enzyme providing protection against products of oxidative stress, it has also been shown to be involved in cellular regulation through the JNKs signaling pathway. Adler et al. have demonstrated that human GST P1-1 is an endogenous inhibitor of JNKs, which belong to the multi-member family of stress kinases and play a role in cell growth, apoptosis, and transformation. It has been reported that GST inhibitors (S-hexylglutathione and ethacrynic acid) caused significant male germ cell apoptosis and that apoptosis, induced by H_2O_2, could be enhanced by the presence of GST inhibitors. Baez et al. have also showed that GST can protect cells against apoptosis induced by o-quinones derived from catecholamines. It should be noted that the endogenous catechol estrogen 4-OHE, did not decrease the intercellular GSH levels nor inhibit GST activity in human breast cancer cells and it has been shown to be ineffective at inducing apoptosis in these cells. It will be the subject of future work to study the signal transduction pathways activated after the decrease in cellular GSH levels and the inhibition of GST activity by catechol estrogens in cells.

Catechol-O-methyltransferase

Unlike GSTs where it is not known if catechol estrogens are substrates, both endogenous catechol estrogens and the equine catechol estrogens are catechol-O-methyltransferase (COMT) substrates. COMT catalyzes the transfer of a methyl group from the donor SAM to the catechol estrogen and thus represents a crucial detoxification pathway for catechol estrogens. Similar to GST, genetic polymorphism in COMT has also been associated with increased risk for developing breast cancer, although some epidemiological studies have not shown a correlation. 4-OHEN was found to be an irreversible inhibitor of COMT-catalyzed methylation of the endogenous catechol estrogen 4-hydroxyestradiol (4-OHE$_2$) with a K_i of 26.0 μM and a k_2 of 1.62×10^{-2}/s. 4-OHEN *in vitro* not only caused the formation of intermolecular disulfide bonds as demonstrated by gel electrophoresis, but electrospray ionization mass spectrometry (ESI-MS) and matrix-assisted laser desorption ionization time-of-flight mass spectrometry (MALDI-TOF-MS) also showed that 4-OHEN alkylated multiple residues of COMT. Peptide-mapping experiments further indicated that Cys 33 in recombinant human soluble COMT was the residue most likely modified by 4-OHEN *in vitro*. Furthermore, we have also shown that the variant form of COMT, where valine has been substituted for methionine, is more susceptible to 4-OHEN-mediated inhibition. These data suggest that inhibition of COMT methylation by 4-OHEN might reduce endogenous catechol estrogen clearance *in vivo* and further enhance toxicity. Experiments are in progress to determine if COMT is a target for 4-OHEN *in vivo*.

Role of the Estrogen Receptor in Estrogen Carcinogenesis

It is well known that the ER plays a major role in the mechanism of estrogen-induced carcinogenesis. The theory is that excessive binding to the ER leads to an increase in cell proliferation in hormone-sensitive target tissues such as the breast and endometrium. In these rapidly dividing cells, the chances for mutations to occur increases dramatically leading to initiation/promotion of the carcinogenic process. Recently, we have hypothesized that the ER could also play a role in catechol estrogen/o-quinone-induced carcinogenesis. It is quite possible that the catechol estrogen and/or o-quinone bind to the ER, which carries it directly to estrogen-sensitive genes, where DNA damage occurs resulting in mutations.

We have preliminary data that this mechanism may play a role in catechol estrogen-induced toxicity, DNA damage, and apoptosis. We have examined the effect of ER status on the relative ability of 4-OHEN and 4,17β-OHEN to induce DNA damage in ER-negative cells (MDA-MB-231), ERα-positive cells (S30), and ERβ-positive cells (β41). The ER-positive cell lines are stable transfectants derived from the MDA-MB-231 cells. The data showed that both 4-OHEN and 4,17β-OHEN induced concentration-dependent DNA single-strand cleavage in all three cell lines. However, cells containing ERα or ERβ had significantly higher DNA damage, although there was no significant difference between the two ER containing cell lines. In addition, the more estrogenic 4,17β-OHEN generated an increased amount of DNA single-strand breaks as compared to 4-OHEN consistent with its enhanced estrogenic activity. Very similar results were obtained when apoptosis was examined in that ER-positive cells were much more sensitive to 4-OHEN-mediated induction of apoptosis compared to ER-negative cells. Finally, the endogenous catechol estrogen metabolite 4-hydroxyestrone was considerably less effective at inducing DNA damage and apoptosis in breast cancer cell lines as compared to 4-OHEN. Our data suggest that the cytotoxic effects of 4-OHEN could be related to its ability to induce DNA damage and apoptosis in hormone-sensitive cells *in vivo*, and these effects may be potentiated by the ER.

Substitution of the 4-Hydroxy Group on Catechol Estrogens with Fluorine Abolishes Quinoid Formation while Maintaining Estrogenic Activity

Chemical modification of estrogens in order to prevent oxidation to toxic quinoids while maintaining the beneficial effects of estrogens would be highly desirable for new hormone replacement therapies. It has been reported that fluorination of the A-ring of estradiol in the 4-position dramatically reduces catechol estrogen formation without loss of estrogenic activity. In addition, 4-fluoroestradiol is much less carcinogenic compared to estradiol *in vivo*. In order to block catechol

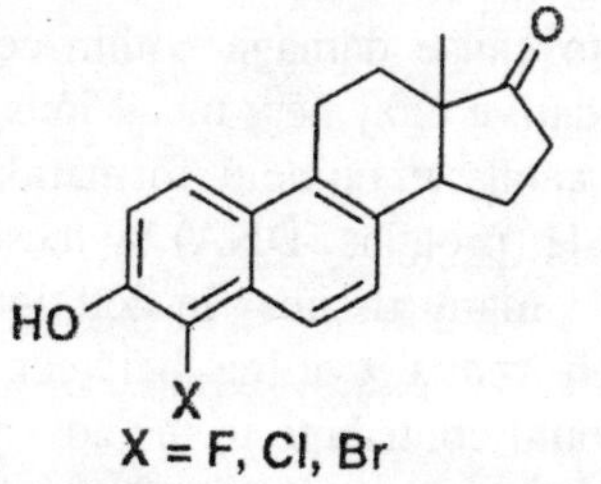

HO, X, O
X = F, Cl, Br

Fig. 9.4. Structures of halogenated equilenin derivatives.

formation from equilenin, 4-halogenated equilenin derivatives were synthesized. These derivatives were tested for their ability to bind to the ER, induce estrogen-sensitive genes, and their potential to form catechol metabolites.

We found that the 4-fluoro derivatives were more estrogenic than the 4-chloro and 4-bromo derivatives as demonstrated by a higher binding affinity for ERs α and β, an enhanced induction in alkaline phosphatase activity in Ishikawa cells, pS2 expression in S30 cells, and PR expression in Ishikawa cells. Incubation of these compounds with tyrosinase in the presence of GSH showed that the halogenated equilenin compounds formed less catechol GSH conjugates than the parent compounds, equilenin and 17β-equilenin. In addition, these halogenated compounds showed less cytotoxicity in the presence of tyrosinase than the parent compounds in S30 cells. Also as stated above, the 4-fluoro derivatives showed similar estrogenic effects as compared with parent compounds; however, they were less toxic in S30 cells as compared to equilenin and 17β-equilenin. Since 17β-halogenated equilenin derivatives showed higher estrogenic effects than the halogenated equilenin *in vitro*, we studied the relative ability of the 17β-halogenated equilenin derivatives to induce estrogenic effects in the ovariectomized rat model. The 4-fluoro derivatives showed higher activity than 4-chloro and 4-bromo as demonstrated by inducing higher vaginal cellular differentiation, uterine growth, and mammary gland branching. However, 17β-hydroxy-4-fluoroequilenin showed a lower estrogenic activity as compared to 17β-hydroxyequilenin and estradiol, which is probably due to the alternative metabolic and distribution pathways in different tissues. These data suggest that the 4-fluoroequilenin derivatives have promise as alternatives to traditional estrogen replacement therapy due to their similar estrogenic properties with less overall toxicity.

The roles of quinones in mediating the adverse effects of estrogens have not been investigated in detail. It is possible for these electrophilic/

redox active quinones to cause damage within cells by a variety of different pathways. Oxidative enzymes, metal ions, and in some cases molecular oxygen can catalyze quinoid formation; so alkylation of cellular nucleophiles (GSH, proteins, DNA) by these species may occur to a significant extent in many tissues. In addition, the formation of ROS especially through redox cycling between the quinones and semiquinone radicals, could contribute to the adverse properties of the parent compounds. Redox cycling can cause lipid peroxidation, consumption of reducing equivalents, oxidation of DNA, and DNA strand breaks. DNA binding occurs, but the sites of alkylation and relationships to cytotoxicity are dependent on the chemical structure of the quinones and the cellular environment in which they are formed. Finally, ERα and/or ERβ may play a role in potentiating the deleterious effects of catechol estrogens and/or o-quinones. Given the direct link between excessive exposure to estrogens, metabolism of estrogens, and increased risk of breast cancer, it is crucial that factors, which affect the formation, reactivity, and cellular targets of estrogen quinoids, be thoroughly explored.

10

Drug Reactions

The use of the term *idiosyncratic drug reaction* (IDR) is quite inconsistent. The term idiosyncratic means specific to an individual. The term will be further restricted in this chapter to exclude reactions that involve known pharmacologic actions of the drug. This excludes adverse reactions such as torsade de pointes, because this adverse reaction involves the effect of a drug on potassium channels, and therefore at least in principle it is predictable. However, torsade de pointes is certainly specific to an individual, and so in another context it could quite reasonably be termed idiosyncratic. When allergists/ clinical immunologists use the term IDR, it usually excludes any immune-mediated reaction. In contrast, in this review it will be used to describe reactions that I suspect are mostly immune-mediated. Other terms that have been used almost interchangeably with IDRs are hypersensitivity reactions, type II and type B reactions.

Characteristics of IDRs

The major characteristic of IDRs is that they are unpredictable and do not occur in most people at any reasonable dose of the drug; however, there is no absolute incidence cutoff, and under the right conditions or in a specific population a specific IDR might occur in more than 50% of patients. It would be better to define adverse reactions by their mechanism, but because the mechanism of most IDRs is unknown we are left with using this characteristic. IDRs can affect virtually any organ and can mimic many other diseases making it very difficult to determine whether or not a given adverse event was due to a drug. A major characteristic of IDRs that is often claimed is that IDRs are dose-independent. In fact, no effect of a drug is independent of dose! As indicated above, an IDR cannot be induced in most patients simply by increasing the dose, and it does not make sense to talk about a dose–response curve in a population where the response does not occur at any dose. Often the incidence does not vary within the narrow dose range used clinically, and an IDR may occur at subtherapeutic doses, especially in a sensitized patient. There is no reason that the dose–response curve for an IDR should be in the same range as the dose–response curve for the therapeutic effect. In fact, the incidences of many IDRs such as hydralazine-induced lupus are clearly dose-dependent within the therapeutic range. In a susceptible patient, there will be a dose–response relationship, and it is axiomatic that a dose can always be found that will not cause an IDR in anyone. A good example is that one way to deal with a patient who is allergic to penicillin is to administer a small dose (about one ten thousandth of a therapeutic dose) and then administer gradually increasing doses until tolerance is induced. Even at one ten thousandth of the usual dose there are more than 10^{16} drug molecules, so there is a lot of room to decrease the dose. I believe it is important to avoid characterizing IDRs as dose-independent, because this is often taken literally and it can be quite misleading. For example, if a very potent drug can be designed it is less likely to cause IDRs as will be discussed again later.

Another important characteristic of IDRs is that there is almost always a delay between starting a drug and the onset of the adverse reaction, unless the patient has been previously exposed to the drug. The length of the delay varies with the type of IDR but is reasonably consistent for a specific drug and type of IDR. It is commonly about 1–2 weeks for IgE-mediated reactions and most other types of skin rash. It is usually 1–3 months for agranulocytosis or liver toxicity, although some types of liver toxicity are associated with a longer delay. For drug-induced lupus, the delay is usually several months, and it is not uncommon for it to occur after more than a year of treatment. It is typical for the delay to be greatly reduced in a patient who has had an IDR to a drug if the patient is rechallenged with that drug, but this is not always the case. In two animal models of drug-induced autoimmunity that we have used, penicillamine-induced autoimmunity in the Brown Norway rat and propylthiouracil-induced autoimmunity in the cat, the time to disease onset on rechallenge is the same as it was on initial exposure. This may be related to the fact that these diseases are autoimmune in nature and, therefore, if autoreactive T cells were not deleted or made anergic, the adverse reaction would continue after the drug was discontinued and this usually does not occur. A clinical example where a clearly immune-mediated reaction does not recur rapidly on rechallenge is heparin-induced thrombocytopenia.

Significance

IDRs represent a major clinical problem and are a significant cause of hospital admissions. They not only cause suffering and sometimes death for the patients who have these adverse reactions, but also markedly increase the uncertainty of drug development. In the period from 1975 to 2000, over 10% of the drugs approved by the FDA either had to be withdrawn or were given a "*black box*" warning because of IDRs not predicted by preclinical testing and clinical trials. If it were not for the potential that a drug candidate might cause IDRs, much of the current testing could be eliminated and the process of development accelerated; yet, the testing that is currently performed is ineffective at predicting whether a drug candidate will pose an undo risk of IDRs. In order to better predict which drug candidates will cause a high risk of IDRs and which patients are at increased risk, we need a better mechanistic understanding; this will be the emphasis of this chapter.

Postulated Mechanisms

Although hypotheses abound, it must be said that, with few exceptions, the mechanisms of IDRs are unknown. Two major hypotheses are that the majority of IDRs are caused by reactive metabolites and are immune-mediated. Although current opinion favors these two hypotheses, in the absence of definitive supportive evidence and with some evidence to the contrary, they are often hotly debated. By their very nature, IDRs are difficult to study, and in particular there are very few animal models. Therefore, it is very difficult to definitively test these hypotheses. In the absence of sufficient animal models, for the time being, we are left with inferring mechanism from clinical data. The question of whether IDRs are immune-mediated and are caused by reactive metabolites are fundamental; therefore, while describing IDRs, this chapter will focus on the evidence relevant to these two hypotheses.

Are IDRs Immune-mediated?

Drug-induced autoimmunity

It is reasonable to assume that autoimmune reactions, such as lupus and myasthenia gravis, are immune-mediated. There is a significant autoimmune component to several other IDRs, although the presence of autoantibodies does not prove that the IDR is immune-mediated unless it can be demonstrated that these autoantibodies mediate the adverse reaction. Autoimmune reactions involving the skin and blood cells will be discussed in the sections involving skin and blood cells, respectively.

Drug-induced lupus

Lupus is the classic generalized autoimmune disease. Most lupus is idiopathic, i.e. its cause is unknown. There are various animal models that spontaneously develop lupus and provide clues to possible mechanisms. In several models, there is defective apoptosis, which presumably interferes with the elimination of specific T cells. Another hypothesis is that there is cross-reactivity between a pathogen and self-antigens so that an immune response against the pathogen leads to autoimmunity. In fact, pathogens could use such molecular mimicry to try to "hide" from the immune system.

Lupus can affect essentially all parts of the body, but involvement of the central nervous system and kidneys are most likely to cause death. It is characterized by a variety of autoantibodies, but the most characteristic autoantibodies are antinuclear antibodies that bind to various components of the nucleus, including DNA and histone protein. Antinuclear antibodies can form immune complexes that are trapped in the kidney, bind complement and induce an immune response leading to kidney damage. However, the mechanism by which an autoimmune response leads to damage of other organs is poorly understood.

Although most lupus is idiopathic, about 10% is due to drugs. Drug-induced lupus is less serious than idiopathic lupus because central nervous system and kidney involvement are uncommon. Discontinuation of the drug usually leads to prompt resolution of symptoms, even though antinuclear antibodies often persist for years albeit at steadily decreasing concentrations. The autoantibodies in drug-induced lupus are often antihistone antibodies, while those in idiopathic lupus are more commonly antidouble-stranded DNA antibodies; however, there is significant overlap between idiopathic and drug-induced lupus such that they cannot be readily distinguished except for the history of exposure to a drug that is known to cause lupus and resolution of symptoms when the drug is stopped.

There are several theories for the mechanism by which drugs can induce lupus, including: inhibition of DNA methylation, activation of antigen-presenting cells, interference with immune tolerance and molecular mimicry; however, conclusive evidence for any one hypothesis is lacking and it is likely that the mechanism is different for different drugs.

Drug-induced myasthenia gravis

Myasthenia gravis is an autoimmune disease characterized by antibodies against the acetylcholine receptor at the neuromuscular junction leading to muscle weakness. It is treated with drugs that inhibit the hydrolysis of acetylcholine by cholinesterase resulting in an increased amount of acetylcholine and providing increased stimuli to the inhibited receptors. As with lupus, most myasthenia gravis is idiopathic, but it can also be caused by drugs. Penicillamine, in particular, can lead to a variety of autoimmune reactions including myasthenia gravis; however, the mechanism is unknown.

Involvement of the immune system in idiosyncratic liver toxicity

Hepatic necrosis

Although there are several patterns of drug-induced liver injury, hepatocellular injury leading to hepatic necrosis is the type most commonly associated with liver failure leading to either death or liver transplantation; therefore, this will be the focus of most of the discussion. Idiosyncratic hepatic necrosis is the most common cause of drug withdrawal, so it is of particular interest to the pharmaceutical industry.

(a) *Apparent immune idiosyncrasy*. Halothane-induced hepatotoxicity is associated with various drug-induced antibodies, which suggests that it is immune-mediated. Some of the antibodies are directed against trifluoroacetylated protein generated by the reactive metabolite of halothane and some are autoantibodies. However, it would be very difficult to prove that these antibodies mediate liver damage; therefore, their presence does not prove that halothane-induced hepatitis is immune-mediated. In fact, if it is immune-mediated, given the nature of the reactive metabolite, it is just as likely that T cells mediate most of the liver damage and the antibodies are an epiphenomenon. But the overall picture strongly suggests that halothane-induced hepatotoxicity is immune-mediated. Specifically, the idiosyncratic nature of the IDR is more readily explained by differences in immune response than by any other known mechanism. In addition, the toxicity almost never occurs on first exposure, which strongly suggests that immune sensitization is involved Overt toxicity with jaundice is usually preceded by fever, and it is often noted that a previous exposure was also associated with fever even though no overt clinical toxicity was observed; this provides further evidence of sensitization during the earlier exposure. Furthermore, there is a reasonable correlation between the presence of antibodies and hepatotoxicity, so even if the antibodies do not mediate the toxicity they represent a marker of immune-activation by halothane in the patients who develop toxicity. Although the cellular infiltrate is usually less than seen with viral hepatitis, there is an inflammatory component to halothane hepatitis and eosinophils are sometimes observed. Despite this evidence, involvement of the immune system in halothane-induced hepatitis has been questioned.

Tienilic acid-induced liver failure is similar to that of halothane in that it is associated with drug-induced antibodies. It this case the antibodies are directed against Cyp 2C9, the enzyme that forms the reactive metabolite. However, as with halothane, there is no direct evidence that these antibodies mediate the hepatotoxicity of tienilic acid. Another feature of tienilic acid hepatotoxicity that suggests that it is immunemediated is that the rechallenge leads to a rapid recurrence. Likewise, the hepatitis associated with dihydralazine is associated with antibodies against Cyp 1A2. Because of other immune-manifestations, the hepatotoxicity associated with sulfonamides, phenytoin, and methyldopa is also usually assumed to be immune-mediated; however, conclusive evidence is lacking.

(b) *Apparent metabolic idiosyncrasy*. Idiosyncratic hepatotoxicity associated with many drugs does not have characteristics that suggest involvement of the immune system. Classic signs of an immune-mediated reaction include fever, rash, and eosinophilia; however, their absence is not strong evidence against an immune mechanism and such manifestations are often absent in clearly immune-mediated reactions. Another characteristic of immune-mediated reactions is a very rapid onset on rechallenge, presumably due to the presence of memory T cells. This is observed with most IDRs that are believed to be immune-mediated; however, rechallenge of patients with a history of isoniazid- or troglitazone-induced hepatotoxicity usually does not lead to a rapid onset of toxicity and may not cause hepatotoxicity at all. The time-to-onset on initial exposure for these drugs also tends to be longer than with drugs that cause hepatotoxicity with more features that suggest an immune-mediated reaction; troglitazone-induced hepatotoxicity has been reported to occur after more than a year of treatment. However, this is also a characteristic of drug-induced autoimmunity. The hepatic

IDRs associated with pyrazinamide and ketoconazole also fit in this category. Zimmerman referred to such hepatic IDRs as metabolic idiosyncrasy. Although this is an interesting concept, there are no examples in which differences in a specific metabolic pathway have been shown to account for why some patients have an IDR to a drug and most do not. For example, although some controversy still exists, it appears that the slow acetylator genotype is associated with an increased risk of isoniazid-induced hepatotoxicity. However, in North America, about 50% of the population are slow acetylators, therefore, this cannot explain the idiosyncratic nature of isoniazid-induced hepatotoxicity. It is certainly possible that some combination of several different polymorphisms in drug metabolism/reactive metabolite detoxication could explain the idiosyncratic nature of IDRs. It also seems probable that polymorphisms in some other biochemical pathways could be involved, but there are virtually no data to support this hypothesis. Although it is likely that a reactive metabolite is involved as discussed below, without evidence of a polymorphism that can explain their idiosyncratic nature, the basis for the idiosyncratic nature of the hepatotoxicity of drugs such as isoniazid is simply unknown and an immune mechanism cannot be ruled out.

(c) *Mitochondrial toxicity*. The characteristics of hepatotoxicity associated with valproic acid are quite different from those of most other drugs associated with causing hepatocellular damage. Instead of children being resistant to valproic acid toxicity, as they are with most other drugs associated with hepatic IDRs, children are at significantly higher risk. Although valproic acid ultimately leads to necrosis, the early histological picture is usually (although not always) one of microvesicular steatosis. This suggests that the drug interferes with mitochondrial β-oxidation of fatty acids, and its structure, a branched-chain aliphatic carboxylic acid, supports this hypothesis. The early appearance of hyperammonemia also suggests impairment of mitochondrial function. The toxicity associated with valproic acid is similar to salicylate-induced hepatotoxicity (also a carboxylic acid) as well as Jamaican vomiting sickness, which is due to a toxic metabolite of hypoglycin A, specifically, 2-methylenecyclopropylpropionic acid. Valproic acid is metabolized to 4-en-valproic acid, which is similar in structure and toxicity to hypoglycin A. Thus, valproic acid hepatotoxicity truly does appear to represent metabolic idiosyncrasy and Zimmerman also classed this IDR as such. However, it is not clear what metabolic polymorphism(s) is/are responsible for the idiosyncratic nature and what is responsible for the delay between starting the drug and the onset of toxicity. In particular, the incidence of valproate-induced hepatotoxicity peaks from 2 to 4 months after the start of therapy and declines rapidly after that. Although there is strong evidence that mitochondrial toxicity is important in the mechanism of valproic acid hepatotoxicity, it is possible that the immune system also plays a role.

Amiodarone and perhexiline are cationic amphiphilic drugs that are concentrated in the mitochondria and cause idiosyncratic steatotic hepatitis whose toxicity also likely involves their inhibition of mitochondrial function. There are other examples, such as zidovudine, in which hepatotoxicity appears to involve damage to the mitochondrial DNA.

(d) *The "inflammagen" hypothesis for hepatic IDRs*. Another hypothesis that has been suggested to explain the idiosyncratic nature and delay in the onset of hepatic IDRs is the chance exposure to some "*inflammagen*," which potentiates the intrinsic hepatotoxicity of the drug. This hypothesis is based on the finding that the combination of an agent, e.g. ranitidine, with lipopolysaccharide caused immediate hepatotoxicity in rats where the same dose of the agent alone did not. To date, this has not been demonstrated with any drugs commonly associated with idiosyncratic liver failure in humans. Furthermore, potentiation by an inflammagen is also consistent with an immune mechanism as discussed later. This hypothesis does not explain why IDRs almost never occur immediately on first exposure even though some drugs, such as antibiotics and anti-inflammatory drugs, are usually administered in the context of an inflammatory environment. This hypothesis also does not explain the rapid onset of toxicity on rechallenge that is an important feature for some drugs, such as halothane and tienilic acid. However, it is likely that there are many mechanisms of IDRs and this may be one of them.

Cholestatic liver injury

The other common pattern of liver injury induced by drugs is cholestatic. It is usually claimed that it rarely results in liver failure. However, a recent paper suggests that cholestatic injury is associated with almost the same risk of liver failure as hepatocellular injury. Although some drugs can cause either types of injuries and individual cases of drug-induced liver injury can have both hepatocellular and cholestatic components, most drugs can usually be classified as predominantly causing either a hepatocellular or a cholestatic pattern. A classic drug associated with causing cholestatic liver injury is chlorpromazine. Chlorpromazine-induced cholestasis is usually preceded by fever and constitutional symptoms and accompanied by eosinophilia. These are classic signs of an immune reaction; therefore, it is assumed that this is an immune-mediated IDR. However, it is not known how chlorpromazine initiates an immune response, or what branch of the immune system mediates the damage.

Another drug commonly associated with cholestatic injury is erythromycin, especially the estolate salt. It usually occurs after 1–3 weeks of treatment and is commonly associated with fever and eosinophilia, thus leading to the assumption that it is immune-mediated; however, as with chlorpromazine, there is little basic understanding of the mechanism. A more recent drug associated with a cholestatic or mixed picture of liver injury is terbinafine.

Immune-involvement in dermatological IDRs

Although usually not serious, skin rashes are said to be the most common type of IDR. It is possible that liver injury is actually more common, but because we cannot see the liver and the transaminases are not measured daily; liver injury is not noticed unless it is severe or it is detected accidentally by blood tests. The skin is a major barrier to the outside world and it is very immunologically active. In fact, dermal or subcutaneous administration of a drug more often leads to an immune response where oral administration often leads to immune tolerance. There are many types of drug-induced skin rashes and only a few will be high-lighted as examples.

IgE-mediated urticaria

Classic urticaria (hives) is mediated by IgE antibodies that bind to mast cells/basophils and, when cross-linked by antigen, lead to the release of mediators such as histamine and leukotrienes that mediate the symptoms associated with such reactions. Depending on the location and extent of mediator release, it can lead to hives or a more generalized reaction called anaphylaxis, which is characterized by hypotension and airway constriction. However, not all urticaria is immune-mediated, or more specifically, not mediated by IgE antibodies. In fact, factors such as heat, cold, and exercise can induce urticaria, and it is hard to imagine an antibody against exercise. It is clear that true anaphylaxis and IgE-mediated urticaria are immune-mediated, because it can be demonstrated that IgE antibodies mediate the IDR. There are other idiosyncratic reactions to drugs, such as X-ray contrast material, that involve a direct pharmacologically mediated degranulation of mast cells and are not immune-mediated; however, X-ray contrast material can also cause true allergic reactions. Nonsteroidal antiin flammatory drugs can also cause an anaphylactoid reaction by shifting the metabolism of arachidonic acid from the synthesis of prostaglandins toward the synthesis of leukotrienes, and it is the leukotrienes that appear to mediate the reaction.

Morbilliform rashes

Morbilliform (measles-like, also known as maculopapular) rashes are very common, especially with the aminopenicillins (amoxicillin and ampicillin). The amoxicillin rash was often referred to as a "*toxic*" rash, because rechallenge with amoxicillin did not usually lead to a recurrence of rash. More recently, there is evidence that at least some morbilliform rashes are mediated by $CD4^{+}$ T cells. This would explain their mild nature because CD4 binds to MHC-II and only a minority of cells expresses MHC-II. However, if these rashes are mediated by the adaptive immune system, it does not explain why there is no memory. We now know that many people lose their allergy to penicillin with time and this may explain the lack of memory. Amoxicillin is often given inappropriately to patients with viral infections, and it may be that a rash only occurs with the combination of drug and viral infection similar to the inflammagen hypothesis. Many severe reactions start out looking like morbilliform rashes and evolve into much more severe reactions. Morbilliform rashes may have more than one pathogenic mechanism, and although immune involvement is likely in most cases, it has not been conclusively demonstrated.

Stevens–Johnson syndrome/toxic epidermal necrolysis Stevens–Johnson syndrome is a more serious rash with a low but significant mortality rate. It is characterized by mucus membrane involvement and systemic symptoms such as fever. Toxic epidermal necrolysis is even more severe and is associated with a 30% mortality rate. It is characterized by separation of the layers of skin at the dermal–epidermal junction. Although it has been a subject of controversy, it appears that Stevens–Johnson syndrome and toxic epidermal necrolysis are mechanistically very similar and the major difference is one of severity. There is evidence that these severe reactions are mediated by drug-specific $CD8^{+}$ T cells that kill keratinocytes by a perforin- and granzyme B-mediated mechanism.

Nevirapine, a non-nucleoside reverse transcriptase inhibitor used for the treatment of AIDS, is associated with a quite high incidence of rash, most of which is mild, but it is also associated with a significant incidence of Stevens–Johnson syndrome and toxic epidermal necrolysis. The incidence is lower in patients with decreased CD4 lymphocyte counts, which suggests that $CD4^+$ T cells are involved in the pathogenesis. Abacavir, another drug used for the treatment of AIDS, is associated with a rash and generalized hypersensitivity reaction. Although the initial reaction typically occurs after about 10 days, rechallenge results in a severe syndrome within hours. Patch testing is usually positive. These characteristics strongly suggest that this is an immune-mediated reaction.

Drug-induced pemphigus

Pemphigus is an idiopathic autoimmune bullous skin disease in which antibodies against desmogleins (proteins that belong to the cadherin supergene family of adhesion molecules) lead to blister formation. Drugs can also cause autoantibody-mediated pemphigus and the antibodies have the same specificity as the idiopathic disease. The drugs associated with the highest incidence of pemphigus, i.e. penicillamine and captopril, have sulfhydryl groups, but other nonsulfhydryl-containing drugs have also been reported to cause pemphigus. Drugs can also cause the related bullous skin diseases, pemphigoid and linear IgA bullous dermatosis. This is another example of an immune-mediated IDR.

Acute generalized exanthematous pustulosis

Acute generalized exanthematous pustulosis (AGREP) is an uncommon condition characterized by intradermal, neutrophil-filled pustules, as well as fever and marked leukocytosis, sometimes including eosinophilia. It is usually caused by aminopenicillins, sulfonamide antibiotics, and diltiazem. It is also characterized by the production of IL-8, which is a neutrophil-attracting chemokine. Patch tests are often positive and the first cells to infiltrate the skin are IL-8-producing $CD4^+$ T cells.

Drug hypersensitivity syndrome

The term hypersensitivity is used in several different ways. It will be used here to refer to a syndrome composed of fever and rash, as well as involvement of one or more internal organs. The most common organ involved is the liver, but involvement of other organs can lead to manifestations such as lymphadenopathy, leukopenia, nephritis, myositis, carditis, pneumonitis, thyroiditis, and aseptic meningitis. Because it is not limited to the skin, its inclusion in this section is arbitrary. This reaction is most commonly seen with aromatic anticonvulsants and sulfonamide antibiotics. The clinical characteristics, especially the delay in onset on first exposure but rapid recurrence on rechallenge, suggest that it is immune-mediated. Further evidence for immune-mediation is the finding of drug-specific T cells in patients with these reactions.

Immune-involvement in hematological reactions

Various blood cells are frequent targets of IDRs. This can occur either in the bone marrow involving the precursors of peripheral blood cells or it can involve destruction of mature blood cells.

Aplastic anemia

Aplastic anemia is due to the destruction of all blood cell precursors in the bone marrow. A bone marrow biopsy showing the replacement of blood cell precursors by fat cells is required for the diagnosis. Most aplastic anemia is idiopathic, probably either autoimmune or caused by a virus, and aplastic anemia sometimes follows viral hepatitis or seronegative idiopathic hepatitis. One treatment for aplastic anemia, which is effective in about two thirds of cases, is immunosuppression with antithymocyte antibodies and/or immunosuppressant drugs such as cyclosporin. Response to this therapy suggests that aplastic anemia is immune-mediated. In addition, the bone marrows of patients with aplastic anemia contain activated lymphocytes that produce interferon-γ and tumor necrosis factor. In fact, the production of interferon-γ in peripheral lymphocytes is a very good predictor of which patients with aplastic anemia will respond to immunosuppressive therapy. The gene expression profiles of $CD4^+$ and $CD8^+$ T cells from the bone marrows of patients with aplastic anemia suggested that both the innate and adaptive immune system are involved in the immune response. The response rate to immunosuppression appears to be the same whether the aplastic anemia is idiopathic or drug-induced, suggesting that drug-induced aplastic anemia is another immune-mediated IDR.

Thrombocytopenia

Probably, the most common drug associated with thrombocytopenia is heparin. Heparin binds to platelet factor 4 and the complex induces the production of antibodies. These antibodies can be against the heparin-platelet factor 4 complex or they can be true autoantibodies that recognize platelet factor 4 alone. The complex binds to the FC receptor on platelets and this leads to platelet aggregation, release of more platelet factor 4, and destruction of platelets. In a study of 202 patients with heparin-induced thrombocytopenia, most occurred after 5–10 days of therapy; however, in some patients, especially those who had received heparin in the last 10 days, thrombocytopenia occurred less than 24 h after starting heparin treatment. It was speculated that this is due to persistent antibodies, because the time course was faster than the usual amnestic immune response. In contrast, all patients who had not received heparin in the previous 100 days had a delayed onset of thrombocytopenia and it was also found that the titer of antibodies decreased rapidly with time. In addition, seven patients who had a previous episode of confirmed heparin-induced thrombocytopenia but did not currently have circulating antibodies were purposely rechallenged: none of them developed thrombocytopenia. Clearly, this is an immune-mediated IDR; thus, not all immune-mediated IDRs occur immediately on rechallenge, especially if there has been a significant period of time between the exposures. In the case of heparin-induced thrombocytopenia, the autoimmune nature of the reaction may prevent the persistence of memory T cells. Gold salts and procainamide can induce the formation of pure autoantibody-mediated thrombocytopenia.

An unusual form of thrombocytopenia is caused by quinine. It is due to a class of antibodies that bind to platelet membrane glycoproteins, usually the fibrinogen receptor or von Willebrand factor receptor, but only when quinine is present in soluble form. When the platelets are washed to remove the quinine the antibody binding no longer occurs. It is not clear whether the quinine forms a complex with the glycoprotein or changes its conformation. Unlike heparin-induced thrombocytopenia, the sensitivity lasts for years and one dose is sufficient to cause thrombocytopenia in a sensitized patient.

An interesting example of drug-induced thrombocytopenia that violates the rule that there is always a delay between starting the drug and the onset of the IDR on first exposure is the antithrombotic drugs, e.g. tirofiban and eptifibatide, which work by binding to the glycoprotein IIb/IIIa complex and block the binding of fibrinogen. There appear to be natural or preexisting antibodies that bind to the drug-glycoprotein complex, because drug-dependent antibodies were found in pretreatment blood samples. There are rare cases in which other IDRs appear to occur immediately on first exposure, but they are not well-documented and the mechanism is not clear.

Agranulocytosis

Another target for IDRs is the granulocytic series of leukocytes. The major granulocyte is the neutrophil. One of the first drugs to be recognized as causing agranulocytosis was aminopyrine. The drug, or more likely a reactive metabolite, induces the formation of drug-dependent antineutrophil antibodies. This was demonstrated by an investigator who took aminopyrine and then infused into himself blood from a patient who had acute aminopyrine-induced agranulocytosis resulting in a precipitous drop in his neutrophil count. The serum also caused aggregation of neutrophils in vitro in the presence of drug. Although these studies demonstrate that aminopyrine can lead to the destruction of mature neutrophils, examination of the bone marrow indicates that neutrophil precursors are also a target.

Hemolytic anemia

The mechanisms of drug-induced hemolytic anemias have been divided into three different categories: autoimmune, hapten-mediated, and immune complex-mediated. The classic example of drug-induced autoimmune hemolytic anemia is caused by α-methyldopa. Antibodies are generated that bind to red cells in the absence of drug. The major antigen to which these antibodies bind appears to be the Rh protein; however, it is not clear how the drug leads to the formation of these antibodies. Cefotetan is presently the most common cause of immune-mediated hemolytic anemia and it is associated with antibodies that bind to cetotetan-treated red blood cells.

Are Reactive Metabolites Responsible for IDRs?

Pioneering work by the Millers and others in the 1950s provided conclusive evidence that many carcinogens exert their activity through chemically reactive metabolites that bind to DNA. The concept that reactive metabolites are also responsible for other types of chemical toxicity was established in Brodie's laboratory, and its most notable extension to drugs was with acetaminophen hepatotoxicity. Although the mechanism by which the reactive imidoquinone metabolite acetaminophen causes liver necrosis has still not been established, there are few who would dispute that this reactive metabolite is responsible for toxicity.

If it is accepted from the previous sections that many IDRs are immune-mediated, the question becomes: how do drugs lead to an immune response? It is known that agents that cause allergic reactions are almost universally either chemically reactive small molecules or large molecules such as proteins. Small molecule allergens include urushiol (poison ivy), dinitrofluorobenzene/dinitrochlorobenzene, trimellitic anhydride, toluene diisocyanate, and oxazolone. Metals that cause immune-mediated reactions are also those that interact very strongly with proteins. This includes mercury, gold, nickel, and beryllium. If reactive metabolites are responsible for many IDRs, the follow-up question is: how do reactive species lead to an immune response?

Hapten vs. pharmaceutical interaction hypotheses

It was suggested some 70 years ago that small molecules are not immunogenic unless they bind irreversibly to proteins. This led to the concept that when small molecules react with proteins they make the proteins appear foreign to the immune system and this can lead to an immune response. Agents that are not immunogenic unless bound to proteins or other macromolecules are known as haptens. Most drugs are not chemically reactive but many are metabolized to one or more reactive metabolites that can bind to proteins; such molecules are known as prohaptens. This principle remained essentially unchallenged for more than a half century until Werner Pichler found that patients who have had an IDR often have T cells that are activated by unreactive drugs in the absence of metabolism that could convert them from prohaptens into hapten. This led to the *pharmaceutical interaction* (PI) hypothesis, i.e. drugs can activate T cells by a direct and reversible interaction with the MHC–T cell receptor complex analogous to the PI between a drug and a receptor. An important question is whether such a reversible interaction can initiate an immune response or whether such T cells are byproducts of an immune response initiated by a reactive metabolite.

Danger hypothesis

Another principle of immunology that was accepted for decades is that the immune system is able to differentiate "self" from "foreign" and, in general, only responds to foreign molecules. Polly Matzinger challenged this hypothesis, saying that it is difficult and inefficient to differentiate self from foreign, and the only defense that an organism needs is to identify agents that cause damage to oneself. This is referred to as the danger hypothesis. She further hypothesized that it is the affected tissue that also determines what type of immune response will occur. Not all drugs that form reactive metabolites are associated with a significant incidence of IDRs, and it is possible that for a reactive metabolite to lead to an immune response it must cause cell damage or cell stress – the danger signal.

Even before the danger hypothesis was proposed it had been recognized that, to induce a significant immune response a second signal was required.(the first signal is the recognition of antigen by T cells presented in the context of MHC). The second signal is provided by costimulatory factors such as B7 on antigen-presenting cells interacting with CD28 on T cells. B7 is upregulated by a variety of stimuli that could be considered danger signals. It is known that some IDRs are more common in patients who have infections or other major stresses such as surgery. The classic example is that if a patient with mononucleosis is given an aminopenicillin (ampicillin or amoxicillin), they are almost certain to develop a rash. It has also been suggested that there is an association between the aromatic anticonvulsant hypersensitivity syndrome and the reactivation of human herpes virus 6. Patients with AIDS have an increased risk of a sulfonamide rash. An interesting example is that patients given an aromatic anticonvulsant after brain irradiation appear to have a much higher incidence of serious skin rashes. However viral infections do not always increase the risk of IDRs. Mild infections, such as the common cold, that are not accompanied by fever are probably not a risk factor. Patients with AIDS and a low CD4 count actually have a lower incidence of liver toxicity and rash when nevirapine is given. Patients with viral hepatitis do not appear to have an increased risk of liver toxicity when given a drug known to be associated with a significant incidence of hepatic IDRs.

Although the underlying biology of the above observations is unknown, there is probably a major difference between an acute and a chronic danger signal. An acute infection (e.g. mononucleosis) coinciding with the initiation of drug therapy probably increases risk while a chronic infection, such as viral hepatitis that preceded the onset of

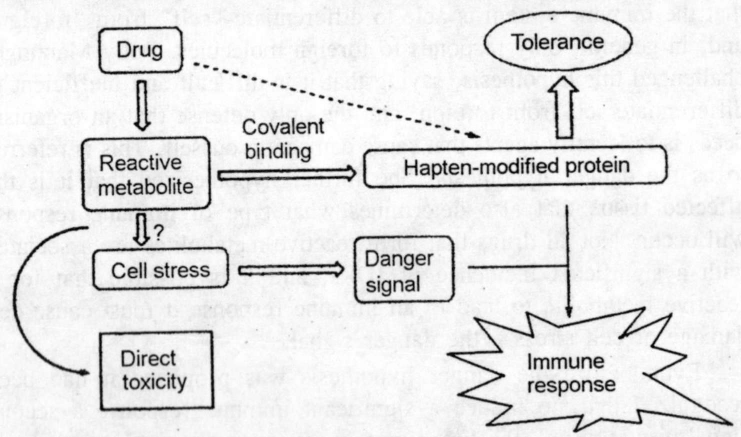

Fig. 10.1. Depiction of the mechanisms by which the hepaten and danger hypotheses could be related to ADRs.

drug therapy, is likely to have a very different effect. A major unanswered question is the relative role of drug-induced danger signals vs. other sources of danger signals.

Importance of reactive metabolite characteristics

Drugs that cause IDRs can often cause several different types of IDRs; however, each drug usually has a characteristic spectrum of IDRs. The characteristic IDR associated with hydralazine is a lupus-like autoimmune IDR, while sulfamethoxazole can cause almost any type of IDR including mild morbilliform rashes, generalized hypersensitivity, toxic epidermal necrolysis, anaphylactic reactions, isolated liver toxicity, agranulocytosis, aplastic anemia, etc. If IDRs are caused by reactive metabolites, why do different types of reactive metabolites cause different types of IDRs and some do not seem to cause any significant toxicity?

One important characteristic is the amount of reactive metabolite formed. The likely reason that drugs given at low dose are rarely responsible for a high incidence of IDRs is that even if conversion of the drug into a reactive metabolite is efficient, the total amount of drug available for such conversion is limited. It is virtually impossible to quantify the amount of covalent binding - a measure of reactive metabolite formed - in humans in the target organ of toxicity. For example, it would be impossible to give a human a dose of radiolabeled drug sufficient to quantify covalent binding, and furthermore sampling internal organs would require an invasive procedure such as a liver biopsy. In general, we are left with extrapolation from experiments in animals, but of course the metabolism of drugs is often significantly different in animals.

Another important characteristic is the reactivity and half-life of the reactive metabolite. Most reactive metabolites are electrophiles (electron deficient) and bind to protein nucleophiles. Some are "soft" and react with "soft" nucleophiles such as glutathione and others are "hard" and bind to hard nucleophiles such as amino groups. Although some of the proteins to which reactive metabolites bind are known, we do not know the range of proteins that are modified by most reactive metabolites and virtually nothing about what protein modifications may be responsible for IDRs. Many reactive metabolites are so reactive that they do not reach sites far from where they are formed; in some cases they do not even escape the enzyme that formed them. Therefore, most reactive metabolites must be formed in the target organ of toxicity. Furthermore, when reactive metabolites with a short half-life are formed intracellularly, reactive metabolite-modified proteins will likely be presented in the context of MHC-I, which is present on all cells except for red cells, and lead to a cell-mediated immune reaction. This is the basis for expecting IDRs to drugs such as halothane to be mediated by T cells. However, some reactive metabolites, such as acyl glucuronides, have a long half-life and freely circulate. Other drugs, especially β-lactams, are reactive without metabolism and these also freely circulate. This type of less reactive species can also bind extensively to extracellular proteins, which can then be taken up by phagocytic antigen-presenting cells and presented in the context of MHC-II leading to an antibody-mediated immune reaction. Consistent with this picture is that the classic IDRs associated with β-lactams are antibody-mediated. This principle was also nicely demonstrated with a study that found that sensitizing agents leading to a delayed-type cell-mediated immune response were found to bind mainly to intracellular proteins and those that lead to an antibody-mediated allergic reaction bound mainly to extracellular proteins. However, immune responses are often a mix of cell- and antibody-mediated reactions.

Involvement of reactive metabolites in drug-induced autoimmunity

The major drugs that have been associated with drug-induced lupus are procainamide, hydralazine, and minocycline. These drugs are oxidized to reactive metabolites by macrophages and this may lead to the activation of these cells and generalized activation of the immune system. The major enzyme involved in this oxidation is myeloperoxidase and drug-induced lupus is often associated with antibodies against this peroxidase. An alternative hypothesis for the mechanism of drug-induced lupus is that inhibition of DNA methylation also leads to activation of the immune system. This hypothesized mechanism does not require the formation of reactive metabolites, because at least in the case of procainamide and hydralazine, the parent drug inhibits DNA methylation. Most of the other drugs associated with the induction of a lupus-like syndrome, such as sulfonamide antibiotics, isoniazid, aromatic anticonvulsants, and propylthiouracil, form reactive metabolites and they also cause other types of IDRs that have been attributed to reactive metabolites. There is no evidence that these other drugs also inhibit DNA methylation. Of course, these two hypotheses are not mutually exclusive.

Penicillamine is associated with a wide range of autoimmune IDRs and it is reactive without metabolism. It has a free sulfhydryl group that can react with protein disulfides to form mixed disulfides between the drug and protein. In addition, penicillamine also has an amino group, which together with the sulfhydryl group, can react with aldehyde groups to form a thiazolidine ring. One of the interactions between T cells and antigen-presenting cells involves the reversible formation of an imine by reaction of an amino group on the T cell with an aldehyde group on the antigen-presenting cell. It is possible that the irreversible reaction between penicillamine and the antigen-presenting cell aldehyde group could lead to a generalized activation of the immune system. Hydralazine and isoniazid also react irreversibly with aldehyde groups and can also cause a lupus-like syndrome.

Various cytokines and anti-cytokine antibodies can also cause autoimmune IDRs. However, it is unlikely that the autoimmune reactions associated with these agents involve reactive metabolites.

In summary, there is evidence to suggest that some drug-induced autoimmune reactions involve reactive metabolites; however, conclusive evidence is lacking and it is likely that the autoimmunity caused by some drugs, especially agents like cytokines, is not caused by reactive metabolites. In cases where it is likely that reactive metabolites are involved, there is no evidence that the reactive metabolite is acting as a hapten. If the mechanism involves activation of macrophages or other antigen-presenting cells, it would fit the danger hypothesis.

Involvement of reactive metabolites in hepatic IDRs

If reactive metabolites are responsible for many IDRs, it is not surprising that the liver is a major target of IDRs, because it has the highest activity of metabolic enzymes that can generate reactive metabolites. It also has a high concentration of glutathione and other systems to detoxify reactive metabolites, but no system is perfect and glutathione conjugates can sometimes be more reactive than the reactive species from which they are formed.

Halothane-induced hepatitis

It is hard to imagine a simple molecule like halothane causing hepatic IDRs without the formation of a reactive metabolite. Similar agents, such as carbon tetrachloride and chloroform, are direct hepatotoxins due to the formation of reactive metabolites. In the series of related anesthetics, halothane, isoflurane, and desflurane, all three agents form virtually the same reactive metabolite – trifluoroacetyl chloride (it would be the fluoride for desflurane). However, the amount of reactive metabolite formed varies by over 100-fold and the risk of idiopathic hepatotoxicity for this series of anesthetics correlates with the amount of reactive metabolite formed. In addition, halothane-induced halothane CF_3–$CHClBr$ (F–C(F)(F)–C(H)(Cl)–Br) ⟶ F–C(F)(F)–C(=O)Cl ~ 20%

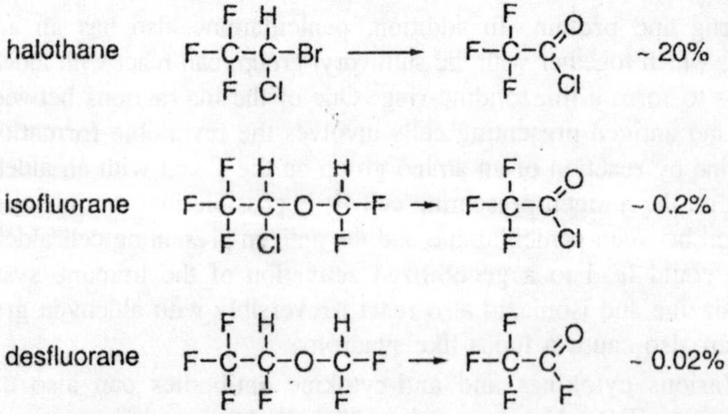

isofluorane F–C(F)(F)–C(H)(Cl)–O–C(H)(F)–F → F–C(F)(F)–C(=O)Cl ~ 0.2%

desfluorane F–C(F)(F)–C(H)(F)–O–C(H)(F)–F → F–C(F)(F)–C(=O)F ~ 0.02%

Fig. 10.2. Comparison of the percentage of halothane and its analogs that are metabolized to reactive acid chloride.

hepatotoxicity is associated with antibodies against trifluoroacetylated protein, which provides very strong evidence that the reactive metabolite acts as a hapten. On the other hand, about 20% of patients, who are anesthetized with halothane, have a transient elevation in transaminases even though they never develop clinically apparent toxicity and this suggests that the reactive metabolite also acts as a danger signal. An alternative hypothesis is that halothane induces an immune response in many patients, but in most cases this immune response is down-regulated, thus limiting the hepatic damage but still causing transaminase elevation.

Tienilic acid-induced hepatitis

Tienilic acid is oxidized to a reactive metabolite by cytochrome P450 2C9. It was first believed that this reactive metabolite was an S-oxide, but I believe the evidence favors an epoxide. This reactive metabolite is so reactive that it binds almost exclusively to the P450 that formed it. The observation that tienilic acid-induced hepatitis is associated with antibodies against Cyp 2C9 strongly suggests that the reactive metabolite is responsible for the toxicity; however, it would be very difficult to prove that. This antibody suggests that the reactive metabolite acts as a hapten. In contrast, because P450 is not an essential protein for cell function, it is not clear how the reactive metabolite could act as a danger signal. In order to test this hypothesis, we performed a microarray analysis on the acute changes in mRNA levels in the liver of animals treated with tienilic acid. We found several changes that are consistent with a danger signal; therefore, either significant binding to other proteins must occur or tienilic acid must cause cell stress through some other mechanism.

Nonsteroidal antiinflammatory drugs

Diclofenac is associated with a significant incidence of liver toxicity. It is an aromatic amine and is metabolized to two different phenols that can form iminoquinones. In addition, it is a carboxylic acid and forms an acyl glucuronide, which covalently binds to protein. However, other *nonsteroidal antiinflammatory drugs* (NSAIDs) that form acyl glucuronides as well as the fibrates, which also form acyl glucuronides, are not associated with a significant incidence of liver toxicity. In addition, bromfenac, another aromatic amine-containing NSAID was withdrawn from the market because of an unacceptable incidence of liver failure. This suggests that the reactive metabolites formed from the aromatic amine portion of the molecule play a role in the mechanism of diclofenac-induced liver toxicity.

Drugs classified as causing metabolic idiosyncrasy

Although the mechanism by which drugs such as isoniazid and troglitazone cause liver toxicity is unknown, the toxicity associated with these drugs has been classified as metabolic idiosyncrasy, because there is not a rapid onset on rechallenge. However, there is no direct evidence of metabolic idiosyncrasy, and such characteristics may also be compatible with an immune-mediated reaction, especially if the reaction is autoimmune in nature. However, it should be repeated that there is also no direct evidence of an immune-mediated mechanism.

Both isoniazid and troglitazone are known to form reactive metabolites. Isoniazid is a hydrazide and oxidation of hydrazines is known to form free radicals and carbocations. An animal model suggests that the pathway leading to toxicity involves acetylation followed by hydrolysis to form acetylhydrazine; however, there is no evidence that this pathway is responsible for the idiosyncratic liver toxicity seen in humans, and direct oxidation of the parent drug also leads to reactive metabolites. Although acetylation is a polymorphic metabolic pathway, acetylator phenotype is not a major risk factor for isoniazid-induced hepatitis, and therefore it cannot be responsible for the idiosyncratic nature of the reaction. Furthermore, there is no other known metabolic pathway that could explain this characteristic.

Troglitazone is oxidized to at least two reactive metabolites. The sulfur of thiazolidinedione is oxidized leading to a reactive sulfenic acid and a reactive isocyanate. In addition, the other end of the molecule is analogous to vitamin E, and it is oxidized to a reactive quinone methide. It is unknown which, if either, reactive metabolite is responsible for the liver toxicity associated with troglitazone.

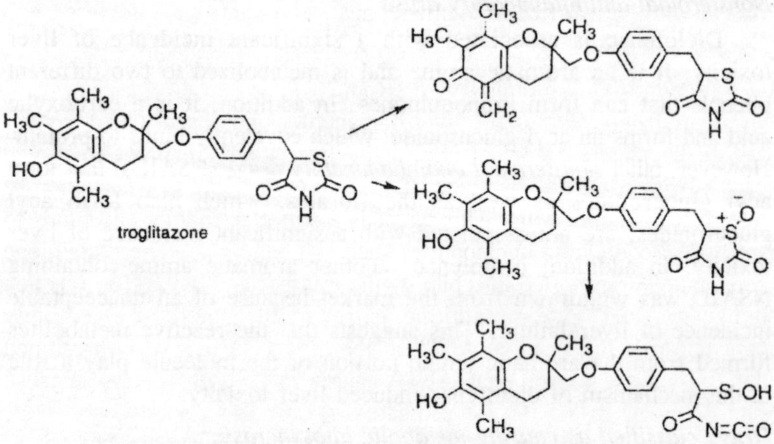

troglitazone

Fig. 10.3. Metabolism of troglitazone to reactive metabolites whose identities are based on the structure of glutathione conjugates.

Pioglitazone and rosiglitazone also have a thiazolidinedione ring, but they are much safer than troglitazone. They cannot form a quinone methide, so it might be inferred that this is the responsible reactive metabolite; however, the therapeutic doses of pioglitazone and rosiglitazone are less than a tenth that of troglitazone.

As with halothane, about 20% of patients treated with isoniazid have a transient elevation of transaminases, suggesting direct toxicity (danger signal) or an immune reaction in which there is down-regulation and tolerance. In the case of isoniazid, the time-to-onset of the elevated transaminases is usually a week or more into treatment, which is harder to explain on the basis of direct cytotoxicity; therefore, it is more likely that it represents an "aborted" immune response. The incidence of elevated transaminases associated with troglitazone therapy is also higher than the incidence of clinical liver toxicity, but in this case the incidence is only 1-2% instead of 20%. In fact, it appears that in general, drugs that cause severe hepatic IDRs also cause an elevation of transaminases in 1% or more of treated patients, thus providing a way to predict at an early stage which drugs will cause hepatic IDRs. However, the converse is not true: drugs that cause an elevation of transaminases in some patients do not always cause a significant incidence of liver failure. In contrast, drugs that cause even a few cases of elevated transaminases along with jaundice (in the absence of other causes of jaundice such as obstruction) during clinical trials are likely to cause a significant incidence of liver failure (Hy's rule). This is presumably because the presence of jaundice is an indication that sufficient damage has been done to interfere with function.

Drug-induced cholestatic liver toxicity

Fortunately, cholestatic liver damage does not usually lead to liver failure. A classic model of cholestatic liver injury involves treatment of rats with α-naphthylisothiocyanate (ANIT) leading to destruction of bile duct epithelial cells. This agent is a soft electrophile and binds to sulfhydryl-containing nucleophiles such as glutathione. The glutathione conjugate is transported into bile by the transporter MRP2. The reaction between ANIT and glutathione is reversible, thereby effectively concentrating the reactive ANIT in the biliary system. It is presumed that this is the reason that ANIT causes cholestatic injury, because rats deficient in MRP2 are protected against this toxicity; however, the details of exactly how ANIT damages bile ducts remains unknown.

The antifungal agent, terbinafine causes both cholestatic and mixed cholestatic/hepatocellular liver injury. It undergoes N-dealkylation to form a unique Michael acceptor that reacts with glutathione, but even after this reaction it retains an α,β-unsaturated aldehyde structure and remains chemically reactive. Therefore, it can be seen as analogous to ANIT.

Chlorpromazine is associated with a high incidence of cholestatic injury and was one of the first drugs to be recognized as causing this type of IDR. It is oxidized to a large number of metabolites, some of which are likely to be chemically reactive; however, the reactive

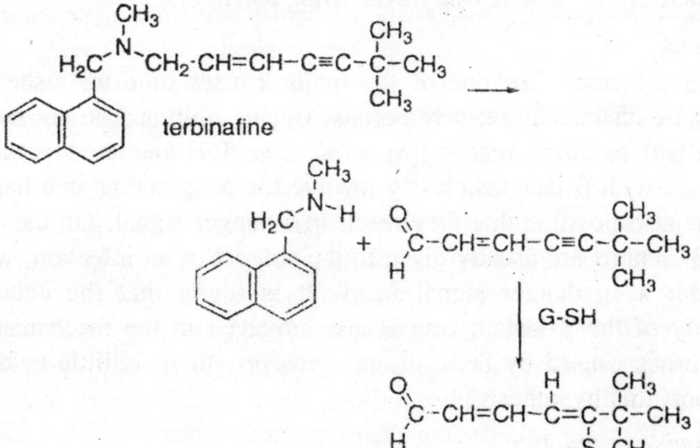

Fig. 10.4. The oxidation of terbinafine to a reactive metabolite whose glutathione (GSH) conjugate is still a reactive α,β-unsaturated aldehyde.

metabolites have not been well characterized and the mechanism remains unknown. Erythromycin, especially the estolate, is also associated with a high incidence of cholestatic liver injury; however, given its structure, a reactive metabolite seems less likely for this drug.

Valproate-induced liver toxicity

The liver toxicity associated with valproate has characteristics strongly suggesting that it interferes with β-oxidation of fatty acids. Being a carboxylic acid that branches at the α-position, which could inhibit β-oxidation, it is conceivable that the parent drug might mediate this inhibition. However, the 4-ene metabolite of valproic acid is much more toxic than the parent drug and is analogous to hypoglycin A, which is well known to cause a similar type of hepatotoxicity. The 4-ene is further oxidized to a reactive diene. In addition, the glucuronide of valproic acid is associated with lipid oxidation. In short, although the mechanism of valproate-induced liver toxicity is not understood, it appears that metabolites are responsible and there is a proposal to make the drug safer by placing fluorine in the α-position, which inhibits both oxidation and glucuronidation.

Involvement of reactive metabolites in dermatological IDRs

Unlike the liver, the skin has only low activity of drug-metabolizing enzymes. Therefore, it is likely that if a reactive metabolite is responsible for a dermatologic IDR, it must (a) be formed readily, such as the oxidation of a *p*-aminophenol to an iminoquinone, (b) be formed by enzymes that are present in the skin, or (c) have a relatively low reactivity so that it can travel from the liver.

β-Lactams

The β-lactams are one of the major causes of drug rashes. β-lactams are chemically reactive because of ring stain and do not require metabolism to form reactive species. The IgE-mediated reactions associated with β-lactams clearly involve the drug acting as a hapten, and it is also possible that they result in a danger signal. On the other hand, β-lactams are usually given in the context of an infection, which could act as a danger signal itself. It is likely that the chemical reactivity of the β-lactam ring is also involved in the mechanism of other rashes caused by these drugs; however, there is little evidence to support this hypothesis.

Sulfonamide antibiotics

The sulfonamide antibiotics are associated with a relatively high incidence of serious dermatological reactions including Stevens–Johnson syndrome, toxic epidermal necrolysis, and hypersensitivity. Although sulfonamide antibiotics are named for their sulfonamide functional group, the functional group that appears to be important with respect to toxicity is the aromatic amine. However, even recently when celecoxib (a sulfonamide but not an aromatic amine) was released it carried a contraindication against use in "patients who have demonstrated allergic-type reactions to sulfonamides". There is no good evidence to support such cross-reactivity; and in fact, there is good evidence against it. Essentially, all drugs that are primary aromatic amines are associated with a relatively high incidence of IDRs; one exception is metoclopramide, but this is presumably because the usual clinical dose is only 5–10 mg. Therefore, it seems likely that the aromatic amine functional group is responsible for IDRs. It is also known that aromatic amines are readily oxidized to various reactive metabolites. There are several aromatic amine carcinogens that are converted into nitrenium ions by oxidation to a hydroxylamine followed by o-conjugation with a good leaving group such as sulfate or acetate. Most drugs that are aromatic amines have an electron-withdrawing group in the para position, so formation of a nitrenium ion is unlikely. However, further oxidation of the hydroxylamine to a nitroso metabolite also represents metabolic activation and, furthermore, redox cycling between oxidation states can also lead to toxicity. The oxidation of aromatic amines can occur in the skin.

Given this background of the aromatic amine being a structural alert, presumably because it readily forms reactive metabolites, it is surprising that the major drug that Pichler found to be associated with lymphocyte activation in the absence of metabolic activation was the aromatic amine sulfamethoxazole. There are two possible explanations for this observation: (1) the hypothesis that aromatic amines are generally associated with IDRs is not due to their ability to form reactive metabolites, or (2) reactive metabolites are associated with the initiation of an immune response, either by generating a danger signal or by acting as haptens; however, once an immune response is initiated, T cells are generated that respond to the parent drug, and these cells are selected for Pichler's experiments by culturing in the presence of drug. Another complication in interpretation of clinical data with respect to sulfonamide antibiotics is that the major formulation of sulfonamide antibiotics that is used clinically is the combination of sulfamethoxazole and trimethoprim. Trimethoprim is known to cause some of the IDRs associated with this formulation and trimethoprim also forms a reactive metabolite.

Aromatic anticonvulsants

Although phenytoin, carbamazepine, and phenobarbital are the agents that most people refer to as the aromatic anticonvulsants, lamotrigine also contains an aromatic ring. There appears to be cross-sensitivity but not cross-reactivity between the traditional aromatic anticonvulsants, i.e. if a patient has an IDR to one of these drugs, there is a high probability that they will have a similar IDR to another anticonvulsant within this class; however, it is not true cross-reactivity because if a patient is rechallenged with the same drug, the time-to-onset of an IDR is very short. In contrast, if they are treated with another drug in the class, the time-to-onset is delayed. This cross-sensitivity suggests that if reactive metabolites are responsible for these anticonvulsant IDRs, the reactive metabolites may be related in some way. There is no evidence that there is an increase in the risk of an IDR to lamotrigine in patients who have had an IDR to the other aromatic anticonvulsants.

It was proposed some time ago that the IDRs associated with the classic aromatic anticonvulsants were due to a reactive arene oxide and the idiosyncratic nature of the IDRs was due to genetic differences in the detoxication of the arene oxide. In fact, epoxide hydrolase, the major enzyme responsible for the detoxication of arene oxides is genetically polymorphic; however, two studies have found that the impaired epoxide hydrolase activity genotype is not a significant risk factor for aromatic anticonvulsant IDRs.

There are many possible reactive metabolites of the traditional aromatic anticonvulsants. In addition to the arene oxide, it has been proposed that the reactive metabolite of phenytoin responsible for IDRs is an o-quinone formed by oxidation of the 4-hydroxy metabolite to the catechol and then further oxidation to the quinone. There is also evidence for the oxidation of one of the hydantoin nitrogens to a free radical, which opens up to an isocyanate, and there is evidence that a free radical is responsible for the teratogenic effects of the drug. However, the 4-hydroxy metabolite, being a phenol, could also be oxidized to a free radical.

Likewise, there are many possible reactive metabolites of carbamazepine. In addition to the arene oxide, the 2-hydroxy metabolite is oxidized with loss of isocyanic acid to an iminoquinone. In addition, a catechol is also formed that could be oxidized to an o-quinone and the 3-hydroxy metabolite is readily oxidized to a free radical. Without a valid animal model, it is very difficult to determine which, if any,

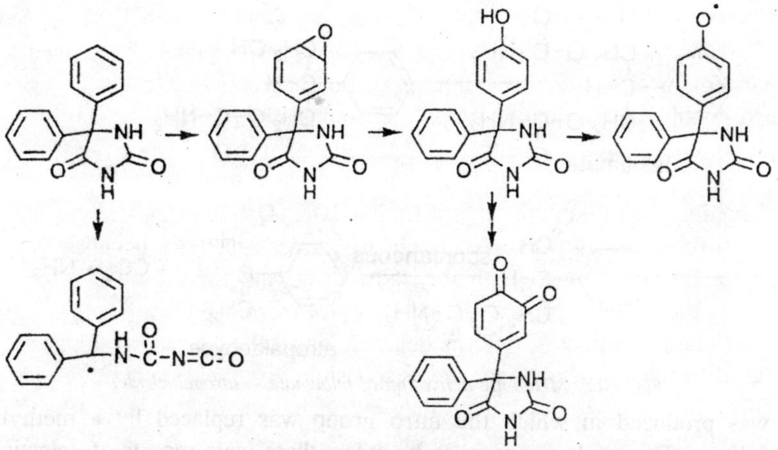

Fig. 10.5. Possible routes of phenytoin metabolic activation.

of these multiple reactive metabolites is responsible for the IDRs associated with the aromatic anticonvulsants.

Nickel

Although not a drug, nickel is responsible for more delayed-type hypersensitivity skin reactions than any other agent, and it is a good example of an agent that acts without irreversible covalent binding. Specifically, nickel forms a strong but reversible tetra-coordinate complex with histidine residues.

Involvement of reactive metabolites in hematological IDRs

Aplastic anemia

Chloramphenicol is a classic drug associated with aplastic anemia. It contains two functional groups that are metabolized to reactive metabolites. The nitro group is the more obvious and it is reduced to the same intermediates as are formed by oxidation of an aromatic amine. In addition, it has a dichloroacetamide, which is oxidized to a reactive acetyl chloride analogous to the reactive metabolite of halothane. Of the two pathways leading to reactive metabolites, the one involving the nitro group is more likely to be responsible for aplastic anemia. Specifically, the nitro group is reduced to an aromatic amine and intermediate oxidation states by gut bacteria, and it is known that aromatic amines can be oxidized by myeloperoxidase present in neutrophils. In contrast, the oxidation of the dichloroacetamide is likely to be mediated by cytochromes P450, which is likely to be present in low levels in the bone marrow. An analog of chloramphenicol

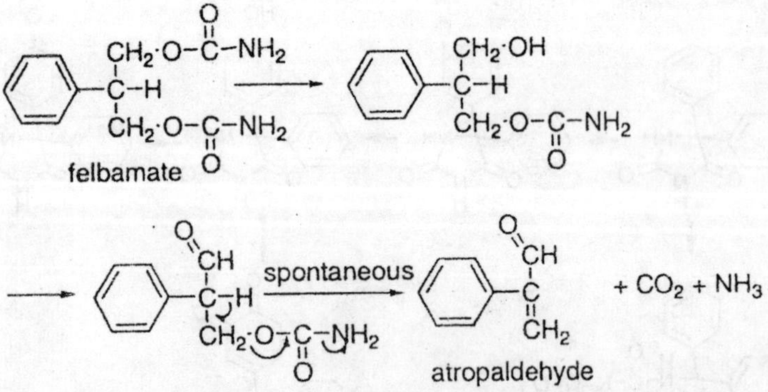

Fig. 10.6. Metabolic activation of felbamate to atropaldehyde.

was produced in which the nitro group was replaced by a methyl sulfone. This analog appears to be safer; there were reports of aplastic anemia caused by this agent, but because of the background incidence of aplastic anemia, these are difficult to interpret. It is also interesting to note that there have been reports of aplastic anemia associated with the use of chloramphenicol eye drops, seemingly in contradiction to the rule that very low doses of a drug are safe; however, the significant background incidence of aplastic anemia again makes these reports hard to interpret and epidemiological studies failed to find an association between the use of chloramphenicol eye drops and aplastic anemia.

Felbamate was a promising anticonvulsant, but after it was released it was found to cause both aplastic anemia and liver toxicity. It is converted by a series of steps into the reactive metabolite atropaldehyde (phenylacrolein). The first step is hydrolysis of one of the carbamates, followed by oxidation of the alcohol to an aldehyde. Thus, the last enzymatic step is probably mediated by alcohol dehydrogenase, which has a wide distribution and is likely present in the bone marrow. This is a minor pathway in rodents but is more extensive in humans. In addition, the therapeutic dose of felbamate is several grams a day. Although atropaldehyde is toxic and it seems likely that it is responsible for the IDRs associated with felbamate, there is no direct evidence for this hypothesis.

Thrombocytopenia

As discussed already, heparin forms a tight complex with platelet factor 4. There is compelling evidence that this interaction is responsible for heparin-induced thrombocytopenia. Heparin is a very large, multiply charged molecule, and therefore it can interact strongly without forming

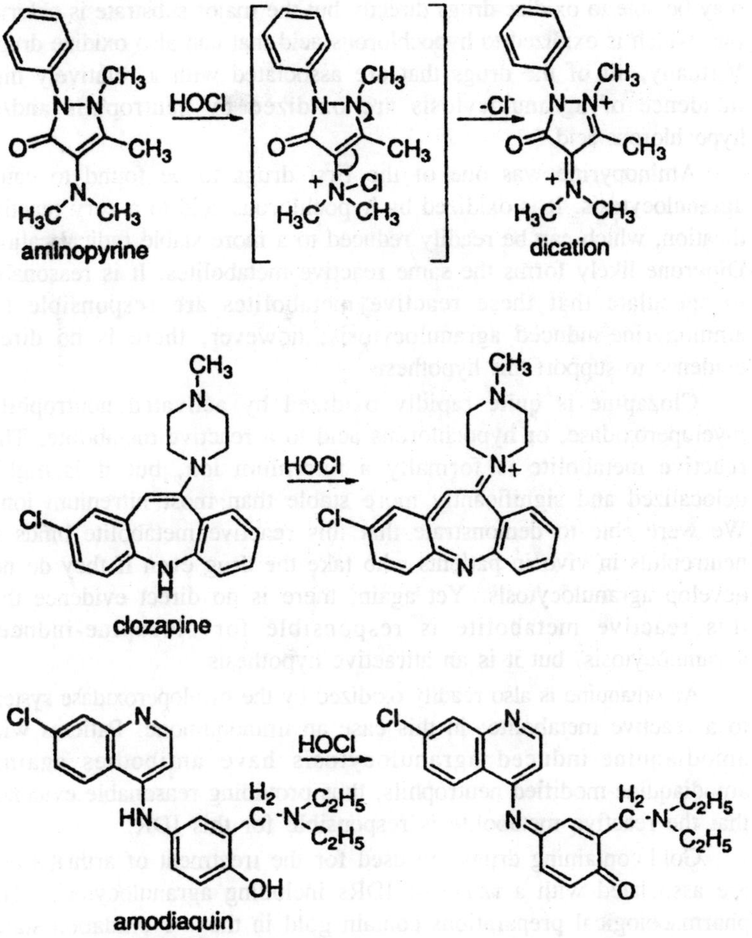

Fig. 10.7. Metabolic activation by hypochlorous acid of three drugs that cause agranulocytosis.

a reactive metabolite; furthermore, there is no evidence that a reactive metabolite is involved.

Agranulocytosis

Unlike the liver where the main oxidative enzymes are cytochromes P450, the major oxidative enzyme in neutrophils is the combination of nicotinamide adenine dinucleotide phosphate (NADPH) oxidase (which generates superoxide that is further converted into hydrogen peroxide) and myeloperoxidase (which is oxidized by hydrogen peroxide to the active form of the enzyme). The oxidized form of myeloperoxidase may be able to oxidize drugs directly but the major substrate is chloride ion, which is oxidized to hypochlorous acid that can also oxidize drugs. Virtually, all of the drugs that are associated with a relatively high incidence of agranulocytosis are oxidized by neutrophils and/or hypochlorous acid.

Aminopyrine was one of the first drugs to be found to cause agranulocytosis. It is oxidized by hypochlorous acid to a very reactive dication, which can be readily reduced to a more stable radical cation. Dipyrone likely forms the same reactive metabolites. It is reasonable to speculate that these reactive metabolites are responsible for aminopyrine-induced agranulocytosis; however, there is no direct evidence to support this hypothesis.

Clozapine is quite rapidly oxidized by activated neutrophils, myeloperoxidase, or hypochlorous acid to a reactive metabolite. This reactive metabolite is formally a nitrenium ion, but it is highly delocalized and significantly more stable than most nitrenium ions. We were able to demonstrate that this reactive metabolite binds to neutrophils in vivo in patients who take the drug even if they do not develop agranulocytosis. Yet again, there is no direct evidence that this reactive metabolite is responsible for clozapine-induced agranulocytosis, but it is an attractive hypothesis.

Amodiaquine is also readily oxidized by the myeloperoxidase system to a reactive metabolite: in this case an iminoquinone. Patients with amodiaquine-induced agranulocytosis have antibodies against amodiaquine-modified neutrophils, thus providing reasonable evidence that the reactive metabolite is responsible for this IDR.

Gold-containing drugs are used for the treatment of arthritis and are associated with a range of IDRs including agranulocytosis. The pharmacological preparations contain gold in the +1 oxidation state, but it is oxidized to the chemically reactive +3 state by macrophage-generated HOCl; it is this form of the drug that appears to be recognized by the immune system.

The use of ticlopidine is limited by its association with agranulocytosis, aplastic anemia, and thrombocytopenia. The thiophene ring is oxidized to a reactive species by hypochlorous acid.

Hemolytic anemia

A classic drug associated with autoimmune hemolytic anemia is α-methyldopa. It is a catechol; therefore, it is likely to be oxidized to a reactive o-quinone. Its metabolic activation has not been extensively studied, although it was noted that some of the drug became tightly bound, especially under oxidative conditions, and is likely due to oxidation of the catechol to a reactive quinone that could covalently bind to red cells. It may seem that catechols would not be a problem, because there are several endogenous catecholamines; however, α-methyldopa is often given at doses of over a gram per day.

β-Lactams are often associated with hemolytic IDRs and, as aforementioned, they are reactive without metabolism. There is good evidence that many of the antibodies responsible for β-lactam-induced hemolytic anemia are directed against the drug.

Diclofenac is frequently associated with hemolytic anemia. In one patient, the pathogenic antibodies were heterogeneous, but the major hapten they recognized was derived from the 4′-hydroxy metabolite, which is a precursor to a reactive iminoquinone metabolite. This type of reactive metabolite can readily be formed in the circulation, because even air can oxidize p-aminophenols. In another patient with diclofenac-induced hemolytic anemia, binding of antibody to red cells required a metabolite that was both oxidized and glucuronidated in the 4′-position. A related NSAID, etodolac, also causes hemolytic anemia, and in one patient the metabolite that was found to cause stimulation of the patient's lymphocytes was hydroxylated para to a nitrogen so that it can form an iminoquinone, and it was also stated that it required glucuronidation, although this was not clear from the data presented.

Conclusions

To summarize the data presented, there is a large amount of evidence that many IDRs are immune-mediated. This is obvious for drug-induced autoimmunity and clear for anaphylaxis, although it can be difficult to differentiate true anaphylaxis from anaphylactoid reactions. The evidence is compelling for many types of rash and some types of cytopenia. An immune mechanism is also likely for a few types of liver toxicity, especially halothane-induced hepatotoxicity. In contrast, there are several types of liver toxicity and cytopenias in which the characteristics suggest that they are not immune-mediated. In particular, most immune-mediated reactions are associated with memory T cells that result in a rapid onset of an adverse reaction in patients who have previously had an IDR to the same drug. Although this is an important characteristic of many immune-mediated reactions, it does not prove that something is immune-mediated, and more importantly, its absence does not prove that something is not immune-mediated. Valproic acid hepatotoxicity is interesting in that there is good evidence that it involves mitochondrial toxicity, but it is not clear what makes it idiosyncratic or what causes the delay between starting the drug and the onset of toxicity. It is conceivable that the immune system plays a role in the mechanism of valproate-induced IDRs. It is interesting to note that it has recently been shown that NK (*Natural Killer*) and NKT (*Natural Killer T*) cells play an important role in acetaminophen-induced hepatic necrosis, which is not idiosyncratic and not believed to be immune-mediated; therefore, the immune system, especially the innate immune system, may play an important role where it was not previously suspected. On the other hand, it is likely that at least some IDRs that have some characteristics of immune-mediated reactions actually involve other variables that lead to the idiosyncratic nature and are not immune-mediated.

However, there are no examples where environmental and/or genetic factors have been defined that explain the idiosyncratic nature of an IDR; if such factors were defined it might no longer be considered idiosyncratic. There are a few examples in which specific genetic polymorphisms are associated with a much higher risk of a specific IDR. For example, the haplotype HLA-B*5701,HLA-DR7, and HLA-DQ3 is associated with high risk of abacavir hypersensitivity and carbamazepine-induced Stevens–Johnson syndrome with HLA-B*1502. However, it is not clear exactly how these polymorphisms are responsible for the increased risk. One example in which the genetic polymorphism explains an increased risk of an idiosyncratic adverse reaction is the polymorphisms that are associated with a high risk of beryllium-induced pulmonary toxicity. These polymorphisms involve negatively charged glutamic and aspartic acid residues at specific sites in MHC-II (HLA–DP) molecules on antigen-presenting cells that allow the binding of positively charged beryllium ions. Predisposition to most immune-mediated diseases, such as idiopathic lupus, multiple sclerosis, etc. are polygenic and it is likely that most IDRs also involve many genes. Likewise, specific genetic polymorphisms have been associated with an increased risk for several IDRs; however, unlike the examples of abacavir-induced hypersensitivity and carbamazepine-induced Stevens–Johnson syndrome, the relative risk is usually small.

Although there is a large amount of circumstantial evidence that reactive metabolites are involved in the mechanism of most IDRs, there is even less definitive evidence for this hypothesis than there is for involvement of the immune system. Furthermore, it is unclear in most cases whether the reactive metabolite is acting as a hapten or a danger signal or whether both effects are necessary, if a drug is going to be associated with a high incidence of IDRs.

Despite significant efforts utilizing several different approaches, little progress has been made in our ability to deal with the issue of IDRs. It is likely that a much better understanding of the mechanisms involved will be required in order to have a significant impact on the problem. It is discouraging that despite thousands of person–years of research, the mechanism by which the reactive metabolite of acetaminophen causes hepatotoxicity remains elusive. Acetaminophen-induced hepatotoxicity is relatively easy to study, because it is easy to reproduce in animals. In contrast, there are very few animal models of IDRs in which the mechanism of the adverse reaction in the animal is the same mechanism as the IDR in humans. Such animal models are very powerful tools for the study of mechanism and it is hard to imagine how many hypotheses could be tested without valid animal models. We have succeeded in developing an animal model of nevirapine-induced skin rash and it appears to involve essentially the same mechanism as the nevirapine-induced skin rash in humans. Specifically, the characteristics appear very similar and both appear to be mediated by $CD4^+$ T cells. We are in the process of using this model to definitively determine if a reactive metabolite is responsible and probe how the parent drug or reactive metabolite induces an immune response. If we knew more about the mechanisms involved in IDRs, it would probably be much easier to develop animal models. Keeping in mind, however, that even if there are basic mechanistic features common to both animal and human IDRs, it is likely that many mechanisms are involved. Our one success with the nevirapine model actually involved capitalizing on a chance observation during metabolism studies rather than a definite plan to develop an animal model. All of our other efforts in which we were trying to develop an animal model based on strategies such as inducing enzymes leading to reactive metabolites, depleting glutathione, vitamin C, or selenium, and stimulating the immune system as well as combinations of such interventions, have been fruitless.

The study of IDRs is an important endeavor and it requires several different approaches and many different disciplines including chemistry, drug metabolism, biochemistry, immunology, pathology, molecular biology, genetics, and clinical medicine. Despite the complexities, eventually we may be able to move beyond describing clinical syndromes and debating hypotheses to a clearer mechanistic understanding that will make IDRs less idiosyncratic.

11

Sensor Protein

Cellular protection against electrophiles and oxidants relies on detoxication by phase II biotransformation enzymes, antioxidant enzymes and related stress response proteins. Many of these inducible genes, such as the glutathione S-transferases, NAD(P)H oxidoreductase, heme oxygenase 1 (HO-1) and γ-glutamyl cysteine ligase are regulated at the transcriptional level through cis-acting DNA sequences known as antioxidant/electrophile response elements (ARE/EpREs). Inducers of ARE/EpRE-driven genes generally are electrophiles or their precursors, which modify sulfhydryl groups in proteins that regulate signaling pathways involved in toxicity and stress.

ARE-dependent transcription is regulated by the transcription factor Nrf2, a member of the basic-leucine zipper NF-E2 family. Nrf2 forms heterodimers with one of the small Maf proteins and this complex activates expression of ARE-driven genes. Studies with Nrf2$^{-/-}$ mice indicate that Nrf2 regulates a variety of genes, including chaperones, antioxidant genes and genes regulating protein degradation. Nrf2$^{-/-}$ mice are more susceptible to toxic chemicals and stress.

Recently, a Cul3 ubiquitin ligase adaptor protein Keap1 (Kelch-like ECH-associated protein 1) was identified as an inhibitory regulator that binds to the N-terminal Neh2 domain of Nrf2. The Keap1 protein has five domains: an N-terminal domain, a BTB domain, a central linker domain, a Kelch repeat domain and a C-terminal domain. The Kelch repeat domain binds directly to Nrf2, as well as to actin, the BTB domain is required for the dimerization of Keap1 and the central linker domain is essential for cytoplasmic sequestration of Nrf2. The question of how Keap1 regulates Nrf2 has attracted intense interest and several models have been proposed. Keap1 initially was proposed to tether Nrf2 to cytoplasmic actin filaments, thus preventing its access to the nucleus. Keap1 also was found to modulate nuclear Nrf2 levels by enhancing nuclear export of the transcription factor. Keap1 regulates the active degradation of Nrf2 by functioning as an adaptor for Cul3-dependent ubiquitination and degradation of Nrf2. Other recent work suggests that Keap1 suppresses nuclear Nrf2 by transiently moving from the cytoplasm into the nucleus to promote Nrf2 ubiquitination.

Electrophiles react with Keap1 to form covalent adducts and adduction is thought to trigger as yet unidentified events that result in enhanced nuclear Nrf2 levels. The mechanism by which Keap1 modifications trigger Nrf2 activation presents an interesting problem. Although the structure of the Kelch domain has been reported, the structure of the entire protein has not yet been determined. Keap1 has 27 cysteine residues, most or all of which appear to be available to react with electrophiles. Initial studies of modification of murine Keap1 by the model alkylating agent dexamethasone mesylate suggested that preferential modification of highly reactive central linker domain cysteines, particularly Cys273 and Cys288, triggers Keap1-Nrf2 dissociation and accounts for the electrophile-sensing mechanism. However, considerable recent work indicates that the relationship of covalent adduction to the sensor function of Keap1 is more complicated. Here we discuss our recent studies of Keap1 modification by two prototypical thiol-reactive electrophiles and the cancer chemopreventive agent sulforaphane. These studies indicate that covalent modification of the Keap1 sensor can result in Nrf2 stabilization through at least two distinct mechanisms.

PATTERNS OF KEAP1 MODIFICATION BY ELECTROPHILES

Keap1 Alkylation by Prototypical Thiol-reactive Electrophiles

The apparently large number of thiol targets in Keap1 suggests that different electrophiles may display different patterns of adduction on this sensor protein. We explored this question by analyzing the adduction of human His_6-Keap1 in vitro by several electrophiles. Initial studies employed the thiol-reactive biotinylating probes N-iodoacetyl-N-biotinylhexylenediamine (IAB) and 1-biotinamido-4-(4′-[maleimido-ethylcyclohexane]-carboxamido)butane (BMCC). These compounds display chemistries typical of a number of electrophilic metabolites of drugs and environmental chemicals and of endogenous electrophiles. However, they differ in their functional effects on Nrf2 activation *in vivo*. Whereas IAB induces ARE-dependent gene transcription, nuclear

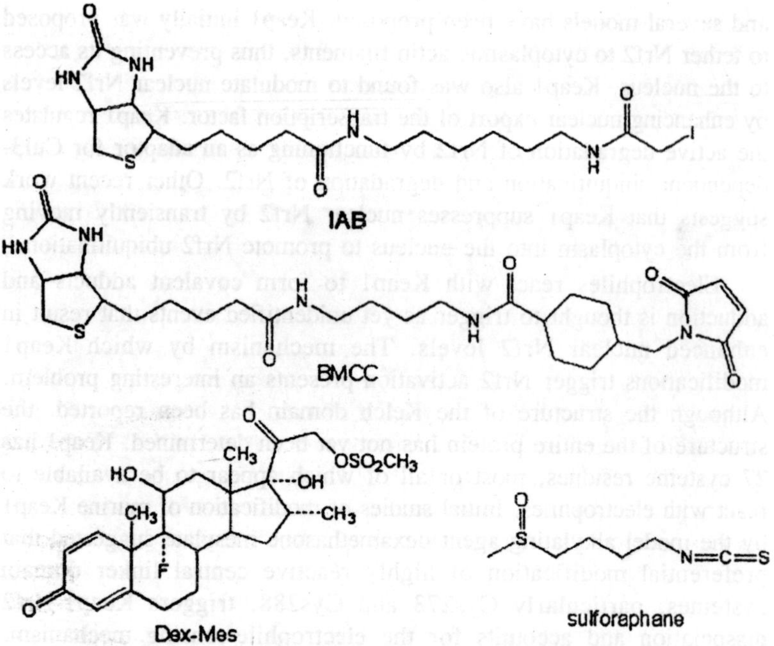

Fig. 11.1. Structures of electrophiles.

Nrf2 accumulation and levels of ARE-regulated gene products, BMCC does not. Dex-Mes induces nuclear Nrf2 accumulation in HEK293 cells, but also causes significant cytotoxicity.

Treatment of human His_6-Keap1 with IAB at a molar ratio of 5:1 (electrophile:protein) for 2 h at 37°C consistently yielded a total of 6 IAB-modified cysteines, each of which had a mass increase of 382.5, corresponding to IAB adducts. All of these cysteines (Cys196, Cys226, Cys241, Cys257, Cys288 and Cys319) are in the central linker domain, which is required for cytoplasmic sequestration of Nrf2. LC–MS–MS analyses routinely generated MS–MS spectra corresponding to approximately 80% of the protein sequence. All of the cysteine-containing tryptic peptides were detected, except for Cys151, Cys395 and Cys406. In analyses of electrophile-treated Keap1, cysteine-containing peptides were detected as S-carboxamidomethylated derivatives (corresponding to unadducted cysteines) or as electrophile-adducted cysteines. All adducts were characterized by mass shifts to b- and/or y-ions that confirmed sequence location of the adducts.

Because Dinkova-Kostova et al. employed the model electrophile Dex-mes to identify reactive thiols in murine Keap1, we also studied adduction of human His_6-Keap1 by this compound under the same conditions as for IAB and BMCC. Dex-Mes alkylated human Keap1 at cysteines primarily in the central linker domain (Cys196, Cys226, Cys241 and Cys249) as well as Cys489 in the Kelch domain and Cys622 in the C-terminal domain. Interestingly, Dex-Mes did not target Cys273 and Cys288 or the central linker domain, as had been reported in similar studies with murine Keap1 *in vitro*.

Keap1 Acylation by the Prototypical Chemopreventive Agent Sulforaphane

Sulforaphane (R-1-isothiocyanato-4-methylsulfinylbutane), an isothiocyanate isolated from cruciferous vegetables, is among the most potent inducers of phase II enzymes. Sulforaphane is an isothiocyanate, which reacts with thiols to form thionoacyl adducts. In contrast to the adducts formed by IAB, BMCC and Dex-Mes, thionoacyl adducts are labile to decomposition under the conditions we used to analyze the former adducts. We developed a modified LC–MS–MS method to map sulforaphane modification sites formed on human His_6-Keap1 *in vitro*. Sulforaphane is considerably more reactive than the other electrophiles studied and elicited Nrf2 activation in cells at low micromolar concentrations. The most reactive cysteines in Keap1 toward sulforaphane were judged to be those that are most reproducibly adducted by 2 μM sulforaphane for 15 min. These were located in the Kelch repeat domain, especially Cys489, which was found to be sulforaphane-modified in all experiments at the 2 μM concentration. Cysteines 513, 518 and 583, also in the Kelch domain were modified in at least three experiments, as were cysteines in the central linker domain (Cys226 and Cys249), the BTB domain (Cys77) and the C-terminal domain (Cys624). At higher sulforaphane concentrations, adduction selectivity was increasingly less selective, yet reproducible between experiments.

Comparison of Reported Modification Patterns on Keap1

In addition to our work described above, two other groups have applied MS methods to map Keap1 adducts formed with electrophiles. Dinkova-Kostova et al. characterized Cys257, Cys273, Cys288 and Cys297 of murine Keap1 as targets of the electrophile dexamethasone mesylate and led the authors to denote these as the "most reactive residues of Keap1". Eggler et al. recently reported that IAB preferentially alkylated Cys151, Cys288 and Cys297 in human Keap1, although data supporting the identification of the adducts and the relative reactivities of the targets were not published with the paper (these authors reported an MS–MS spectrum of the Cys288-IAB adduct, but later provided us MS–MS spectra for all of the reported adducts).

The differences between reported electrophile targets in Keap1 reflect differences in experimental design and adduct analysis. The Talalay group employed murine Keap1 in their studies, whereas our studies and the studies of Eggler et al. employed human Keap1. Murine and human Keap1 differ by 12 of 153 residues in the central linker domain, which may result in conformational differences that affect adduction chemistry. Each study used somewhat different conditions for incubation of Keap1 with electrophiles and analysis of adducts. For example, molar ratios of electrophile to Keap1 varied from 33:1 (Dex-Mes:Keap1) to 5:1 in our studies with IAB, BMCC and Dex-Mes to 1:1. Our studies demonstrated that incubation time also affected the distribution of adducts. A significant difference between our work and that of Eggler et al. is that they employed an avidin affinity step in the preparation of Keap1 peptide adducts for LC–MS–MS analysis. This enriches adducts and increases the detection of even low abundance adducts and may be the major reason for differences in reported IAB adducts with human Keap1 *in vitro*. Without adduct enrichment, the detection of lower abundance adducts may be suppressed by higher abundance unadducted Keap1 peptides in the sample.

Although differences in experimental design and analysis undoubtedly contribute to the differences in reported Keap1 adduct sites, the major contributing factor to adduction site diversity is the diversity of the electrophile chemistries studied. This is clear from our studies, where the experimental design and analysis of IAB, BMCC and Dex-Mes were identical. Dex-Mes and IAB are S_N2-type electrophiles that alkylate by nucleophilic displacement of a leaving group. BMCC reacts with thiols by Michael addition. Although the experimental conditions we used to generate and detect sulforaphane adducts were slightly different, the pattern of sulforaphane adducts was quite different than observed for the other electrophiles. Thiols react with sulforaphane by addition to the isothiocyanate carbon to yield thionoacyl adducts. The acylation reaction occurs much more rapidly than do the alkylation reactions with the other electrophiles at equivalent reagent concentrations.

An implicit assumption in previous work on Keap1 adduct sites is that the most easily detected adducts represent the most reactive targets for modification. However, MS–MS detection of adducts per se does not indicate their relative amounts or the relative reactivities of the modified cysteines. The sampling methods LC–MS–MS instruments use to acquire MS–MS spectra introduce a certain random nature to sampling low abundance species. Thus, in three analyses of the same sample, a high abundance peptide adduct will be detected all three times, whereas lower abundance adducts may be detected in one run and not in the others, even though the concentration of that adduct is the same in all three samples. For this reason, we have used the frequency of adduct detection in replicate analyses to compare the relative reactivities of Keap1 sites toward both sulforaphane and IAB. The frequency of detection in replicate analyses is roughly proportional to amount and this mode of analysis provides a survey level of quantitation. Given these considerations, our analyses suggest that Cys196, Cys241 and Cys288 were most reactive toward IAB, whereas Cys489, Cys583 and Cys624 were most reactive toward sulforaphane. Our data do not exclude the possibility that other adducts were present, but suggest that these adducts were not abundant under the conditions of our analyses. Definitive resolution of adduction selectivity and target reactivity will require rigorous kinetic analyses of competing Keap1 adduction reactions.

Relationship of Keap1 Modification Sites and Functionally Significant Cysteine Residues

Inferences about critical targets in Keap1 have been drawn from functional analyses of Keap1 mutants. Cys273Ser and Cys288Ser mutations in the central linker domain blocked Keap1-dependent ubiquitination of Nrf2 and Cys273Ala and Cys288Ala mutations blocked Keap1-dependent repression of an ARE reporter. Zhang et al. also reported that Cys151 in the Keap1 BTB domain is required for inhibition of Keap1-dependent degradation of Nrf2 by sulforaphane and oxidative stress, although this mutant does function as a constitutive repressor of Nrf2. These data would suggest that Cys273, Cys288 and Cys151 are key targets for electrophilic Nrf2 activators.

However, MS-based mapping studies of Keap1 adducts are not consistent with this view. In murine Keap1, Cys273 and Cys288, but not Cys151 were preferred targets for Dex-Mes. In human Keap1, we found that only Cys288 was modified by IAB. We also found that neither Cys151, Cys273 nor Cys288 were modified by sulforaphane in human Keap1, except at high concentrations. Eggler et al. reported that Cys151 and Cys288 were preferred targets for IAB, although the supporting data are not clear. Taken together, the available adduct mapping and reactivity data do not support the view that Cys151,

Cys273 and Cys288 are obligatory targets for Nrf2 activation and suggest instead that the adduction–activation relationships are more complicated.

Electrophile-induced Ubiquitination of Keap1

Zhang and colleagues observed that Keap1 expressed in COS1 cells was converted to a group of *high molecular weight* (HMW) forms upon treatment with the prototypical ARE-inducer tert-butylhydroquinone (tBHQ). We subsequently observed the formation of HMW Keap1 forms in studies with IAB. FLAG-Keap1 transfected cells were treated with 100 μM IAB for 2 h at 37°C, FLAG-Keap1 proteins were captured with anti-FLAG antibodies, and analyzed on reducing sodium dodecyl–polyarylamide gel electrophoresis sulphate (SDS-PAGE) gels. The majority of the Keap1 protein from IAB-treated cells migrated in a series of HMW bands with a molecular mass of greater than 150 kDa, whereas the Keap1 protein from untreated cells migrated with an observed molecular weight of 70 kDa, which corresponds to the Keap1 monomer. Immunoblotting with anti-ubiquitin indicated intense ubiquitin immunoreactivity co-migrating with the HMW Keap1 protein bands from IAB-treated cells, but not from controls. HMW Keap1 forms were not observed in cells treated with 100 mM BMCC, nor was anti-ubiquitin immunoreactivity detected. The HMW Keap1 protein forms were detected under reducing conditions on SDS-PAGE (15 mM β-mercaptoethanol in the loading buffer). Pretreatment of the samples with 8 M urea, reduction with tris (carboxyethyl) phosphine (TCEP) and alkylation of the reduced protein with iodoacetamide prior to SDS-PAGE failed to alter the migration of the HMW Keap1 products. However, these denaturation conditions did result in detection of Cys151 as the S-carboxamidomethyl derivative (data not shown) and is consistent with the work of Wakabayashi et al., which indicated that C151 does not undergo adduction. Treatment of His_6-Keap1 with IAB *in vitro* did not generate HMW Keap1 products detectable by immunoblotting. In FLAG-Keap1-expressing 293 cells, both IAB and tBHQ induced a concentration-dependent formation of HMW Keap1 forms.

To better understand the nature of the HMW Keap1 forms, we analyzed tryptic digests of the corresponding gel bands by LC–MS–MS. Eight gel sections corresponding to a molecular weight range from 70 kDa and above were analyzed. The majority of peptides detected in these analyses mapped to Keap1 and ubiquitin, both of which were represented by detection of multiple peptides in different bands. Keap1 proteins from both control and IAB-treated cells were

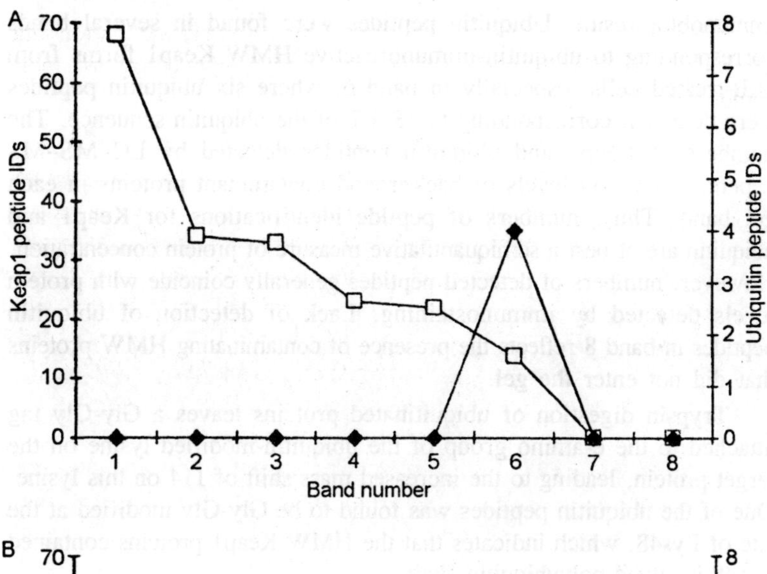

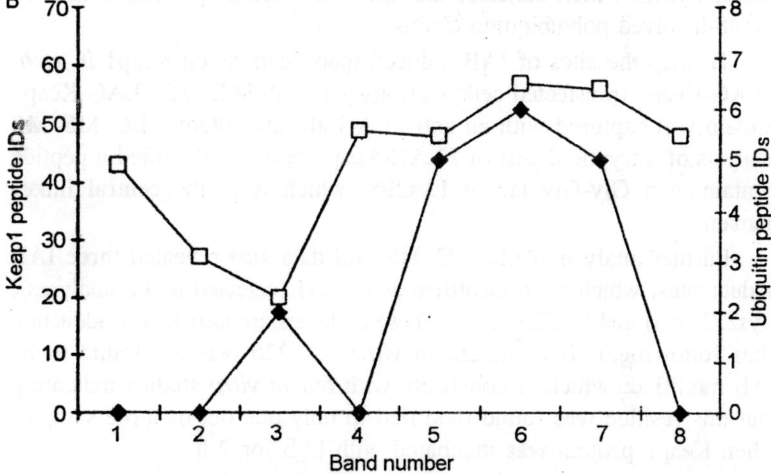

Fig. 11.2. Distribution of Keap1 (□) and ubiquitin (◆) peptide identifications in SDS-PAGE gel fractions from (A) control and (B) IAB-treated transfected cells.

found in multiple bands of 70 kDa molecular weight and higher. However, the distribution of HMW Keap1 and ubiquitin are different between these samples. In control cells, Keap1 protein with a molecular weight of 70 kDa is the dominant species, whereas Keap1 protein was detected primarily in bands corresponding to a molecular weight greater than 150 kDa in the IAB-treated cells. Ubiquitin peptides were only detected in band 6 in control samples, which is consistent with the immunoblot result. Ubiquitin peptides were found in several bands corresponding to ubiquitin-immunoreactive HMW Keap1 forms from IAB-treated cells, especially in band 6, where six ubiquitin peptides were detected, corresponding to 68.4% of the ubiquitin sequence. The numbers of Keap1 and ubiquitin peptides detected by LC–MS–MS depend in part on levels of background contaminant proteins in each gel band. Thus, numbers of peptide identifications for Keap1 and ubiquitin are at best a semiquantitative measure of protein concentration. However, numbers of detected peptides generally coincide with protein levels detected by immunostaining. Lack of detection of ubiquitin peptides in band 8 reflects the presence of contaminating HMW proteins that did not enter the gel.

Trypsin digestion of ubiquitinated proteins leaves a Gly-Gly tag attached to the e-amino group of the ubiquitin-modified lysine on the target protein, leading to the increased mass shift of 114 on this lysine. One of the ubiquitin peptides was found to be Gly-Gly modified at the site of Lys48, which indicates that the HMW Keap1 proteins contained Lys48-involved polyubiquitin chains.

To map the sites of IAB-induced modifications on Keap1 *in vivo*, FLAG-Keap1 transfected cells were treated with IAB and FLAG-Keap1 protein was captured with an anti-FLAG affinity column. LC–MS–MS analysis of a tryptic digest of FLAG-Keap1 proteins identified a peptide containing a Gly-Gly tag at Lys298, which is in the central linker domain.

Further analysis of the LC–MS–MS data also revealed three IAB adduct sites, which were identified as Cys241 (detected in 3/3 analyses), Cys257 (2/3) and Cys288 (3/3). These cysteines are also Keap1 adduction sites following IAB treatment *in vitro*. Cys226 was not found to be IAB modified, which is consistent with our *in vitro* studies indicating that this residue was found modified in only one out of three samples when Keap1 protein was incubated with IAB for 2 h.

Some SCF (Skp1p-cullin-F-Box protein) complexes, which function as E3-ubiquitin ligases, may form complexes with different substrates. F-box proteins are substrate adaptors that provide substrate specificity and ubiquitin-dependent degradation by SCF complexes of certain G-cyclins involved in the control of cell cycle progression. In some cases, F-box proteins are degraded by autoubiquitination within their own SCF complex, which suggests that SCF complex can switch rapidly between substrate (G-cyclin) and substrate adaptor (F-box protein) to balance their levels. Cul3-associated BTB proteins are substrate adaptors for Cullin-3 ubiquitin ligases and these proteins are themselves regulated through ubiquitination and proteasome-mediated degradation. Keap1 is a BTB protein and functions as an adaptor to target Nrf2 for ubiquitination by Cul3-based E3 ligase. Our results suggest that site-specific modification of Keap1 by electrophiles switches ubiquitin targeting from Nrf2 to Keap1 and that this target switching mechanism governs Nrf2 activation by electrophiles.

The IAB treatment-induced Nrf2 stabilization as indicated by elevated cytosolic and nuclear Nrf2, coincident with formation of HMW FLAG-Keap1. FLAG-Keap1 transfected cells were exposed to 100 μM IAB for 2 h, FLAG-Keap1 proteins then were captured with anti-FLAG antibodies, and associated proteins were analyzed by immunoblotting. In untreated cells, very little Nrf2 was found associated with Keap1, as detected by immunoblotting. These results are consistent with those reported previously and were interpreted to indicate rapid destabilization of Nrf2 when it is associated with non-adducted Keap1. Treatment with IAB, which resulted in the adduction and ubiquitination of Keap1, also increased the amount of Nrf2 associated with Keap1. This was interpreted to be a consequence of Nrf2 stabilization. tBHQ has been reported to cause increased association of Nrf2 with Keap1 under conditions where Keap1 is ubiquitinated. These observations suggest that stabilization of Nrf2 can occur without dissociation from Keap1.

Unresolved Questions about Electrophile-induced Activation of Nrf2

Different electrophiles that are Nrf2 inducers produce different patterns of Keap1 modification. Modification sites reported in several studies appear to differ and this certainly may reflect differences in methods and experimental conditions. However, these differences also appear to reflect different chemistries of the electrophiles studied. One of the main questions posed in most of these studies is whether there is a true hierarchy of Keap1 target reactivities. Unfortunately, observation of adducts tells little about the competing reactivities of different target sites. The only way to address this is to measure chemical reactivities of site-specific modifications with specific electrophiles under defined conditions. In other words, the kinetics of modification will provide the answer to this question.

What does this tell us about the sensing mechanism of the system? Other sensor systems display sensitivity to specific oxidants and function primarily through one electron oxidation of an iron–sulfur center or through thiol-disulfide redox changes. Keap1 appears to serve the role of electrophile sensor, which requires a greater degree of flexibility, given the diverse chemistry of electrophiles. The variety of electrophile modification patterns formed on Keap1 by Nrf2 activators is consistent with this concept. This implies that different cysteine modifications could contribute to Nrf2 activation. Further, if multiple patterns of Keap1 modification are similarly able to cause activation, is there a requirement for a critical level of certain types of modifications (e.g., central linker domain adducts)? Again, studies of the kinetic reactivities of different cysteine–electrophile pairs would provide a quantitative basis for comparing modification patterns. These considerations support the idea that, as a sensor for diverse electrophiles, Keap1 must be able to convert diverse chemistries to a common signal for Nrf2 activation.

Another unsettled issue is how adduction results in Nrf2 activation. The available evidence indicates that some adduction reactions cause Keap1 ubiquitination, whereas others do not. Nevertheless, recent studies with sulforaphane indicate that Keap1 ubiquitination is not required for Nrf2 stabilization. Additional studies may reveal other examples of compounds that display different modification maps, different degrees of Keap1 ubiquitination and different degrees of Nrf2 activation. In this context, a screen to compare adduction patterns and molecular events proximal to Nrf2 activation would help to identify key hierarchal inducer-dependent and independent regulatory steps. One may hypothesize that repression of Nrf2 ubiquitination is a common regulatory step. Electrophile chemistry appears to dictate whether Keap1 ubiquitination represents a pivotal step in regulation.

Finally, the question of electrophile-mediated release of Nrf2 from Keap1 is not well understood. Mutation of Keap1 residues Cys273 (C273A) or Cys288 (C288A) completely abolished Nrf2 ubiquitination and Keap1-mediated repression of Nrf2/ARE-directed gene expression. Nevertheless, these mutations did not significantly alter the association between Nrf2 and Keap1. Electrophile adduction of Keap1 cysteine residues did not cause release of Nrf2 when studied in an in vitro model. However, phosphorylation of Nrf2 is known to produce stoichiometric release from Keap1. This raises the interesting question of whether phosphorylation of Nrf2 is direct consequence of electrophile modification of Keap1 or an indirect consequence of electrophile-mediated Keap1 ubiquitination.

12

CLINICAL ELECTROPHORESIS

Capillary electrophoresis (CE) is a special case of using an electrical field to separate the components of a mixture. Electrophoresis in a capillary is differentiated from other forms of electrophoresis in that it is carried out within the confines of a narrow tube. To understand the behavior of molecules under the influence of an electrical field inside a capillary it is essential to understand the phenomena that result from the geometry of a capillary.

FUNDAMENTALS OF ELECTROPHORESIS

Basic Principles

It has long been known that molecules can be either positively or negatively electrically charged. When the numbers of positive and negative charges are the same, the charges cancel, creating a neutral (uncharged) molecule. If given the freedom to move, charged particles will seek regions, such as an electrode, having an opposing charge; in other words, opposites attract. In this example a mixture of ionic substances is dissolved in a suitable solvent, such as water. In the absence of an electrical field, the motion of these ions is essentially random. When the electrical field is applied, charged species begin to move. A crude separation occurs, resulting in a less random distribution of charged particles. Cations (positively charged ions) move toward the cathode (negatively charged electrode), and anions (negatively charged ions) move toward the anode (positively charged electrode).

Figure 12.1 also illustrates another aspect of electrophoresis in solution, the significance of the mass charge ratio (m/z). In this figure there are actually four types of charged particles: large and small positively charged and large and small negatively charged. If each

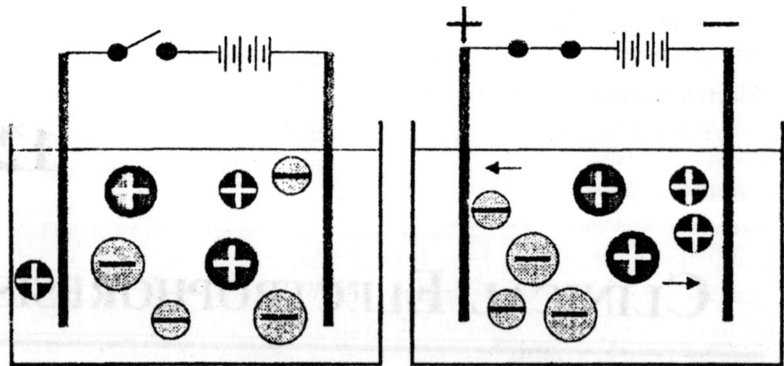

Fig. 12.1. Simple electrophoresis.

particle has only a single charge, then the absolute value of the force on each particle will be the same. The acceleration created by this force can be determined by the relationship Force = mass × acceleration (F = ma). The viscosity of the separation medium opposes the acceleration with the result that a steady velocity is achieved under constant conditions. This means that the system can not only separate particles having opposite charges, but can also separate particles of the same charge if there are other differences between them. The science of electrophoresis is largely concerned with creating systems that exploit the differences between the molecules. Alternatively, the analyst may wish to develop a system that creates differences between molecules. Varying the pH of the separation method is an example. At pH = 10.0, glycine and acetic acid will have the same charge (−1). At pH = 7.0, glycine will have a very small net charge whereas acetic acid will still have a charge of −1. Separation of these two molecules would therefore be different at pH = 7.0 and at pH = 10.0.

Numerous other factors besides pH affect electrophoretic separations. These include the hydrodynamic radius of the molecules, the viscosity of the separation medium, and temperature. In real systems there are other forces, in addition to the electrical field, acting on the charged molecules, e.g., the entire fluid mass may be moving relative to the vessel in which it is contained. Some of these factors can affect the electrophoresis in a very complex manner; for example, the passage of current through a liquid can raise the temperature of that liquid. This change in temperature can influence the electrical resistance of the system (and hence the current), the viscosity, and the velocity of the molecules moving in the field. These factors will be discussed later in the specific context of CE. Janini and Issaq presented a detailed discussion of the theoretical underpinnings of these factors.

Electrophoresis in a Capillary

The electrophoretic process in a capillary has all of the features previously described. In addition, the small diameter of the capillary and its large aspect ratio (length/width) contribute additional factors. What actually defines a capillary? For this chapter the discussion will be limited to capillaries formed from fused silica and having an inner diameter (i.d.) of 100 μm or less. The usual range of inner diameters is from 20–100 μm. Typically the capillaries that are used in CE are circular in cross-section. However, capillaries with square cross-sections have been produced. These may offer some advantages in terms of thermal regulation and detection sensitivity, but to date they have not been widely used.

Advantages of the capillary

Capillaries were introduced into electrophoresis as an anti-convective and heat controlling innovation. In wide tubes thermal gradients cause band mixing and loss of resolution. The use of glass capillaries of 200–500-μm i.d. was reported by Virtanen in 1969. Jorgensen's introduction of 75 μm capillary tubes was the start of modern "*high-performance*" CE.

Figure 12.2 illustrates the separation of a mixture of two components (both negatively charged) in a capillary. A small plug of sample is introduced into one end. When an electrical field is applied, the components begin to move in the field as previously described. The narrow capillary reduces lateral diffusion and insures that temperature

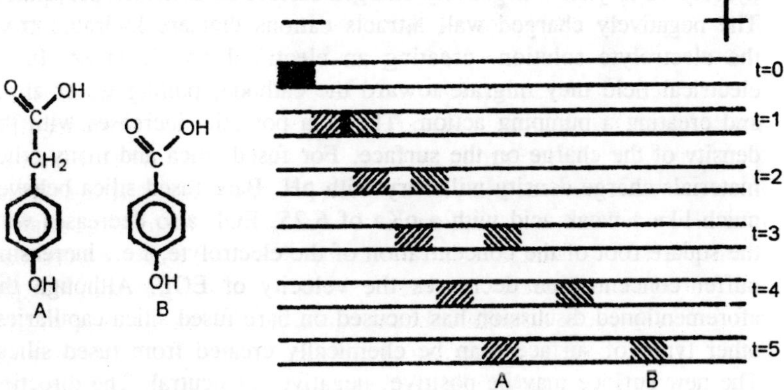

Fig. 12.2. Capillary electrophoresis.

differences between the center of the capillary and the wall are quite small. Because the two components in this example move at different velocities, they can be separated. The geometry and other properties of the capillary electrophoretic separation also lead to a condition known as *plug flow*. Under ideal plug flow conditions, the only factor leading to sample dispersion is diffusion. This contributes to the high efficiency of CE separations.

Electroosmosis

The small diameter of the capillary contributes to another aspect of the separation process. This is the phenomenon known as electroosmosis, electroendoosmotic flow, or simply EOF. EOF exists in any electrophoretic system. It will occur whenever the liquid near a charged surface is placed in an electrical field resulting in the bulk movement of fluid near that surface. Because the surface to volume ratio is very high inside a capillary, EOF becomes a significant factor in CE.

The velocity of the electroosmotic flow through a capillary is given by the Smoluchowski equation (Eq. 1),

$$\nu_{eof} = -(\varepsilon\zeta / 4\pi\eta)E \qquad ...(1)$$

where ε is the dielectric constant of the electrolyte, ζ is the zeta potential (Volts), η is the viscosity (Poise), and E is the potential applied (Volts/cm). In CE the zeta potential (ζ) is a measure of the charge on the wall of the capillary. This charge arises from both the nature of the material that composes the capillary and the composition of the electrolyte (buffer). The most commonly employed capillary material is fused silica. The surface of a fused silica capillary can be hydrolyzed to yield a negatively charged surface as described previously. The negatively charged wall attracts cations that are hydrated from the electrolyte solution, creating an electrical double layer. In an electrical field they migrate toward the cathode, pulling water along and creating a pumping action. The zeta potential increases with the density of the charge on the surface. For fused silica and many other materials charge density will vary with pH. Bare fused silica behaves much like a weak acid with a pKa of 6.25. EOF also decreases with the square root of the concentration of the electrolyte, i.e., increasing buffer concentration decreases the velocity of EOF. Although the aforementioned discussion has focused on bare fused silica capillaries, other types of surfaces can be chemically created from fused silica. The new surface may be positive, negative, or neutral. The direction of the electroosmotic flow will therefore depend on the sign of the

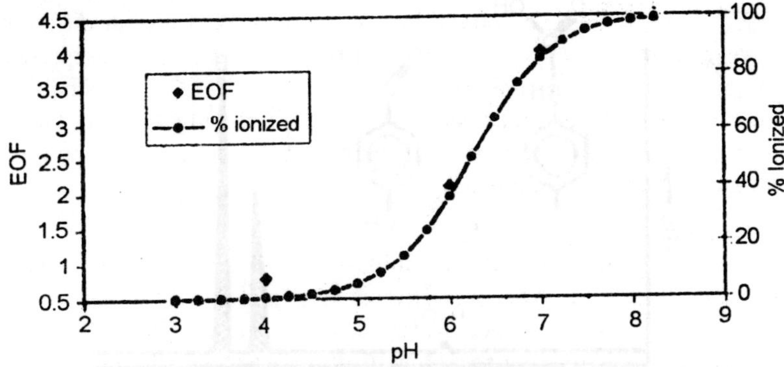

Fig. 12.3. EOF as a function of pH.

charge on the wall of the capillary. Flow is always toward the electrode that has the same charge as the capillary wall. Thus an uncharged wall will have, in theory, no EOF. In reality this is difficult to accomplish.

In the narrow confines of the capillary the velocity of liquid is nearly uniform across the i.d. of the capillary resulting in what has been termed "*plug flow*". This is in contrast to the laminar flow exhibited by pumped systems, which creates a velocity profile across the diameter of the tube. On the other hand, plug flow greatly reduces the band broadening seen in systems (such as *high-performance liquid chromatography* [HPLC]) that are pumped by a pressure differential.

In the example, the EOF is assumed to be zero. In practice it is very difficult to completely eliminate EOF, although it can be reduced

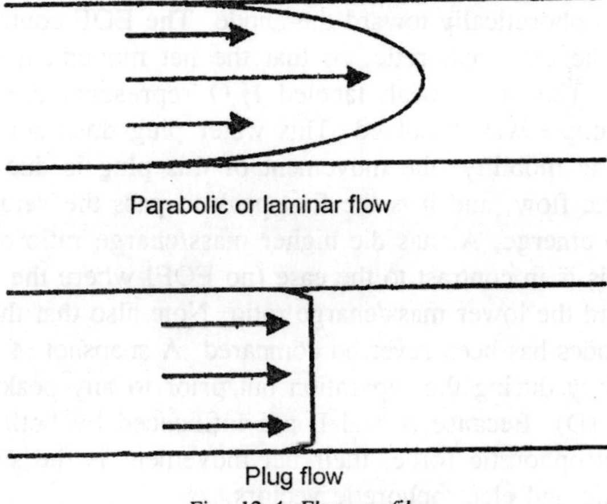

Fig. 12.4. Flow profiles.

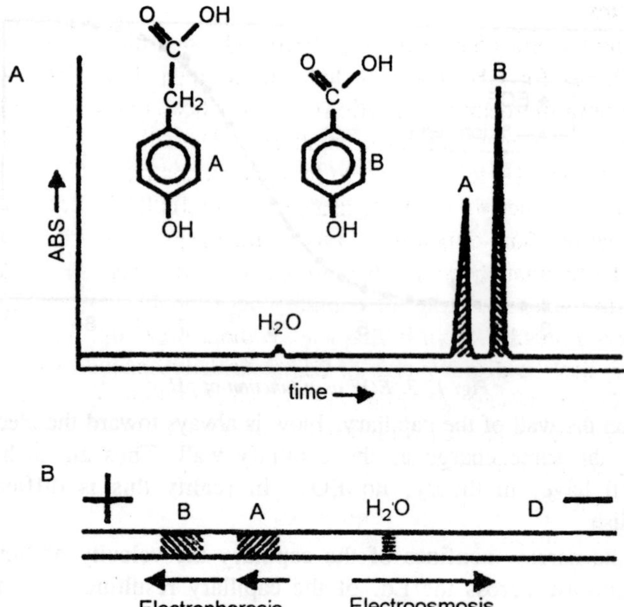

Fig. 12.5. Separation with EOF.

to a value near zero. In many separations it is a significant factor, and it may affect the net movement of the analyte molecules more than does the electrophoretic force. The movement (vectors) due to the electrophoretic and electroosmotic forces may even be in opposite directions. Both analytes have a charge of -1 under these conditions. The EOF in this case is toward the cathode, while the analytes are moved electrophoretically toward the anode. The EOF contribution is larger than the electrophoretic, so that the net movement is toward the cathode. The small peak labeled H_2O represents the water in which the sample was dissolved. This water plug does not have any electrophoretic mobility; the movement of this plug is due solely to electroosmotic flow, and it is the first peak to pass the detector. The next peak to emerge, A, has the higher mass/charge ratio of the two analytes. This is in contrast to the case (no EOF) where the first peak to emerge had the lower mass/charge ratio. Note also that the polarity of the electrodes has been reversed compared. A snapshot of the inside of the capillary during the separation but prior to any peak reaching the detector (D). Because A and B are influenced by both the EOF and the electrophoretic force, their net movement is the sum of the electroosmotic and electrophoretic vectors.

Capillaries

Many materials have been suggested and tested for the construction of capillaries for CE. These include fused silica, borosilicate glass, and polytetrafluoroethylene (Teflon). Fused silica is now the preferred material for the construction of capillaries. The silica used is of very high purity, similar to that used to produce silicon chips for electronic components. Tubes of silica are heated to over 1000°C, then stretched to produce the final dimensions. Fused silica capillaries are extremely brittle. To facilitate handling they are coated with a layer of polyimide 10–25 μm thick, rendering the capillary very flexible. It can easily be wound on a spool 2.5 cm in diameter without breaking. The coating, however, has the disadvantage of being virtually opaque to UV light. It must be removed to create a "*window*" to allow on-capillary detection. This makes an area that is very fragile, warranting careful handling to prevent breakage.

The thickness of the wall of the capillary and the polyimide coating is generally much greater than the i.d. of the capillary. A typical capillary will have an external diameter of 350 μm. If the internal diameter is 50 μm, this leaves a wall thickness of 150 μm. The thickness of the wall is critical, because the heat that is produced when an electrical current passes through the electrolyte must be removed through this wall. Reducing the wall thickness increases the fragility of the capillary at the same time as it increases the heat transfer capacity. External diameter is thus a trade-off between strength and heat transfer.

Variables in Capillary Electrophoresis

Capillary electrophoresis offers many directions from which to approach an analytical problem. This can be advantageous because as the number of options available increases, the likelihood that a solution to the analytical problem can be found also increases. This can also be a disadvantage, particularly to the newcomer, because the wide choice of options can appear daunting. This is compounded by the interactive nature of some of these factors. For example, a change in pH can affect the current; a change in current can affect temperature; a change in temperature can affect pH, the factor we were trying to vary in our experiment. Understanding these key factors will contribute to successful analysis.

Capillary Surface

The inner surface of a capillary is an extremely important factor in CE. The inner wall is in contact with the separation chemistry and the samples. As noted earlier, the capillary wall is the site of the mechanism by which EOF is created. In order to understand how to control the effect of the surface on the separation, it important to understand the behavior of the capillary surface. The inner surface of a CE capillary is more analogous to the surface of the particles packed inside an HPLC column than it is to the HPLC column wall. Unlike the wall of an HPLC column, the capillary wall participates in the separation process. In CE the goal is usually to prevent interaction between the analytes and the inner wall of the capillary while simultaneously controlling EOF. In order to have control over the separation process it is necessary to have control over this surface.

Surface modifications

The nature of the surface of a bare fused silica capillary depends somewhat on the treatment it has experienced. Most of the surface is in a siloxane form; there are few groups present that can create a charged surface. Treatment with base (NaOH or KOH) causes the hydrolysis of the siloxane group. Sometimes referred to as an etched surface, this layer is rich in silanol groups, which are the weak acids referred to in the discussion of EOF. To convert completely the surface of the capillary into this form may require long periods of exposure with 0.1–1.0 M base at elevated temperatures. Incomplete conversion may lead to poor reproducibility in peak migration times.

Not all separations can be optimized using bare silica. However, the silica surface is chemically reactive and can be derivatized in a variety of ways. Silane derivatization reactions are commonly employed

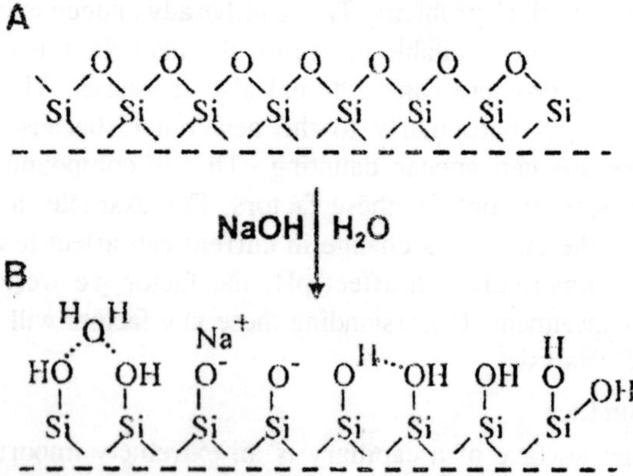

Fig. 12.6. Silica surface chemistry. Surface of fused silica before (A) and after (B) NaOH hydrolysis.

to link other groups to silica. This can result in a linkage through a Si-O-Si-C bond or through a Si-C bond depending on the chemistry employed. The Si-C bond is said to be the more stable of the two at high pH values. Using a molecule that has a silane at one end and a second functional group at the other allows a second layer to bond. This approach allows more complex coatings to be applied in layers. In this way many types of coatings have been created including polyacrylamide, polyvinyl alcohol, polyethylene glycol, and polyvinylpyrolidone. Each of these coatings will have different properties of charge and adsorptivity. Most were designed to reduce protein binding to the capillary wall. Basic proteins, being positively charged, are particularly difficult to analyze in untreated capillaries because they bind tightly to the negatively charged wall. Coatings are also employed to modify the charge of the wall such that EOF is drastically altered or reversed.

Presently, the analyst seldom prepares covalently coated capillaries, as many types are commercially available. With commercially available fixed coatings, it is possible to obtain charges ranging from acidic to neutral to basic and from *hydrophilic* to *hydrophobic*. The analyst may also wish to incorporate noncovalent coatings into a separation method using a bare silica capillary. These transient or dynamic coatings rely on ionic interactions to hold them on the capillary wall. Polyamines will stick to the negatively charged silica, effectively shielding the negatively charged wall from the solution and creating a positively charged surface. In such a capillary, the EOF will be toward the anode. Coatings of this type may be stable for several runs. Cationic detergents such as tetradecyltrimethylammonium bromide (TTAB) can be used to form a positively charged surface as well. Such coatings are actually bilayers. The first layer has the positively charged head of the detergent attached to the negatively charged silanol surface. The hydrophobic tails of the molecules extend radially inward, forming a *hydrophobic* surface. A second layer of detergent forms with the hydrophobic tails in contact with the tails of the first layer and the positively charged heads forming the inner surface of the capillary. Again, EOF will be toward the anode. These detergent bilayers are easy to form but lack stability. They are easily disrupted by organic solvents and usually require that the detergent be added to the run buffer (where it may interact with analytes).

Whenever a capillary is used, the buffer being used modifies the surface. Most workers have come to recognize that capillaries perform best when they are "dedicated" to a specific type of buffer species.

For example, if a capillary that has been equilibrated with a phosphate buffer is used with a borate buffer of similar concentration and pH the migration times will drift from run to run until a new equilibrium condition has been established. Although neither borate nor phosphate would be expected to form a coating on the capillary wall, it is apparent that the capillary does "remember" the buffer it has held. This dedication of a capillary to one type of system is a relatively inexpensive way to improve results.

Capillary regeneration

Regeneration is the process of creating the same surface on the inner wall of the capillary prior to the start of every analytical run with a given method. Although it is only necessary to recreate the same surface condition every time, it is in fact easier in the long run to fully regenerate the surface. There are two goals to regeneration: (1) to clean the capillary of any residual buffer and sample from the previous analysis; and (2) to create the same surface from run to run, thereby enhancing reproducibility. If the method has been properly designed these steps should not be necessary. If sample components are sticking to the capillary wall in sufficient quantity to affect subsequent runs, it is advisable to change the method to prevent the sample from sticking (perhaps by using a coating or by increasing the buffer concentration) rather than incorporating a cleaning procedure. In practice this can be difficult to accomplish, particularly with samples containing protein (such as serum) that is inherently troublesome.

This chapter will focus on the regeneration of bare silica capillaries. The special handling of coated surfaces will be discussed previously. However, when using commercially coated capillaries, it is important to follow the manufacturer's instructions for cleaning and regeneration. This is because coated capillaries are easily converted into bare silica capillaries.

Freshly purchased fused silica capillaries, even those sold as "ready to use," may not be clean when first received. Therefore, some variation of the following procedure should be used whenever a new piece of bare silica capillary is used.

1. Flush the capillary with methanol. This will remove any organic residues (such as oil) and will aid in the subsequent wetting of the surface.
2. Flush with water.
3. Flush with 1 N hydrochloric acid. This removes any residual cations.

4. Flush with water.
5. Flush with 1 N NaOH. This step hydrolyzes the siloxanes to create the charged silanol groups that provide EOF.
6. Flush with water.
7. Flush with electrolyte.

Many variations on this procedure exist. For example, a second hydrochloric acid wash can be added after the NaOH if the removal of residual sodium is desired (as prior to a sodium analysis). The time and temperature of each step is important. A minimum of three capillary volumes should be used over at least 5 min. Static soaking should be avoided in favor of a continuous flow. As expected, the use of elevated temperature (35–40°C) will enhance the cleaning rate. The final flush with electrolyte, although critical to obtain assay reproducibility, is often neglected. The procedure described above creates a virgin surface that may change as analysis proceeds. There is usually an equilibration between the capillary wall and even simple buffers, such as sodium phosphate. Applying voltage to the capillary facilitates the exchange of ions at the surface after filling with the electrolyte.

The regeneration process between sample runs can be milder than the initial cleaning, particularly if the method is not detrimental to the surface and the samples are not sticky. In the best of cases it is only necessary to flush with fresh run buffer. At other times exposure to acid or base, or even an organic solvent, may be required to restore the surface to the original condition. The regeneration procedure, however, should be matched to the separation method. For separations using sodium borate buffer, pH 8.3, regeneration with NaOH is appropriate. For separations using phosphate buffer, pH 2.5, the use of NaOH or other base rinses should be avoided. At low pH, EOF is suppressed because the silanol groups are poorly ionized. Using NaOH to regenerate the capillary will increase the time needed to reequilibrate the surface with the low pH electrolyte (phosphate), thus rinsing with a higher concentration of low pH buffer or even with 1 N acid (i.e., phosphoric) will generally give better results.

Rinsing coated capillaries adds a further complication, in that the coating itself may be labile in the presence of the cleaning solution. Exposure to NaOH will strip many covalently bonded phases from the capillary surface. It is critical to follow the manufacturer's recommendations for cleaning and regenerating coated capillaries. Dynamic coatings such as TTAB should be reconstructed by rinsing with a more concentrated solution of the coating material than is used in the run buffer. For example, if the running buffer contains 0.5 mM of detergent, a pre-rinse with 20 mM detergent followed by the actual running buffer would be appropriate.

Separation Buffers

The significance of the capillary wall in controlling the process of separation in CE cannot be overstated. The separation, however, takes place in the separation buffer. It is here that the conditions are such that the differences in mobility can exist. Buffers can either be made or purchased. Buffer quality is independent of the instrument system used. However, even the best instrument system will not perform properly with a poorly prepared buffer.

Significance of pH

The most common measurement in analytical chemistry is probably the measurement of pH. It is also the measurement that is most often made improperly. In CE it is extremely important to properly control pH since it affects analyte charge, electroosmotic flow, and, by affecting current, heat production. Thus small changes in pH tend to have greater impact in CE than do comparable pH variations in HPLC.

The titration curve of the silica surface behaves as a typical weak acid (e.g., acetic acid). The ionization of acetic acid (pKa = 4.76) is shown in Eq. 2. At the pKa, the analyte will be 50% charged. This does not mean that each molecule carries one-half of a charge, but rather that at any point in time one half of the molecules are charged and the other half are uncharged. A titration curve represents the probability than any given molecule will be charged at a given pH.

$$H_3C - COOH \rightleftarrows H_3C - COO^{(-)} + H^{(+)} \qquad ...(2)$$

When the molecule is uncharged it is under the influence of the electroosmotic flow but not the electrical field. When charged the molecule responds to both forces. As the fraction of the time the molecule spends in each state varies with pH, the net migration velocity will change. As discussed earlier, the EOF also changes with pH. Failure to properly control pH is one of the major causes of poor reproducibility in CE.

Buffer species

Buffers are compounds that are used to control the pH of a solution. They are generally weak acid or bases that can accept or donate protons. Buffers reduce the change in pH that is caused by the introduction of additional acid or base; CE buffers are selected on the basis of the pH range that is to be maintained, as well as other factors.

A wide range of buffers has been employed in CE systems. The most commonly employed are phosphate, borate, citrate, acetate, and Tris (trishydroxymethylamino methane). The zwitterionic buffers that have been recommended by several authors have the advantage of carrying less current than do mono-functional buffer molecules. However, the selection of a buffer for CE should be based on several factors, including: (1) pH value desired; (2) operating temperature; (3) charge of the buffer relative to the analytes and the capillary wall; and (4) effects on detection. These factors are further described as follows:

1. For any buffer the effective buffering range is defined as within one pH unit of the buffers pKa. Thus a buffer with a pKa of 5 would be usable from pH 4.0 to pH 6.0. For CE it is much better to have the pH as close to the pKa of the buffer as possible, certainly within ± 0.5 pH units, to reduce the buffer's contribution to variability.
2. Buffer molecules exhibit a temperature coefficient. The pH of a buffered system will tend to change with temperature. In addition, buffers tend to differ in their sensitivity to temperature. For example, phosphate has a low temperature coefficient compared to Tris. The temperature coefficient of the buffer is also important because during electrophoresis the analyst has only limited control of the temperature inside the capillary.
3. Interaction between the buffer and the analytes can change the effective charge on the analyte molecules, changing their migration velocity. Ion pairing can also occur between the buffer molecules and the analytes affecting the separation.
4. Buffers differ widely in their absorbance spectra. This is much less of a problem in CE than in HPLC because of the short path-length in CE detection. However, for high-sensitivity work the background absorbance may become an issue.

Once the buffer composition has been selected, it is essential that it be prepared properly. In order to make a buffer consistent it is critical to make the buffer the same way every time. For example, preparing a 50 mM sodium phosphate buffer by starting with 50 mM sodium phosphate and adjusting the pH with phosphoric acid will result in a buffer with a phosphate concentration higher than 50 mM. Such a buffer is best prepared by titration of phosphoric acid with NaOH. A buffer that has found wide application in CE is sodium borate. However, the preparation of borate buffers can be confusing because boric acid combines with sodium hydroxide according to Eq. 3.

$$4\ H_3BO_3 + 2\ NaOH \rightleftarrows Na_2B_4O_7 + 7\ H_2O \qquad \ldots(3)$$

Four moles of boric acid react with sodium hydroxide to form one mole of sodium tetraborate. A borate buffer will contain both boric acid and tetraborate. In discussing these systems it is customary to refer to the concentration of Boron. Thus, 4 M boric acid and 1 M sodium tetraborate have the same concentration of boron.

Buffer concentration

Increasing the concentration of a buffer will increase the buffering capacity of the system, making it less likely to change pH with the addition of acid or base. In addition, there are other factors in CE that can be affected by the concentration of the buffer. These factors can be critical when trying to achieve optimum resolution and reproducibility.

If the composition of the sample plug is different from the composition of the buffer in the capillary, the phenomenon of stacking may occur. Properly exploited stacking can result in sharper peaks and greater sensitivity. One way to achieve stacking is to keep the conductivity of the sample lower than the conductivity of the running buffer by reducing the concentration of the sample buffer relative to the run buffer. To understand this phenomenon, consider the buffer filled capillary as a wire. If the buffer concentration is uniform from one end of the capillary to the other end, the voltage drop will be linear. Inserting a plug of dilute sample is like inserting a resistor into the wire. The voltage drop now becomes steeper in the region of the plug than it is elsewhere. Since velocity is proportional to the voltage gradient, the velocity of the analytes will be faster in this region. Analytes will move rapidly until they reach the boundary between the dilute sample plug and the more concentrated running buffer. On reaching this point they will stack, increasing the local concentration of analyte and creating a zone that is narrower than the original injection plug.

Because stacking is caused by a difference in conductivity between the buffer and the sample, it might be assumed that dissolving the sample in pure water would create the highest peak efficiencies. In practice, however, this is not usually the case. The resistance across a plug of nearly pure water can be so high that localized heating results. This heating causes convective mixing and de-stacking. There should be always be some buffer ions in the sample plug; keeping samples at about 1/10 the concentration of the running buffer is a good rule of thumb.

One way to maximize stacking would be to increase the concentration of the buffer, particularly if the samples as received are high in salt. As stated previously, EOF decreases with the square root of the buffer concentration. If EOF is to remain constant it will be necessary to increase it in some other way, such as a change in pH, temperature, or voltage. If desired, EOF can be reduced simply by increasing the buffer concentration. However, by increasing the buffer concentration the current that passes through the capillary will also increase. This in turn will increase the heat generated inside the capillary and, if not adequately dissipated, a variety of problems can result. Without adequate cooling the ability to exploit higher buffer concentrations is limited.

When trying to separate basic compounds or proteins that tend to interact with the capillary wall using bare silica capillaries, problems are frequently encountered. In extreme situations they may be totally adsorbed on the capillary wall and never pass the detector. In other cases the wall may provide a drag force that results in peak tailing, loss of resolution, and decreased signal-to-noise ratio. Although coated capillaries are one solution to this problem, merely increasing the concentration of the electrolyte can often reduce these interactions.

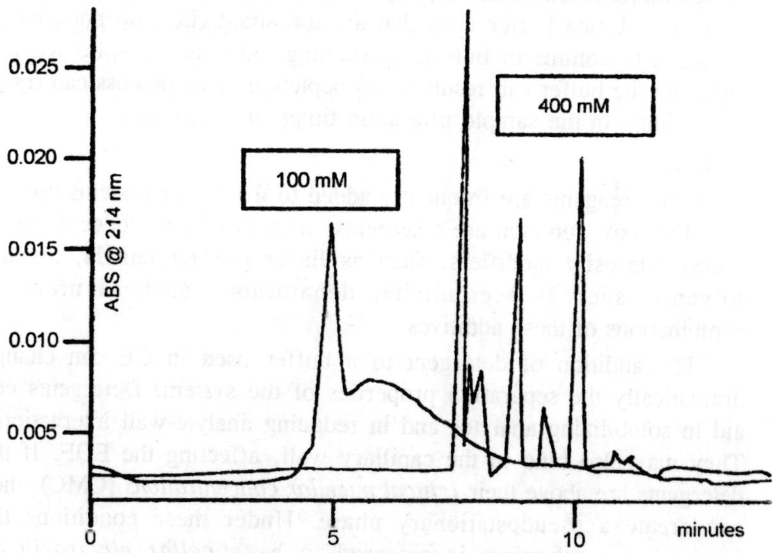

Fig. 12.7. Effect of buffer concentration on peak shape.

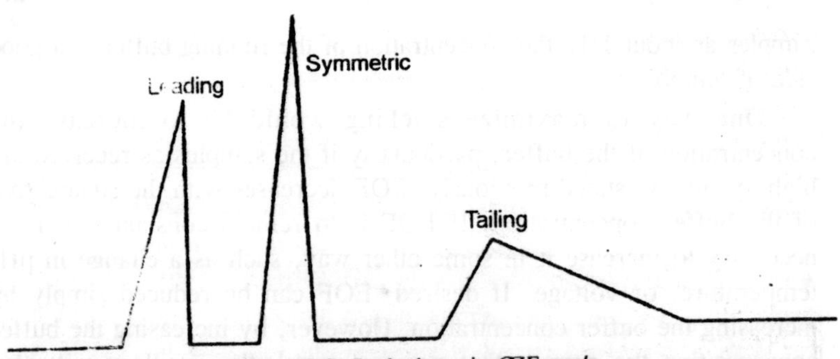

Fig. 12.8. Peak shape in CZE mode.

Peak shape in many modes of CE differs from the bell shape that is commonly seen in HPLC and other chromatographic separations. In open capillary modes (such as *capillary zone electrophoresis* [CZE]), it is not uncommon to see peak shapes. In CE the electrical field influences the buffer ions just as it does the analyte ions. The peak shape in these separations is due to the relative migration rates of the buffer ions and the analyte ions. The degree of asymmetry will increase with increased difference in mobility. Buffer mismatch can so distort the peak shape that analytes may be difficult to quantitate or may even be lost.

Because the buffer ions migrate in the electrical field, the concentration of the buffer ions in the inlet and outlet vials will change over time. Using buffer vials that are too small (i.e., do not contain an adequate volume of buffer) or running too many samples without replacing the buffer can result in ion depletion. This process can result in a change in the sample migration times or resolution.

Additives

Other reagents are frequently added to the buffer systems used in CE. The most common are detergents, such as sodium dodecyl sulfate (SDS), viscosity modifiers, such as linear polyacrylamide, organic solvents, such as acetonitrile, denaturants, such as urea, or combinations of these additives.

The addition of detergent to a buffer used in CE can change dramatically the separation properties of the system. Detergents can aid in solubilizing analytes and in reducing analyte-wall interactions. They may also bind to the capillary wall, affecting the EOF. If the detergents are above their *critical micellar concentrations* (CMC), they can create a pseudostationary phase. Under these conditions the separation mechanism is referred to as *micellar electrokinetic chromatography* (MEKC). Detergents for CE may be anionic, cationic, or nonionic. Protein separations can also be achieved with detergents. By titrating the concentration of SDS in the run buffer it is sometimes possible to achieve protein separations based on differential binding of the detergent to different proteins. This is not a separation by MEKC because the protein molecules are too large to be included in the micelle.

Viscosity modifiers provide a physical retardation to the movement of molecules. Suitable viscosity modifiers include polymers, such as linear polyacrylamide or soluble cellulose derivatives, as well as small molecules like urea. By retarding large molecules more than they do small molecules the dimension of size separation is added to the electrophoretic separation. This is exploited fully in *capillary gel electrophoresis* (CGE) which is discussed earlier. At lower concentrations, viscosity modifiers can aid in the separation of very similar analytes. Viscosity modifiers can also have significant effects on EOF, both by the change in viscosity and by interacting with the capillary wall.

Organic additives routinely used include acetonitrile, methanol, formamide, and dimethylformamide. These solvents improve the solubility of organic molecules that would otherwise be poorly soluble in an aqueous system. At sufficiently high concentrations, they can also reduce the degree of ionization of charged analytes. In MEKC they can alter the relative hydrophobicity of the micellar and non-micellar phases. Organic additives can also affect viscosity and wall charge (and hence EOF). The effect of solvents on viscosity can be complex. Acetonitrile has a lower viscosity than water, and any combination of water and acetonitrile will have a viscosity between that of water and acetonitrile. Methanol also has a lower viscosity than water, but combinations of water and methanol can be substantially more viscous than either solvent alone. In nonaqueous CE organic solvent completely replaces water in the separation solution.

Temperature

Temperature control is crucial to reproducible separations in CE. However, temperature regulation is complicated by several factors. First is that the passage of electrical current through the buffer-filled capillary results in the production of heat. This self-heating effect is inherent in electrophoretic separations and is called Joule heating. Thus temperature control in CE is as much a task of removing heat as it is maintaining a constant temperature environment. Second is that the temperature of the contents inside the capillary is difficult to measure. A layer of silica and a layer of polyimide separate the small fluid volume inside the capillary from the thermostatted medium. Any heat must be transferred to and from the separation buffer through these layers.

Although the temperature inside the capillary cannot easily be measured it can be estimated. Equation 4 is used to estimate the Joule heating (Q). In this equation

$$Q = E^2 \Lambda c \qquad \ldots(4)$$

Q is the Joule heat generated (Ω/cm³), E is the voltage gradient (V/cm), Λ is the molar conductivity of the electrolyte ($cm^2\ mol^{-1}\ W^{-1}$) and c is the concentration of the electrolyte (mol/L). Since the conductivity of the electrolyte will vary with temperature, a positive feedback mechanism occurs. In other words, as the temperature increases, the current will also increase. This in turn generates more heat thus generating more current. This feedback loop is moderated by the ability of the cooling system to remove heat and thus limit current.

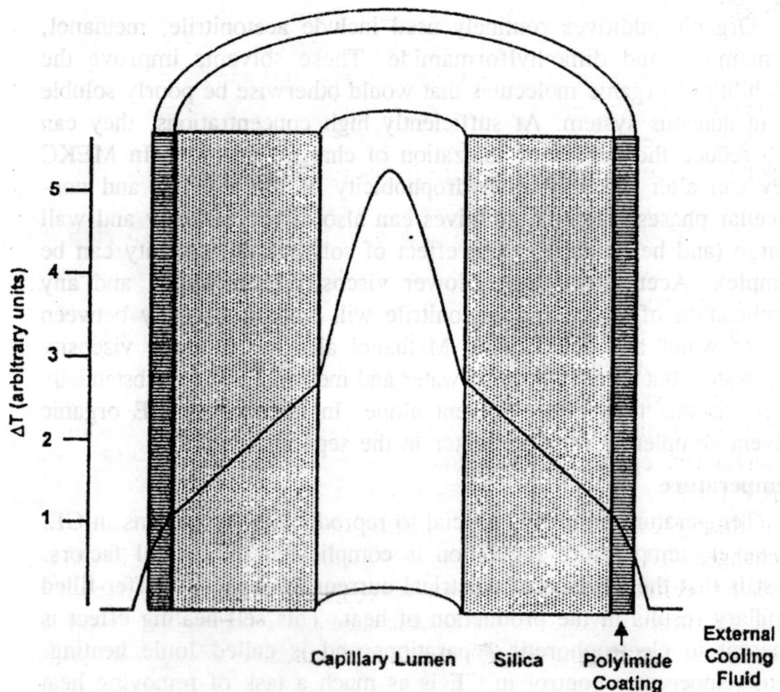

Fig. 12.9. Theoretical radial temperature profile.

Because the cooling system must act at the surface of the capillary and not internally, a temperature gradient exists from the center of the capillary to the outside.

The temperature gradient within the capillary is parabolic. The difference in temperature between the center of the capillary and the wall will increase with increasing capillary internal diameter. Current will also increase as the diameter increases (current α radius^2). The combination of these two factors can lead to the conclusion that heating will cause band broadening and that the band broadening will increase as the internal capillary diameter increases. In systems with adequate temperature control, this thermal band broadening does not become a problem unless the capillary diameter is larger than about 100 μm. A more detailed discussion of heat transfer in CE can be found in an article by Knox.

A second temperature gradient can also exist in poorly designed systems if the entire length of the capillary is not maintained in the same thermal environment. The regions of the capillary that are in buffer vials, passing through cartridge walls, or in detector cells are frequently much less efficiently cooled than are other regions of the capillary. Depending on the system and the capillary length, this uncooled region can account for as much as 25% of the capillary's effective length and can account for much of the variation in performance seen between instruments of different design.

Dynamically cooled CE systems are conveniently divided into two groups: those employing gas and those employing liquid as a heat exchange medium. Liquid cooling is generally considered to be more efficient than gas cooling simply because the heat capacity of liquids exceed that of air. The most effective liquid coolant would be water because of its enormous heat capacity. However, when dealing with electrical equipment, the use of water as a heat exchange medium is not advisable. The requirements of safety has led to the use of perfluorinated organic molecules, having the general formula (F_3C-$[CF_2]_n$-CF_3), because of their very low electrical conductivity. Because of their greater heat capacity, liquids tend to be slower to adjust to changes in temperature than gases. Liquid cooling also necessitates sealed recirculating systems, adding to the expense and complexity of the instrument. Whatever the cooling medium, most modern instrument systems use computer controlled Peltier devices to control the temperature of the cooling fluid. Peltier devices are semiconductor mechanisms that can be made to heat or cool by reversing the direction of current flow through them.

Changes in temperature can also impact other factors inside the capillary. For most liquids, an increase in temperature causes a decrease in viscosity. For example, water has a viscosity of 1.002 centipoise at 20°C. This drops to 0.798 centipoise at 30°C. In the absence of any other changes this change in viscosity will result in a substantial increase in EOF. In addition, the pH of a buffered solution may also change with temperature. A 10°C change in temperature will cause a 0.3 pH unit change in the pKa of Tris. This may be sufficient to change both EOF and the charge on the analyte molecules.

A simple way to determine if a CE system is capable of coping with the heat that will be produced during separation is by creating an Ohm's Law plot. Ohm's Law states that V = IR. If we vary voltage (V), the current (I) should change in a linear manner so long as resistance (R) remains constant. An increase in temperature within the capillary generally results in a decrease in resistance (and hence an increase in current at constant voltage). By measuring the current at a variety of voltages a graph of current vs voltage can be created. Regardless of the type of cooling system the current will become nonlinear at some voltage. For the buffer system being considered the point at which the line deviates from linearity indicates the maximum voltage possible for that buffer system/capillary combination on that instrument. In practice it is possible to run at somewhat higher voltage if it is understood that the temperature within the capillary is higher than the thermostatted temperature under these conditions. It is good practice to monitor current during a run because an increasing current during a run may indicate that the heat dissipation capacity of the instrument is being exceeded. In the worst case the heat in the capillary may become sufficient to boil the buffer locally, usually at some poorly cooled location. This usually breaks the electrical circuit (and sometimes the capillary).

Volume Relationships

The dimensions employed in CE are much smaller than those with which most chemical analysts are accustomed to work. Capillary diameters typically are measured in microns and as such the entire volume of a capillary is usually a few microliters. Injected sample volumes are in nanoliters (10^{-9}L). At these scales the tolerances required of instrument systems are extremely small and difference of 1 μm in the diameter of a capillary can create very large differences in the results of an analysis.

Flow Dynamics

Most often the sample being analyzed by CE is injected into the capillary by pressure. To calculate the volume of liquid injected it is necessary to use the Poiseuille equation (Eq. 5), which estimates the flow of liquid through a cylinder.

$$V = (\Delta P d^4 \pi t)/(128 \eta L) \quad ...(5)$$

In this equation, ΔP is the pressure drop down the length of the cylinder (Pascals), d is the cylinder's inside diameter (m), t is time the pressure is applied (s), η is the fluid viscosity (Pascal-seconds), and L is the total length of the cylinder (m). This equation has wide applicability in fluid dynamics and can be used to calculate fluid flow in CE capillaries, blood vessels, or a water main. It shows that the delivery of fluid into a capillary by pressure is directly proportional to the pressure that is applied and the length of time the pressure is applied. Fluid delivery is inversely proportional to the liquid viscosity and the length of the capillary, and proportional to the fourth power of the diameter. Temperature is indirectly involved in this relationship because the viscosities of most fluids change with temperature.

The volumes typically encountered in CE. This example assumes the viscosity of water at 25°C (1.000 centipoise). Typically injection and rinse pressures are 0.5 and 20 psi, respectively.

As predicted by Eq. 5, the volume of fluid delivered at a given pressure increases dramatically as the diameter of the capillary increases. Doubling the diameter of the capillary increases the delivered volume 16-fold. The implications of this are significant. The volume injected under constant condition changes dramatically when the capillary diameter changes over a narrow range. Because tolerances of 1–2 μm are not uncommon in commercially available capillary, selecting different pieces of capillary nominally 20 μm in diameter could give peak areas that vary substantially. Cutting pieces from a large spool of capillary is no guarantee of uniformity because the diameter may vary along the length of the spool.

The injection plug length is the linear distance within the capillary that is occupied by the injected sample volume. An injection plug that is too long may result in wide bands and loss of resolution, particularly if the analytes cannot focus. Increasing the capillary diameter allows the injection of substantially larger volumes of sample without increasing the plug length. Because the volume of a cylinder increases with the square of the radius a doubling of the capillary diameter will allow the injection of four times as much sample without changing the plug length. The viscosity of the fluid being delivered is the most difficult parameter to know with accuracy. The aforementioned examples have assumed the viscosity of water at 25°C. Within the range of temperatures typically used in CE separations (15–60°), the viscosity of water varies in a nonlinear manner from 1.138 to 0.467 centipoise. Almost anything added to the water will alter both the viscosity and the temperature-viscosity relationship. The additions of macromolecules, such as cellulose derivatives or acrylamide polymers, are extreme cases. These molecules display remarkable viscosity behavior with changes in flow rates. Linear polymers, for example, can extend and align themselves when forced through a capillary. They can show a reduction in viscosity with increased flow. Other systems may increase in viscosity with flow because of polymer entanglement. Even systems as simple as methanol-water can show complex behavior. For example, a 1:1 mix of methanol and water has a higher viscosity than either pure solvent. It is also important to remember that when calculating volumes injected into fluid-filled capillaries, the viscosity of the fluid in the capillary is usually more significant than the viscosity of the sample (unless one is analyzing highly viscous samples).

Entering the Poiseuille equation into a spreadsheet program simplifies fluid delivery calculations such as these. There is also a Windows-compatible computer program called "*CE Expert*" that can perform these calculations.

Sample Handling

Four basic strategies are used to deliver these fluid volumes into capillaries: Positive pressure, vacuum, gravity, and electrophoresis. Positive pressure and vacuum have been the most common methods of filling and rinsing capillaries. Positive pressure up to 100 psi (7 bar) has been used for rinsing. This pressure is delivered either from a source of compressed gas, such as nitrogen, or from an on-board air pump that applies pressure to the headspace of a buffer reservoir. Vacuum delivery is limited to 10 psi or less but can be useful for drawing fluid from containers that cannot be made pressure tight.

Gravity and electrophoresis are not practical for filling and rinsing capillaries, but they are used, along with pressure and vacuum, for injecting samples into capillaries. Gravity injection (sometimes called hydrostatic injection) is accomplished by inserting the inlet end of the capillary into the sample vial and raising the vial and capillary relative to the outlet end. Reproducible gravity injection requires that the vial be raised to the same height for the same duration of time at each injection (gravity itself being a fairly reliable source of motive power). Pressure and vacuum injections are more complicated. Regardless of how the pressure differential is created, a finite time is required for the pressure to reach a steady state. Changes in pressure on the order of 0.05 psi can be significant at the low pressures commonly employed (0.1–1 psi). Systems that rely on pressure or vacuum must have some sort of feedback mechanism to compensate for these variations. These systems either adjust the delivered pressure or the delivery time to maintain the desired product of pressure and time. In well-engineered systems a 3-s injection at 1 psi and a 10-s injection at 0.3 psi should give identical results, because both are 3 psi-second injections. In practice the longer, lower pressure injection usually gives better performance because it allows a longer time for the system to respond to variances.

Electrophoretic or electrokinetic injections do not conform to the Poiseuille equation. In this method of sample introduction, the inlet of the capillary is inserted into the sample and the outlet into a buffer vial. Voltage is briefly applied. Through a combination of electrophoresis and electroosmotic flow sample is drawn into the capillary. This technique is valuable when delivering sample to a gel-filled capillary or when pressure delivery is not possible. There is a possibility of bias when using this technique. Components that migrate more rapidly in the electrical field will be over-represented in the sample compared to slower moving components. To maximize the volume injected, the sample should be at a considerably lower ionic strength than the run buffer. Subsequent injections will show reduced peak areas because each injection delivers salts from the capillary buffer into the sample vial, raising the ionic strength of the sample. This effect can be minimized (and injected quantity increased) by pre-injecting from pure water immediately prior to the sample injection.

Most commercial systems employ some sort of carousel or X-Y-Z robotic system to move the buffer and sample vials to the capillary. These systems may also provide refrigerated storage for labile samples. In this case the sample storage temperature should be regulated independently of the capillary thermostatting system.

Detection

In order to gain useful information from the separation technique, it is necessary to detect and measure the analytes. Detection may be qualitative and/or quantitative. Most CE detection is done on-capillary; that is, a section of the capillary is linked to the detection device and the capillary itself is the detection cell. It is also possible to couple to detectors that are outside of the separation capillary although this does require a specialized interface.

Geometry and Path-Length

The most frequently used method of detection involves absorbance of energy as the analytes move through a focused beam of light. The scale of the detection apparatus and of the signal produced has created some unique challenges for the instrument developer.

On-capillary detection eliminates the problems of coupling the capillary and its power supply to flow cells or other devices. However, detection through the capillary is complicated by the curvature of the capillary itself. The capillary and the fluid it contains make up a complex cylindrical lens. The curvature of this lens must be accounted for in order to gather the maximum amount of light and thereby maximize signal-to-noise ratio. The effective length of the light path through the capillary is actually about 63.5% the stated i.d. of the capillary. Thus a 50-μm capillary has an effective path length of only 32 μm. This can be compared to typical HPLC detectors that have detectors in the 5–10 mm range. Because of this very small light path, the absorbance signal obtained from a CE system is also correspondingly small. Therefore, a peak with an absorbance of 0.002 AU is a significant peak. Noise levels are correspondingly small and are usually measured in microabsorbance units. The maximum absorbance of typical CE detectors is 0.2 AU. The capillary lumen occupies only a small part of the diameter of the capillary; the remainder is transparent silica. This geometry allows for large amounts of stray light to enter the detector so that a fully opaque sample would not reduce the light passing through the capillary to zero. This factor must be considered in the design of effective CE detector hardware and software. Several novel approaches have been taken to increase the path length (and the sensitivity) of CE detectors. One approach has been to use a specially constructed low-volume flow cell. These cells carry the analytes through two right-angle bends. The segment between the bends, which may be over 1000 μm long, is thus at right angles to the direction of the capillary and parallel to the direction of the light beam. Properly designed, these cells can dramatically increase sensitivity but at the risk of some loss of resolution. Another approach has been to create a wide zone or "*bubble*" in the capillary at the window. A 50-μm i.d. capillary may have a window that is 150 μm in diameter, giving a sensitivity increase of approximately threefold.

Absorbance

Absorbance detectors are the most commonly encountered types of detector in CE instrument systems. They rely on the absorbance of light energy by the analytes. This absorbance creates a shadow as the analytes pass between the light source and the light detector. The intensity of the shadow is proportional to amount of material present.

The simplest absorbance detector uses only portion of the available energy. The broad-spectrum light from a source lamp is passed through a filter or diffracted by a grating so that a narrow range of the spectrum is used. In some cases lamps (such as hollow cathode types) are used,

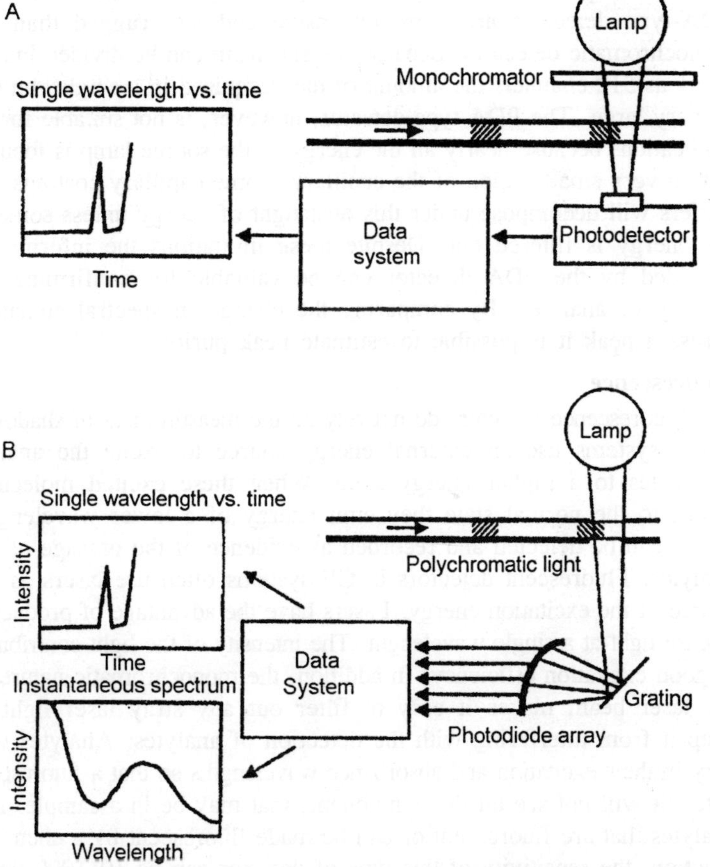

Fig. 12.10. Comparison of single wavelength (A) and photodiode array (B) absorbance detectors.

that produce light at only a few discrete wavelengths. Monochromatic absorbance detectors are relatively inexpensive and rugged. However, because only a part of the spectrum is used, information may be lost from complex samples that have components with differing absorbance maxima.

Another type of absorbance detector looks at changes over a wide range of wavelengths simultaneously. The photodiode array detector (PDA) delivers the entire spectrum of light available from the source lamp to the capillary window. The light passing through the capillary is diffracted into a spectrum that is projected on a linear array of photodiodes. In this manner it is possible to record the entire absorbance spectrum of analytes as they pass by the detector window. PDA-type detectors are more expensive and less rugged than are monochromatic detectors. Because the spectrum can be divided into as many as 512 channels the amount of data acquired in a single run can be very large. The PDA type detector, however, is not suitable for all applications because nearly all the energy of the source lamp is focused onto a very small region of the capillary. Some capillary coatings and buffers will decompose under this onslaught of energy unless some of the energy is filtered out. Despite these limitations the information provided by the PDA detector can be valuable for confirming the identity of analytes. By comparing the change in spectral signature across a peak it is possible to estimate peak purity.

Fluorescence

Fluorescence detectors do not rely on the measurement of shadows. These systems use an external energy source to excite the analyte molecules to a higher energy state. When these excited molecules return to the normal state they emit energy of a lower wavelength, which can be detected and recorded as evidence of the passage of the analytes. Fluorescent detectors in CE systems often use lasers as the source of the excitation energy. Lasers have the advantage of producing intense light at a single wavelength. The intensity of the light contributes to good excitation efficiency. In addition, the monochromatic nature of the laser beam makes it easy to filter out any stray laser light to keep it from interfering with the detection of analytes. Analytes will vary in their excitation and absorbance wavelengths so that a fluorescent detector will not see all the components that may be in a sample. For analytes that are fluorescent or can be made fluorescent by a chemical reaction, the sensitivity of this type of detector can be 10–1000 times better than an absorbance detector.

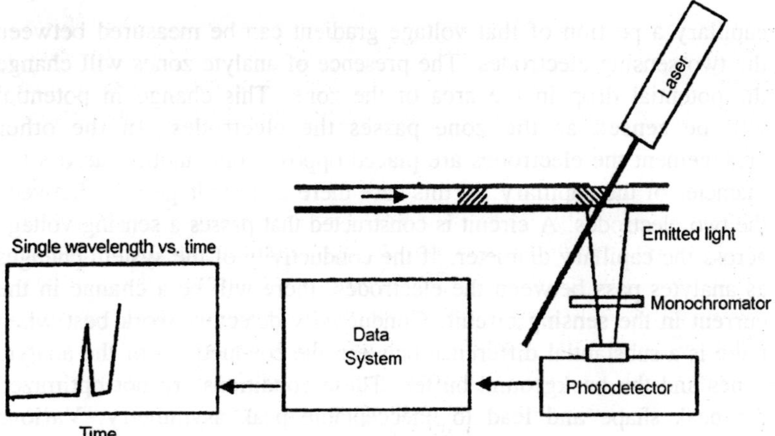

Fig. 12.11. Laser-induced fluorescence detector.

Amperometry and Conductivity

These two detection techniques potentially can offer a high degree of sensitivity and be applied to a wide variety of analytes, including those without appreciable UV absorption. Amperometry and conductivity are difficult to do in practice, and to date these devices are not commercially available. Both of these detection schemes require the use of sensing electrodes that are scaled to the dimensions of the electrophoresis capillary. In addition, these detectors place some limitations on the type of separation buffer employed.

In amperometric detection, an electroactive analyte undergoes an electrochemical reaction inside a detector cell. The CE separation is generally carried out at microampere currents and kilovolt potentials, whereas the detection cell must operate at picoampere currents and millivolt potentials. The two circuits must therefore be isolated, usually by connecting the capillary to the high voltage at a point prior to the end of the capillary where the detection cell is located. This system depends on EOF to carry the analyte past the high voltage electrode to the detection cell. Amperometric detectors have been used successfully for the detection of biogenic amines at levels as low as 10^{-8} m. With continued advances in microfabrication this type of detector should become routinely available.

There are two types of conductivity detector. Both require that two electrodes be placed within the separation capillary. In the first type a short distance down the length of the capillary, separates the electrodes. Because there is a voltage gradient down the length of the capillary a portion of that voltage gradient can be measured between the two sensing electrodes. The presence of analyte zones will change the potential drop in the area of the zone. This change in potential will be sensed as the zone passes the electrodes. In the other arrangement the electrodes are placed opposite one another across the diameter of the capillary. In this case there is no voltage drop between the two electrodes. A circuit is constructed that passes a sensing voltage across the capillary diameter. If the conductivity of the system changes as analytes pass between the electrodes, there will be a change in the current in the sensing circuit. Conductivity detectors work best when there is a substantial difference between the conductivity of the analyte zones and the background buffer. These conditions are not optimized for peak shape and lead to unacceptable peak asymmetry. Various schemes have been described for avoiding this problem. Conductivity detectors have been used for the measurement of inorganic ions and in isotachophoretic separations.

Capillary Electrophoresis-Mass Spectrometry

Hybrid systems such as CE-mass spectrometry (CE-MS) offer an additional dimension of analysis in addition to detection. CE data consists of migration time, quantity, and (using a PDA detector) spectral signature. MS adds the additional data of molecular weight and, using collision dissociation and MS-MS systems, structural information as well. This combination of techniques provides an orthogonal approach to analysis in a single analytical run.

The predominant form of MS that has been coupled to CE has been electrospray MS. The outlet end of the CE capillary is inserted into the electrospray interface. Because the volume of liquid emerging from the capillary is very small, a make-up liquid is pumped through an axial needle. This sheath flow also provides a return connection to the high-voltage power supply of the CE system. The liquid is mixed with a flowing gas stream and nebulized into a spray. The spray vaporizes and the ionized analyte particles are carried into the MS detector. The MS system is usually set to scan across an expected range of mass values. Because the width of peaks in CE can be very small, the MS instrument must be able to scan across the desired mass range very rapidly or peaks may be missed.

Most mass spectroscopists prefer to use buffer systems that are volatile, such as ammonium formate, in order to reduce the accumulation of buffer salts inside the MS instrument. These buffers may not be optimized for the separation of the analyte mixture, although an incomplete separation can be acceptable in CE-MS because the MS systems provide an additional dimension of separation.

Many of the existing commercial CE systems have been interfaced to commercial MS systems. The design of these systems allows the use of UV or other detectors prior to the MS interface, but usually require quite long and awkward reaches of capillary to connect the two systems. Unlocking the true potential of this method will require the development of a CE system that is fully integrated with the MS system.

Indirect Detection

In the previous discussions it has been assumed that detection will be direct, that is, the presence of the sample in the detector cell or window will cause an increase in the output signal. This is not always the case. There are certain applications where the decrease of the background signal provides evidence of the passage of analytes through a detector. In some cases a detector that is useful for indirect detection would not detect the analytes in direct mode. An example of this is the detection of inorganic ions such as sodium or sulfate with a UV detector.

To detect such analytes, the capillary is filled with a buffer that has mobility close to that of the analytes and also has a significant UV absorbency. The buffer/chromophore must carry the same charge as the analyte. For the analysis of sulfate, a buffer containing sodium chromate is used. In the area of the capillary occupied by the sulfate band the chromate is displaced, creating a chromate depleted region. Because chromate absorbs light at 254 nm, by monitoring background electrolyte absorbance at this wavelength the presence of sulfate will be indicated by a negative peak, with an area corresponding to the amount of chromate displaced and hence to the amount of sulfate present. Most CE data analysis packages can invert these negative peaks, producing a normal-appearing electropherogram.

Data Analysis

The collection and analysis of CE data has many characteristics in common with other chromatography-like analyses. Many analysts have utilized data systems developed for HPLC and GC systems. These data systems may not be optimal for CE for three reasons:

1. The signals obtained from CE are usually very small. A typical HPLC peak may have a maximum absorbance of 0.2 AU, whereas a CE detector may have a full range of 0.2 AU. A typical peak in CE may have a maximum absorbance of 0.002 AU.

2. CE peaks can be quite narrow with a width of only a few seconds. Some older data systems (particularly HPLC systems) cannot respond sufficiently fast to deal with this data. If data is to be collected digitally, it must be collected at a high data rate to define adequately the peak shape.
3. CE peaks are often non-Gaussian. Because of the low band broad spreading in CE and the effects of electrofocusing CE peaks tend to be more triangular and less bell-shaped than peaks in HPLC and GC. At times CE peaks may have one edge that is nearly vertical. Some data systems have difficulty locating the peak start and stop times for these shapes.

Two types of peak-detection methods dominate analytical data analysis: slope sensitive algorithm and the moving median filter algorithm. Slope sensitive algorithms look at the slope of the baseline over some interval of time. When the slope exceeds a pre-determined value, a peak is said to have begun. The point at which the slope goes to zero identifies the peak apex, and the point at which the slope returns to the starting value defines the peak end. The slope-sensitive method looks for peaks independently of the baseline shape. Most commercial software packages use this method.

Moving median filter algorithms take a different approach. Peaks are relatively high frequency (impulse) events when compared to baseline drift. These algorithms seek to define how the baseline would look in the absence of peaks by filtering out all impulse events. Whatever differs from the baseline is defined as a peak. In practice, the algorithm makes several passes through the data set (iterations) to determine the best fit. This type of algorithm, commercially available as "Caesar," is more successful at dealing with the abrupt slope changes in CE data than are slope-sensitive algorithms.

A data system for CE needs to include some calculations that can be deemed "*CE specific*." These include the calculation of mobility (a measure of the velocity of an analyte through the capillary) and corrected peak area. Corrected area is necessary because the peaks passing through a CE detector do not all pass through at the same velocity. Early eluting peaks move through more rapidly than do later eluting peaks. This is unlike the situation in HPLC where the velocity through the detector cell is dependent only on the flow rate and not on the retention time. Because later eluting peaks are moving more slowly, they appear to be larger relative to earlier eluting peaks. Corrected peak area normalizes peak area to unit migration time and allows accurate comparison of the components in a mixture.

Fraction Collection

Fraction collection is placed under the heading of detection under the assumption that fractions are being collected for analysis outside the CE instrument. At first glance, fraction collection in CE appears to be analogous to fraction collection in HPLC, but there are significant differences.

The velocity of peaks through the HPLC detector is constant if the flow rate is constant. This is not true in CE where earlier eluting peaks are moving more rapidly than later eluting peaks. The delay time between peak detection and elution (the time for transit from the window to the capillary outlet) will therefore vary, becoming longer with each successive peak. This time can be quite long. Consider a capillary 60-cm long with the window located 10-cm from the outlet end. If a peak passes the detector at t = 5 min it will not emerge from the end of the capillary until t = 6 min. A peak detected at t = 10 min will emerge at t = 12 min. Peaks that pass the detector between 5 and 10 min will all be in the outlet segment of the capillary between t = 6 and t = 12 min. A further complication is that collection requires that the outlet of the capillary be moved to a new collection vial for each peak that is to be collected. At each move the circuit will be broken. The time needed for the power supply to ramp down and ramp up at each move, and the diminished peak velocities during the ramping segments cannot be disregarded. Complex algorithms are needed to do this process smoothly.

A more serious limitation to the collection of fractions from CE is the very small amount of sample that the fraction will contain. Consider a capillary 100 μm in diameter and 50 cm long, with the window located 10 cm from the end. A 5 psi-sec injection into this capillary will inject about 189 nL of sample. If the analyte concentration is 1 mg/mL in the starting sample and the peak is collected with 100% efficiency, the recovered sample will be 189 ng. Repeating this run 10 times would yield less than a two micrograms of product. Although fraction collection in CE is possible, one must question whether it is worth the effort.

Modes of Separation in Capillary Electrophoresis

A CE system can be operated in several different modes. These modes offer the analyst a variety of ways to approach an analytical problem. The choice of mode will be based on the analytical problem under consideration. This section will describe the major modes of capillary electrophoretic separation that are currently in use and provide some applications for each.

Capillary Zone Electrophoresis (CZE)

Mechanism

Section 1 of this chapter dealt almost entirely with this form of CE. CZE is characterized by the use of open capillaries and relatively low viscosity buffer systems. Analyte molecules move from one end of the capillary to the other according to the vector sum of electrophoresis and electroosmotic mobility.

Applications

CZE is the most widespread mode of CE. It has been used for analytes as diverse as sodium ions, drugs, and protein molecules. Analyte species can be separated by CZE if they migrate at different velocities in the electrical field.

Capillary Gel Electrophoresis (CGE)

Mechanism

Capillary gel electrophoresis (CGE) is separation based on viscous drag. In this mode of CE the capillary is filled with a gel or viscous solution. EOF is often suppressed so that the migration of the analytes is solely by electrophoresis. Larger molecules tend to be retarded more by the viscous separation medium than are smaller molecules, so that the separation is effectively based on the molecular size.

Applications

This is the method of choice for molecules that differ in size but not in mass/charge ratio. DNA molecules, for example, can vary greatly in length, but the charge per unit length is quite constant. In a pure CZE separation, all the molecules move at very nearly the same velocity and no separation results. In a viscous medium, the longer molecules are retarded more than shorter molecules. Thus shorter pieces of DNA pass the detector sooner than do larger pieces of DNA.

Protein molecules are composed of more complex subunits than DNA molecules. Even though proteins vary widely in their size, the wide range of charge states possible in a protein sequence complicates size separation. In order to separate proteins by size, it is necessary to mask the native charge and create a more nearly uniform charge-mass ratio. This is done by treating the proteins with the detergent SDS. Although there are exceptions, typically proteins bind to a constant number of SDS molecules per unit length. Because the SDS molecules are highly negatively charged the amino acid subunit charge contributes little to the mobility of the molecules and a separation based on chain length is possible. This technique of SDS-CGE is exactly analogous to SDS-polyacrylamide gel electrophoresis (SDS-PAGE).

Capillary Isoelectric Focusing (cIEF)

Mechanism

Molecules that carry both positively and negatively charged groups exhibit, at a specific pH, an equal number of positive and negative charges. At this pH, known as the isoelectric pH or pI, the molecule, although charged, behaves as if it is neutral because its positive and negative charges cancel each other. The molecule, therefore, has no tendency to migrate in an electrical field. In isoelectric focusing, special reagents called *ampholytes* are used to create a pH gradient within the capillary. These ampholytes are mixtures of buffers with a range of pKa values. In an electrical field, ampholytes will arrange themselves in order of pKa; this gradient is trapped between a strong acid and a strong base. Analytes introduced into this gradient will migrate to the point where the pH of the gradient equals their pI. At this point the analyte, having no net charge, ceases to migrate. It will remain at that position so long as the pH gradient is stable, typically as long as the voltage is applied.

Applications

Capillary isoelectric focusing (cIEF) is used almost exclusively for the separation of closely related protein species. Hemoglobin can be separated into several bands by this technique, whereas separation by SDS-CGE usually results in a single form being identified. In this application, the protein sample is mixed with the ampholyte solution and the mixture is pumped into the capillary. When voltage is applied, the proteins and the ampholytes migrate to their appropriate positions in the gradient. When focusing is complete, the proteins in the mixture are distributed throughout the length of the capillary. In order to detect the proteins it is necessary to mobilize them so that they pass by the detector in turn. There are two ways to accomplish this mobilization. Pressure mobilization utilizes positive pressure applied to one end of the capillary to drive the entire fluid column through the window. In order to prevent band distortion, this pressure must be applied carefully, preferably while the voltage is still being applied. Chemical mobilization requires that one end of the capillary be transferred to a salt solution after focusing has taken place. Upon application of voltage, salt will migrate into the capillary, disrupting the pH gradient and allowing the proteins to migrate past the detector by electrophoresis.

cIEF is also widely used for examining the distribution of carbohydrate isoforms of glycoproteins. In other techniques, such as SDS-CGE or CZE, these proteins tend to move as diffuse bands and to generate broad peaks. cIEF can often resolve these bands into peaks that differ by as little as one charged sugar group.

Capillary Isotachophoresis (cITP)

Mechanism

In this technique the sample plug is introduced between two different buffers. One of these, the leading electrolyte, has the highest mobility in the separation. The second, trailing electrolyte, has a mobility lower than anything else does. The sign of the charge on the analytes and the buffers must be the same. When the voltage is applied the ions in the sample form discrete zones that are not separated into peaks; one zone is adjacent to the next. The concentration of the analyte within a zone is constant within that zone and the length of the zone is proportional to the concentration within the zone. Because the voltage drop is uniform within a zone, isotachophoretic methods are quite compatible with conductance detectors.

Applications

Capillary isotachophoresis (cITP) of peptides and proteins has been used with MS detection. Since this mode of separation delivers zones of uniform concentration to the MS, it may be an ideal separation mechanism for this detection technique.

Micellar Electrophoresis

Mechanism

Electrophoresis is not possible for analytes that are not charged. In order to analyze such analytes, it is necessary to employ some agent in the separation buffer that will transport them through the capillary. The most commonly used mode of CE for these analytes is MEKC. In this technique a suitable charged detergent, such as SDS, is added to the separation buffer in a concentration sufficiently high to allow the formation of micelles. These micelles are arrangements of detergent molecules that have a hydrophobic inner core and a hydrophilic outer surface. Micelles are dynamic and constantly form and break apart. For any given analyte, there is a probability that the molecules of that analyte will associate within the micelle at any given time. This probability is the same as the partition coefficient in classical chromatography. When associated with the micelle, the analyte molecule will migrate at the velocity of the micelle. When not in the micelle, the analyte molecule will migrate with the EOF (if any). Differences in the time that analytes spend in the micellar phase will determine the separation.

Applications

MEKC is useful for a wide range of small molecules such as drugs, pesticides, and food additives that are not charged and are sufficiently hydrophobic to associate with the micelle. While SDS is probably the most widely used detergent for this purpose, cationic detergents such as TTAB can also be employed. Nonionic detergents by themselves do not provide mobility to uncharged analytes, but in combination with charged detergents they will modify the separation. Some detergents are useful in specific applications. For example, sodium cholate is useful in the separation and analysis of a variety of steroids. The micelles formed in this case are not the classical spherical shape but are probably sodium cholate molecules arranged on each other like a stack of coins. Different uncharged steroids differ in their tendencies to participate in these stacks.

Chiral Electrophoresis

Mechanism

Chiral molecules are molecules that can exist in two stereo-specific forms. These chiral forms or enantiomers are identical in molecular weight and chemical formula but differ in the arrangement of the atoms in space. Separation of these enatiomeric forms depends on the tendency to associate differentially with other chiral molecules known as chiral selectors. By incorporating a chiral selector into the CE buffer, it is often possible to separate enantiomers of a chiral molecule. This is analogous to MEKC described previously. The complex of the analyte and the selector will migrate at a different rate than will the analyte alone. Because one of the two enantiomers associates more strongly with the selector than does the other form a separation can be achieved.

Applications

The most commonly employed chiral selector in CE is cyclodextrin, ring shaped carbohydrates made up of 6, 7, or 8 D-glucose subunits. Cyclodextrins may be chemically modified to alter their hydrophobicity or charge. Uncharged cyclodextrins are not suitable for the analysis of uncharged analytes since the complex will move with the EOF.

However, cyclodextrins modified to carry a charge by addition of sulfate groups, can serve both as chiral selectors and as carrier molecules (similar to the detergent in MEKC). Other molecules, such as the antibiotic vancomycin, have also been employed as chiral selectors.

Chiral CE can be used to separate the enantiomeric forms of pharmaceuticals as well as natural substances, such as amino acids. Impurities as small as 0.1% are easily detected by this method.

Nonaqueous Electrophoresis

Mechanism

Electrophoresis usually is considered to occur only in aqueous solutions. However, CE can be performed using nonaqueous systems based on such solvents as acetonitrile, methanol, formamide, and dimethylformamide, to which are added small amounts of anhydrous acid or buffer salts. The separation is by simple electrophoresis as EOF is very low under these conditions.

Applications

There are times when two analytes have the same charge to mass ratio and are not easily separated. In some cases this same analyte pair can be separated in a nonaqueous environment where they may have different pKa values than those expressed in water. The degree of solvation, and hence the radius of the solvated species, may also differ in aqueous and nonaqueous environments. Hence, nonaqueous CE offers an alternative for analytes that are difficult to separate under aqueous conditions. In addition, some analytes are difficult to solubilize in aqueous systems but dissolve readily in organic solvents, thus nonaqueous CE offers an alternative to MEKC for these analytes. Separations by nonaqueous CE have been reported for drugs, dyes, preservatives, surfactants, and inorganic ions.

Capillary Electrochromatography

Mechanism

Capillary electrochromatography (CEC) is a hybrid technique between liquid chromatography and electrophoresis. It is a partitioning technique in which molecules distribute between a stationary and a moving phase. As described for MEKC, different analytes will tend to associate to a greater or lesser extent with the stationary phase, effecting a separation.

CEC capillaries are packed with particles like those used in HPLC columns. Unlike conventional LC techniques, CEC uses electroosmotic flow to drive the mobile phase down the column. The resulting plug flow improves the separation efficiency over that of the laminar flow of pressure driven systems.

Applications

As of this writing, most of the work done on CEC has used model systems, such as polyaromatic hydrocarbons. A great deal of effort is underway to identify applications where this technique can be the method of choice. Because the buffers used are typically high in organic content and hence volatile, CEC may be useful when coupled to mass spectroscopy (CEC-MS).

13

FORENSIC SIGNIFICANCE

Forensically significant cases are those in which remains are recovered that have come from humans who died violently or unexpectedly, or for which the cause of death or manner of death is potentially a legal or otherwise significant issue (this may exclude very old or prehistoric remains). This text discusses the subset of forensically significant remains that are partially or completely decomposed, fragmented, or unidentified. This chapter is not meant to reiterate what other experts have described. Rather, we present the authors' philosophy regarding the evaluation of cases in which the lower extremities, or parts thereof, represent the majority of the forensically significant and useful remains recovered. Results expected from the analysis of such remains form a biological profile that is potentially capable of providing positive identification leading to and perhaps facilitating the determination of the cause and manner of death, a task that usually requires the integration of data from multiple sources and which is outside the scope of this book.

Fragmentary or partial remains, such as a single lower extremity, clearly pose a somewhat more daunting task than a more complete set of remains. Human anatomy is easily recognizable when complete, fleshed remains are involved. Skeletonized remains are less familiar and can be confused with nonhuman skeletal elements or even wood or rocks. The lower extremity is composed of the thigh, the knee, the leg, the ankle, and the foot. Basic familiarity with the overall skeletal anatomy of the femur, tibia, fibula, patella, and foot bones can aid investigators in determining exactly which segments are present (and of course, those that are missing) in medicolegal investigations involving lower extremity remains. This chapter is a summary of some of the more forensically important skeletal landmarks and is intended to aid in the identification of the bone to which they belong.

Forensically Significant Skeletal Anatomy

The thigh contains the largest bone in the human body: the femur. The proximal end of the femur consists of a rounded head made of spongy bone that forms the ball of the balland-socket hip joint. This head is distinctive in shape and size; the femur is the only bone in the human body with this skeletal configuration. The distal epiphysis forms part of the knee and is made up of two large condyles. Anteriorly the femur is devoid of significant landmarks. Posteriorly, the linea aspera is the point of muscle attachment for the short head of the biceps femoris, and next to it is a nutrient foramen. In heavily muscled individuals, the linea aspera can be quite large, forming a large bony ridge that runs the length of the femur. Juvenile and adult femoral morphology is largely similar, with the exception that unfused juvenile femora consist of multiple segments and adult femora (barring trauma or abnormal development) consist of a single segment.

The patella (knee cap) is the largest sesamoid (bone nodule) in the human body. It lies anteriorly to the lower extremity of the distal end of the femur and slightly superior to the proximal tibia. The patella has two articular surfaces posterior—a larger lateral and slightly smaller medial surface. Multiple nutrient foramina on the anterior surface may be mistaken by the inexperienced as rocks with pits caused by erosion. If the entire patella is covered with mud, it may be mistaken at the forensic scene for a clump of mud or a rock. Variation in the patella is common; triangular, elliptical, circular, and oblique shapes have been documented.

The lower leg contains two bones, the tibia and the fibula. The tibia is the larger and is commonly known as the "*shin bone*". The tibial shaft is somewhat triangular compared with the relatively more rounded femoral shaft. The proximal posterior shaft is marked by the popliteal line, which forms a boundary for insertion of the popliteus muscle. A nutrient foramen also appears at the same location lateral to the popliteal line and nearly always slopes distally, exiting the bone proximally. The proximal epiphyseal end is formed by two large, flat condyles and the tibial tuberosity on the proximal anterior side. The distal epiphyseal end is characterized by the medial malleolus, a projection of bone that is felt on the medial aspect of the ankle.

The fibula is the smaller of the two leg bones and its distal end forms the outside part of the ankle. In contrast to the relatively wider tibia, the fibula is irregular and narrow in shape. The proximal epiphysis consists of a slightly rounded formation with a styloid process (posterior projection of bone), and its the distal end consists of a lateral malleolus, which forms the outside part of the ankle. The fibular shaft is largely unremarkable, offering no distinguishing features because it bears no weight. Unlike the femur, it is not expected to be significantly larger in well-muscled individuals.

The human foot is made up of 14 phalanges, 5 metatarsals, and 7 tarsals (calcaneus, talus, cuboid, navicular, and the first, second, and third cuneiforms). Additionally, two sesamoids sit inferiorly on the distal first metatarsal. The calcaneus forms the heel and the talus articulates with the distal tibia, forming the medial aspect of the ankle. The human foot is unique amongst mammalian extremities, because it is constructed for upright walking. The four toes are in line with the first (big) toe (the hallux), unlike the toes of other apes (humans are considered apes), in which the hallux is offset from the remaining toes. To a large extent, the human foot has lost its grasping ability, which is characteristic of the other apes. In humans, the tarsals usually form an arch—an ideal structure for weight-bearing in a bipedal animal. The relatively large number of skeletal elements and articular surfaces results in a number of unique skeletal features, including trabecular patterns and osteophytes, which may be useful within forensic contexts, e.g., for comparing radiographs. Similar to the patella, the tarsals also exhibit foramina for blood vessels that may be confused with surface erosion by the untrained eye. Additionally, the foot may often be well preserved when it remains in footwear, frequently surviving intact for forensic analysis.

EMBRYOLOGY

The development of the human is complex, yet orderly. There are critical periods of human development during which certain major elements are formed. For the lower extremity, the critical period begins during the third week after fertilization with the formation of the cardiovascular system, including vessels for limbs. During the third and fourth weeks, limb buds appear. By the end of the eighth week, all the major organ systems have begun to develop. It is between the third and eighth weeks of gestation that *in utero* exposure to toxins (teratogens) may cause abnormal development of the limbs persisting into extrauterine (postnatal) life. Examples of such toxins are numerous and include thalidomide and cocaine. However harmful teratogens are, their effects may become useful when evaluating forensically significant case material. For example, fetal malformations caused by maternal substance abuse may provide anatomic features unique to that individual that can be used to assist identification efforts. Alcohol consumption by the mother can cause fetal alcohol syndrome, and cocaine use may cause vascular malformations. Both of these teratogens may result in potentially unique anatomic features that can be used for premortem and postmortem comparisons.

Normal bone growth involves the development of blood vessels that penetrate the cortices via nutrient canals. Both the location and angle of entry of vascular elements into the bony cortex are highly variable from person to person and even from one side of the bone to the other in the same individual. This variation may be of significant forensic utility. For example, the nutrient artery for the femur arises from the deep femoral artery and enters the femur posteriorly along the linea aspera, but the location of entry of the vessel is somewhat variable. If two femora are recovered whose general physical characteristics indicate that they are from the same individual, the disparate positions of the nutrient canals should not dissuade the examiner from the concluding that they are from the same person.

Because muscles attach to bone, the absence of one or more muscles can cause limb deformities. Any muscle of the body may fail to develop. If the opposing muscle is present, the limb contracts at the joint. Such deformities can be corrected with braces or surgical repair. Although functionally insignificant, slight variations in muscle development or attachment can be used forensically. Additionally, population differences in skeletal development can cause a slight variation in limb appearance, especially with regard to limb length. The ratio between the lengths of the tibia and femur varies and may provide clues to ethnicity.

Procedural Approaches

When confronted with decomposed or partial human remains, attention to anatomical detail, careful consideration of the available human remains, and scrutiny of the surrounding scene or environment are important for identification and trauma analysis purposes. Because of the complexity of procedures involved in examining human remains within various contexts, the authors advocate a multidisciplinary team approach to the recovery and analysis of suspected human remains. Thus, when remains are discovered, securing the scene and maintaining it in an undisturbed fashion until all appropriate personnel (e.g., medical examiner/coroner's agent, law enforcement, forensic anthropologist,

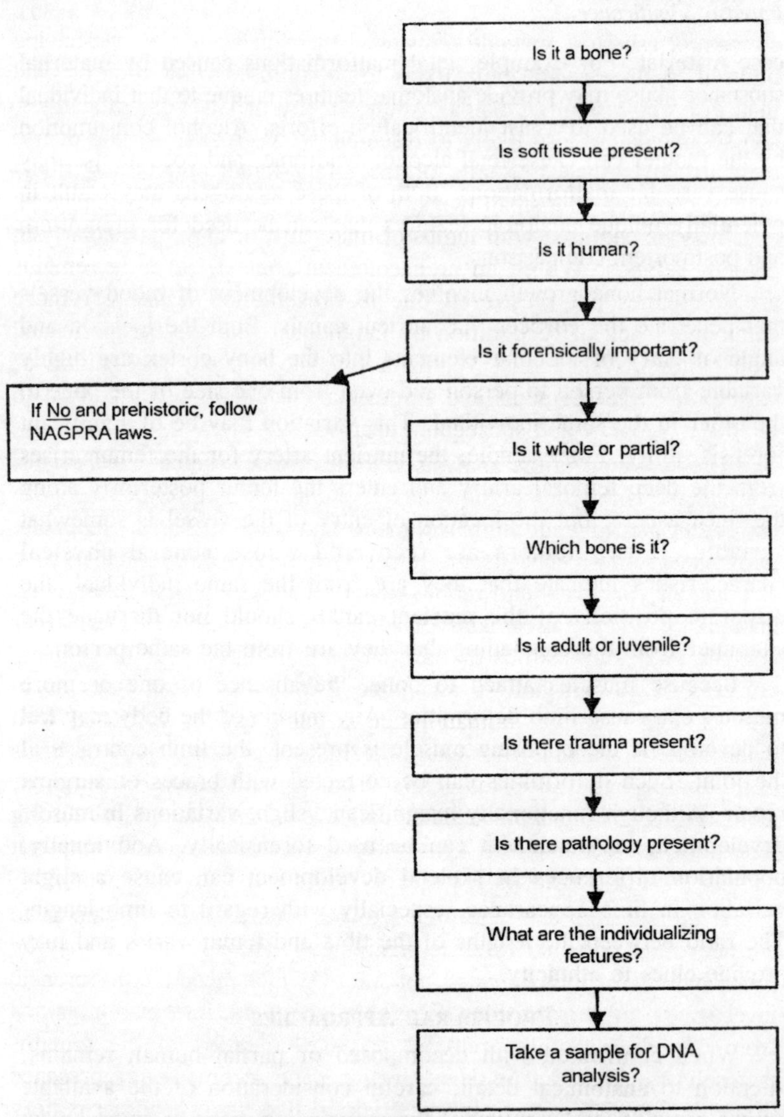

Fig. 13.1. Chart used to illustrate an algorithm in the analysis of fragmentary remains.

odontologist, and radiologist) are present is important. Although it may seem obvious, the authors cannot emphasize enough that human remains can look remarkably like sticks, rocks, or chunks of mud or dirt.

Fragmentary, burned, mummified, or partial lower extremities can resemble wood, rock, or other features of the surrounding scene, such as foam or asbestos. Juvenile remains—being smaller in size and having unfused epiphyses—are more likely to be confused with wood or mud than are whole adult remains. Adult tarsals, metatarsals, phalanges, and sesamoids are also likely to resemble wood, rocks, or mud due to their irregular shapes. Shafts of the infant femur, tibia, and fibula may be confused with small twigs or animal bones, while the epiphyseal ends may be confused with lumps of mud, dirt, or clay, particularly in outdoor settings. Within an archaeological context, juvenile remains are sometimes not recovered due to preservation issues or, more commonly, lack of recognition by individuals who are inexperienced with children's skeletons. Within a forensic context, recognition of various juvenile segments and fragmentary adult segments is vital to facilitate recovery and subsequent analyses.

The next step in the analysis is to determine whether the remains are human. Numerous authors have documented similarities between both adult and juvenile human remains and those of various animals, particularly with respect to the lower extremity. Adult animals—such as dogs, sheep, goats, and rabbits—have smaller extremities than adult humans. The skeletal remains of adult cattle, horses, or other larger animals will exhibit limbs that are larger than those of adult humans. Differences in morphology and bone texture can yield clues as to species. For example, human infant remains can be confused with avian skeletal remains; however; the lighter, hollow bones of birds help distinguish these materials from human skeletal remains. Comparative mammalian skeletal collections are also useful during this stage of the analysis. Extremely fragmented remains may not contain enough diagnostic features to assign a species designation.

If the remains are determined to be human, the next step is to consider their potential forensic significance. Human remains may be found within many contexts, not all of which necessitate forensic investigation or personal identification. Commonly, information gained from the context of the remains and the condition of the remains themselves will aid in the determination. The accompanying presence of archaeologically significant materials such as arrowheads or pottery may indicate ancient remains. Tombstones, coffin hardware, buttons, and clothing may provide data with respect to the time frame. Extreme drying of remains, with little adherent soft tissue, often indicates remains of no forensic significance. In the United States, Native American Graves Protection and Repatriation Act (NAGPRA) laws dictate that law enforcement agencies, coroners, and medical examiners must identify the nearest Native American group and notify them of any finds before proceeding with removal. Experienced forensic or physical anthropologists will need to examine the remains in situ. In some situations, the determination of forensic significance can be made before any further investigative effort is undertaken.

The discovery of forensically significant remains should culminate in a recovery using standard archaeological procedures to maximize the preservation of information and maintain the chain of custody at the scene. A thorough search of the scene as well as detailed photography, mapping, packaging, and transporting of human remains are necessary to optimize the forensic recovery and subsequent evaluation. Scene context (indoor or outdoor, size of the scene, landscape, weather), available personnel, budget, resources, and legal issues all contribute to the nature of a recovery operation. Forensic anthropologists can often be located by contacting the nearest university with an anthropology department. These individuals, who have advanced degrees and training in archaeology and human osteology, are typically best equipped to handle the recovery and analysis of fragmentary human remains. Following the team approach, the forensic anthropologist should be consulted early in the investigation and ideally would participate in recovery efforts.

Suspected and known human remains should be transported to a laboratory. All remains should be photographed immediately—*in toto* and each element separately—upon their arrival at the laboratory. Traditionally, 35-mm film cameras can provide a high level of resolution. However, high-quality digital cameras can also achieve high resolution. Inclusion of an American Board of Forensic Odontology standard grey scale in photographs is essential for accurate measurements and dimensions. Radiography is a routine procedure in forensic examinations and is useful for separating human from nonhuman and nonskeletal materials. Radiographs should be performed prior to the removal of any clothing, soft tissue (if defleshing is desired), debris, or other adherent material. Highly decomposed remains frequently result in variable soft tissue density, which may obscure skeletal detail in the radiograph. Therefore, we recommend that the examiner who requires fine skeletal detail on radiograph remove the soft tissue and radiograph the remains again with various image orientations.

Radiographically, bone may demonstrate a discernable medullar cavity and trabecular latticework. Radiographs will also highlight potential features for individual identification. It should be noted that prior to defleshing, tissue samples should be preserved in case of a need for pathological, DNA, or toxicological analysis. Thorough documentation of the soft tissue should be accomplished prior to tissue removal, and photographs should be taken and any individual characteristics noted. Subsequent to radiography, an inventory of the remains should be made. This serves two purposes: first, a permanent inventory of the collected and any missing remains can be maintained and distributed to other agencies and is vital for comparison with any subsequent discoveries; second, information regarding the remains present also dictates the next steps of the analysis, i.e., determination of race, age, sex, and stature (which constitutes the biological profile). Investigators should make notes of any signs of pathology or disease processes, such as osteomyelitis or antemortem fractures, which can be compared with antemortem medical records for presumptive identification.

Documentation of any and all individualizing characteristics present on the soft tissue or skeletal elements can also aid in making a positive identification. Soft tissue characteristics may include tattoos, scars, birthmarks, or concentrations of melanin; characteristics intrinsic to the bone itself include the trabecular pattern. Fractures in various stages of healing can be compared with medical records, leading to a positive identification. Surgical alterations or implants such as rods, pins, or hip replacements can also be useful. Some implants are imprinted with serial numbers, which are recorded at the time of surgery and can be linked to an individual using available antemortem medical records. Comparison with records of missing individuals is the final stage in the process. However, there is the possibility of finding no match between the remains and an individual, given the fragmentary nature of the skeletal materials. For example, a small segment of a human fibula may be forensically significant but otherwise unidentifiable. Some jurisdictions may choose not to treat the remains as forensically significant, because the removal of all or part of a skeletal element in the lower extremity is theoretically compatible with life (e.g., surgery). Fragmentary remains can be scattered across great geographical distances because of a traumatic event or animal scavenging; therefore, communicating with other agencies regarding the inventory of the remains is vital.

14

Radiology in Forensic Studies

While the field of forensic medicine is said to have begun at some indefinite time five or six centuries ago, the origins of forensic radiology can be described more precisely. Wilhem Conrad Rontgen—professor of physics, director of the Physics Institute, and Rector of the University of Wurzburg—observed an unusual phenomenon while experimenting with cathode ray tubes on November 8, 1895. After 50 d of intensive investigation, he determined that he had discovered a new kind of ray ("eine neue Arte von Strahlen"), one that could penetrate solid, opaque materials and produce photographic representations of their contents. He called them "X-rays" because "x" was the symbol of the unknown. A manuscript was produced and immediately accepted for presentation at the January 23, 1896, meeting of the Wurzburg Physical Medicine Society. As sometimes happens today, word of his findings were "*leaked*" to the popular press and flashed by telegraph and cable throughout the electrified world, reaching New York on January 8, 1896. The potential for applying this new ray to the task of forensic problem solving was recognized almost immediately.

Professor Arthur William Wright, director of the Sloan Physics Laboratory at Yale University, is accorded primacy in the production of X-ray images (of inanimate objects) in the United States on January 28, 1896. A few days later, he bought a rabbit at a market and exposed the carcass to an X-ray beam for an hour. Examination of the photographic plate revealed lead shot within the body. Professor Wright had, for the first time, established a cause of death through radiography—put another way, by forensic radiology! In consonance with the purpose of this book, we will attempt a chronology of early forensic applications of radiology limited to the lower extremity.

Chronology of Early Forensic Radiology of the Lower Extremity

On a cold Christmas Eve in Montreal, George Holden shot Tolson Cunning in the leg. The wound healed, but the injured limb remained symptomatic. His surgeon, Dr. R. C. Kirkpatrick, requested an X-ray photograph of the area to be taken by Professor John Cox of the Physics Department at McGill University. This was accomplished on February 7, 1896 and showed the bullet lodged between the tibia and fibula. This image was submitted to the court during Mr. Holden's trial for attempted murder. Successful prosecution resulted in a sentence of 14 yr in the penitentiary.

In England, during September 1895, a burlesque and comedic actress known to us now only as Miss Folliott fell on the steps leading to her dressing room in the Nottingham Theater. Her foot injury kept her bedfast for a month, after which she was still unable to tread the boards. Dr. Frankish sent her to University College Hospital, where both feet were "*photographed*" by X-rays (perhaps the first comparison of films?) and the films demonstrated that the left cuboid clearly was displaced. This finding could be appreciated by both judge and jury when the negatives were displayed in court. The conviction of the theater owners for maintaining an unsafe workplace was somewhat mitigated by the charge that Miss Folliott was guilty of contributory carelessness. Because this case was commented on in British publications as early as April 1896, the actual radiography must be almost contemporaneous with the Holden case.

On September 2, 1895, Frank B. Bolling was thrown from his buggy "while driving a fractious horse" on the streets of Chicago and sustained a fracture of his right ankle. The fracture was set by two surgeons, and Mr. Bolling was able to return to work by May 1, 1896, but his ankle still hurt. To evaluate this persistent pain, Dr. Otto L. Smith and Professor W. C. Fuchs examined the offending ankle with 35 to 40 min of exposure to an X-ray tube placed just 5 in. from the ankle. Subsequent radiation damage and pain led to an amputation in November 1896 and two more amputations later because of pain and recurrent infections. Bolling filed the first malpractice suit for radiation damage and was awarded $10,000.

The first trial in which X-ray evidence was accepted by a United States Court took place in Denver in the waning months of 1896. The case began on June 15, 1895, when James Smith fell from a ladder while pruning a tree and injured his hip. Perhaps for pecuniary reasons, he waited almost a month before soliciting the professional services of Dr. W. W. Grant, who was widely known and well respected and a founder of the American College of Surgeons. He is credited with performing the first appendectomy in the United States, in 22-yr-old Mary Gartside.

Dr. Grant found no evidence of a fracture and did not restrict Mr. Smith's activity, but requested that he return in 1 wk. The diagnosis of "no fracture" was again asserted. Dr. Grant heard no more about Mr. Smith until April 1896, when the poorly paid law clerk engaged two of the best young lawyers in Colorado to file a $10,000 civil action against Dr. Grant, claiming limb shortening and disability as a result of his failure to diagnose a femoral fracture. Quick to take advantage of new technology, these bright young attorneys had engaged the services of Dr. Chauncey Tennent Jr, MD, of Denver Homeopathic College and a local photojournalist, Harry H. Buchwalter, to examine their client with X-rays. On four occasions between November 7 and 29, 1896, several attempts to obtain an image of Mr. Smith's hip (with exposures ranging up to 80 min) were finally successful in showing the outlines of an impacted fracture of the proximal femur. (It is not clear whether this was a femoral neck fracture or an intertrochanteric fracture.)

The fundamental legal issue was admission of a radiograph as evidence. Photographs were already recognized for their ability to show something a witness could testify to as an accurate representation of what had actually been seen. The X-ray image revealed structures or objects hidden from the eye and had been refused admission in some jurisdictions, which felt that it was "like offering the photograph of a ghost." The argument raged all day before District Judge Owen E LeFuvre who, after sleeping on the matter, handed down his decision, eloquently phrased in the elegant language of those days:

We… have been presented with a photograph taken by means of a new scientific discovery… it knocks for admission at the temple of learning. What shall be do or say? Close fast the door or open wide the portals? These photographs are offered in evidence to show the present condition of the head and neck of the femur bone, which is entirely hidden from the eye of the surgeon… Modern science has made it possible to look beneath the tissues of the human body, and has aided the surgeon in telling of the hidden mysteries. We believe it is our duty to be the first... in admitting in evidence a process known and acknowledged as a determinate science. The exhibits will be admitted in evidence.

The first appellate decision regarding the admission of radiographs as evidence in a US courtroom was rendered in 1897. It involved the case of Mr. Beall, who was in an elevator in the warehouse of WS Bruce and Company when it fell five stories. He sustained injuries to his leg and sued for compensation, claiming negligence in the construction and maintenance of the elevator. A witness, Dr. Saltman, testified that "overlapping bones of one of the plaintiff's legs, at the point where it was broken by this fall" were shown on a radiograph he was permitted to submit to the jury. The defense objected to admission of the radiograph and appealed. The Supreme Court of Tennessee ruled "...no sound reason was assigned at the bar why a civil court should not avail itself of this invention, when it is apparent that it would serve to throw light on the matter in controversy."

Dr. H. Graeme Anderson was one of the pioneer physicians assigned to the British Royal Flying Corps during World War I. He also became a licensed pilot, hence, one of the earliest flight surgeons. In his 1919 book, The Medical and Surgical Aspects of Aviation, Dr. Anderson devoted several pages to 17 cases of injuries to the talus that had been sustained during aircraft accidents. He termed this generic injury "*Aviator's Astralagus*" and illustrated it with radiographs. This probably is the first recognition of "*pattern injuries*," of which more will be said later. (It surely is worth mentioning that Dr. Anderson also reported that "Nemirovsky and Tilmant have lately organized an aeroplane...to carry a pilot, a surgeon, and a radiographer who can act as an assistant surgeon.... The elective current from the aeroplane can be used...to work the X-ray apparatus." Surely this is a first—and maybe the last— example of in-flight radiography. The author will welcome information about other examples).

Feet played an important role in solving the infamous Ruxton murder. On September 15, 1935, the wife of a Dr. Ruxton and her nursemaid disappeared from the family home in Lancaster and were never again seen alive. Two weeks later, a discovery of human remains triggered a search that began in the surrounding area and continued for another month until most of two female bodies could be reassembled. However, the faces had been mutilated, the teeth extracted, the terminal digits of the hands amputated, and other distinguishing topographical features had been excised from soft tissues, all to preclude identification.

Three feet were recovered. Casts were made and fitted into the shoes of the missing women. The presumptive left foot of Mrs. Ruxton was mutilated where she was known to have had a bunion and elsewhere (perhaps as a distraction), but a radiograph showed an exostosis of the first metatarsal head consistent with the bunion deformity. Other identifying anatomic features were found, and this case featured an early use of the photographic superimposition of facial features on a skull. Incriminating evidence also was found in the Ruxton home. The doctor was convicted and hanged for the murders.

In 1946, Dr. John Caffey MD—self-taught radiologist at New York's Babies Hospital (and the father of Pediatric Radiology)—published the first of several papers alerting the profession (and the public) to the peculiar concatenation of unusual skeletal injuries in the extremities of children that had often been associated with skull injuries, subdural hematomas, or both in the absence of any history of trauma. This led to the now widespread recognition of the intentional physical abuse of children—perhaps radiology's greatest contribution to forensic medicine.

In 1949, the Great Lakes liner Noronic caught fire and burned in Toronto, with many fatalities. Dr. Arthur C Singleton, a professor and head of the Radiology Department at the University of Toronto, was asked by the Attorney General of Ontario to assist in the identification of the bodies, thus becoming the father of mass casualty radiology. He was able to positively identify 24 of 119 fatalities by radiologic comparison alone. One of the illustrations in his paper on the matter showed comparison radiographs of a dismembered foot, noting similar features.

In 1981, Evans and Knight's book, *Forensic Radiology*, became available to the English-speaking world. It described applications of radiology for the purpose of identification and to identify evidence of abuse, mishaps, and malpractice, as well as for age determination and other anthropological conditions and correlation with forensic pathology, gunshot wounds, and other inflicted trauma. Unfortunately, of the more than 100 radiographs reproduced in this small but fairly comprehensive volume, only six were of the lower extremity.

In the ensuing quarter century, the utilization of radiology in the forensic sciences has increased and now includes some applications of newer modalities—nuclear radiology, ultrasonography, magnetic resonance imaging, and *computed tomography* (CT). Still, the great potential for radiology in forensics that was predicted by enthusiasts in the first couple of years after Rontgen's discovery remains largely unrealized.

Anthropological Considerations

It was recognized early after Röntgen's discovery that the X-ray could greatly assist in the identification of human remains, especially those in which superficial identifying features were distorted or destroyed by fire, immersion, decomposition, mutilation, or fragmentation. The first step in the procedure is the establishment of certain anthropological parameters, sometimes called the "*biologic profile*": age, sex, stature, and race or population ancestry. When the body or its parts are skeletonized, or when there are time and available facilities to remove flesh from the remains, the physical anthropologist can do the job with equal or sometimes superior accuracy. Otherwise, the radiologic method must suffice. In either event, it is useful to radiograph the remains for purposes of subsequent comparison with antemortem examinations.

First, one must determine whether the remains are human or animal. Skeletal similarities can be confusing to the inexperienced viewer.

Next, it must be determined whether the remains are those of a single human or commingled with other humans or animals—a sometimes difficult and time-consuming task. Only then can a biologic profile be established. For the purposes of this discussion, it is assumed that human body parts from the lower extremities are being analyzed.

Age Determination

The radiologic determination of maturity or prematurity at birth is based on the ossification of secondary centers at the knee. The distal femoral epiphysis will be partially ossified in 90% or more of full-term fetuses. The proximal tibial epiphysis will be similarly visible in 80% or more of mature neonates. Thereafter, chronological age is estimated according to skeletal maturation, as indicated by the appearance, growth, and ultimate fusion of epiphyses and apophyses (non-articulating secondary ossification centers).

Between mid-adolescence and middle age, the fusion line of the physis gradually disappears, tendinous attachments may become more prominent, and degenerative change insidiously commences. Estimation of skeletal age by radiologic evaluation of the lower extremities during these decades is fraught with difficulty and inaccuracy. The effects of advancing age become more apparent with advancing degenerative

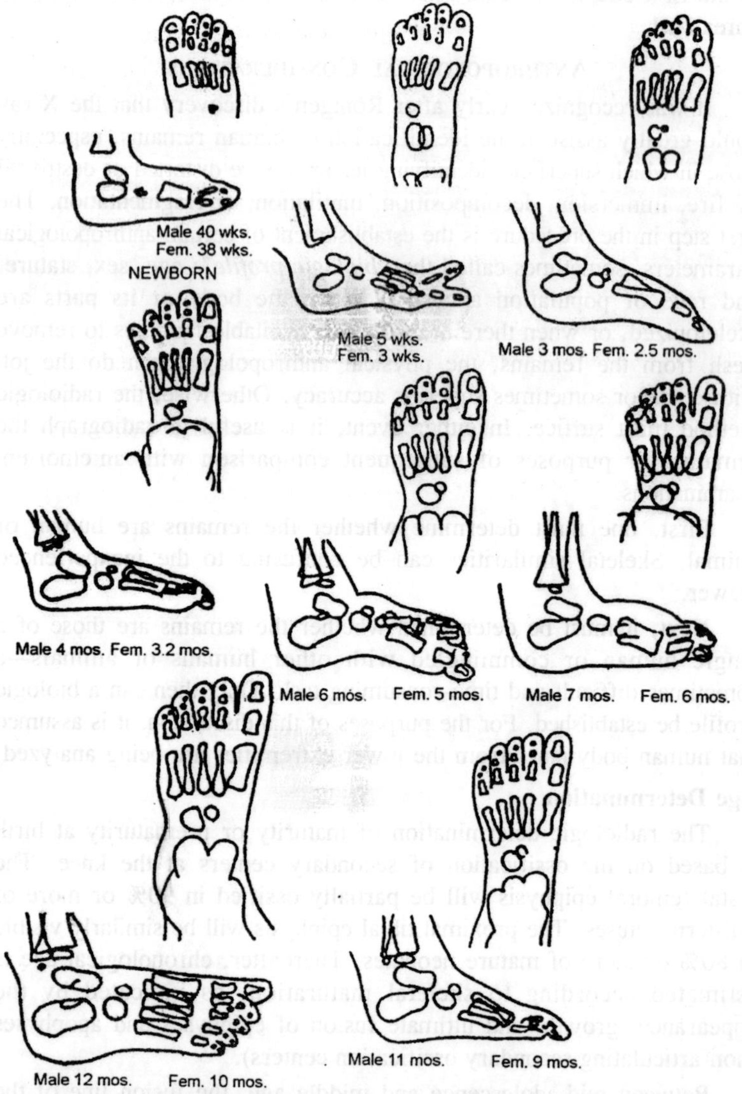

Fig. 14.1. Chronological development of the foot and ankle.

change and skeletal demineralization, but even then the use of radiology to estimate age may result of an error of a decade or so.

Sex Determination

Skeletal maturation accelerates in females at a greater rate than in males after the third or fourth year of life. However, this difference is not a useful determinant. In general, the male skeleton becomes more robust and heavier with aging and develops more prominent attachments for muscles and tendons. With further aging, there is a tendency for more degenerative hyperostotic changes in the male. Male long bones are approx 110% longer than their female counterparts. The male femoral head is larger. All of these findings are helpful but not definitive in establishing the sex of unidentified remains.

Other parts of the skeleton are far more helpful than those of the extremities. Bipartite patella, an anatomical variant occurring in approx 2% of the adolescent population, is nine times more common in boys than in girls.

In individuals of African ancestry, the tibia is long relative to the femur, but the ratios vary and overlap in US populations, probably due to racial mixing. The femoral shaft is bowed anteriorly in white and Asian populations compared with black populations; however, there is still considerable variability. However, a markedly bowed femur is unlikely to belong to a black decedent.

Craig developed a method of determining race based on the angle of the intercondylar shelf on the femur that can be used with either skeletal or fleshed remains. It requires radiography with true lateral positioning of the distal femur. The angle between the roof of the

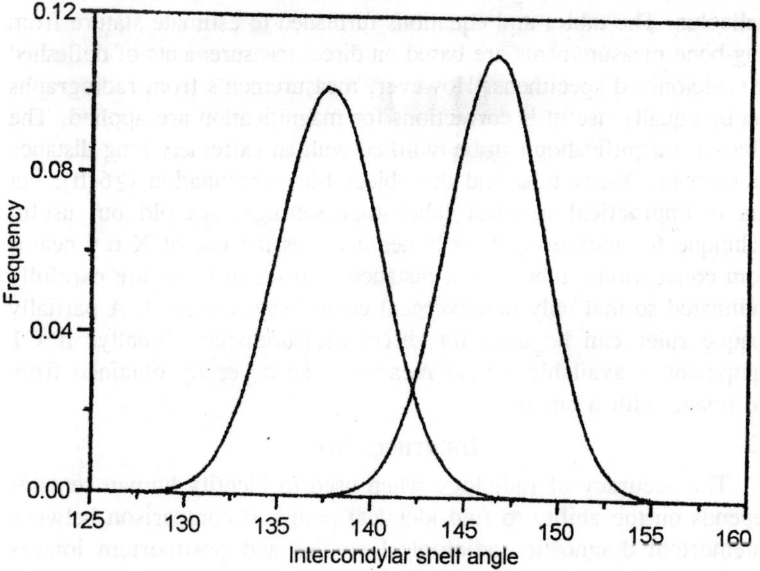

Fig. 14.2. Graphic representation of racial distribution of intercondylar shelf angles.

intercondylar notch (or intercondylar shelf) and the long axis of the femoral shaft are measured. Thus, this may serve as a fairly useful determinant for assigning race or population ancestry.

Steinbach and Russell suggested that a measurement of the soft tissue in the heel pad that exceeds 21 mm is a reasonably accurate indication of acromegaly. However, the fallibility of this diagnostic indicator has been described by Puckett and Seymour, who demonstrated a greater-than-"average" heel pad measurement in Blacks, 40% of whom had heel pads exceeding 21 mm compared with only 9% of Caucasians. Local soft-tissue swelling can skew this measurement even further. Hence, heel pad thickness is of doubtful value in the process of determining race or population ancestry in unidentified body parts.

Determination of Stature

Extensive research on World War II and Korean War casualties has enabled investigators to develop methods of estimating stature based on measurements of long bones. The length of the femur is the most reliable basis for calculating stature. The tibia is also useful, but there has been some controversy over the accuracy of tibial measurements, particularly the most appropriate location of the more distal measuring point. Apparently, the plafond of the tibia is the preferred site of measurement rather than the tip of the medial malleolus. The tables and equations furnished to estimate stature from long-bone measurements are based on direct measurements of defleshed or skeletonized specimens. However, measurements from radiographs can be equally useful if corrections for magnification are applied. The effect of magnification can be nullified with an extremely long distance between the X-ray tube and the object–film combination (≥6 ft), but this is impractical in most laboratory settings. An old but useful technique for measuring long bones involves the use of X-ray beams from conventional tube–object distances (36–40 in.) that are carefully collimated so that only nondivergent central rays are used. A partially opaque ruler can be used for direct measurements. Finally, if CT equipment is available, direct measures can be easily obtained from the image with a cursor.

Identification

The accuracy of radiology when used to identify human remains depends on the ability to find identical points of comparison between antemortem diagnostic radiological studies and postmortem images obtained with similar techniques. Hence, postmortem studies must be obtained with the parts positioned to simulate the routine radiologic positions and projections used in medical diagnostic studies. Equipment and technical factors employed in the production of such postmortem radiologic images will be discussed later in this chapter. Unless identity is readily established, it is wise to obtain radiographic studies of all available body parts prior to their release, because it is not easy to predict which body regions will be represented on the antemortem radiographs subsequently acquired.

Statistical Considerations Related to Body Parts

The abdominal trunk—particularly the soft tissue and bony structures of the back, including the spine and pelvis—are most likely to survive the rigors of separation, incineration, decomposition, and the activities of carnivores. The extremities are susceptible to damage by all of these factors. Further, the odds of finding antemortem studies of the extremities are less than those of some other body parts. In a survey of films in a large university hospital radiology department, investigators found that the lower extremity accounted for only 11% of all roentgenograms and an even smaller percentage of studies using other radiologic modalities. In the Bass and Driscoll study of incomplete skeleton retrieval in Tennessee, the femur was the second most common skeletal element found in 58 fragmented skeletons; the tibia ranked fifth, the fibula eighth, and the patella 13th. In a series of 30 cases in which the identification of the victim was established by comparing antemortem and postmortem radiologic findings, Murphy and coworkers found that the extremities contributed to 20% of cases.

Identification of Individual Skeletal Elements

Individual bones can be matched on antemortem and postmortem radiographs by comparing overall configurations or comparable abnormalities associated with (1) anomalous, congenital, or developmental lesions; (2) disease or tissue degeneration; (3) tumors or tumor-like conditions; (4) trauma; (5) iatrogenic lesions; and (6) trabecular patterns and vascular grooves.

Again, the position of the postmortem specimen must duplicate that of the antemortem radiograph. This may require trial and error or the "*shadow positioning technique*" of Fitzpatrick and Mascaluso.

Anomalous, Developmental, and Congenital Variations

Riddick et al. were able to identify the charred remains of a kidnapped murder victim on the basis of a developmental anomaly in a patella—a "*dorsal defect*" found in only 1% of the population. Clubfoot deformities were discovered in one examination of decomposed human remains. Finding custom-made orthopedic shoes in the room, investigators were able to locate the vendor who, in turn, helped them antemortem radiographs of the feet. These were successfully compared with postmortem studies.

Disease or Degenerative Change

Degenerative changes are frequently helpful or even definitive in the identification of unknown remains. We have already seen examples in the Ruxton case and in the case of heel spurs of the calcaneus. Judging from the literature, it is rare to be able to match skeletal remains by lesions that arise secondary to disease processes. However, certain diseases have such distinctive features that they could be used for identification purposes.

Tumors and tumor-like lesions

Malignant tumors may change so rapidly that they are of little use for comparison studies, especially when the films were obtained over a long interval of time. Other such lesions, however, are relatively stable and may be useful on occasion.

Trauma

Dr. Fovau d'Courmelles accurately predicted in the October 1898 American X- Ray Journal that "knowing the existence of a fracture in a person, who has been burned or mutilated beyond recognition, we can hope to identify him by the X-ray".

Residual deformities from fractures, retained bullets, embedded knife blades, or posttraumatic calcifications can all provide identification if appropriate comparative radiographs become available.

Iatrogenic alterations

Residual findings from previous treatments or manipulations can be helpful in using radiology for identification purposes. Orthopedic hardware, prostheses, drill holes and drill bits, osteotomies, fusions, and manipulations may all leave recognizable traces that can be seen on the radiograph.

Trabecular Patterns and Vascular Grooves

The trabecular pattern of some bones can be quite distinctive and can be matched on antemortem and postmortem films. Weight-bearing or stress-bearing large trabeculae in the femur, tibia, and os calcis are particularly useful. Kahana and Hiss have described a computerized system of matching trabecular patterns by superimposing densitographs and reported a case identified by that system using only the bones of a thumb. However, we find that in most cases, one can satisfactorily match the pattern by sight alone while manipulating the specimen.

Identification in Mass Casualty Situations

The same techniques and variables that are taken into consideration when identifying individual skeletal elements apply to mass casualty situations, except for the logistical problems that are complicated by the size of the matrix (i.e., the number of remains involved and the fact that they are sometimes commingled and often fragmented). Most mass casualty operations take on the characteristics of a field exercise, because a fear of contaminated blood and body fluids has closed the doors of most hospitals to mass casualty remains. The organization of a mass casualty operation is beyond the scope of this chapter, but there is extensive literature on the subject. Apart from obtaining radiographs of mass casualty victims for identification purposes, it is also useful to look for foreign bodies that may provide valuable information, such as serial or part numbers, sources of bombs or weapons, trace evidence of explosives or chemicals, or even an unexploded bomb.

Pattern Injuries

Some traumatic episodes result in radiologically demonstrable lesions that are relatively consistent. These are called pattern injuries, and they can frequently be used to predict or deduce the mechanism of injury, the offending agent, or both.

Abuse

Child abuse

In Caffey's first paper on the subject, he remarked on a pattern of skeletal lesions found in children who also had a subdural hematoma. The pattern was one of metaphyseal fragmentation, another finding he called "*involucrum,*" and fractures in different stages of healing. Later, Caffey added other components to the pattern: "*bowing fractures*", *metaphyseal cupping*, and "*ectopic ossification centers,*" which nowadays translates to epiphyseal separation. Caffey and others added still more observations to the total pattern, including transverse and spiral fractures of long bones that are inappropriate to the age and activity of the child.

The interpretation of pediatric radiographs requires considerable training and experience. Radiographically, it is quite true that "children are not just little adults." Other conditions, both normal and abnormal, may be confused with child abuse. One of the best examples of this is the so-called "*toddler's fracture*"—an undisplaced spiral fracture of the tibia that is the common result of the somewhat uncoordinated, often pigeon-toed effort at locomotion by children in this age group—which is not an indication of abuse. By contrast, a spiral fracture of the tibia in a nonambulatory child is almost invariably an indication of child abuse. A single thin line of periosteal calcification may exist in normal healthy infants up to age 4 mo. However, it is bilateral, symmetrical, unilamellar, and asymptomatic and is not indicative of child abuse. A number of other conditions may be confusing, including that darling of defense attorneys: osteogenesis imperfecta.

It must be remembered that the most important feature of radiologic findings in child abuse is that the injury is inconsistent with the age, development, and activity of the child.

Physical abuse of adults

Spousal abuse or abuse of intimate partners does not usually involve the lower extremity. Abusive blows to women are almost exclusively directed to the head, neck, and face. Domestic violence and automobile accidents are the most common causes of facial injury in women. Patterns emerge here: automobile accident victims tend to show massive and multiple injuries to the facial bones and mandible, whereas battered women show mostly fractures of the mandibular body or angle and the contralateral mandibular ramus. Of course, nasal, orbital, zygomatico-facial, and dental fractures are seen along with dislocations of the mandible. Defensive injuries of the upper extremity (*fending fractures*) are seen, but the lower extremities are rarely involved. Blows to the body are uncommon except in pregnant women, where the breast and abdomen may be pummeled.

Abuse of the aged

Here, the patterns of injury are somewhat like those seen in child abuse, i.e., twisting, pulling, and squeezing injuries of the extremities as a result of punishment or attempts at restraint. However, blows to the head may simulate those seen in spousal abuse. Senile osteoporosis complicates the diagnostic issue in the elderly—particularly in the extremities, where routine handling, lifting, turning, and restraint may produce fractures.

Pedal Injury Patterns

This topic is something of a double entendre, because it refers to injuries to the pedal extremity—which are caused mostly by pedals, either brake or rudder!

Dr. Andrew's collection of "*aviator's astragalus*" cases was amassed from air crashes, and he believed that the mechanism was one of dorsiflexion against the rudder pedal during impact. More contemporary studies have suggested a spectrum of injuries caused by this mechanism. In Group 1 injuries of this type, there is a relatively undisplaced fracture of the neck of the astragalus or talus. In Group 2, there is fracture of the talar neck with displacement of the body of the talus into equinous deformity. In Group 3, there is a posterior dislocation of the talus, which may involve the entire bone or only a major portion of the body of the talus, with the anterior fragment remaining roughly in place between the tibial plafond and the navicular. True posterior extrusion of the talus is quite rare, because it requires rupture of the Achilles tendon. Talar dislocations and extrusions also occur in plantar flexion in association with either pronation or supination, in which case the soft tissue injury and extrusion will be either anteromedial or anterolateral, respectively.

According to Simson, flight surgeons during World War II recognized a lesion they called "*Aviator's fracture*"—a pattern of dorsally displaced mid-foot metatarsal fractures that occur as a result of impact against a rudder pedal. It is impossible to tell from the rather poorly reproduced roentgenogram the extent of additional injuries to the tarsal bones. It appears that there are fractures of not only the metatarsals but also fracture/dislocations in the hind foot.

Tarsometatarsal fracture/dislocation (the so-called *Lisfranc lesion*) can be acquired through a variety of mechanisms, with dislocations occurring in both the dorsal and plantar direction. It is not uncommon for the history to include the fact that the foot was forced against or trapped beneath a brake or gas pedal. However, such injuries can also occur as a result of a fall, the foot being run over by a vehicle, or a heavy weight being dropped on the foot. Thus, the pattern is not specific. The key injury is disruption of the locking mechanism of the base of the second metatarsal between the first, second, and third cuneiforms. Ordinarily the lateral metatarsals are displaced both laterally and dorsally. There is a divergent Lisfranc deformity involving a fracture of the base of the second metatarsal and lateral subluxation of the four lateral metatarsals.

Bumper fracture

The bumper fracture has been recognized for years as a well-established pattern suggesting the injury, the object, the direction in which it was traveling, and the position of the victim.

Patterns of Torture and Terrorism

Physical beating is a widespread form of torture. Palmatoria is a form of localized torture virtually unique to the small West African country Guinea-Bissau. Palmatoria involve repetitive blows by a slender rod to the shin, where the tibia lies closest beneath the skin. Ordinary radiographs (of somewhat limited quality) have shown a periosteal reaction, presumably as a result of subperiosteal hemorrhage and hematoma. Somewhat peculiar endosteal and medullary changes have also been seen. Recent case reports in the United States and France have shown that this specific injury can produce a hidden endosteal fracture that is likely to be undetected on plain films but becomes obvious on a CT scan. It seems possible (perhaps likely) that some of the cases that took place in Guinea-Bissau would show similar findings when more sophisticated imaging modalities were used.

Falaca is a form of torture characterized by beating the foot, primarily the sole of the foot. This is a widespread form of torture in the Middle East, especially in Turkey and Iraq, as well as in Asia and in some Spanish-speaking areas (where it is called *bastinado*). Substantial injuries can be produced by this form of torture, including edema, hematoma, fractures, and injuries to ligaments, tendons, fascia, and aponeuroses. The clinical findings are usually diagnostic if they are made immediately after such torture. Radiography can confirm or exclude fractures and allows the investigator to estimate the extent of soft tissue injury and the time interval since torture. Early nuclear medicine studies show a massive increased uptake in the affected areas. Later radiographic studies demonstrate bone and soft tissue injury and evidence of subsequent healing.

Knee capping

The punitive destruction of a major joint by gunshot wound was originally thought to be the signature injury of certain criminal elements in the United States. More recently, it has been seen as an act of terrorism in other parts of the world, especially Northern Ireland. The punishment is not limited to the knee; other major joints have also been targeted.

GUNSHOT WOUNDS

From the day that Professor Wright examined his rabbit, radiology has played an important role in the evaluation of gunshot wounds. The number, location, and caliber of bullets; the angle and direction of fire; the discovery of concealed gunshot wounds; weapon ballistics;

types of bullets; and unconventional loads all fall within the purview of modern radiologic investigation.

Number of Bullets

Since more than one bullet can enter through a single entrance wound, it is important to determine the number of bullets and correlate them with entrance and exit wounds. Any discrepancy requires a search for spent bullet casings at the scene, additional entrance wounds, or radiographic investigation.

Caliber of Bullets

The use of radiographs to estimate the caliber of a bullet can be fraught with difficulty, particularly because the range of bullet sizes among calibers that are commonly used in handguns, for instance, is quite minimal. The magnification factor further confuses the picture and increases the risk of comprising the accuracy of the findings.

Location

Locating the bullet would seem to be a rather simple task. However, bullets may end up at sites quite distant from the entrance wound. They may be diverted from their expected path by striking bone or tissue. They may migrate great distances through blood vessels, the alimentary tract, the genitourinary tract, the spinal canal, the tracheobronchial tree, or within pleural and peritoneal spaces.

Types of Bullets

The ordinary load for handguns and rifles is a bullet made of lead. The lead may be fully or partially covered by another metal, called a jacket, which has several purposes: it protects the barrel of the weapon from leading; it hardens and lubricates the bullet, thereby somewhat diminishing the possibility of bullet deformity when it strikes tissue, particularly bone; and it may be shed as the bullet traverses tissues in the body. Each weapon has grooves inside the barrel that leave identifiable marks on the bullet as it passes through. This is important for ballistics identification. In the unjacketed bullet, the pattern will be on the lead itself; in semi- or fully-jacketed bullets, the ballistic markings will be on the jacket. Hence, it is important to identify and retrieve the separated jacket for ballistic purposes. Copper jacketing is usually quite easily identified. The so-called *silvertip load*, which has become quite popular in the United States, is jacketed with aluminum and can be quite difficult or impossible to locate with conventional radiography.

Military weapons tend to have high-velocity characteristics and, according to the Hague Piece Conference of 1899, must be fully jacketed. "Civilian" weapons and loads are mostly of a lower velocity. Some of the bullets used in civilian handguns and rifles have identifying characteristics, including the following:

1. The unjacketed bullet commonly used in high-velocity hunting ammunition fragments so extensively that the resulting pattern is called a "*lead snowstorm*."
2. The Black Talon mushrooms into a characteristic six-petal flower or star configuration.
3. The Glaser safety slug carries multiple small lead pellets in a copper cup, producing an unusual mixed pattern of densities.
4. The Winchester Western .25 caliber cartridge contains a copper-coated lead hollowpoint bullet filled with a single no. 4 steel pellet and, thus, produces the unusual finding of a single small bullet accompanied by a single small shot.

Finally, unconventional loads—plastic bullets, rubber bullets, and ceramic bullets—are being seen with increasing frequency because they are used in crowd control.

Production of the Radiograph

As previously mentioned, it has become increasingly difficult to use hospital or clinical radiologic installations for forensic investigation. The medical examiner's office, whether a one-room morgue or a separate building, needs its own in-house radiologic facility. The basic requirements are functional radiographic equipment and space to store and use it; X-ray films, cassettes, film storage space; a dark room and film processing facility, a film identification system; and envelopes and storage space for archival radiographs.

X-Ray Equipment

Either mobile or fixed X-ray equipment will suffice. The mobile X-ray unit is entirely self-contained and mounted on wheels for easy maneuverability. Stand-alone units may also be used; these are mounted on the floor, wall, or ceiling. A disadvantage lies in the fact that the staff must bring the body or body parts to the machine. An advantage is that high-performance X-ray equipment is not required, because there is no need to overcome the problem of physical or physiologic motion in the body or body part being examined. Thus, adequate equipment can be obtained at fairly reasonable cost, particularly because second-hand equipment has been made available as a result of recent technological advances and the introduction of new modalities to the field of clinical radiology.

Film

X-ray film is sensitive not only to X-rays but almost every color of light. It is packaged in light-proof cardboard boxes and must be handled in a darkroom equipped with an approved X-ray safety light. X-ray film is also sensitive to heat, low humidity, and stray radiation; hence, it must be carefully stored. X-ray film comes in a variety of sizes. It is easier for the forensic facility to employ one standard size; 14- × 17-inch film is recommended.

Film cassettes

Unexposed film is loaded in the darkroom onto rigid holders called cassettes, which are made of plastic and metal. The cassettes are flat, rectangular structures that are hinged at one end. The unexposed film is sandwiched between two fluorescent intensifying screens, which help reduce the amount of X-ray exposure required. Some cassettes come with a built-in grid of parallel lead lines, which improves the quality of images made of thick body parts. Both grid and non-grid cassettes are required for different examinations.

Film processing

Exposed films must be unloaded from a cassette in the dark and processed. There are many small automatic processors on the market, and these are highly recommended. If available, a nearby hospital or clinic processing facility may be a satisfactory alternative to in-house processing.

Film Identification

If the radiographic output is quite low, one can successfully write the name or other identifier of the body or body parts directly on the film with an indelible marker after the film has been processed. A better and more dependable method involves affixing readily available lead letters and numbers on the exposable surface of the cassette with adhesive tape, thus putting identification on the film at the same time as the exposure.

Exposure Factors

All radiographic equipment will have a control panel allowing the technician to select exposure factors—milliamperes (ma), exposure time(s), and kilovoltage (kVp)— appropriate for the body part and its thickness. Milliamperage and time may be combined as milliampere-seconds (mAs).

Simplified exposure chart is suggested as a starting point for the production of useable images. Suggested milliampere-seconds, kilovoltage settings, and the selection of a grid or non-grid cassette are supplied for different body parts and tissue thicknesses. It is recommended that the X-ray tube be 40 in. from the film or cassette holder. A ruler or simple aluminum caliper should be used to measure the thickness of the part to be examined.

Positioning

Standard radiographic positions for the lower extremity are required in order to match features on antemortem radiographs. Figures provide information that can be used to determine how to position the body part and central beam of the X-ray for each standard position. Each positioning photo is accompanied by a sample of the image to be expected from it.

INDEX

M

N

O

P

Q

R

S